LECTURES

ON THE

COMPARATIVE GRAMMAR

OF THE

SEMITIC LANGUAGES

LECTURES

ON THE

COMPARATIVE GRAMMAR

OF THE

SEMITIC LANGUAGES

WILLIAM WRIGHT

GYAN

Published by

GYAN

Gyan Publishing House
5, Ansari Road
Daryaganj, New Delhi-110002
Phone: 011-47034999, 9811692060
E-mail: books@gyanbooks.com

Distribution Network
gyanbooks.com
India, USA, Canada, UK, Australia

ISBN: 978-93-6433-532-4 (HB)

First Published, 1890

2nd Impression 2024

Printed at: Gyan Press, Delhi.

LECTURES ON THE COMPARATIVE GRAMMAR OF THE SEMITIC LANGUAGES
Author: WILLIAM WRIGHT

LECTURES

ON THE

COMPARATIVE GRAMMAR

OF THE

SEMITIC LANGUAGES.

LECTURES

ON THE

COMPARATIVE GRAMMAR

OF THE

SEMITIC LANGUAGES

FROM THE PAPERS OF THE LATE

WILLIAM WRIGHT, LL.D.,

PROFESSOR OF ARABIC IN THE UNIVERSITY OF CAMBRIDGE.

CAMBRIDGE
AT THE UNIVERSITY PRESS
1890

PREFACE.

THE Lectures printed in this volume were composed and delivered for the instruction of students in the University of Cambridge, and with special reference to the Examination for the Semitic Languages Tripos.

It appears from the *Cambridge University Reporter* that Professor Wright began "a short course of elementary lectures" on the Comparative Grammar of Hebrew, Syriac and Arabic in the Easter Term of 1877, and he continued to lecture on the subject at intervals till he was withdrawn from work by his last illness. The manuscript from which this volume is printed represents the form which the Lectures ultimately assumed, after they had passed through repeated and sedulous revision. They were never redelivered without being retouched, and in parts rewritten; and the whole manuscript, except a few pages at the end, was so carefully prepared as to be practically ready to go to press. It was Professor Wright's intention that the lectures should one day be printed, and during his last illness he often spoke of this intention in such a way as to make it clear that he meant to publish them without any substantial modification or addition. It was not his design to produce a complete system of the Comparative Grammar of the

Semitic Languages or to give a complete account of all recent researches and discussions, but to do through the press for a wider circle of students what he had done by the oral delivery of the lectures for his Cambridge pupils.

Under these circumstances the task of editing the book for publication has been very simple. I have divided the text into chapters, for the convenience of the reader, but have printed it for the most part word for word as it stood in the manuscript. In a very few places I have removed repetitions or other slight inconcinnities of form, but in such cases I have been careful to introduce nothing of my own, and to limit myself to what would certainly have been done by the author's own hand if he had lived to see the book through the press. Occasionally I have thought it necessary to add a few words [within square brackets] to complete a reference or preclude a possible misconception, and I have also added a few notes where the statements in the text seemed to call for supplement or modification in view of facts or arguments which had not yet come under the writer's notice when the lectures were last revised. So long as his health allowed, Professor Wright closely followed all that was done in Semitic learning, and incorporated with his manuscript, from time to time, references to everything that he deemed important for the practical object of the lectures. But it was no part of his plan to give a complete view of the literature of the subject; as a rule he only referred to essays which he wished to encourage his hearers to read in connexion with the lectures. Bearing this in mind, I have been very sparing in the introduction of additional references to books and papers; but, on the other hand, I have borne in mind that every written lecture must occasionally be supplemented in delivery by unwritten remarks or explanations, and a few of the notes may be regarded as taking the place of such remarks. I have, for example, occasionally thought it necessary to warn the reader that certain words cited in the text are loan-words. In all questions of phonetics this is a point of importance, and I am informed by those who heard the lectures that Professor Wright was careful to distinguish loan-words as such in his teaching, in cases where the fact is not noted in his manuscript. A considerable number of the notes are due to the suggestion of the author's old and intimate friend Professor Nöldeke, of Strassburg, who has kindly read the lectures in proof, and the notes signed N. or Nöld. are directly taken from his observations. Some of these, which were not communicated to me till the book was in page, have been necessarily placed among the *Additional Notes and Corrections*, to which I desire to call the special attention of the reader.

It will be observed that the Lectures do not embrace any systematic discussion or classification of the forms of nouns in the Semitic languages; nor can I find any indication that the author intended to add a section on this important and difficult subject. He seems to have regarded it as lying beyond the region that could be conveniently covered in a course of lectures to undergraduates; and he did not live to read the recent works of his old and valued friend Professor de Lagarde (*Uebersicht über die im Aramäischen, Arabischen und Hebräischen übliche Bildung der Nomina*, Göttingen 1889: *Abh. der k. G. d. W.*, Bd. xxxv), and of Professor

Barth (*Die Nominalbildung in den Sem. Sprachen*, 1ste Hälfte, i., Leipzig 1889). On the other hand he doubtless intended to complete the subject of verbal inflexion, and I have therefore thought it right to make a few additions to the rough sketch of the derived forms of verbs whose third radical is ו or י, with which the manuscript ended, and also to supply, by way of appendix, a short section on verbs one of whose radicals is an א. Here also I have derived great advantage from Prof. Nöldeke's suggestions.

The printing of the volume, necessarily slow from the nature of the work, has been still further retarded by a prolonged illness, which fell upon me after the early sheets were printed off, and which would have caused still more delay had not Mr A. Ashley Bevan, of Trinity College, kindly undertaken to read the proofs during my enforced absence from Cambridge. I have to thank Mr Bevan not only for this service but for suggesting several useful notes.

W. ROBERTSON SMITH.

CHRIST'S COLLEGE, CAMBRIDGE,
June, 1890.

CONTENTS.

CHAPTER I.

INTRODUCTORY REMARKS. THE TERM SEMITIC. DIFFUSION AND ORIGINAL HOME OF THE SEMITES.

IN commencing a course of Lectures on the Comparative Grammar of the Semitic Languages, I feel it almost unnecessary to begin with an apology for my subject. The results which may be attained by the comparative treatment of an entire class, or even of a single group of languages, have been patent to all, since the time when men like Bopp, Pott and Schleicher, have investigated the connexion of the Indo-European languages; Jacob Grimm that of the Teutonic; and Diez that of the Romance. What has been done in these fields may yet be accomplished in another; and every attempt to illustrate the history and grammar of the Hebrew language in particular ought to be welcome to its students, even though the results should fail to be in exact conformity with preconceived notions and ancient prejudices.

To myself it is a matter of more importance to apologise for the meagreness of the outline which is all that I can pretend to offer. I have no great discoveries to announce, no new laws to enunciate. The field of our investigations is limited. Instead of ranging from the farthest limits of Hindūstān to the coasts of Ireland, and from the shores of Iceland to the isles of Greece, we are confined, I may say, to a small portion of Western Asia. Our position is that of the Teutonic or Romance philologist rather than that of the Indo-European. The languages with which we have to deal form a small group, which are as intimately connected with one another as old Norse, Gothic, old High German and old English, on the one hand; or as Italian, Spanish, Portuguese, Provençal, French and Wallachian, on the other. And not only this, but I propose to confine myself chiefly to three of these languages—Hebrew, Syriac and Arabic; and to consider these as they appear to us in the ancient forms of their literary monuments, and not, save incidentally, in the modern aspects of their spoken dialects.

You probably infer, then, that our path is a smooth one; that there is not much to investigate; not much room for inquiry or speculation. And yet this is far from being the case. On the contrary, it is surprising how relatively little progress the comparative philology of the Semitic languages has yet made; partly owing to the inherent difficulties of the subject, and partly to the imperfection of our knowledge on many preliminary points of importance.

A hundred years ago the Sanskṛit language was barely known to Europeans by name; so recently as 1816 appeared Bopp's *Conjugations-Syştem*, the first work of the great master and founder of the science of Comparative Grammar. And behold, the mustard seed has already grown into a great tree, and has yielded an ample and goodly crop of fruit.

Beside the results of Indo-European philology, those as yet attained by Sçmitic grammarians seem scant and dwarfish. Since the days of Reuchlin, who died in 1522, we Europeans have been engaged in the study of Hebrew and its sister-languages. The Dutchman De Dieu and the Swiss Hottinger, our own Edmund Castle and the Germans Buxtorf and Ludolf, Alting of Groningen and Danz of Jena, were among those who laid the foundations of our science; and they found worthy successors in the three great Dutch linguists, Schultens, Schroeder and Scheid. But yet the labours of these scholars were not far in advance of those of the classical philologists of their day, who speculated upon the obvious affinities of Latin and Greek, and their connexion with other languages, without being able to arrive at any satisfactory results; simply for want of the proper key wherewith to unlock this linguistic treasury. It was reserved for the men of our own day to take a decided step in advance. Thanks to the studies of a Gesenius and an Ewald, a Roediger and an Olshausen, a Dillmann and a Noeldeke, the Comparative Grammar of the Semitic languages is at last beginning to assume the proportions of a science; and we may therefore hope, before many years are past, to see the results of their labours embodied in a work which shall not be inferior in fulness and accuracy, I will not say to those of Bopp and Schleicher, but rather to those of Grimm, of Diez, and of Curtius.

You understand, then, that there exists as yet no work which I can recommend to you as a complete text-book of Semitic Comparative Grammar; no treatise which we can confidently follow as a guide from the beginning of our course to its end. The French Orientalist Renan proposed to himself to write such a work; but he has not yet advanced beyond the introduction, the *Histoire Générale des Langues Sémitiques* [8vo, Paris, 1st ed. 1855]. The second part, the *Système Comparé*, has remained, and is now, I fear, likely to remain, a desideratum. Differing as I do from Renan, not merely in small details, but also in various matters of principle, I can still admire the industry and scholarship which are manifest in every page of the *Histoire Générale*; the justice of many of its views, and the clearness of its style and arrangement; and I therefore advise those of you who have not yet read it, to do so without delay, as a good introduction to the studies to which I now invite your attention[1]. In connexion with our special course I would recommend to you more particularly the Hebrew Grammar of Justus Olshausen, *Lehrbuch der Hebräischen Sprache* (Brunswick, 1861); that of B. Stade, *Lehrbuch der Hebräischen Grammatik*, 1ter Theil (Leipzig, 1879); and Bickell's *Grundriss der Hebräischen Grammatik* (Leipzig, 1869, 70), of which an English translation by Curtiss appeared at Leipzig in 1877 under the title of *Outlines of Hebrew Grammar.* To this little book I shall sometimes have occasion to refer, as I prefer it to Land's *Hebreeuwsche Grammatica* (Amsterdam, 1869), of which there is also an English translation by Reginald Lane Poole, *Principles of Hebrew Grammar* (London, 1876). I would also mention with commendation the latest or 22nd edition of Gesenius' *Hebräische Grammatik*, by Professor Kautzsch of Tübingen, as furnishing some useful hints; [24th ed. Leipzig, 1885].

The term *Semitic* is, as has been often observed, more convenient than scientific. It is not, however, easy to invent a

[1] [See also Nöldeke's article "Semitic Languages" in the ninth ed. of the *Encyclopaedia Britannica*, vol. xxi. (Edin. 1886).]

better; and it is, at any rate, no worse than "Hamitic," and much superior to "Japhetic" or "Turanian." The word is derived, as you are aware, from the tenth chapter of the Book of Genesis, in which the nations of the world, so far as known to the Jews, are divided into three sections, not, as it would seem, ethnographically, nor even geographically, but with reference to political history and civilisation[1]. Thus alone can we satisfactorily explain the mention of the Phoenicians and other Canaanites among the children of Ham. That the languages of Canaan were akin to the Hebrew, almost to identity, is certain; that their connexion with ancient Egyptian was a very remote one, is equally certain—many philologists would deny it altogether; but that Canaan and the Phoenicians were long subject to Egypt, and that they derived a great part of their civilisation from the Egyptians, are historical facts which do not admit of dispute.

The Semitic races occupy but a small portion of the earth's surface. They are known to us historically as the inhabitants of the south-western corner of Asia. Their territory is bounded on the north by Mount Taurus and the mountains of Armenia; on the east, by the mountains of Kurdistān and Khūzistān, and the Persian Gulf; on the south, by the Indian Ocean; and on the west, by the Red Sea and the Mediterranean. Early colonisation led them across the strait of Bāb el-Mandeb into the country which we call Abyssinia; and they also occupied, at an extremely remote period, various points on the shores of the Mediterranean Sea and even of the Atlantic Ocean, the trading ports of the energetic Phoenician race.

If you ask me whether the Semites were autochthones,—whether they were the original, primitive inhabitants of the Asiatic region above described,—I must beg of you to formulate the question differently.

It seems certain, on the evidence of ancient monuments, that the great basin of the Tigris and Euphrates was originally occupied by a non-Semitic people or peoples, of no mean civilisation, the inventors of the cuneiform system of writing. Hebrew tradition, as contained in the Old Testament, mentions

[1] See Tiele, *Vergelijkende Geschiedenis van de Egyptische en Mesopotamische Godsdiensten* [8vo, Amsterdam, 1872], p. 20.

various gigantic tribes as the primitive inhabitants of Palestine (הַנּוֹלָדִים בָּאָרֶץ, 1 Chron. vii. 21), such as the Emīm, הָאֵמִים, Nĕphīlīm, הַנְּפִילִים, Rĕphā'īm, הָרְפָאִים, 'Anāḳīm, הָעֲנָקִים, Zūzīm, הַזּוּזִים, and Zamzummīm, זַמְזֻמִּים; the Ḥōrīm or Troglodytes, הַחֹרִים, and others; some of whom at least were probably non-Semitic.

It appears then that in certain parts of their territory the Semites were not autochthones, but a foreign conquering race. Was this the case with the whole Semitic region? Does the cradle of the Semites lie within the boundaries designated above, or outside of them? That is the shape which your question should take.

Here, on the very threshold of our inquiries, the opinions of the best modern authorities diverge widely, some maintaining (as I myself was formerly inclined to do) that the Semites were ancient immigrants from the North East; others that their home was in the South, whence they gradually overspread the whole of Syria and Mesopotamia by successive migrations in a northerly direction. In recent times the former view has been upheld, to mention only a very few names, by von Kremer, Guidi, and Hommel; the latter by Sayce, Sprenger, Schrader, and De Goeje.

It was in 1875 that von Kremer published in a German periodical called *Das Ausland* (nos. 1 and 2) two articles on "Semitische Culturentlehnungen aus dem Pflanzen- und Thierreiche," i.e. on plants and animals which the Semites obtained, with their names, from other races. His conclusions, so far as they interest us at the present moment, are briefly these. Before the formation of the different Semitic dialects, they had a name for the camel, which appears in all of them; whereas they have no names in common for the date-palm and its fruit, or for the ostrich. The one the Semites knew while they were as yet one people, dwelling together; the others they did not know. Now the region where there is neither date-palm nor ostrich, and yet where the camel has been known from the remotest antiquity, is the great central tableland of Asia, near the sources of the Oxus and Jaxartes, the Jaiḥūn and Saiḥūn. Von Kremer regards the

Semitic emigration from this region as having preceded the Aryan or Indo-European, perhaps under pressure from the latter race; and he holds that the Semites first settled in Mesopotamia and Babylonia, which he looks upon as the oldest centre of Semitic civilisation. "In der babylonisch-mesopotamischen Niederung, wo die Semiten sich angesammelt hatten, entstand das erste und älteste semitische Culturcentrum."

In 1879 the Italian orientalist Ignazio Guidi wrote a memoir upon the primitive seat of the Semitic peoples, "Della sede primitiva dei popoli Semitici," which appeared among the publications of the Reale Accademia dei Lincei. His line of argument is much the same as von Kremer's (whose articles appear to have been unknown to him). Comparing the words in the various Semitic languages which express the configurations of the earth's surface, the varieties of soil, the changes of the seasons and climate, the names of minerals, plants and animals, etc., Guidi arrives at nearly the same conclusions as von Kremer, viz. (1) that Babylonia was the first centre of Semitic life, "siamo sempre riportati alla Babilonide come centro degli antichissimi Semiti (p. 48)"; and (2) that these primitive Semites were immigrants from the lands to the S. and S.W. of the Caspian Sea, which he regards as "probabile punto di partenza degli antenati dei Semiti (p. 51)."

In the same year, 1879, Hommel wrote a paper on this subject, which I do not possess in its original shape. His conclusion, however, is nearly identical with that of von Kremer and Guidi, that lower Mesopotamia, and not Arabia, was the original seat of the Semites. You will find his views stated briefly, with some slight polemic against von Kremer, in his book *Die Namen der Säugethiere bei den Südsemitischen Völkern* [Leipzig, 1879], p. 406 sqq. Consult also his later work, *Die Semitischen Völker u. Sprachen*, 1883, especially p. 63.

Assuming for the moment the correctness of this view,—taking it for granted that the Semites first settled as one race in Mesopotamia and Babylonia,—how are we to depict to ourselves their dispersion over the territory which they subsequently occupied? Somewhat as follows:—

Having forced their way through the mountainous region of Kurdistān, and reached the Tigris, the Semites would cross it and settle in the country between the Tigris and Euphrates. Thence they would gradually make their way southwards by two different lines, through what we call Syria and Babylonia. The one branch would extend its wanderings as far as Canaan; the other to the head of the Persian Gulf, where in process of time they would cast off a fresh swarm, which occupied Arabia and then crossed over into Africa. All this of course is supposed to happen in pre-historic times; as Guidi says, "tale parmi che possa essere stato il movimento preistorico di questi popoli."

Let us now consider the opposite view, which I am at present strongly inclined to adopt.

The plainest statement of it in English is that of Sayce in his *Assyrian Grammar* (1872), p. 13: "The Semitic traditions all point to Arabia as the original home of the race. It is the only part of the world which has remained exclusively Semite. The racial characteristics—intensity of faith, ferocity, exclusiveness, imagination—can best be explained by a desert origin."

Similarly Sprenger in his *Alte Geogr. Arabiens* (Bern, 1875), p. 293: "All Semites are according to my conviction successive layers of Arabs. They deposited themselves layer upon layer; and who knows, for example, how many layers had preceded the Canaanites, whom we encounter at the very beginning of history?" "Alle Semiten sind nach meiner Ueberzeugung abgelagerte Araber. Sie lagerten sich Schichte auf Schichte, und wer weiss, die wie vielte Schichte zum Beispiel die Kanaaniter, welche wir zu Anfang der Geschichte wahrnehmen, waren[1]?"

Schrader expresses views of the same nature in an article in the *ZDMG.* for 1873, vol. xxvii. pp. 397—424. After a long discussion of the religious, linguistic and historico-geographical relations of the different Semitic nations to one another, he arrives at the conclusion that Arabia is the home of these races: "Die Erwägung der religiös-mythologischen, weiter der linguistischen, nicht minder der allgemein geschichtlich-geographischen Verhältnisse, weist uns nach Arabien als den Ursitz des Semitismus" (p. 421).

Lastly, De Goeje in his academical address for 1882, *Het Vaderland der Semietische Volken*, has distinctly declared himself

[1] [The same view is already expressed and defended in Sprenger's *Leben und Lehre des Mohammad*, Bd i. (Berlin, 1869), p. 241 *sq.*]

in favour of the view that Central Arabia is the home of the Semitic race as a whole. Laying it down as a rule without exception that mountaineers never become inhabitants of the steppe and nomade shepherds, De Goeje rejects the notion that the Semites can have descended from the mountains of the Arrapachitis to become dwellers in the plains and swamps of Babylonia. On the other hand he shews how nomades are continually passing over into agriculturists with settled habitations; how villages and towns are gradually formed, with cultivated lands around them; and how the space needful for the pasturing nomade is thus gradually curtailed until the land becomes too narrow for him and he is forced to seek a home elsewhere. So it fared with Central Arabia. The result was that the nomade population was incessantly overstepping its bounds in every direction, and planting itself in Syria, Babylonia, 'Omān, or Yaman. Successive layers of emigrants would drive their predecessors in Syria and Babylonia farther northwards towards the borders of Kurdistān and Armenia, and thus the whole of Mesopotamia would be gradually semitised, and even portions of Africa would in course of time more or less completely share the same fate. This process, I may remark, has often been repeated in more recent, historical times, in which the Arab migration has overflooded the whole of Syria and Mesopotamia. In the earliest centuries of the Christian era, the wealthy city of Palmyra was ruled, I may say, by a company of Arab merchants. Three petty kingdoms, those of Ghassān, of the Tha'labites, and of al-Ḥīrah, divided between them the southern part of the Syrian steppe; and in the struggles between the Byzantine and Persian empires the Arabs of Mesopotamia had always to be reckoned with, and yielded a reluctant obedience to the one side or the other. De Goeje also lays stress upon the fine climate of Central Arabia and the splendid physical and mental development of the race; and, like Schrader, compares their language with those of the other Semites in the earliest stage at which we know them, drawing the inference that the speech of the Arabs is the nearest approximation that we can have to the primitive Semitic tongue. "En dat van alle Semietische talen het Arabisch het naast staat aan de moedertaal, waaruit zij gesproten zijn, is overtuigend bewezen door hoogleeraar Schrader te Berlijn (p. 16)."

This view is of course diametrically opposed to that of Sayce, who claims for the Assyrian "the same position among the Semitic tongues that is held by Sanskṛit in the Aryan family of speech." Which of these scholars is in the right we shall be better able to judge by and by. Meanwhile I will only say that I range myself on the Arabic side with Schrader and De Goeje.

Accepting this view of the cradle of the Semites,—assuming that they spread from Arabia as their centre,—how shall we depict to ourselves their dispersion over the Semitic territory? Let Schrader speak. He imagines the northern Semites—i.e., the Arameans, Babylonians and Canaanites—to have parted in a body from their brethren in the south, and to have settled in Babylonia, where they lived together for a long period. The Arameans would be the first to separate from the main body of emigrants; at a considerably later period the Canaanites; last of all the Assyrians. At the same time an emigration would be going on in a southerly direction. Leaving the northern Arabs in Central Arabia, these emigrants would settle on the southern coast of the peninsula, whence a band of them subsequently crossed the sea into Africa and pitched in Abyssinia[1].

[1] [On all these theories of the cradle of the Semitic race see also Nöldeke's remarks in *Enc. Brit.* xxi. 642. He himself suggests, "not as a definite theory but as a modest hypothesis," that the primitive seat of the Semites is to be sought in Africa, though he regards the Arabian theory as "not untenable." It may be observed that, if the Semites originally came from Africa, Arabia may yet be the centre from which they spread over other parts of Asia.]

CHAPTER II.

GENERAL SURVEY OF THE SEMITIC LANGUAGES.

I NOW proceed to give you a more detailed account of the several languages, or groups of languages, which constitute the Semitic family. I divide them broadly into the *northern* Semites and the *southern* Semites. By the former I understand the Arameans, the Canaanites and Hebrews, the Babylonians and Assyrians; by the latter, the northern Arabs, the southern Arabs or Ḥimyarites, and the Ge'ez or Abyssinians. In the course of my description it may, perhaps, be better to follow a geographical than a historical arrangement; for this reason, that linguistic and political history are very different things; that one nation may have played its part in the world's history, and have disappeared from the stage, long before a kindred people has come prominently into notice; and yet, from a linguistic point of view, the language of the latter may exhibit their common speech in a more antique phase, and may prove in the hands of the comparative philologist a more efficient implement than that of the former. An example of what I mean is afforded us by the Icelandic, which among all the existing Teutonic dialects has retained the greatest number of original forms with the least alteration. Another and still better instance is the Lithuanian language. It is spoken by only a couple of millions of people (at most) on the borders of Prussia and Russia; its earliest written literary document dates from the middle of the sixteenth century; and yet it has preserved many of the forms of Indo-European speech in a less corrupted condition than any of its European congeners, aye, than any dialect of the entire family which is not at least two thousand years older.

The causes which produce results such as these are, probably, manifold; but some of them at any rate are, as it seems to me, sufficiently clear. Language is after all, as Whitney has remarked, the work of tradition; we speak as we were taught by our fathers and mothers, who were in their turn trained by a preceding generation. This process of transmission is always, and necessarily, more or less imperfect. Hence language is always undergoing a process of modification, partaking of the nature both of decay and of growth. The less imperfect the transmission, the slighter will the modification obviously be. Now two circumstances above all others are favourable to the continuity and completeness of linguistic tradition: isolation is the one; the possession of a literature is the other. If a race, speaking a single language, occupies a circumscribed territory, so long as that race is confined within those narrow limits, and thrown but little into contact with surrounding races, the forces which produce linguistic decay and growth are, if not entirely repressed, at least limited in their operation. Dialectic differences will probably arise, but they will be comparatively few and trifling. On the other hand, if the said race extends its territory largely, by conquest or colonisation, and is thrown into constant contact or collision with other races, the decay and growth of its speech proceeds with greatly accelerated rapidity; and the language runs no small risk of being ultimately broken up into several languages, the speakers of which are no longer mutually intelligible. Here the possession of a literature steps in as a counteracting force, exercising a strong conservative influence. English, as is well known, has changed less since Shakespear's time than it did in the interval between him and Chaucer; and certainly much less since Chaucer's age than it did during the five preceding centuries. So too with Arabic. As long as the Arabs were confined within the limits of their peninsula, the variations of their speech were but small. We know indeed of dialectic differences, but they are neither numerous nor important. The words and names handed down to us from antiquity as Arabic,—whether in the cuneiform inscriptions, the Bible, or the writers of Greece and Rome,—are easily recognisable as such, unless when they have undergone corruption in the course of transmission. Since Muḥammad's time, however, the changes have been more rapid and numerous; and by this time the natives of Syria, Egypt, and Morocco, would perhaps have been scarcely intelligible to one another, had it not been for the link of a common literature, commencing with the ancient poets and the Ḳor'ān. The existence of this link has greatly retarded the processes of growth and decay; and hence it happens that the Arabic of the present day is a far closer representative of the language as spoken, say, two thousand years ago, than modern Italian and French are of the Latin of the same period.

We commence, then, our survey of the Semitic tongues with the *Northern* section, and herein with the *Eastern* group, which, as it happens, is the first to appear prominently in the field of history. This group comprises two very closely allied languages, the Babylonian and Assyrian, which have been preserved to us in numerous inscriptions, written in cuneiform or wedge-shaped characters. The earliest of these inscriptions go back beyond the time of the Babylonian king Ḥammurabi, who cannot, according to the best authorities, have flourished later than circa 1500 B.C.; and the latest come down to the beginning of the fourth century B.C., when the Persian monarch Artaxerxes Mnemon reigned[1]. They are all written, unfortunately for us, in a non-Semitic character, primitively hieroglyphic, and of peculiar complexity, one of the varieties of the cuneiform type. Into a full description of these, and the history of their decipherment, so far as it has till now been accomplished, I cannot here enter. The Assyrian character, as I shall call it for shortness' sake, is not alphabetical, but syllabaric. Such syllables as *ka, ki, ku, ak, ik, uk*, are each expressed by a single sign, as well as syllables of the form *kam, kim, sak, sik*. These latter compound syllables may, however, be also denoted by two signs, the one indicating a syllable which ends with a certain vowel, and the other a syllable which begins with the same vowel; e.g. *ka-am, si-ik*. Under these circumstances alone, the learning to read Assyrian texts with fluency would be no light task; but the difficulty is enormously enhanced by the fact that a great number of the signs employed in writing are not syllables but ideograms; not phonetic signs, but characters denoting an object or idea. Some of these ideograms have no phonetic value whatever; whilst others are both ideographic and have a phonetic

[1] [The Br. Mus. has an inscr. of Antiochus I., Soter, of the year 269 B.C.]

value as well. For instance 𒀭 as a syllable sounds *an*, but as an ideogram it means "God," *ilu*, which is otherwise written phonetically with two signs, *i-lu*. One class of ideograms are mere determinatives, their object being solely to indicate the nature of the following group of signs; e.g. 𒁹 before every name of a man, 𒆳 before most names of countries, etc.

How much perplexity is caused by the intermixture of these ideograms with the phonetic signs you can easily conceive; and that the Assyrians themselves found a difficulty herein is obvious from their use of what is called "the phonetic complement." This consists in the addition to an ideogram of one or two phonetic signs, indicating the termination of the word denoted by the ideogram. For example, a certain combination of wedges sounds KI; but as an ideogram it means "the earth." Consequently the phonetic complement *tiv* is added to it, to lead the reader to the correct pronunciation, which is not *ki-tiv*, but *irṣi-tiv* (אֶרֶץ). Two ideograms, the phonetic values of which are SU-AS, mean "I burned." Now in Assyrian the idea of "burning" is expressed by *sarap, isrup* (שָׂרַף), or *kavâ, ikvû* (כָּוָה). Consequently, when the 1st pers. sing. imperf. of the former verb is intended, the syllable *up* is added to the ideograms SU-AS, and the whole word, though written SU.AS.*up*, is pronounced *asrup*. We do something of this kind ourselves, but on a very limited scale, when we write LSD, and read "pounds, shillings and pence"; or write & and *i.e.* and *viz.*, and pronounce "and" and "that is" and "namely." The Persians made more use of the same procedure in writing the Pahlavi character. Using a strange jumble of Semitic and Persian, they wrote *lhmâ* and *bsrâ* [i.e. the Aramaic *laḥmâ*, "bread"; *besrâ*, "flesh"], but spoke *nân* and *gôsht*; they wrote *ab* and read *pit* ["father"], but *abitr* did duty for [the synonym] *pitar*.

To return to the Assyrian. A yet greater difficulty lies ahead of the decipherer than any of those already mentioned; for it seems to have been established that some at least both of the syllabic signs and of the ideograms are polyphonic, that is, have several different sounds and significations.

For further details and explanations I must refer you to the works of Ménant, Smith, Oppert, Sayce and Schrader, especially the treatise of the last-named scholar in the *ZDMG.*, vol. xxvi. pp. 1—392; Sayce, *An Assyrian Grammar for comparative purposes*, 1872; *An Elementary Grammar of the Assyrian Language*, in "Archaic Classics," 1875 (2nd ed. 1877)[1]. The researches of these and other writers, such as Rawlinson, Hincks and Norris, not to mention younger scholars, such as Delitzsch, Haupt and Hommel, have rendered it clear that the language of the Assyrian and Babylonian empires, as handed down to us in this particular variety of cuneiform writing, was a member of the North Semitic group, closely connected with Phoenician and Hebrew, and only in a somewhat less degree with Aramaic.

As I shall not often refer hereafter to the Assyrian tongue, I may take this opportunity of stating that, in regard to its vowels, the Assyrian seems to have preserved more than the Hebrew of that ancient simplicity which is so conspicuous in the Arabic. It appears to possess only the three radical vowel sounds *a*, *i*, *u*, a fact which need not surprise us, if we look to the written vocalisation of the Arabic and to the analogy of Sanskṛit in the Indo-European family[2]. In respect to its consonants, however, the Assyrian approaches more nearly to the lower level of the Phoenician and Hebrew, as contrasted with the higher level of the Arabic. This is especially obvious in regard to the sibilants, as "three," *šalašti*, שָׁלֹשׁ, ثَلَاث; "manly," *zikaru*, זָכָר, ذَكَر. Some salient and distinctive features in its grammar we may have occasion to notice from time to time; and I therefore only remark in conclusion that this eastern branch of the North Semitic languages has left no modern representative whatever.

Proceeding northward and westward, we meet with the great *Aramean* or *central* group of the North Semitic dialects.

The Bible has made you familiar with the name of *Arām* (written אֲרָם, constr. אֲרַם, for which we should rather have expected אָרָם, agreeably to the analogy of דָּבָר, דְּבַר). It speaks of אֲרַם דַּמֶּשֶׂק or "the Aram of Damascus," אֲרַם צוֹבָה,

[1] [See also Lyon, *Assyrian Manual* (Chicago, 1886); Delitzsch, *Assyr. Gr.* (Berlin, 1889).]

[2] [But Haupt (*Amer. Journ. of Philol.* viii. (1887), p. 265 *sqq.*) and Delitzsch maintain the existence of *e* in Assyrian.]

אֲרַם מַעֲכָה, etc., all places situated in Syria. אֲרַם נַהֲרַיִם, "Aram of the two rivers," is usually supposed to mean *Mesopotamia*, but it is possible that the two rivers were not the Euphrates and Tigris, but the Euphrates and its chief affluent the Chabōras or Khābūr, which would limit the designation to the western half of what is generally understood by Mesopotamia. A part of this territory bore the name of פַּדַּן אֲרָם, which we may probably identify with the village of ܦܕܢ, called by the Arab geographers فدّان [Faddān], near Ḥarrān. *Arām* seems, therefore, not to be a geographical or political designation, but the ancient name of the race, which they brought with them in their wanderings from the banks of the lower Tigris, the district known in the time of the Sāsānians, and even later, as ܒܝܬ ܐܪ̈ܡܝܐ [Beth Armāyē], or "the home of the Arameans." Now the Jews, as is well known, employed the word אַרַמַּאי (אֲרַמִּי) in the sense of "gentile," "heathen"; and under the influence of their usage, it was retained by the Syrian translators of the New Testament to express Ἕλληνες, ἐθνικοί, and similar words. But a term which was used in the Bible to designate "heathens" could no longer be borne by a Christian people. Hence the old name was modified into ܐܪܡܝܐ [Ārāmāyā]; but even this was gradually discarded and replaced by another, the Greek designation of "Syrians." This is merely an abbreviation of "Assyrians." At first the Greeks called all the subjects of the Assyrian empire Ἀσσύριοι, or more usually by the shorter form Σύριοι or Σύροι. Subsequently, as they became better acquainted with these regions, they used the fuller form Ἀσσυρία to designate the lands on the banks of the Tigris, whilst the shorter form Συρία served as the name of the western lands; and at last this term was adopted by the Arameans themselves, who as Christians applied to themselves the term ܣܘܪ̈ܝܝܐ [Suryāyē]. See Noeldeke in *Hermes* for 1871, p. 443, and in *ZDMG.* xxv. 113.

From its northern settlements the Aramean race gradually extended itself over the whole of Syria, Palestine and Mesopotamia; and its language is consequently known to us in various forms, attaining their literary development at different periods.

Firstly, there is the dialect of northern Mesopotamia, specifically of the district around Orhāi (Urhōi) or Edessa, which we commonly call Syriac. It is known to us as a literary language from about the second century after Christ down to the thirteenth or fourteenth. The best grammars of it for our purpose are those of Noeldeke [Leipzig, 1880] and Duval [Paris, 1881].

Secondly, there are the dialects of Syria Proper and of Palestine, the region to the west of the Euphrates. These are usually spoken of by the absurd designation of *Chaldee*, which would properly mean something very different, as we have seen above. Leaving out of account two words in the book of Genesis (ch. xxxi. 47) and a verse in Jeremiah (ch. x. 11), the oldest literary monuments of this branch of Aramaic are certain passages in the book of Ezra (ch. iv. 8—vi. 18, vii. 12—26), going back to the end of the sixth or the beginning of the fifth century B.C., which are, as Renan says, really specimens of the Aramaic of the time of Darius Hystaspis, Xerxes, and Artaxerxes Longimanus[1]. About the Aramaic portions of the book of Daniel there is a doubt, for they are, according to the best foreign critics, of much later date, having been written by a Palestinian Jew in the time of Antiochus Epiphanes, about 166 or 165 B.C. This point, however, is one which I am not called upon to settle, and I content myself with merely indicating the doubt. Then follow the Biblical Targūms, Onḳelos, Jonathan, Pseudo-Jonathan, and the Yĕrūshalmī. Now, do not for a moment suppose that the Jews lost the use of Hebrew in the Babylonian captivity, and brought back with them into Palestine this so-called Chaldee. The Aramean dialect, which gradually got the upper hand since the fourth or fifth century B.C., did not come that long journey across the Syrian desert; it was *there*, on the spot; and it ended by taking possession of the field, side by side with the kindred dialect of the Samaritans, as exemplified in their Targūm of the Pentateuch, their festal services and hymns. For the grammati-

[1] [See however Kuenen, *Onderzoek*, 2nd ed. (Leiden, 1887) vol. i. p. 502 *sq.*, where the view is taken that the author of Chronicles-Ezra-Nehemiah made extracts from an Aramaic work: this work may have been written in the Persian period, and it contained authentic history, but the documents it cites are not literally authentic. Upon this view the language of the Aramaic portions of Ezra is not so old as Renan supposes.]

cal study of the Biblical Aramaic I recommend to you the grammar of S. D. Luzzatto, *Elementi grammaticali del caldeo biblico e del dialetto talmudico-babilonese*, which has been translated into German by Krüger (Breslau 1873) and into English by Goldammer, rabbi at Cincinnati (New York, 1876). The works of Winer and Petermann may also be named. The former has been done into English by Riggs and by Longfield. Turpie's Manual (1879) may be found convenient; but Kautzsch's *Grammatik des Biblisch-aramäischen* (Leipzig, 1884) is the best in its particular field. The best Samaritan grammars are those of Uhlemann (Leipzig, 1837), and Petermann (Berlin, 1873). That of Nicholls may also be mentioned.

Subordinate dialects of this second class are:—

(*a*) The Egyptian Aramaic, as exhibited, for example, in the stele of Saḳḳāra, now in the Berlin Museum[1]; in the inscription preserved at Carpentras in France[2]; in the papyri Blacassiani, formerly in the collection of the Duc de Blacas, now in the British Museum[3]; and the papyrus of the Louvre edited by the Abbé Bargès[4]. The Berlin stele is dated in the fourth year of Xerxes, B.C. 482. The other monuments specified, and a few more of the same class, may perhaps be ascribed, as M. Clermont-Ganneau maintains[5], to the periods of Persian sway in Egypt, B.C. 527 to 405 and B.C. 340 to 332; but it is possible that some of them at any rate may be of later date, the work of Jews dwelling in Egypt.

(*b*) The Nabathean dialect, or that of inscriptions found in Ḥaurān, Petra, and the Sinaitic Peninsula, as well as at Taimā and Madāïn Ṣāliḥ or al-Ḥijr in North Arabia. The great inscription of Taimā[6] is of the Persian period and therefore some centuries anterior to the Christian era. The inscriptions discovered by Doughty at Madāïn Ṣāliḥ, and just published by the French Academy[7], date from B.C. 3 to

[1] [Figured and published in the Palaeographical Society's *Oriental Series*, Plate lxiii.]

[2] [*Ibid.* Plate lxiv.]

[3] [*Ibid.* Plates xxv., xxvi.]

[4] [*Papyrus égypto-araméen*, Paris, 1862.]

[5] [*Revue Archéologique* 1878, 79, xxxvi. 93 *sqq.*, xxxvii. 21 *sqq.*]

[6] [Published by Nöldeke in *Sitzungsb. d. k. Pr. Acad. zu Berlin*, 10. July, 1884.]

[7] [*Documents épigraphiques*, &c., 4° Paris, 1884; now superseded for most of the inscriptions by Euting's *Nabatäische Inschriften aus Arabien*, 4° Berlin, 1885.]

A.D. 79[1]. The Sinaitic inscriptions are certainly not of earlier date, whatever the Rev. Ch. Forster may have written to the contrary[2].

(*c*) The dialect of the inscriptions found at Tadmor or Palmyra, a large collection of which has been published by the Comte de Vogüé in his work *Syrie Centrale, Inscriptions Sémitiques*, 4to, Paris, 1868—77, on which Noeldeke has based his admirable article in the *ZDMG.*, vol. xxiv., p. 85. They range from 9 B.C. to the latter part of the third century of our era. Since De Vogüé's publication considerable additions have been made to our stock, notably one large bilingual inscription in three columns, containing a tariff of taxes and imposts on merchandise of various sorts[3].

(*d*) The dialect spoken by the Christians of Palestine, the principal literary monument of which is a Lectionary, edited by the Count Miniscalchi-Erizzo under the misleading title of *Evangeliarium Hierosolymitanum* [4to, Verona, 1861, 64], since there is nothing to connect it specially with Jerusalem. The remaining relics of this literature have been collected by Land in the fourth volume of his *Anecdota Syriaca* [4to, Lugd. Bat. 1875]. They comprise portions of the Old and New Testaments, hymns and fragments of theological writings. The grammar of this dialect has been written by Noeldeke in the *ZDMG.*, vol. xxii. p. 443. The extant MSS. of the lectionary belong to about the eleventh century, but as a spoken language this dialect was probably extinct several centuries before that time.

The third and last subdivision of the Aramean branch comprehends the dialects which occupied the Assyrian mountains and the plains of al-'Irāḳ. Of the former, so far as ancient times

[1] [These are the dates given by the French academicians. The inscription which they assign to B.C. 3 (Doughty 7 = Euting 12) is really, according to Euting's more perfect copy, of the fortieth year of Ḥārithat IV. = A.D. 31. But Euting 1 (which was not in Doughty's collection) dates from the first year of this king, so that the series begins in B.C. 9. Again the inscription of the fourth year of Rab'ēl (Euting 28 = Doughty 19), which the academicians place in A.D. 79, is assigned by Euting with more probability to A.D. 75. The date of king Rab'ēl depends on the reading of the inscription of Ḍmēr, published by Sachau in *ZDMG.* xxxviii. (1884) p. 535.]

[2] [Euting has copies of dated Sinaitic inscriptions of the 3rd Christian cent.]

[3] [Published by De Vogüé in *Journal Asiatique*, Ser. 8, t. i. ii. (1883). See also *ZDMG.* xxxvii. 562 *sqq.*, and xlii. 370 *sqq.*, where the literature is fully cited.]

are concerned, we know little or nothing. Of the latter, to which Arab writers apply the name Nabathean (نَبَطِي or نَبَاطِي), the older representative is the language of the Babylonian Talmūd (exclusive of certain portions, which are written in late Hebrew). Its more modern representative, which has only died out as a spoken language within the last few centuries, is the Mandaitic, the dialect of the Mandeans or Gnostics (מאנדאייא), otherwise called Ṣābians (i.e. "Washers," from their frequent ablutions and washings, الصَّابِئُون, rad. צבא = צבע, or المُغْتَسِلَة) and, though very absurdly, St John's Christians. A miserable remnant of this race still lingers in Chūzistān [and near Baṣra], where they have been visited by Petermann and other recent travellers; but even their priests seem now to understand but little of their Aramaic dialect. Our MSS. of their religious works are all modern, the oldest in Europe being of the sixteenth century. The grammar of this dialect too has been written by the indefatigable Noeldeke, *Mandäische Grammatik*, Halle, 1875.

All these Aramean dialects may be divided into two classes, which are readily distinguishable by the form of the 3rd pers. sing. masc. of the Imperfect. In the western dialects—Biblical Aramaic, the Targūms, the Samaritan, the Egyptian Aramaic, the Nabathean, the Palmyrene, and the Christian dialect of Palestine—the prefix of this person is *yodh*, יִקְטֻל; whereas in the eastern dialects—at least in Syriac—it is *nun*, ܢܶܩܛܽܘܠ. The usage of the Babylonian Talmūd and the Mandaitic appears to fluctuate between *n* and *l*, though *nūn* preponderates in the latter. The form with *l* appears occasionally in Biblical Aramaic, and very rarely in the Targūms, but it is restricted to the verb הֲוָא (לֶהֱוֵא or לֶהֱוֵי, לֶהֱוֹן, לֶהֶוְיָן).

Each of these two classes of Aramaic dialects has its modern representative. Around the village of Ma'lūlā, among the hills a short distance N.N.E. of Damascus, Syriac is still spoken, more by the women and children than by the men of the locality. The prefix of the 3rd pers. sing. masc. Imperf. is *yōdh*, and this dialect therefore represents the Western Aramaic. For instance:

ܐܒܘܢܢ ܒܫܡܝܐ. ܢܬܩܕܫ ܐܫܡܟ

ابونَح بِشما يِتقَّيش اِشمَخ[1]

In the mountains of Diyār-Bakr and Kurdistān, northwards of Moṣul, from Māridīn and Midyād on the west as far as Urmiah or Urūmiah and Selmās (سَلْماس) on the east, other Aramaic dialects are still spoken by the Christian and Jewish populations, who, in the eastern districts at least, have a hard struggle for existence among the Muḥammadan Kurds. The eastern dialect—the grammar of which has been written first by the American Missionary Stoddard [London 1865], and afterwards more fully and accurately by Noeldeke[2]—is usually called Modern Syriac or Neo-Syriac. This term is, however, erroneous, in so far as the said dialect, though a representative of the old Eastern Aramaic, is not directly descended from the more ancient language which we usually call Syriac, but from a lost sister tongue. Owing to the state of its verbal inflection, we cannot say for certain that the 3rd pers. sing. masc. Imperf. was formed with *n* instead of *y*, though this is highly probable, considering its relation to Syriac on the one side and Mandaitic on the other; but several points connect it more closely with the Mandaitic and the dialect of the Talmūd Bāblī than with Syriac. For example, the infin. Pa"ēl in old Syriac is ܡܦܪܘܩܘ, but in modern Syriac it is ܚܪܘܬܐ (חֲרוּתָא), ܦܪܘܩܐ (פְּרוֹקָא), which stand (as the usage of some subdialects shews) for מְחַרוּתָא, מְפַרוֹקָא, and correspond very closely to Talmudic forms like שַׁבּוֹחֵי, סַיּוֹעֵי, צַלּוֹיֵא, and Mandaitic forms like באורוכיא, יאקוריא, קאומיא. In one respect there is a curious approximation to Hebrew, viz. in the existence of participles Pu"al and Hof"al, of which old Syriac has no trace, though we find the latter in Biblical Aramaic and perhaps in Palmyrene. When the modern Syrian says ܒܝܬ ܦܪܝܩ *bit*

[1] [See Ferrette in *Journ. R. As. Soc.* xx. (1863), p. 431 *sqq.*, Nöldeke in *ZDMG.* xxi. 183 *sqq.*, Huart in *Journal As.* Ser. 7, t. xii. (1878), p. 490 *sqq.*, and Duval, *Ibid.* t. xiii. (1879), p. 456 *sqq.* Fuller information is promised by Prym and Socin.]

[2] [*Gr. der neusyrischen Sprache am Urmia-See und in Kurdistan*, Leipz. 1868.]

parkin, "I will save," he uses a Pa"ēl participle active, with the loss of the initial *m*, ܒܝܬ *bit* being a contraction of ܒܥܐ ܕ [*it is* required that], and ܦܪܩܝܢ standing for ܡܦܪܩܝܢ أنا [saving *be* I]. But when he says ܦܘܪܩܝܬ لك *purkit lī*, "I have saved thee," he employs a Pu"al participle, ܦܘܪܩܝܬ being a contraction of ܡܦܘܪܩܐ أنت, so that the literal meaning is "thou hast been saved by me." The original form ܡܦܘܪܩܐ is of course identical with the Hebrew מְחֻדָּשׁ, מְבֹרָךְ, מְפֹרָשׁ, and quite distinct from the old Syriac and Arabic passive participles ܡܩܛܠ، مُقْتَل. These Neo-Syriac dialects have been largely illustrated of late years by the publications of Socin and Prym, of Merx, and of Duval[1].

I pass on from the Central or Aramaic to the next great division of the Semitic family, the ***Western***, the members of which inhabited the narrow strip of land on the coast of the Mediterranean Sea, from the mouth of the Orontes southwards.

Here we have two different, though kindred, layers of population to deal with.

(1) The *Canaanites*, under which term we include the Bĕnē Ḥēth or Hittites, the Amorites, Jebusites, and some other tribes frequently mentioned in Scripture in close connexion with one another, and the Phoenicians of the seacoast. The Philistines, who occupied part of the south of Palestine and afterwards gave their name to the whole country, I purposely exclude for the present, as being ἀλλόφυλοι, of a yet uncertain race, though not improbably Semitic.

Just as the various Aramean tribes called themselves אֲרָם, so these Canaanites called themselves by the common name of Χνᾶ, i.e. כְּנַע. Stephanus Byzantius says that Χνᾶ was an old name for Phoenicia; Sanchuniathon, [Philo Byblius, ap. Euseb. *Pr.*

[1] [Prym and Socin, *Der neu-aram. Dialect des Ṭûr 'Abdîn*, Gött. 1881; Socin, *Die neu-aram. Dialecte von Urmia bis Mosul*, 4° Tüb. 1882 (cf. Nöldeke in *ZDMG.* xxxvi. 669 *sqq.*); Duval, *Les dialectes neo-araméens de Salamas*, Paris, 1883; Merx, *Neusyrisches Leseb.* 4to, Breslau, 1873; Guidi in *ZDMG.* xxxvii. 293 *sqq.*]

Ev. i. 10 (*Fr. Hist. Gr.* iii. 569)] that it was the name of a god or of a heroic ancestor. In the Old Testament it appears as a geographical term, under the form כְּנַעַן [which is taken to mean "lowland"]. Whether this territorial sense was the original one, may be doubted. Palestine, as a whole, is anything but a low, flat country; and the supposed contrast with אֲרָם is out of the question. It may be that the name was brought by these tribes, as a national designation, from their original home in lower Mesopotamia; or it may be that, as a national designation, it has some other source as yet unknown to us.

Of the different Canaanite races the only one that attained and maintained a great political importance was the *Phoenician*. From the district of Sidon and Tyre the Phoenicians gradually spread, principally northwards, along the coast of Syria, occupying such places as Bērytos (Beirūt), Byblos (גְּבַל [Gebal, Ezek. xxvii. 9], جُبَيْل), Botrys (بَتْرُون, Batrūn), Tripolis, Simyra (Σίμυρα, הַצְּמָרִי ["the Zemarite," Gen. x. 18]), Arke (Ἄρκη or τὰ Ἄρκα, הָעַרְקִי ["the Arkite," Gen. x. 17]), Sinnas (Σιννᾶς, הַסִּינִי ["the Sinite," Gen. x. 17]), Aradus (הָאַרְוָדִי ["the Arvadite," Gen. x. 18], أَرْوَاد) and Antaradus (أَنْطَرْطُوس, Tortosa), Laodicea, and Amathe (חֲמָת [Hamath], حَمَاة), farther inland. With the extension of their domains by colonisation we are not now concerned. Suffice it to say that the Phoenicians occupied, in whole or in part, many of the islands of the Mediterranean, such as Cyprus, Rhodes, Crete, Malta, Sicily, the Lipari isles, Sardinia, and the Balearic group. They had settlements in Egypt and throughout all northern Africa, where Carthage rose to be the dreaded rival of Rome. They set foot in Gaul at Massilia or Marseilles[1]; and a large portion of Southern Spain was in their hands. From the port of Cadiz their ships sailed

[1] [The evidence for the existence of a Phoenician colony at Marseilles before the Phocaean settlement is wholly archaeological and has broken down bit by bit. Last of all it has been shewn, since these lectures were written, that the famous Phoenician sacrificial tablet is of Carthaginian stone and must have been brought from Carthage; how or when can only be matter of conjecture. See *Corpus Inscr. Sem.* i. 217 *sqq.*]

southwards along the coast of Africa and northwards towards Britain; whilst from Elath (أَيْلَة) and Ezion-geber on the Red Sea they traded with S. Arabia and India, which they also reached by way of the Persian Gulf. In short, go where you will throughout the ancient world, you find the Phoenician סֹחֵר, as keen and energetic a trader as his kinsman the modern Jew.

All the languages of this Canaanitic group, it would seem, closely resembled what we call Hebrew; but the only one of them with which we are well acquainted is the Phoenician. It has been preserved to us in numerous inscriptions from all parts of the ancient world, varying in date from the seventh (or eighth) cent. to the first cent. B.C., or, if we include the Punic, to the second or third cent. of our era. The grammar which you should consult is that of Schröder [*Die Phönizische Sprache*, Halle, 1869], and you should also read Stade's treatise "Erneute Prüfung des zwischen dem Phönicischen u. Hebräischen bestehenden Verwandtschaftsgrades," in ***Morgenländische Forschungen***, Leipzig 1875[1].

Of the so-called Hittite empire, the chief seats of which were at Kadesh on the Orontes and subsequently at Karkĕmīsh on the Euphrates, I here say nothing; because it is doubtful whether the *Kheta* of the Egyptians and the *Khatti* of the Assyrians can really be identified with the בני חת or חִתִּים of the Book of Genesis. Ramses II., in the fifteenth cent. B.C., waged war with the Kheta and captured their city Kadesh; and the Khatti were always a bar in the way of the Assyrian kings down to the year 717 B.C., when Sargon succeeded in taking Karkĕmīsh. This northern kingdom may be meant in such passages as 1 Kings x. 29, 2 Kings vii. 6, and 2 Sam. xxiv. 6; but scarcely in Gen. x. 15, xv. 20, and xxiii., or Deut. vii. 1, where we have clearly to deal with a strictly Canaanitic tribe.

(2) The Canaanites were already long masters of the land, when a body of strangers appeared among them. These immigrants had originally started from Ur Kasdīm, i.e. the city called in the Assyrian inscriptions *Uru* (now al-Muġair, المُقَيَّر)

[1] [A complete collection of Phoenician inscriptions will form the first part of the *Corpus Inscriptionum Semiticarum* undertaken by the French *Acad. des Inscr.* The first vol. has appeared, fol. Paris, 1881–87, with atlas of plates.]

in Babylonia, and had gone northwards to Ḥarrān in Mesopotamia. Here a split took place among them. The family of Naḥor remained in Mesopotamia; that of Teraḥ, under the leadership of Abrām, marched south-westwards into Canaan. These strangers received the name of עִבְרִיִּים or עִבְרִים, most probably because they came מֵעֵבֶר הַנָּהָר, from across the great river Euphrates. This is what the LXX. intended when they rendered the words לְאַבְרָם הָעִבְרִי (Gen. xiv. 13) by Ἀβρὰμ τῷ περάτῃ; and what Origen meant when he explained Ἑβραῖοι by περατικοί. Some of these strangers remained in the country, and in the end permanently occupied different portions of it on the East side of the Jordan and to the east and south of the Dead Sea; viz. the Children of Ammon, of Moab, and of Edom. Others of them, the Children of Ishmael, wandered away among the adjacent Arab tribes to the E. and S. E., and ultimately became inseparable and indistinguishable from them. Others still, the Children of Jacob, after dwelling for some considerable time in Palestine itself, moved southwards, and swelled the ranks of the Semitic immigrants into Egypt. After a sojourn in that country, which is variously estimated at from 215 to 430 years[1], the Children of Jacob fled or were expelled, and resumed a nomade life in the Sinaitic peninsula under the leadership of Moses. This event may be placed in the fifteenth or fourteenth cent. B.C., for the calculations of different scholars vary. Marching northwards they came once more to the borders of Palestine, and passing by their kinsmen of Edom and Moab, they fell upon the Amorites, who had succeeded in crushing Ammon and seriously crippling Moab. The Amorites went down before the fierce assault of Israel, for whom God fought (as the name betokens), and the land to the north of the Arnon was the reward of their prowess. From this vantage-ground they entered upon a long struggle with the Canaanites, which, after various vicissitudes, ended in the substantial triumph of the Israelites and the conquest of large portions of the Canaanite territory, in which they settled side by side with the conquered race.

[1] [See the commentaries on Exod. xii. 40.]

The language of the Hebrews is well known to us, its literature extending over a period of many ages, from the date of the earliest Biblical books down to the redaction of the Mishnah, about the end of the second century after Christ, when Hebrew had long ceased to be the language of ordinary life, and was only written and spoken in the schools. But the same cannot be said of the languages of Ammon, Moab and Edom, of which, till within the last few years, we knew no more than the Old Testament itself could teach us. However, in 1868, the German missionary Klein discovered a stone with a long inscription at Dībān (the ancient Dibon, דִּיבֹן) in the territory of Moab. This passed, after it had been broken and mutilated, into the hands of M. Clermont-Ganneau, then one of the officials of the French Consulate at Jerusalem, and is now deposited in the Louvre. This inscription belongs to the time of Mēsha', king of Moab, in the first quarter of the ninth century B.C., and gives an account of his wars with the Israelites and his domestic undertakings. The language is so similar to the Hebrew of the Old Testament that Prof. Roediger simply treated it as such in the last edition which he published of Gesenius' Hebrew Grammar (the twenty-first, 1872)[1].

If, then, the difference between the Phoenicians on the one side, and the Hebrew and Moabite on the other, be so slight, how is this to be explained? In one or other of two ways. We might suppose, firstly, that the ancestors of the Hebrews, who wandered from Ur Kasdīm northwards in company with Arameans, were, though of the same stock, yet of a different family from these; and this circumstance might have led to their separation from the Arameans, and to their seeking a home among more closely allied peoples in Canaan. Against this view, however, it may be fairly urged that, in the Old Testament itself (Deut. xxvi. 5), Abram is spoken of as אֲרַמִּי אֹבֵד "a wandering," or "nomade, Aramean"; and that Jacob's relatives in Paddan Aram are always expressly called Arameans (Gen. xxv. 20, xxviii. 5, xxxi. 20, 24). I incline, therefore, to the second explanation, put forward by Schröder and other scholars, which is this: that

[1] [The latest edition of the "Moabite Stone" is that of Smend and Socin, Freiburg, 1886. In the same year a facsimile of a portion of the inscription with transliteration and translation was published by the Palaeographical Society (2nd Ser. pl. 43).]

these nomade Arameans, the tribes of Abram and Lot, having settled among a Canaanite population of a much higher order of civilisation, were soon constrained to disuse their mother tongue, the Aramaic, and to adopt the kindred language of the people among whom they had settled. To the advanced civilisation of the Hittites and Phoenicians the monuments of Egypt and the Old Testament itself bear ample testimony. We know for certain, thanks to the labours of such Egyptologists as the Vicomte de Rougé and Mr Goodwin, that in the time of Ramses II., that is, in the fifteenth century B.C., the Kheta of Kadesh were in possession of the art of writing and of a literature. And as for the Phoenicians, when Solomon desired to build his Temple to Jehovah, Hiram king of Tyre supplied the materials and the artisans; when Solomon sought to trade with South Arabia, it was again Hiram who manned the fleet of ships at Ezion-geber. That a small and less civilised tribe, such as the Hebrews in the time of Abram undoubtedly were, should have soon adopted the language of the more numerous and cultivated race among whom they took up their abode, has in itself nothing surprising, and is a fact not altogether unknown in history. In France and Spain, for example, the conquering German race soon gave up the use of its mother-tongue, which left but slight traces of the conquest upon the language of the conquered. The Norsemen invaded and took possession of a district in France, to which they gave their name; but the Normans invaded England as a French-speaking people, and were again in process of time merged among the English whom they conquered.

The last great section of the Semitic languages is the *Southern* or Arabian, which we may divide into three branches; viz. the North Arabian or Arabic, commonly so called; the South Arabian or Ḥimyaritic; and the Ge'ez or Ethiopic.

I. *Arabic* is, in its historical career and literary development, one of the latest of the Semitic languages to rise into prominent notice. Though we read of wars between the Arabs and the Assyrians, the Romans, and the Persians, who were each acknowledged at different periods as liege lords of a considerable part of the Arabian Peninsula; yet it was not till the seventh century of our era that the nation acquired a really historical importance. It was under Muḥammad and his successors that the Arabs, maddened by religious enthusiasm, rushed forth from their deserts like a torrent; broke the Byzantine power on the banks of the Hieromax (Yarmūk); crushed the might of Persia on the day of al-Ḳādisîyah; and adding conquest to conquest, planted the standard of their Prophet, within a hundred years, upon the banks of the Indus in the east and of the Tagus in the west.

The literary development of the race dates from the same period. Before Muḥammad's time the northern Arabs had only a literature of ballads, mostly handed down by oral tradition. With the promulgation of the Ḳor'ān a new era commenced, and there are few, if any, nations of ancient and medieval Europe which can boast of a literature like the Arabic, especially in history, geography, philosophy, and other sciences, to say nothing of poetry, and of the peculiar systems of theology and law which depend upon the Ḳor'ān and the Sunnah.

The Arabic language was thus peculiarly fortunate. Leading a life of comparative seclusion—not ground, like the Arameans and Canaanites, between the two grindstones of Assyria, Babylon, or Persia, on the one side, and Egypt on the other; nor, like the Phoenicians, thrown by commerce and colonisation into close contact with a dozen foreign nations—the Arabs had preserved, down to the sixth or seventh century of our era, far more of the ancient form and fashion of Semitic speech than any of their congeners. If not the Sanskṛit, Arabic is at least the Lithuanian among the Semitic tongues. At this particular period too the dialect of the tribe of Ḳoraish[1], which had already acquired a certain supremacy over the rest, was fixed by the Ḳor'ān as the future literary language of the whole nation. Had it not been for this circumstance, we might have known Arabic in the form of half a dozen languages, differing from one another almost as widely as the members of the Romance group or the modern languages of northern India. But its literature has in a great measure prevented this, and preserved the unity of the language, so that the dialectic divergences

[1] [The Ḳoraish, i.e. the branch of Kināna settled in and about Mecca, were the tribe of the prophet.]

of what is called "vulgar Arabic" are by no means so great as we might have expected after all the struggles and vicissitudes of the last twelve centuries. From the mouth of the Tigris, throughout Mesopotamia, Syria and Palestine, Arabia proper, Egypt, and North Africa, as far as Morocco, the language is essentially one and the same—Arabic, sunk by the gradual decay of its inflection to the level at which we become acquainted with Aramaic and Hebrew. In its purest form it is probably to be heard among the Bedawīn; in its most corrupt in the island of Malta. The standard grammar of the classical Arabic is that of Silvestre de Sacy (second edition, 2 vols. Paris, 1831[1]). Smaller works in various languages are numerous. For the modern dialects there is also an ample choice. For the Egyptian dialect none can compete with Spitta, *Grammatik des Arabischen Vulgärdialectes von Ægypten* (1880). For the Syrian a useful book is the *Grammaire Arabe vulgaire* of Caussin de Perceval (fourth edition, 1858); and for the Algerian the *Éléments de la Langue Algérienne* of A. P. Pihan (1851). The Maltese has been treated by Vassalli, *Grammatica della lingua Maltese*, second edition, 1827; and by Gesenius in his *Versuch über die Maltesische Sprache* (Leipzig 1810).

2. The *Ṣouth Arabian* or *Ḥimyaritic* [also called Sabaean] is one of the less known of the Semitic tongues. I use the term Ḥimyaritic (حِمْيَر, ܚܡܝܪܝܐ, Ὁμηρῖται) here, in its widest sense, to denote the language, or rather group of languages, whose territory extends along the south coast of Arabia, from the strait of Bāb-el-Mandeb on the west to the mouth of the Persian Gulf on the east. There seems to be little doubt that the three great provinces of al-Yemen, Ḥadramaut (חצרמות, Gen. x. 26), and Mahrah, spoke dialects of one tongue, and that these dialects have their modern representatives in the Ehḳilī, also called Ḥakilī or Ḳarāwī, and the Mehrī.

The ancient Ḥimyaritic is chiefly known to us through inscriptions, which have been found in great numbers, especially

[1] [The grammar of De Sacy is now difficult to procure, and the reader who desires to bring his knowledge down to date must take with it the notes of Fleischer, which form the first volume of his *Kleinere Schriften*, Leipzig, 1885. Students will therefore prefer the excellent grammar of the author of these lectures, 2nd ed. London, 1874.]

in the most accessible of the three provinces above named, that of al-Yemen. How far back they may go in point of time is uncertain. According to Mordtmann and D. H. Müller in their *Sabäische Denkmäler* (4° Vienna, 1883), p. 86, the era of the three dated inscriptions as yet known to us is, as guessed by Reinaud, the Seleucian. These inscriptions belong therefore to A.D. 261, 328, and 357[1]. None of the Ḥimyaritic monuments are likely to be later than the seventh century of our era. The grammar of these languages has not yet been formally compiled by any one orientalist, but we may soon expect a work on the subject from the competent hand of Prof. D. H. Müller of Vienna.

3. Crossing over into Africa, we encounter the Ge'ez or Ethiopic, the language of the Abyssinians, an ancient Ḥimyaritic colony, as the word ግዕዝ ፡ "migration" or "the emigrants," itself shews. Its territory is the mountainous region S.W. of Nubia, where its modern representatives still flourish. The most prominent of these are: on the north, the *Tigré*, spoken in the Dahlak islands, and on the mainland in Ṣamhar and by the Habab, Mensa, Bogos, and neighbouring tribes; in the centre, the *Tigriña* [or *Tigrai*], which prevails in the districts of Dembeyā, Hamasēn, Sarawē, Akala-guzai, and Agamē, around the ancient capital of Aksūm, and in the region of Walḳait; and in the south, the *Amhariña* or *Amharic*, the language of Samēn and the districts around Gondar and the Lake Ṣānā or Ṭānā, as far as Gōjām. Of these three languages, the Tigré most resembles the old Ge'ez, whilst the Amharic has deviated furthest from it.

The oldest monuments of the Ethiopic literature are a few inscriptions, belonging to the first five or six centuries of our era. Next to these we must rank the translation of the Bible, executed probably at different times, during a space of several centuries from the fourth century onwards. The bulk of the literature is, however, modern, and consists of translations from the Coptic, and still more frequently from the Arabic, which were produced

[1] [In his article "Yemen" in the *Encyclopaedia Britannica*, 9th ed. vol. xxiv. (1888), Prof. Müller looks with some favour on the view put forward by Halévy (*Ét. Sab.* p. 86), who takes the inscription Ḥiṣn Ghorāb, dated 640, to speak of the overthrow of Dhū Nuwās, and so fixes on 115 B.C. as the epoch of the Sabaean era. In that case the *five* dated inscriptions now known are to be ascribed to A.D. 270, 458, 467, 525, and 554 respectively. Cf. *C.I.S.*, IV. i. p. 18.]

in abundance from the thirteenth to the sixteenth centuries, when the ancient Ge'ez had died out, but was still cultivated by the priesthood, like Latin by the learned of Europe or Hebrew in the Talmudic schools. The standard grammar of the ancient Ge'ez is that of Dillmann [Leipzig, 1857] which has superseded that of Ludolfus or Leuthof, an admirable work in its day. The Tigriña dialect has been handled by Praetorius, *Grammatik der Tigriña-Sprache* (Halle, 1871) [and Schreiber, *Man. de la langue Tigraï* (Vien. 1887)]. For the Amharic I may name the works of Isenberg (1842) and Massaja, *Lectiones grammaticales* (Paris, 1867); but the best book on the subject is that of Praetorius, *Die Amharische Sprache* (1879). [See also Guidi, *Gr. elem. della l. Amariña* (Rome, 1889)].

Having thus taken a rapid and necessarily imperfect survey of the Semitic languages, it may be well for us to spend a few minutes on an inquiry as to their connexion, real or imaginary, with the great contiguous families, more especially with the Indo-European and the Egyptian.

This is a question of great difficulty, and not to be settled in the crude and offhand manner of Fürst and Delitzsch on the one hand or of von Raumer and Raabe on the other. The temptation to identification is great, and too much weight has been attributed by the scholars mentioned, and even by men of higher reputation, to analogies that lie merely on the surface. The Semitic languages, like the Indo-European, belong to the inflective class; but this circumstance, as Whitney has remarked (*Language and the Study of Language*, 3rd ed., p. 300), by no means implies a genetic connexion or even descent from a common stock. The resemblance between the two families is, on the whole, not greater than we might reasonably expect to find in languages produced by human beings of nearly the same natural endowments under very similar circumstances of development. The probability of an ultimate connexion will of course seem greatest to those who believe in a common birthplace of the two races. If they both spread themselves abroad from a point near the Caspian Sea, or in Central Asia, original unity is not impossible. But if the Indo-Europeans rooted in Central

Asia, or, as some recent scholars (such as Penka in his *Origines Ariacae* [Teschen, 1883], and O. Schrader, in his *Sprachvergleichung und Urgeschichte* [Jena, 1883]) have tried to prove, on the shores of the Baltic, whilst the Semites were autochthones in Central Arabia, the chances of original unity are reduced to a vanishing point. An ultimate relationship, if one exist at all, will only be discovered when we have solved the great mystery of the Semitic tongues, the triliterality of the roots. With a few exceptions, the most important of which are the pronouns, every Semitic root, as historically known to us, is triliteral; it consists of three letters, neither more nor less, and these three are consonants. The vowels play only a secondary rôle. The consonants give the meaning of the word; the vowels express its modifications. The letters *ḳtl* (قتل, קטל), for example, are the bones of a skeleton, which the vowels clothe with flesh and endow with life. These three consonants convey the idea of "kill." Add vowels, and you get such words as قَتَلَ *ḳatala* "he killed," قُتِلَ *ḳutila* "he was killed"; قَتْل *ḳatl* "the act of killing" or "of being killed"; قِتْل *ḳitl* "a killer," "an enemy"; قَاتِل *ḳâtil* "killing." The use of prefixes, affixes, and even of infixes, is common to both families of languages; but the Indo-Europeans have nothing like this triconsonantal rule with its varying vocalisation as a means of grammatical inflexion. The Indo-European roots are not thus restricted in their nature; the radical vowels, although more liable to phonetic change than the consonants, are as essential a part of the root as these latter. A root may consist of a single vowel; of a vowel followed by one or more consonants; of one or more consonants followed by a vowel; of a vowel preceded and followed by a single consonant; and so on. The Sanskṛit roots *i* "go," *sthâ* "stand," *ad* "eat," *vid* "know," *grabh* "seize," are something wholly different in character from the Semitic roots *ḳrb* "come near," *ḳtl* "kill," *plg* "divide," which, as Bopp has justly remarked (*Vergl. Gr.*, 2te Ausg., 1ter Bd, p. 196), are unpronounceable, because, in giving them vowels, we make an advance to a special grammatical form. And yet here, if anywhere, will an ultimate connexion between these two families of languages be discovered. It cannot escape the observation of the student that a great many Semitic roots have two consonants in common, whilst the third seems less essential, and is therefore variable. For example, *ḳt* or *ḳd* are common to the series, قتّ, قتل, قدّ, قدح, قذّ, قطّ, قطع, قطف, قطل, قطم, all of which convey the idea of "cutting" in some form or other. *Pl* or *fl* are found in فلّ, فلج, فلح, فلخ, فلذ, فلع, فلق, فلم, فلي, all meaning "cleave" or "divide." *Ḥ, ḳ* are the basis of חקק, חקה, חקר, of which the original signification is also "slit" or "cut." *Pḥ* or *fḥ* are the essential constituents of فحّ, فاح, فاخ, نفح, نفخ, meaning "blow," "puff." When Semitic philology has advanced so far as to have discovered the laws by which the original biliterals (assuming their separate existence) were converted into triliterals; when we are able to account for the position and to explain the function of each variable constituent of the triliteral roots; then, and not till then, may we venture to think of comparing the primitive Indo-European and Semitic vocabularies. Meantime, to assert the identity of such a word as בָּנָה "he built" with *pono*, or of בָּעַר "he burned up" with *πῦρ*, is little better than sheer folly. And why? Because the comparison is not that of original forms, but of an original form (or what is very nearly so) with a comparatively late development. בָּנָה was originally *bănăyă*; *pōno* is a softening of *posno*, as we learn from its perfect and supine, and includes a suffix and a pronominal element. בָּעַר originally sounded *baʿara*; *πῦρ* is stated to be a contraction of *πύϊρ*, which probably stands for an original **pavar*, and comes from a radical *pu*, in Sanskṛit "to be bright," "to purify," *plus* a derivative suffix. If such comparisons as these could be upheld, they would prove that Hebrew and Arabic were not merely connected with, but actually derived from Sanskṛit or Greek or Latin. What has been written on this subject by Fürst and by the elder Delitzsch in his *Jesurun* (1838) is absolutely worthless; as are also the lucubrations of von Raumer and Raabe. The best that can be said about it you will find in the younger Delitzsch's *Studien über Indogermanisch-Semitische Wurzelverwandtschaft* (Leipzig 1873) and in McCurdy's *Aryo-Semitic Speech* (1881).

As to the affinity of the Egyptian language with the Semitic stock, that is also a question which is as yet *sub judice*. Benfey, in his well-known work *Ueber das Verhältniss der ägyptischen Sprache zum semitischen Sprachstamm* (Leipzig 1844), sought to establish this affinity by various considerations, grammatical and lexicographical; and the conclusion to which he came was, that the Semites are only one branch of a great family, which includes not only the Egyptians but also all the other languages of Africa. His views have been combated by Pott, Renan, and other scholars; and certainly in this unrestricted form they seem to land us in almost Turanian absurdities. But with regard to the ancient Egyptian and the Coptic, Egyptologists seem gradually to be arriving at conclusions similar to those of Benfey. De Rougé, Ebers, and above all Brugsch, in the introduction to his *Hieroglyphic Dictionary*, have declared their belief in the descent of the Egyptian from the same stock as the Semitic languages. An examination of the Coptic alone readily suggests several considerations in support of this view. For example, there is the marvellous similarity, almost amounting to identity, of the personal pronouns, both separate and suffixed—a class of words which languages of radically different families are not apt to borrow from one another. "I" in Coptic is ⲁ̀ⲛⲟⲕ, ⲁⲛⲁⲕ.

"Thou" ⲛ̀ⲧⲟⲕ, ⲛ̀ⲧⲁⲕ
"He" ⲛ̀ⲑⲟϥ, etc.
"She" ⲛ̀ⲑⲟⲥ, etc.
"We" ⲁ̀ⲛⲟⲛ, ⲁ̀ⲛⲁⲛ
"Ye" ⲛ̀ⲑⲱⲧⲉⲛ, ⲛ̀ⲧⲱⲧⲛ̄, ⲛ̀ⲧⲁⲧⲛ̄
"They" ⲛ̀ⲑⲱⲟⲩ, ⲛ̀ⲧⲟⲟⲩ, ⲛ̀ⲧⲁⲩ

The suffix pronouns I give as they appear in connexion with the preposition ⲛⲁ "to."

"to me"	ⲛⲏⲓ, ⲛⲁⲓ	"to us"	ⲛⲁⲛ
"to thee," m.	ⲛⲁⲕ	"to you"	ⲛⲱⲧⲉⲛ, ⲛⲏⲧⲉⲛ
f.	ⲛⲉ		
"to him"	ⲛⲁϥ	"to them"	ⲛⲱⲟⲩ, ⲛⲁⲩ
"to her"	ⲛⲁⲥ		

Again, there is the curious resemblance in the forms of some of the simplest numerals; e.g.

1, masc. ⲟⲩⲁⲓ, ⲟⲩⲁ, ⲟⲩⲱⲧ; fem. ⲟⲩⲓ, ⲟⲩⲉⲓ, ⲟⲩⲱⲧ
2, masc. ⲥⲛⲁⲩ, fem. ⲥⲉⲛⲧⲉ, ⲥⲛⲟⲩϯ
7, masc. ϣⲁϣϥ, ⲥⲁϣϥ; fem. ϣⲁϣϥⲓ, ⲥⲁϣϥⲉ
8, masc. ϣⲙⲏⲛ, ϣⲙⲟⲩⲛ; fem. ϣⲙⲏⲛⲓ, ϣⲙⲟⲩⲛⲉ.

In the verb, the formation of the present tense presents a remarkable analogy to that of the Semitic imperfect or, as some still prefer to call it, future,—I mean the form יִקְטֹל. E.g.

sing. 1.	ϯ. ⲧⲱⲙ *I am joining, adhering;*	pl. 1.	ⲧⲉⲛ. ⲧⲱⲙ
2. m.	ⲕ. ⲧⲱⲙ, ϫ. ⲧⲱⲙ	2.	ⲧⲉⲧⲉⲛ. ⲧⲱⲙ
f.	ⲧⲉ. ⲧⲱⲙ		
3. m.	ϥ. ⲧⲱⲙ	3.	ⲥⲉ. ⲧⲱⲙ
f.	ⲥ. ⲧⲱⲙ		

Analogies like these seem to favour the idea of a genetic relationship between the Semitic languages and the Egyptian; or at least of a closer affinity than can be said to subsist between the Semitic and the Indo-European. To discover any connexion between the two latter, we must endeavour to work our way back to the very earliest stage of their history—to a period before Semitic really was Semitic; we must try to disintegrate the triliteral Semitic root; to extract from it the biliteral, which alone can be compared with the Indo-European radical. And if haply we succeed in this, it is apparently the utmost that we can hope for; their subsequent developments, the growth of their grammatical systems, are wholly distinct and discordant. But the connexion between the Semitic and the Egyptian languages seems to be of a somewhat nearer kind. It is true that we are met by the old difficulty with regard to the form of the Egyptian roots, the majority of which are monosyllabic, and certainly do not exhibit Semitic triliterality; but, on the other hand, we have not a few structural affinities, which may perhaps be thought sufficient to justify those linguists who hold that Egyptian is a relic of the earliest age of Semitism, of Semitic speech as it was before it passed into the peculiar form in which we may be said to know it historically.

CHAPTER III.

SEMITIC WRITING.

AFTER these preliminary investigations and surveys, there remains yet another subject on which it is desirable to say a few words before we address ourselves to the special object of these lectures, the comparative grammar of the Semitic languages. That subject is—the origin and history of Semitic writing. My account of this interesting topic must, however, be very brief and sketchy; the more so as I hope to treat it more fully in a subsequent course of lectures. Meantime I would refer those of you who seek further details to the treatise of the Vicomte de Rougé, *Mémoire sur l'origine égyptienne de l'alphabet phénicien*, 1874; to the work of Lenormant, *Essai sur la propagation de l'alphabet phénicien dans l'ancien monde*, of which the first part appeared in 1872, and two more have since been added, though the book must now unhappily remain unfinished; to the *Mélanges d'Archéologie orientale* of the Cte de Vogüé, 1868; and to Mr Isaac Taylor's excellent book *The Alphabet* [London, 1883], especially vol. i.

All writing—Chinese, Assyrian, Egyptian—was originally pictorial. The next stage was that of the ideogram. Each picture received a fixed, often symbolic, value, and was always used in the same way. In Egyptian the figure of a tongue meant "to speak"; two hands holding a shield and spear meant "to fight"; and so on. The third step—a great one—was to make a particular sign stand in all cases for one and the same syllabic sound; e.g., the figure of a mouth 𓂋 for *ro*, the Egyptian for "mouth"; the figure of a hand for *tot*; the figure of an eye for *iri*. The last and greatest step was to divide the syllable into its component parts or letters, and to represent each of these by a special figure. Here the ancient Egyptians happily lighted upon what has been called the "acrophonic" principle; that is to say, they designated each letter by the picture of an object, the name of which began with the sound which the letter was to represent. For example, the picture of a *lion*, would mean the letter *l*, because the word *labo*, ⲗⲁⲃⲟⲓ, begins with that sound; the picture of an *owl* the letter *m*, because the word *mūlag*, ⲙⲟⲩⲗⲁϫ, begins with that sound; the picture of a *mouth* the letter *r*, because the word *ro*, ⲣⲟ, begins with *r*.

To this stage the Egyptians attained at a very early period; but, like the inventors of the cuneiform characters, they did not avail themselves fully of their great discovery. On the contrary, they mixed up the two principles, the ideographic and the phonetic, in a manner that is extremely puzzling to the reader. To an Egyptian the figure of a *lion* might actually mean "a lion"; or it might, as an ideogram, be a symbolic sign, meaning "preeminence," "sovereignty"; or it might, as a mere letter, designate the sound *l*. To an Assyrian a certain combination of wedges might convey the idea of "the earth"; but phonetically it might express the syllable *ki*. Hence the mass of determinative signs of various kinds employed in writing by the Egyptians, Assyrians and Chinese.

Of course, in process of time, the picture gradually faded away. Details were neglected; a few bold strokes sufficed to depict the object intended; and, in the end, the form of the *letter* often bore little or no resemblance to the *thing* from which it was derived. The group of wedges, the hieratic or demotic character, and the modern Chinese sign, are, in most cases, wholly unlike any object in heaven or earth.

The Egyptians, in addition to the stiff pictorial hieroglyphs, had two sorts of more current or cursive characters, called the hieratic and the demotic. The former, used (as the name indicates) by the priests, was employed for sacred writings only; the latter, used by the people, served for all ordinary secular purposes. It was of the former that the inventors or adapters of the Semitic alphabet appear to have availed themselves. They used the forms which are found in papyri anterior to the eighteenth dynasty, belonging, roughly speaking, to the period between 2100 and 1500 B.C. De Rougé endeavours to show that out of the twenty-two Phoenician letters, fifteen are beyond doubt directly derived from Egyptian models, whilst only one, the *'ayin*, is clearly of Semitic invention. It may be that the "spoiling of the Egyptians" went so far; that the plundering Semites appropriated not only the idea of a written alphabet, but the very forms which the letters were to take. However, I cannot profess myself entirely convinced, not even by Mr Isaac Taylor's argumentation. If they did so, the Semites both remodelled and renamed their acquisitions. Out of the Egyptian *eagle* or *vulture* they made the head and horns of an ox, 𐤀, אָלֶף; the *throne*, , became the head and neck of a *camel*, 𐤂, גָּמָל; the group of lotus plants growing out of the water, , a *set of teeth*, 𐤔, שֵׁן; and so on[1].

Deecke's attempt to derive the forms of the Semitic alphabet from the Assyrian, I must regard as an utter failure. You will find his views stated in an article in the *ZDMG.*, vol. xxxi. p. 102.

The remodelled Egyptian alphabet has been, in the hands of the Phoenicians and other Semites, the parent of nearly all the systems of writing used by the nations of Europe and Western Asia. The Greeks received it from the Phoenicians, and having again remodelled it, passed it on to the Etruscans, the Romans, and the Copts. The sacred books of the Persians are written with an alphabet of Aramaic origin. The Uīgūr Tatars [and through them the Mongols] acknowledge a similar obligation. And even the Sanskṛit alphabet, with all its Asiatic offshoots, has been traced to a South Semitic source.

The oldest monument of Semitic writing as yet discovered, with what we may call a certain date, is the inscription of Mēsha', מֵישַׁע, king of Moab, which we may place about B.C. 890[2]. Here we find already a carefully developed system of orthography and punctuation, which contrasts favourably with those of Phoenician inscriptions of later date by several centuries. Final vowels are expressed by the letters י (ī), ו (ū) and ה (ō),

[1] Halévy, with whom Nöldeke inclines to agree, derives the Semitic alphabet from the hieroglyphs.

[2] [i.e. soon after the death of Ahab, which, according to the received chronology, took place 897 B.C. If, as is concluded from the Assyrian monuments, Ahab was alive in 854 and took part in the battle of Ḳarḳar (Schrader, *Keilinschr. und A T.* 2nd ed. Giessen, 1883, pp. 199, 463) the stone of Mesha dates from about 850 B.C.]

e.g. אבי, בנתי, עשׂ, בביתה, לה; and the words are separated by a single point, which is also found in a few of the younger Phoenician inscriptions, and in Samaritan, and which we may compare with the line | of the Ḥimyaritic, and the two dots of the Ethiopic (:)[1]. Equally old, if not older, is the inscription on the fragments of a bronze bowl discovered in Cyprus (*Corpus Inscrr. Semitt.*, i. pp. 22–26, and pl. iv). To the same class of alphabets as these inscriptions belong the various Phoenician monuments and coins of Tyre and Sidon, Gĕbal, Cyprus, Athens, Malta, Sicily, Sardinia, Marseilles, Carthage and other parts of N. Africa, and Spain. The oldest of these date from the sixth or fifth century B.C., whilst of the youngest or Neopunic many are post-Christian. The difference between the earlier and later monuments in the form of certain letters is very marked. Observe these in particular:—

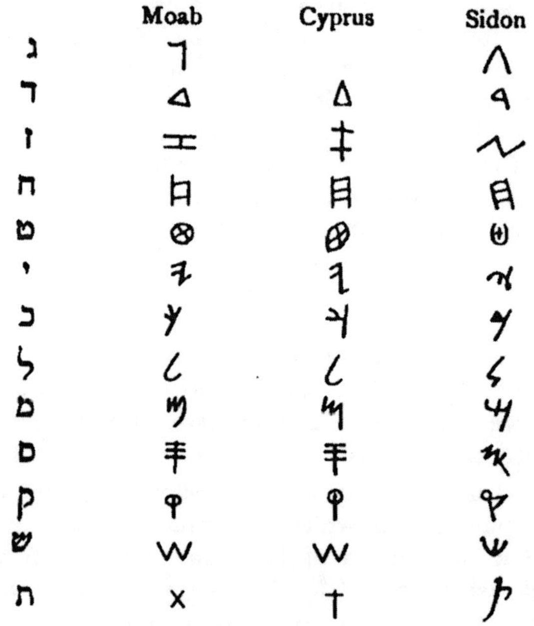

The ancient Hebrew modification of the Semitic alphabet is now known to us in a document to which an approximate date can be assigned, viz. the Siloam inscription, of the seventh

[1] [Cf. the facsimile, *Palaeographical Society*, 2nd Series, pl. xliii. (1886).]

century B.C.[1] As compared with the Mēsha' alphabet, notable varieties in the forms of single letters are:—

Old seals and other gems, dating, say, from the seventh to the fourth century B.C., exhibit identical forms; and the same remark applies to two fragmentary inscriptions from the neighbourhood of Jerusalem, discovered by M. Clermont-Ganneau and now deposited in the British Museum. This alphabet is still found, with slight modifications, upon the Maccabee and other Jewish coins; and is known to us in its latest shape as the *Samaritan* alphabet. It began, however, to be disused by the Jews even before the commencement of our era, and to be supplanted by a modified form of the Palmyrene character, the so-called *square* character, כְּתָב מְרֻבָּע. Some of the extant inscriptions of this type belong to the century preceding our era. For the first three or four centuries after Christ our materials, though not abundant, are sufficiently ample for palaeographical purposes.

The third of the Semitic alphabets is the Aramaic, our knowledge of which commences with some Assyrian weights, which go back as far as the seventh or eighth century before our era. There are also extant some gems and seals of nearly the same age. Among the inscriptions may be mentioned that recently discovered by Prof. Euting at Taimā, clearly belonging to the Persian period, say from the sixth to the fourth century B.C. A sure mark of antiquity in this, as well as in the Phoenician alphabet, is the undulating or wavy form of the letters *m* and *sh*, as contrasted with the later forms, which exhibit a cross-line. In the inscription of Mēsha', as well as in the Assyrian weights, we find 𐤌 𐤌 and 𐤔, which become at a later time 𐤌 𐤌 and 𐤔 𐤔. The letter מ too in the Moabite

[1] [Cf. the facsimile in the *Oriental Series* of the Palaeographical Society, Plate lxxxvii. (1882). "The inscription...may be ascribed to the reign of Hezekiah towards the year 700 B.C.": cf. 2 Kings xx. 20; 2 Chron. xxxii. 30.]

stele and the oldest Aramean seals has the forms 𐤎 𐤎, whereas later on it appears as 𐡎 𐡎 𐡎 𐡎 and the like. A peculiarity of the Aramean alphabet is that some of the letters have open heads, and thus contrast markedly with the closed heads of the Phoenician type. These are :—

	Phoen.	Aram.
ב	𐤁	𐡁
ד	𐤃 𐤃	𐡃 𐡃
ע	𐤏	𐡏
ר	𐤓	𐡓

To this class belong the Egyptian-Aramaic alphabet, the Nabathean (including the Sinaitic inscriptions), and the Syriac Esṭrangĕlā with all its more modern developments, comprising the Mandaitic on the one hand and the Kūfic and Naskhī Arabic on the other. The character of the Palmyrene inscriptions is very interesting, as coming nearest to the Jewish square character.

The alphabet used by the southern Semites, though ultimately sprung from the same stock as the Phoenician and Aramean alphabets, must have been separated from them at a very remote time, and have run its course under peculiar influences. The oldest inscriptions which we possess, whether from North or South Arabia, whether Thamūdite (aṣ-Ṣafā)[1] or Himyaritic or Ethiopic, are written, like all other Semitic writings, from right to left. Others, probably of later date, are written, to use a Greek word, *βουστροφηδόν*, "as the ox turns in ploughing," that is, like some Greek inscriptions, alternately from right to left and left to right. Finally the latter course

[1] [The inscriptions of aṣ-Ṣafā in the volcanic region S.E. of Damascus were first observed by Graham in 1857. Ten were published by Wetzstein (*Reisebericht*, Berl. 1860) more by De Vogüé in his *Syrie Centrale*, *Inscr. Sém.* (4° Paris, 1868–77); cf. Halévy's papers in *J. As.* 1877, 81, 82. Other inscriptions in the same character have been copied by Doughty and Euting in various parts of northern Arabia, especially in the region associated with the name of the ancient race of Thamūd (Θαμουδηνοί); hence the name Thamuditic. Euting's inscriptions have been deciphered by D. H. Müller (*Denkschr.* of the Vienna Acad. 1889). Twenty-six characters have been determined, and a twenty-seventh probably corresponds to the Arabic ظ "A sign for ض probably existed but does not occur in known inscriptions."]

prevailed, and the Ethiopian, like the Greek, wrote from left to right, even as we do at the present day.

The Semitic alphabet, as framed by the Semites upon an Egyptian model, consisted of twenty-two letters, all consonants, which were faithfully retained by the Arameans. The Hebrews long subsequently added one to this number, by distinguishing ש into שׁ *sh* and שׂ *s*. The Arabs, who tried to distinguish the finer shades of sounds in writing, required no less than six additional letters; viz. ث ذ and ظ, as lisping modifications of ت د and ط; ض as a modification of ص; and خ and غ as harder forms of ح and ع. The order of the Syriac alphabet was retained by them in the numerical values of the letters, (ابجد هوز حطي كلمن سعفص قرشت ثخذ ضظغ); but the ordinary sequence of the letters was very much altered, chiefly for the sake of bringing similar sounds or similar figures into juxtaposition, e.g. ب ت ث, ج ح خ, etc. The Ethiopic alphabet has two letters fewer than the Arabic, or twenty-six in all, owing to the addition of ኀ خ and ፀ ض, which it has in common with the Arabic, and of two *p*s, the one of native origin ጰ *pait*, the other borrowed from the Greek, ፐ *pa*, perhaps originally *psa*. The sequence of the letters differs both from the Hebrew and Arabic: ሀለሐመሠረሰቀበተኀነአከወዐዘየደገጠጰጸፀፈፐ.

From what I have just said you will see that I do not regard the ancient Semitic alphabets as adequately representing all the sounds of the Semitic languages. My belief is that the finer shades of utterance were disregarded, and that one sign was in several cases used to represent two cognate sounds. I believe that the lisped dentals of the Arabic, ث ذ ظ; and the letter ض (as distinguished from ص), represent sounds of the proto-semitic tongue. I also think that the stronger gutturals خ and غ, as distinguished from ح and ع, belonged to that speech; and that it probably had three sibilants (besides ز *z* and ص *ṣ*), viz. *sh* (שׁ), *s* (שׂ), and *ś* = ס, of which last sound I do not know the peculiar original nuance. De Lagarde[1] and others think that it was originally *ks* or *ksh*, which was gradually softened into *sh* and then into *s*.

[1] [Lagarde, *Symmicta* (Goettingen, 1877), p. 113 *sq*.]

CHAPTER IV.

THE LETTERS OF THE SEMITIC ALPHABET AND THE CHANGES THEY UNDERGO.

WE will now proceed to examine the letters of this alphabet in detail, and to ascertain, so far as is possible within our present narrow limits, what changes they undergo in the different Semitic languages, more especially in Arabic, Syriac, and Hebrew; so that we may be enabled to compare the words of these languages with one another, not by haphazard, but according to certain fixed rules. For this purpose it will be best to arrange the letters in groups, according to the vocal organs with which they are pronounced.

I. We commence then with the gutturals, which are in Syriac and Hebrew four in number, א, ה, ח, and ע. In Arabic and Ethiopic ח has two representatives, ሐ ح and ኀ خ; whilst in Arabic ע has two representatives, ع and غ. Most scholars regard the sounds of خ and غ as a later development in Arabic and Ethiopic; but with this view I am not disposed to agree. I believe, on the contrary, that these differences of sound existed from the earliest times, but that the inventors of the Semitic alphabet were not careful to distinguish in writing what seemed to them to be merely different shades of the same sound. That the Hebrew possessed the sound of غ seems certain from the fact that the LXX. expresses ע by γ (i.e. *gh*) in several proper names; e.g. עַזָּה, Γάζα, غَزَّة; עֲמֹרָה, Γομόρρα; צֹעַר, Ζόγορα and Σηγώρ, زُغَر. Further, Χοδολλογομόρ = כְּדָרְלָעֹמֶר, corresponding with an Elamitic *Kudur-Lagamar* (a name formed like *Kudur-Mabûg* and *Kudur-nahundi* or *Kudur-nanhundi*); and Γαιδάδ for עירד, Genesis iv. 18, where the Massoretic text has (probably incorrectly) עִירָד. On the contrary, ع is indicated in Greek merely by the *spiritus asper*, and even more frequently the *spiritus lenis*, with a vowel; or in the middle and at the end of a word by a vowel alone; as Ἡλί, עֵלִי; Ἑβραῖος, עִבְרִי; Ἀμαλήκ, עֲמָלֵק; Συμεών, שִׁמְעוֹן; Φαραώ, פַּרְעֹה; Γελβουέ, גִּלְבֹּעַ. It is not so easy to prove the existence of غ as distinct from ح in Hebrew, because the Greeks had no precise equivalent for either sound, and expressed them by κ, χ and the soft breathing indifferently. Thus the name of the river חָבוֹר is in one place Χαβώρας, الخَابُور, and in another Ἀβώρας [Ἀβόρρας, etc.]; חָרָן, حَرَّان, becomes Χαρράν and Κάρραι; פֶּסַח is transliterated by πάσχα and φασέκ, الفِصْح. However, the comparison of the cognate languages, particularly Arabic and Assyrian, makes it exceedingly probable that the distinction of ح and خ once existed in Hebrew and Aramaic. Compare חָבַל *bind*, حَبَلَ, with חָבַל *act wickedly*, خَبِلَ *be corrupted, unsound, mad*; חָפַר *dig*, حَفَرَ, with חָפֵר *be ashamed, bashful*, خَفِرَ; חָלַל *profane, desecrate*, حَلَّ, حِلّ, حَلَال, with חָלַל *bore, wound*, خَلَّ[1].

1. Of these gutturals א is the weakest, indicating nothing more than that very slight, almost imperceptible, movement of the vocal organs, which the Greeks represent in writing, though only at the beginning of a word, by the *spiritus lenis*. The Arabs have a special sign for it, viz. the hamza, ء, which they

[1] [For the evidence to a similar effect from the Assyrian see p. 50, *infra*; also Delitzsch, *Prolegomena eines neuen hebräisch-aram. Wörterbuchs zum A T.* (Leipz. 1886) p. 173 *sq.*]

write either with or without ا, according to circumstances: أ إ ٱ, ءَ ءِ ءُ. This sign is nothing but the letter ع written small, to show that the *alif* is to be pronounced somewhat like an ع; which is also indicated by the name *hamza*, i.e. "compression," viz. of the upper part of the windpipe. In this way the Arabs readily distinguish the consonant أ from the long vowel ا *ā*, of which more hereafter. The only thing resembling the *hamza* in the Hebrew system of punctuation is the single point which appears in our Bibles in a very few cases, and is treated of in our Grammars under the head of *Mappīḳ*; e.g. וַיָּבִיאּוּ Gen. xliii. 26, Ezra viii. 18; תָּבִיאּוּ Lev. xxiii. 17; לֹא רֻאּוּ Job xxxiii. 21; but in some MSS., e.g. the codex Reuchlin, it is quite common.

א أ, as a consonant, may be found in Arabic and Hebrew at the beginning or the end of a syllable, and that either at the beginning, middle or end of a word: أَلِفٌ, أُمٌّ; سَأَلَ, مَسْأَلَةٌ; سُؤْلٌ, ذِئْبٌ, رَأْسٌ, يَأْلَفُ; بَرَأَ, شَيْءٌ, سُوءٌ. Compare in Hebrew, אָמַר, אִמִּי, אָמֵן; שָׁאַל, מִשְׁאָלָה, יִרְאָה; and with يَأْلَفُ such cases as יֶאֱהַב Prov. xv. 9 (where others read יֶאֱהָב); וַיֹּאמֶר Gen. xlvi. 29; וַיֶּאְשַׁם Hosea xiii. 1; תֶּאְשַׁם Hosea xiv. 1; מַאְפֵּלְיָה Jerem. ii. 31.—At the beginning of a syllable in the middle of a word, if the preceding consonant have no vowel, أ is apt to be elided in Arabic, and its vowel transferred to the preceding consonant; e.g. مَلْأَكٌ *mal'ak*ᵘⁿ becomes مَلَكٌ *malak*; يِرْأَى (יִרְאֶה) becomes يَرَى; شَمْأَلٌ becomes شَمَالٌ. Compare in Hebrew מַלְאָךְ, but מְלָכָה for מְלָאכָה; לִקְרָתִי for לִקְרָאתִי; שְׂמֹאל for שְׂמֹאול, and that for שְׂמְאֹל, شَمْأَلٌ. This is still more common in Aramaic; e.g. ܡܰܠܰܟܳܐ for ܡܰܠܐܰܟܳܐ, and with entire disappearance of the א, ܫܡܥܐ for ܫܡܥܢܐ.—At the end of a syllable in the middle of a word ܐ is very apt to pass into a vowel-letter, and to be brought into conformity with the preceding vowel. Thus رَأْسٌ *ra'sᵘⁿ* becomes راس *rās*; ذِئْبٌ *dhi'bᵘⁿ* becomes ذيب *dhīb*; سُؤْلٌ *su'lᵘⁿ* becomes سول *sūl*. The usual spelling ذِئْب, سُؤْل, is a compromise in writing between the ancient and the modern forms (ذِأْبٌ, سُأْلٌ : ذِيب, سُول). Hebrew, Syriac, and Assyrian, took nearly the same course. An original רַאְשׁ first became רָאשׁ *rāsh* in Hebrew, as in the actual plural רָאשִׁים, and then רֹאשׁ *rōsh*. We should have expected this form to be written רוֹשׁ, but here the spelling has lagged behind the pronunciation, and the א remains as a vestige of the original form. So also ضَأْنٌ *ḍha'nᵘⁿ*, "sheep," Hebrew originally צַאְן, then צָאן, and finally צֹאן *ṣōn*. The corresponding Aramaic forms are רֵישׁ, ܪܺܫ, for רָאשׁ, and עָן, ܥܢ, for *ḍhān*. In Assyrian I find cited such forms as *rēshu* or *rīshu*, *ṣēnu* or *ṣīnu*.—Initial א is often dropped at the beginning of words, when pronounced with a short vowel; e.g. נַחְנוּ for אֲנַחְנוּ; חַד, ܚܕ, for ܐܚܕ (Heb. אֶחָד, אַחַד); ܐܢܫ for אֱנָשׁ (Assyr. *nīshu*); ܚܪܢܐ = ܐܚܪܢܐ = אַחֵר; ܚܪܬܐ = אַחֲרִית; ܚܬܐ = אָחוֹת, but plur. ܐܚܘ̈ܬܐ; ܐܚܝܢܐ *kinsman*, from ܐܚܐ, אָח. Similarly in vulgar Arabic, خد for أَخَذَ, كل for أَكَلَ, حد for أَحَدٌ. *Per contra*, an initial א with its vowel may be merely prosthetic, to lighten the pronunciation of an unpleasant combination of consonants, especially in foreign words; e.g. אֶזְרוֹעַ for ذراع, ܕܪܥܐ, זְרוֹעַ; אֶתְמוֹל for תְּמוֹל (Eth. ትማልም: *tᵉmālĕm*, ܐܬܡܠܝ); اِقْلِيم, *κλίμα*;

اقنوم, ܩܢܘܡܐ; ܐܣܦܘܓܐ, σπόγγος; ܐܣܟܡܐ, σχῆμα; ܐܣܛܠܐ, στολή; أسطول, στόλος.—At the end of a word this weak guttural is exceedingly apt to disappear altogether, particularly after a diphthong or a long vowel. Hence سوء *sau'un* is vulgarly pronounced *sau* سو, Heb. שָׁוְא; شيء *shai'un* is vulgarly pronounced شي *shai*: compare in Heb. גַּיְא, גַּי, constr. גֵּיא, גֵּי; חֵטְא, with suff. חֶטְאוֹ. In some of these cases, assimilation of the א to the previous sound formed the intermediate stage. For example, نبيء *nabī'un* became first نبيّ *nabīyun*[1], and then *nábī*, نبي. Hence, whilst the Hebrew holds fast נָבִיא (though with silent א), pl. נְבִיאִים, the Aramaic emphatic is נְבִיָּא, ܢܒܝܐ, with double *y*, for נְבִיאָא, ܢܒܝܐܐ. When preceded by a short vowel, the consonant *ālif* is usually vocalised after the loss of its own proper vowel; e.g. طمِئَ טָמֵא; مَلِئَ מָלֵא; مَلَأَ, ܡܠܐ; قَرَأَ, קְרָא, ܩܪܐ.—In Aramaic indeed א rarely appears as a substantial consonant, and in all possible cases throws back its vowel on a preceding letter, which is either vowelless or has a very short vowel; as ܡܐܐ for ܡܐܐ, מֵאָה, مِئَة; ܫܐܠ for ܫܐܠ, שָׁאַל, سَأَلَ; ܐܚܐ for ܐܚܐ; ܐܬܐܟܠ for ܐܬܐܟܠ. In the middle of a word it may preserve its consonant power, especially when originally doubled, as ܫܐܠ; but at the end of a word forms like ܚܛܐ, ܢܛܐ, are very rare. In some cases assimilation takes place, especially in the Ettaf'al of the verb, as ܐܬܬܐܡܪ for ܐܬܐܡܪ, ܐܬܬܚܕ for ܐܬܐܚܕ. Similarly ܐܬܬܣܝܡ, اتّخذ; ܐܬܬܓܪ, اتّجر; ܐܬܬܢܣ (from انس).

[1] [Apparently a loanword from the Hebrew, through the Aramaic, in which the *hamza* was already lost: Nöldeke, *Gesch. des Qorâns*, p. 1; Guidi, *Sede*, p. 36; Fränkel, *Fremdww.*, p. 232.]

א is prone to interchange with ה, particularly at the beginning of a word. Arabic and Aramaic have frequently א, where Hebrew has ה; e.g. أ = הֲ; إِسِ, إِنْ = הֵן, הִנֵּה; ([but conversely] הֵיךְ for אֵיךְ); أَنْتَ = הַפַּךְ (where Syriac also ܗܦܟ); أَقْتَلَ, ܐܩܛܠ = הִקְטִיל; -אֶת, ܐܶܬ, in passives and reflexives = -הִת.

In Arabic, especially in the vulgar dialects, أ may interchange with و, as وَاخَذَ for آخَذَ, وَاكَل for آكَل, *widn* for أُذُن, *wilf* for إِلْف, رواس for رُؤَاس; *tarwis*, "introductory formula," for تَرْئِيس, and the verb رَوَّس for رَأَّس. Very rarely does it interchange with ي *y*, as in *yasīr* for أَسِير, *malyān* for مَلْآن. Parallels to this latter permutation in Syriac are ܝܠܦܐ = אָלֶף, أَلِفَ; ܝܪܚ = אָרַךְ.

2. ה does not require much remark after what has just been said of its interchange with א.—Occasionally it interchanges even in the ancient languages with ח, as נָהַר *bow down*, נְחִין נְחַן (with ח) ܢܚܢ. Also with ו; e.g. נוּר and נהר *be bright, shine, burn*; בּוֹשׁ and ܒܗܬ, *be ashamed*; רוּץ and ܪܗܛ, *run*; דּוּר and دَهْر; [perhaps also] כּוּן and כהן, whence כֹּהֵן and ܟܘܡܪܐ.—On a substitution of ה for a primitive initial שׁ, I shall say something when we come to that letter.

3. Hebrew and Syriac ח we ought properly to distinguish, according to the Arabic and Assyrian, into ح and خ; as חָרַשׁ *cut, plough*, ܚܪܫ, حَرَثَ; חָרֵשׁ *be deaf and dumb*, ܚܪܫ, خَرِسَ.
—In the Aramean dialects there is a strong inclination to weaken its sound to that of ה. Only the modern Syriac of Urūmiah exhibits the contrary tendency, and uses the rougher

sound of خ in all cases, going so far indeed as to harden ܪܟܝܟ into ܪܟܝܚ *rākhit.*

In old Arabic ح interchanged dialectically with ع, and خ with غ; e.g. حتّي and عتّي; نحم and نعم; خفير *protector, guard,* and غفير. In the modern Arabic of Egypt, the substitution of ح for ع seems to be common, when the ع is immediately followed by another consonant; as *semiḥt* = سمعت, *maḥsare* = معصرة, *mābiḥsh'* = ما أبيع شي. Hence we may be justified in comparing, for example, רָעֵב *be hungry*, رغب *desire, covet*, with ርኃበ: *be hungry*; צָבַע *dip, dye*, صبغ, with ጸብሐ: ; חָמַס *injure, oppress, ill use*, حمس *be firm, strong, brave*, with ዐመፀ: *oppress*, an intermediate link being חֹמֵץ, חָמוֹץ, *oppressor.*

Occasionally too ח corresponds to *k*-sounds; c.g. שֹׁחַד *bribe*, ܫܘܚܕܐ, شكد; بحث *search*, בִּקֵּשׁ; ሐጸረ: *be short*, קָצַר; ሐደፈ: and ቀደፈ: *row*, قذف (as well as غذف, جذف, جدف).

4. Hebrew and Syriac ע ordinarily represents Arabic ع and غ; as עַיִן, ܥܝܢܐ, عَيْن; שָׁמַע, ܫܡܥ, سَمِعَ; but עֹל, غُلّ; עֶלֶם *youth*, ܥܠܝܡܐ, غُلَام; עֶרֶב *evening*, غَرْب; עֲרָבִים *willows*, ܥܪܒܬܐ, غَرَب [*Populus Euphratica*]; עֹרֵב *raven*, ܥܘܪܒܐ, غُرَاب. —Possible relations with ח (ح خ) I have already indicated.—It is sometimes weakened into א, as in מְתָאֵב *abhorring* (Amos vi. 8), compared with the ordinary form מְתָעֵב; and even passed over entirely, as in בִּי *pr'ythee*, for בְּעִי, Syr. ܒܥܘܬܐ; בַּל for בַּעַל. This tendency gains ground to an enormous extent in the Aramean dialects, where we find such forms as מָנָא for

טוּעֲנָא, and in the Punic or later Phoenician of Africa, where we find יַר for יַעַר *wood*, as החרשם שיר (inscr. of Tugga), confirmed by S. Augustine on Ps. cxxiii.—Of the Aramaic substitution of ע for Arabic ض, Hebrew צ, I shall speak hereafter.

It would appear from this short survey of the gutturals, that they were exceedingly apt in the younger Semitic dialects to be confused with one another, and to disappear altogether. In Ethiopic MSS. there is usually no distinction observed between ሀ, ሐ, ኀ, on the one side and አ, ዐ, on the other; modern Amharic pronounces them all as አ at the beginning of a word, and slurs them over in the middle or at the end. Similar is the case of the Samaritan. In modern Syriac ܗ is very feeble, and ܥ scarcely heard at all; and in Mandaitic there is absolutely no distinction between א, ע, on the one hand and ה, ח, on the other. The Talmūd too writes א for ע and ה for ח in not a few words; e.g. ·אַ (with following *daghesh*) for עַל; אַבָּא (not אַבָא) *wood*, for עַבָא, ܥܳܒܳܐ, غَابَة; אול for עול, غَزَل *spin*; אוּנְקָא = عُنُق *neck*; אַרְבָא *willow*, עֲרָבִים, غَرَب; אַרְבָלָא *sieve*, ܥܪܒܠܐ, غِرْبَال (*cribrum*, *cribellum*[1]); הֲדָדֵי *one another*, ܚܕܕܐ; מְהוּלְתָּא *sieve*, ܡܚܘܠܬܐ, مُنْخُل. It is related that the Babylonian rabbi Ḥaiyā was held guilty of blasphemy for pronouncing, in Isaiah viii. 17, הִכֵּיתִי with ה instead of חִכֵּיתִי with ח (וְחִכֵּיתִי לַיהוָה הַמַּסְתִּיר פָּנָיו מִבֵּית יַעֲקֹב)[2]. In Assyrian there is obviously no difference in sound between א ה and ע, nor any way of distinguishing them from one another in writing; e.g. *ilu*, "god," *ish'alū*, "they asked," *mūṣa'u*, "exit"; *la'abu*, "flame," *ti'āmtu*, "sea," *dāru*, "eternity," *nāru*, "river"; *uzzu*, "strong," *zēru* or *zīru*, "seed," *ishmī*, "he heard," *rīmu*, "thunder." Neither has غ any distinct sound or representative, as *uzālu*, "gazelle," *āribu*, "raven."

[1] [Lagarde, *Armenische Studien*, p. 65, No. 976; but see also Fränkel, *Aram. Fremdww. im Arab.* (Leiden 1886), p. 91.]

[2] [*TB. Meg.* 24 b.]

ח ح has likewise sunk to the same level, e.g. *rāimu*, "loving," *rēmu*, "grace," *imēru* or *imīru*, "ass," *aptī*, "I opened," *rūḳu*, "distant, remote." But ח خ has preserved its sound and is represented by a special sign; e.g. *khītu*, "sin," *khamilti*, "five," *akhu*, "brother," *amkhaṣ*, "I destroyed," "defeated," *arkhu*, "month." In this case the comparison of the Assyrian may be important for Hebrew lexicography, as shewing us the distinction between ח ح and ח خ in this language. E.g., as Friedrich Delitzsch has pointed out in his little book *The Hebrew Language viewed in the Light of Assyrian Research* [London 1883], פָּתַח فَتَحَ, *to open*, Assyr. *iptī*, "he opened," is quite different from פִּתּוּחַ *carving, engraving*, Assyr. *iptakh*, "he carved." So too מַלָּח, مَلَّاح, *sailor*, is in Assyr. *malākhu* or *mallākhu* (with خ), and has nothing to do with مِلْح, מֶלַח "salt." It is said to be a word borrowed from the Accadian.

II. Advancing from the gutturals, we next encounter, in the order of the organs of speech, the so-called palatals, ג, כ, ק. These interchange freely with one another in the different dialects. E.g., in Hebrew itself the radicals גנן and כנן; סגר and סכר, also Syriac ܣܓܪ and ܣܟܪ; further כִּחֵד and جَحَدَ; גָּעָה, ܓܥܐ and ܩܥܐ; שָׁקֵד *almond tree*, שִׁגְדָּא, ܫܓܕܐ; קֹשְׁטְ *truth*, ܩܘܫܛܐ, but Mand. ܟܘܫܛܐ; קַשָּׁת *archer*, ܩܫܬܐ; צָחַק and ضَحِكَ. In Mandaitic the interchange of ק with ג is very frequent, under the influence of a neighbouring ܛ or ܨ; as גאיטא [*gaiṭā*] = ܩܝܛܐ *summer*, and so in the radicals גטן, גטל, לגט, for קטן, קטל, לקט; גצף *break off (a branch)* = קצף (comp. קְצָפָה in Joel i. 7: שָׂם גַּפְנִי לְשַׁמָּה וּתְאֵנָתִי לִקְצָפָה). More rarely does ג exchange with غ; e.g. نَبَغَ, נבע, ܢܒܥ and ܢܓܥ; גָּרָה,

ܝܓܝܒ, and غري *be angry*; جَلَبَة and غَلَبَة, *outcry*; جَدَف and غَدَف (dial.), *row*[1].

1. ג is hard in Hebrew, Aramaic, Assyrian, and Ethiopic, like our *g* in *go, give, get*; in Arabic its sound varies, for the Syrians pronounce it soft, like *g* in *gem*, whereas in Egypt and parts of Arabia the hard sound is retained, جبل, رجل. The Hebrew and Aramean, however, modified its sound, when immediately preceded by a vowel (however slight), into one much resembling that of the Greek γ between two strong vowels, as ἀγαθός, or the Arabic غ. Indeed, when writing Arabic with Hebrew letters, the Jews generally use גֿ to represent غ. Modern Syriac gives unaspirated ܓ the sound of *dy* or *j* in a few roots, such as ܓܢܝܘ *dyāniu* or *jāniu* (ܓܢܝܒ) "steal, carry off"; ܓܡܠܐ *dyümla* or *jümla*, "camel." In a very few cases the Arabic soft *g* has been still further softened into *sh*; e.g., in Egypt the word *wishsh*, "face," apparently = وجه. Similarly the old grammarian al-G'awālīḳī mentions تشتر as a faulty pronunciation of تجتر, "it chews the cud[2]."

2. ך is also hard in Hebrew, Aramaic, Assyrian, Arabic and Ethiopic, like our *k*, as כָּתַב, ܟܬܒ, كَتَبَ. The Hebrew and Aramaic modify its sound, after a vowel, into one closely resembling that of the Arabic خ, as יִכְתֹּב, ܢܟܬܘܒ (but Arabic يَكْتُبُ). Hence, when a Jew writes Arabic with Hebrew letters, he uses כֿ for خ.—In modern Syriac unaspirated *k* ܟ is said to have the sound of *ty* or *ch*, e.g., ܟܠܒܐ *tyalbā* or *chalbā*; ܡܠܟܐ *maltyā* or *malchā*; ܟܦܐ *tyappā* or *chappā*.—In modern Arabic

[1] [These last seem to be loan-words, Fränkel, p. 227.]

[2] [*Livre des locutions vicieuses*, p. 145, in *Morgenl. Forschungen*, Leipz. 1875.]

ك is also softened dialectically into a sound like that of *ts* or *tsh*, sometimes of *dj* or *ǵ*; as كاتب *tˢʰātib* or *ťātib*, حكيم *haǵīm*, كامل *ǵāmil*.—In some Amharic words the old Ethiopic *k* has been aspirated, *kh*, and finally becomes *h*, e.g. *hōna*, "to become," for *kōna*, كان; *hūlū*, "all," for *kwĕllū*, كُلّ. Perhaps this may help us to connect such a form as Ar. إيا, *īyā*, with Eth. ኪያ: *kīyā*.

3. ק in the older dialects is a *k* pronounced far back in the mouth, or rather, deep in the throat. In our English alphabet its lineal representative is *q*. In some Arabic dialects it takes the sound of *dsh* or *ds*, sometimes of *ch* or *ć*; e.g. قبلة *dshiblĕ* or *dziblĕ*, قريب *dzarīb*, عقيل *'adzīl*, قائد *ćā'id*, سرقة *sirća*. But its ordinary sound, throughout Arabia and Africa, is that of a hard *g*. This too is common in the modern forms of Ethiopic, whence *Magdalā* for *Maḳdalā*, መቅደላ:, *tagábbala* for *taḳábbala*. In parts of Syria and Egypt, on the other hand, as well as in Amharic, ק is apt to be converted into א أ. A Syrian Christian says *'ult*, *'a'ūl*, for قُلْتُ, أقُولُ; and a native of Shoa pronounces *ta'ábbala* instead of *tagábbala* or *taḳábbala*. The Egyptian railway station Zagazig is written زقازيق *Zaḳāzīḳ*, pronounced either *Zagāzīg* or *Za'āzī'*; the word *ḥaḳīḳī* حقيقي becomes *ḥa'ī'ī*.

III. We next come to the dentals ד, ת, ט, which are common to all the old languages: e.g.

دُبّ, ድብ: Ass. *dubbu*,	דֹּב,	ܕܒܐ;
يَدٌ, እድ: Ass. *idu* (power),	יָד,	ܐܝܕܐ;
تَحْتَ, ታሕተ:	תַּחַת,	ܬܚܘܬ;
تَيْسٌ,	תַּיִשׁ,	ܬܝܫܐ;

أَتَانٌ, Ass. *atānu*, אָתוֹן, ܐܰܬܳܢܳܐ;

طَلٌّ, ጠል: טַל, ܛܰܠܳܐ;

طَعْمٌ, ጣዕም: טַעַם, ܛܰܥܡܳܐ;

خِطْءٌ, ኀጢአ: Ass. *ikhti*, חֵטְא, ܚܛܳܗܳܐ.

Of these, ת and ט interchange freely, as קְטַל, ܩܛܰܠ, but قَتَلَ, ቀተለ:; קֶשֶׁת and ܩܶܫܬܳܐ; קֹשֶׁט and ܩܽܘܫܛܳܐ; طَغِيَ, ܛܥܳܐ, and תָּעָה, rarely טָעָה; חָטַף, ܚܛܰܦ, خَطِفَ, and חָתַף. In modern Syriac ܛܠܳܐ for ܬܠܳܐ. ד often interchanges with ת, as in the Hebrew radicals תור and דור, Arabic تَارَ and دَارَ; תֹּף and دَفٌّ; in Mandaitic כאדפא, "shoulder," for ܟܰܬܦܳܐ, כָּתֵף, كَتِفٌ; שידקא, "silence," ܫܶܬܩܳܐ; and even כדאב, as well as כתאב, ܟܬܳܒ. More rarely does ד interchange with ט, as דִּבָּה and ܛܶܒܳܐ; אָטָד, أُطَدٌ, and ܗܰܛܳܛܳܐ or ܗܰܕܳܛܳܐ, Mand. אטאטא; טַבּוּר, "height, mountain," Sam. [illegible], Eth. ደብር:; דָּבֵק, ܕܒܰܩ, دَبِقَ and طَبِقَ, ጠበቀ:: Of a possible interchange of ת with ך, I shall have something to say when we come to speak of the persons of the perfect in the verb. As another instance I may mention the substitution of *k* for *t* in some modern Syriac forms of the verb ܐܶܬܳܐ, "to come," e.g., particip. ܟܝܳܐ and ܐܶܟܝܳܐ (*tyïa*, *ityā*), for ܐܳܬܶܐ and ܐܳܬܝܳܐ; imper. ܟܝܳܐ (*tyā*) for ܬܳܐ (ܬܐ).

Of these three letters ד and ת undergo a slight modification in Hebrew and Aramaic, when immediately preceded by a vowel. In this position they receive a sound nearly approximating to *th* in *that* and *think* respectively; whence the Jews in writing Arabic use דׄ for ذ and תׄ for ث. E.g. דָּבֵק, יִדְבַּק;

תְּעָה, יְתְעָה. The fate of such aspirated letters is usually to disappear gradually, especially when they stand between two vowels or at the end of a word. Final *d* is almost lost to the ear in a Spanish word like *ciudad*, whilst in the Italian *città* it is gone even to the eye. So in French there is no trace of a *d* in *épée*, but the comparison of the Spanish *espada* and Italian *spada* reveals at once the history of the word. Similarly in the Semitic languages the final ת of the feminine gender in the noun and verb disappeared. The Arabic قَتَلَتْ became in Hebrew קָטְלָה; the Ethiopic ገነት: *gannat*, was written in Arabic جَنَّةٌ *gannat*^{un}, and vulgarly pronounced first *gannat*, then *gannah*, and finally *ganna*, *janna*, exactly the Hebrew גַּנָּה, Syriac ܓܰܢܬܳܐ. This has gone much farther in the Aramaic dialects than in Arabic and Hebrew. E.g. in Syriac, ܡܰܠܟܽܘ for ܡܰܠܟܽܘܬܳܐ, מַלְכוּת; ܩܽܒ for ܩܰܒܶܠ; ܗܳ, ܗܳܢܳܐ, ܡܳܢ, ܡܳܢܳܐ, for הָא דֵין, הָא, הָא דְנָא, מָא דֵין, מָא דְנָא; ܐܳܢܳܐ for אַי דְנָא. In the Talmūd, בֵּי for בֵּית; הָאי for הָדֵין (with the additional loss of the final *n*, as in בֵּי for בֵּין, הָנֵי for הָלֵין), fem. הָא for הָדָא; מַאי for מָא דֵין; and the like. In modern Syriac this aspirated *t* and *d* disappear regularly between two vowels: ܡܰܠܟܽܘܘܳܐ for ܡܰܠܟܽܘܬܳܐ; ܣܗܳܐ for ܣܗܳܕܳܐ; *sūsāwā'ē* (ܣܽܘܣܘܳܐܶܐ) for *sūsāwāthē* (old Syr. ܣܽܘܣܘܳܬܳܐ); ܬܠܳܐܝ *tlā'ī*, 30, for ܬܠܳܬܝܢ; ܕܺܝܝ *dīyī*, "mine," not for ܕܺܝܠܝ, as in old Syriac, but for the Talmūdic דִּידִי (from יַד); ܝܳܕܰܥܢܶܗ (*yāne*) "I know him," for ܝܳܕܰܥܢܶܗ (ܝܳܕܰܥ ܐܢܐ ܠܶܗ); ܠܳܐ ܝܳܕܥܽܘܬܳܐ "ignorance," for ܠܳܐ ܝܳܕܥܽܘܬܳܐ. Hence the fem. pron. ܗܳܝ (old Syr. ܗܳܕܳܐ) becomes first ܐܳܗܳܐ, and finally ܐ, with which compare the Talmūdic הָא above. I should remark that where ד and ת are retained in modern Syriac of Urumiah, their sound is hard, and very little difference is perceptible between them, particularly at the end of words. For instance, the particle *bit*, which forms the future tense (ܒܸܬ ܦܵܪܹܫ) is a contraction for ܒܥܸܐ ܕ, but usually written ܒܸܬ; the imperative of ܥܒܲܕ, "to do," is written and pronounced ܒܘܼܬ *vut*, for ܥܒܘܿܕ; ܡܸܢܹܗ ܕܐܸܫܬܵܐ is pronounced nearly as *minnit Ishō*; the old Syriac ܒܝܲܕ ܝܘܼܡܵܐ is pronounced and actually written ܒܝܼܬ ܝܘܼܡܵܐ.—Lastly, I may mention that the hard ተ and ደ of the ancient Ethiopic are changed in Amharic, in certain cases [where *y* or *i* follows], into *ty* or *ch*, and *dy* or *j*; e.g., in the 3rd pers. sing. fem. perf. of the verb *nabarach* "she was" (for ነበረት፡ *nabarat* "she sat," compare Spanish *ser*, for *seer*, *sedere*); *ĕj* for እድ፡ *ĕd* "hand," *wallāj* for ወላዲ፡ *wallādī* "father."

Thus far I have spoken chiefly of the pure ד, ת, ט, which remain unchanged in all the old Semitic languages, and undergo comparatively slight alterations in the modern dialects, such changes depending mainly upon the aspiration of these letters in the older forms. Now, however, I must touch upon another set of modified dentals, which undergo in the old languages themselves a regular series of permutations.

Besides the simple dentals ت *t*, د *d*, ط *ṭ*, the old Arabic possesses a series of aspirated or lisped dentals, ث *th*, ذ *dh*, ظ *ṭh*. These formed, I have no doubt, part of the protosemitic stock of sounds, which has been preserved in Arabic alone. In the other Semitic languages they underwent various modifications.

The Arameans, as a rule, dropped the difficult lisped sound altogether, and fell back upon the simple dental; e.g. ثَبَرَ *break*, ܬܒܲܪ; حَرَثَ *plough*, ܚܪܵܬ; ذَبَحَ, ܕܒܲܚ; أَخَذَ, ܐܚܲܕ; إِثْمٌ; ظُفْرٌ, ܛܸܦܪܵܐ; نَظَرَ, ܢܛܲܪ. The other Semites took a different course, modifying the lisped letter into a sibilant. In Phoenician and Hebrew

ث became *sh*, in Ethiopic and Assyrian ሰ *s*[1]; e.g. ثور, שׁוֹר, ሰር: Ass. *sûr*; ثقل, שָׁקַל, ሰቀለ: (*hang up*), Ass. *iškul* (hang up, weigh); ثوم *garlic*, שׁוּם, ሰምት: Ass. *sûmu*; حرث, חָרַשׁ, ሐረሰ:; ثمر, ሰመር: (*abundant crop*). Similarly ذ became in all these languages *z*; e.g. ذبح, זָבַח, ዘብሐ: Ass. *zêbu* (for *zibḫu*); اذن, אֹזֶן, እዝን: Ass. *uznu*; اخذ, אָחַז, አኀዘ:: Finally, ظ appears in the other languages as צ, *ṣ*; e.g. ظلمة, צַלְמוּת, ጸልምት: Ass. *ṣalmu*, "dark"; ظل, צֵל, ጸላሎት: Ass. *ṣillu* and *ṣalûlu*; ظفر, ጽፍር: צִפֹּרֶן, Ass. *ṣupru*; نظر, נָצַר, ነጸረ:: Of course, as every rule has its exceptions, these series are occasionally liable to disturbances. For instance قثاء *cucumber*, ቀሲያት: קִשֻּׁאִים, Ass. *ķissî*, ought by rule to be in Aramaic קתיא; but the actual form is קַטְיָא, ܩܛܝܐ, the proximity of ק having hardened the *t*.

Of the Aramaic dialects some have advanced to the Hebrew stage, at least in sporadic instances. In the great inscription of Taimā, for example, we find זי for די, זן and its fem. זא for דן and דא; and the same forms occur in the Egyptian Aramaic inscriptions and papyri. In Mandaitic there are not only pronominal and adverbial forms of this kind, as האזין, fem. האזא (but האדינו *this is*, and occasionally האדא); האיזאך = ܗܝܕܝܢ *then*; האיזין, as well as האידין, *how?* but also a few other words, as זאכרא or זיכרא, *male*, זאביא or זיביא, *offering* (but דאבא *offerer*, מאדבחא *altar*), זיקנא *beard*, and very strangely זיקלא as well as דיקלא, *palm tree*, and זמא as well as דמא, *blood*.

[1] [Of the two forms of *s* which are distinguished in Assyrian writing, though they seem to have ultimately come to be pronounced alike, the one which corresponds to ث = שׁ is that which Schrader and Delitzsch represent by *š*, while Sayce and other English scholars render it by simple *s*. See below, p. 58.]

Among the modern dialects the Arabic alone calls for notice. Generally speaking, it has adopted the same course as the old Aramaic, i.e. it retrogrades by changing the lisped into the simple dental; e.g. تور *tōr*, "ox," كتير *ketīr*, اتنين *itnēn*, شحات "beggar." More rarely it advances the *th* to a sibilant, *s*, as *sibit* = ثبت, *bāḥis* = باحث (argue, dispute), *khabbās* = خباث (scoundrel). The word حديث in the sense of *narrative, story*, is pronounced in Egypt *ḥadīt*, but in the sense of "religious tradition," *ḥadīs*. Even in ancient Arabic we occasionally find *t* for *th*, as in تبر = ثبر, تاب *repent*[1] = ثاب *return*. Similarly lisped ذ seems to become in modern Arabic either *d* or *z*; e.g. *dīb* = ذئب, *dahab* = ذهب, *adān* = أذان, *kidb* and *kizb* = كذب, *izn* = اذن, *zikr* = ذكر (recitation), *zamb* = ذنب. In like manner ظ is pronounced either *ḍ* (ض) or *z*, e.g. *'aḍm* = عظم, *ḍill* = ظل, *ḍalma* = ظلمة, *zulm* = ظلم, *ḍuhr* = ظهر, *zahar* = ظهر, *ḥifz* = حفظ[2].

IV. The sibilants next engage our attention, viz. ז, ס, ש (שׁ, שׂ), and צ.

1. Pure *z* ז runs through all the Semitic languages, as زرع, זֶרַע, ܙܪܥ, Ass. *zêru* or *zîru*, "seed"; عز, ዐዘዘ: עֹז, ܥܙܝܙ, Ass. *izzu*, "strong." But Eth. ዘ, Heb. ז, and Ass. *z*, often correspond, as we have seen above, to Arab. ذ and Aram. ד; as ذئب, זְאֵב, *zibu*, ዝእብ: *hyaena*, ܕܐܒܐ.

[1] [In this sense and form the word is a loanword from the Aramaic ܬܒ, see Fränkel, *Lehnww.* p. 83.]

[2] [The distinctive sound of ظ is preserved in some parts of the Ḥijāz.]

Not unfrequently ז interchanges with ץ and ס; e.g. עָלַץ, עָלַם, עָלַז; נָסַע, نزع; صدق, צָדַק, ܙܕܩ; صغر, צָעַר, זְעֵיר, ܙܥܪ and ܐܙܥ, vulg. Arabic *s*ᵉ*ghaiyar* and *ṣûghaiyar* (صغير زغير).

2. The Aramaic possesses two *s*-sounds, ܣ *s* and ܫ *sh*, to which correspond Arabic س *s* and ش *sh*, Ethiopic ሰ and ሠ, which latter are, however, confounded in modern times. The Hebrew has also ס = ܣ, but splits ܫ into שׁ *sh* and שׂ *s*, the latter of which approximates to ס, and is often confounded with it; e.g. כַּעַשׂ and כַּעַס; רָפַשׂ and רָפַס; שִׂכְלוּת for סִכְלוּת in Eccl. i. 17. Hence, by a further confusion of sounds, the Ephraimite סִבֹּלֶת for שִׁבֹּלֶת (intermediate stage, שִׂבֹּלֶת).

The Assyrian appears also to have had two *s*-sounds, though Assyriologists seem to differ on the question of their pronunciation. Haupt, for example, evidently distinguishes between an Assyrian *s* = Hebrew שׂ, and an Assyrian *sh* = Hebrew שׁ, but holds that these were gradually confounded, as in Ethiopic, so that both came to be *s*. As for the Assyrian sound corresponding to the Hebrew ס, Haupt holds that it was *sh*. On the contrary, Schrader and others seem to maintain that the Hebrew ס is in Assyrian *s*, and that the other letter is *sh*, *š*. See Schrader's article in the *Monatsberichte der Berliner Akademie*, 5 March 1877; Hommel, *Zwei Jagdinschriften Asurbanibal's*, 1879; and Haupt's "Beiträge zur assyrischen Lautlehre" in the *Nachrichten der königl. Gesellschaft der Wissenschaften zu Göttingen*, 25 April, 1883, especially p. 107, note 2[1].

[1] [In Schrader's system of transcription *s* is the Assyrian consonant that corresponds etymologically to Hebrew ס and *š* that which corresponds to Hebrew שׁ. Similarly Delitzsch, *Ass. Gr.* p. 106, recognises an Assyrian *s* = Hebrew ס and an *š* which etymologically considered is of threefold nature, viz. $š_1$ = שׂ, س; $š_2$ = שׁ, ث; $š_3$ = שׁ, ش. In many English books on the other hand, e.g. in those of Sayce, Schrader's *š* is written *s*, while his *s* is *ś*. Prof. Wright abstains, it will be observed, from expressing any opinion of his own on the controverted question of the pronunciation of the sibilants, and his MS. presents variations which shew that he had not come to a final decision as to the best way of transcribing them. See above, p. 13, l. 19 where *s* in *sarap* is the consonant which Schrader and Delitzsch represent by *š*, and

As a rule, ܣ = س = ሰ = ס ; as

ܣܓܶܕ	سَجَدَ	ሰገደ:	סָגַד
ܐܶܣܰܪ	أَسَرَ	አሰረ:	אָסַר

but there are exceptions [perhaps merely graphical], as

ܣܰܬܘܐ סְתָו [for שְׁתָו] but شِتَآءٌ . شَتْوَةٌ.

Hebrew שׂ, as a general rule, corresponds to Arabic ش ; and vice versâ, Arabic س corresponds to Hebrew שׁ. The Aramaic follows the Hebrew, writing of course ܣ for שׂ. E.g.

(1)	שָׂבַע	ܣܒܰܥ	شَبِعَ		
	שָׂב	ܣܳܐܒ	شَابَ	ሢበ:	Assyr. *šîbu* (grey-haired)
	שְׂמֹאל	ܣܶܡܳܐܠܐ	شِمَال		„ *šumēlu* (-*ilu*)
	שָׂנֵא	ܣܢܳܐ	شَنِئَ		
	שָׂרִיד	ܣܪܺܝܕܳܐ	شَرِيدٌ		
	עֶרֶשׂ	ܥܰܪܣܳܐ	عَرْشٌ		„ *irsu, éršu*
(2)	שָׁבָה	ܫܒܳܐ	سَبَى		
	שָׁבַח	ܫܰܒܰܚ	سَبَّحَ	ሰብሐ:	
	שָׁבַע	ܫܒܰܥ	سَبْعٌ	ሰብዐ:	
	שׁוֹק	ܫܳܩܳܐ	سَاقٌ		

similarly p. 56, l. 2 sqq., whereas on p. 14, l. 23 *š* is used in Schrader's sense. Elsewhere he writes *s* with *sh* above it, but on the whole he seems finally to have inclined to use *š* in Schrader's sense whenever it was desirable to indicate a distinction between the two forms of the sibilant. For the sake of uniformity this mode of transcription will be adopted in the following pages, without reference to variations in the MS., which would doubtless have been removed had Prof. Wright lived to see his work through the press.]

לָשׁוֹן ܠܶܫܳܢܳܐ لِسَانٌ ልሳን፡ Assyr. *lišânu*

רֹאשׁ רֵישׁ ܪܺܫܳܐ رَأْسٌ ርእስ፡ „ *rêšu, rîšu*

These rules are not, however, invariably observed. E.g.

שָׁלֵו ܫܰܠܘܳܐ but [as a loanword] سَلْوَى (not شَلْوَى)

שֶׁמֶשׁ ܫܶܡܫܳܐ but شَمْسٌ (not سَمْسٌ, except in some modern dialects), Assyrian *šamšu*.

There is another Hebrew שׂ, which corresponds to an Aramaic ܣ, Arabic ش, Ethiopic ሰ, Assyrian *s* [*ś*], of which I gave some examples above. Add:

ܬܰܠܓܳܐ ثَلْجٌ שֶׁלֶג *šalgu*

ܚܪܰܫ حَرَثَ חָרַשׁ ሐረሰ፡

ܚܕܰܫ حَدَثَ חָדַשׁ ሐደሰ፡ *uaddiš*

שׂ and שׁ, as well as ס, may occasionally interchange with צ, e.g. שָׂחַק, Eth. ሠሐቀ፡ or ሥሕቀ፡, צָחַק; חֹמֶשׁ, ܚܘܡܣܐ, Eth. ሕምስ፡ (womb), Talm. חִימְצָא and הִימְצָא (fat of the intestines), Mand. הִימְצָא; שָׁוַע, צָוַח, صاح, ጸውዐ፡; קָסַם, ܩܶܨܡܳܐ.

ס س is frequently changed into צ ص under the influence of a following ט, and in Arabic of a ق غ خ or ر; as صَطَرَ, صَخَرَ, صَقَبٌ ("young camel," "tent pole"), صَقْفٌ; especially in foreign words with *st*, as אִסְטְלָא or אִצְטְלָא.

Very curious is the change in Assyrian of *š* into *l* before a dental; e.g. *alṭur* or *ašṭur* (שׁטר), *maštîtu* or *maltîtu* (drink, שׁתה), *khamišti* or *khamilti* (five, חמשׁ), *lubuštu* or *lubultu* (dress, לבשׁ). It appears, however, to be thoroughly well established.

Lastly, it would seem that an initial *s* may in certain cases interchange with ה *h*, and later with א. This is most obvious in the verbal form ܫܰܦܥܶܠ, Heb. הִפְעִיל, Ar. أَفْعَلَ, Aram. ܐܰܦܥܶܠ; and in the pronouns of the 3rd pers., Ass. *šu*, f. *ši*, pl. *šunu*, f. *šina*; in the suffix forms *šu*, *ša*, pl. *šunu*, *šina*. The Ḥimyaritic offers us a suffix form שׁ, pl. שׁם, as well as הו, pl. המו. The other Semitic languages have all the *h*-form, except the modern Mehrī, which has, according to von Maltzan[1], masc. *he*, f. *sē*, pl. *hĕm*, f. *sĕn*; as suffixes *he*, f. *es*, pl. *hum*, f. *senu*. Such cases as سَلَكَ, הָלַךְ, هَلَكَ, are very rare, and may either be accidental or capable of some other explanation.

3. We have already seen that צ may be weakened into the other sibilants שׂ, ס, ז; and we have also shown that it corresponds in Ethiopic, Phoenician, Hebrew, and Assyrian, to the Arabic ظ, which is represented in Aramaic by ט, ܛ. One or two additional examples may not be superfluous.

צְבִי,	Assyr. *ṣabîtu*,	ظَبْيٌ		ܛܒܝܐ
צָהֳרַיִם		ظُهْرٌ		ܛܗܪܐ
צָעַן *migrate* (Is. 33. 20)		ظَعَنَ	ጸዐነ:	ܛܥܢ
טָעַן *load*		*travel*	*load*	*carry*.

I now remark that צ in Hebrew may correspond

(*a*) To Arabic ص, Ethiopic ጸ, Assyrian *ṣ*, Aramaic ܨ; as

צוּד	صَادَ		*iṣûd*	ܨܳܕ
אֶצְבַּע	إِصْبَعٌ	አጽባዕት:	*ṣumbu* (for *ṣubbu* = *ṣub'u*)	ܨܶܒܥܳܐ
בְּצָלִים	بَصَلٌ	በጸል:		ܒܨܠܐ
נָצַב	نَصَبَ			ܢܨܒ

(*b*) To Arabic ض, Ethiopic ፀ, Assyrian *ṣ*, Aramaic ܥ; as

צָרָה, צַר	ضَرَّةٌ	ፀር:	ܥܩܬܐ
צֶמֶר		ፀምር:	ܥܡܪܐ

[1] [*ZDMG.*, vol. xxv. (1871) p. 200 sq.]

צָק	ضاق			ܥܩ
צֹאן	ضأن		*ṣēnu, ṣînu*	ܥܢܐ
	ضرس	ፀርስ፡		ܥܪܣܐ
רָצַץ	رضّ			ܪܥ
פצץ	فضّ			ܦܥ
יָצָא		ወፅአ፡	*ūṣî* ("he escaped") part. *āṣû*	ܝܥܐ
רָצָה	رضي		("satisfied")	ܪܥܐ
בֵּיצָה	بيضة		*bîṣu*	ܒܝܥܬܐ
אֶרֶץ	أرض		*irṣitu* (*ĕr-*)	ܐܪܥܐ

If another ע follows in the word, then this Aramaic ע is commonly weakened into א; e.g.

צֵלָע	ضلع	*ṣilu* (for *ṣillu, ṣilʾu*)	עִלְעָא	ܐܠܥܐ
גֵּי הַצְּבֹעִים	ضبع		אפעא (אפא)	ܐܦܥܐ
	عرض		עֲרַע	ܐܪܥ
	ضعف			ܐܥܦܐ
צְפַרְדֵּעַ	ضفدع		עוּרְדְּעָן	ܐܘܪܕܥܐ
עֵץ	عضة	Assyr. *iṣṣu*		אָע

There are however some exceptions to this rule; e.g.

צָמַד	ضمد	ፀመደ፡		ܨܡܕ
נָפַץ	نفض	ነፈጸ፡	"to be scattered, flee" (with ጸ, not ፀ)	ܢܦܨ

רצץ	رضّ		ܪܥ
	عرض		ܥܪܥ[1]
	غمض		ܥܡܥ
	ضرع	Assyr. *siru*	ܥܪܥܐ
	ضرك		ܥܪܟ
חמץ	حمّض		ܚܡܥ and ܚܡܥܐ
	صرف	with ص, not ض[2]	ܨܪܘܦܐ
	صيرفي		ܡܨܪܦܢܐ

In such cases some of the younger dialects seem to be, as it were, faintly conscious of their loss, and strive to make good the defect in different ways. Sometimes a ק, or the combination אק, takes the place of the ע; as in אַרְקָא for אַרְעָא (Jerem. x. 11), Mand. אקנא for עָנָא, אקאמרא for עַמְרָא. Occasionally the same thing happens in the case of a simple ע, as עָפָר, عفر, ܥܦܪܐ, Mand. אפרא, but also אקאפרא, and even אגאפרא. At other times a ג appears upon the scene; e.g. ضغط "to press, squeeze," ܐܬܥܨ *be oppressed*, instead of ܐܥܨ; ضحك, Syriac ܓܚܟ, Talm. גְּחֵיךְ, for ܐܓܚܟ. This last word, owing to the difficulty of its utterance, undergoes some curious modifications. The regular Aramaic form is found in Talmudic and Mandaitic, viz. אַחֵיךְ (not Afel), עהכית, "I laughed"; but also חייך (חַיֵּךְ), and even דְחַךְ. Something similar occurs in Syriac with the word ܐܥܦܐ, ضعف, whence are formed the secondary radicals ܥܦ and ܥܦܦ.

[1] [This example is however disputed by G. Hoffmann, *ZDMG.*, xxxii. 762.]
[2] [See however Fränkel, *Fremdww.*, p. 183.]

Before going further let us examine by the light of these permutations the Hebrew radical צפר. You will find that it represents no less than four different radicals in Arabic and Ethiopic.

(1) צפר "whistle, twitter," صفر, whence

צִפּוֹר, ܨܦܪܐ, צִפַּר, صافر, عصفور, Ass. *iṣṣūr* (for *iṣpūr*).

(2) צפר "turn, return, twine, twist," ضفر, ፀፈረ: whence צְפִירָה "turn, crown or garland."

(3) צפר "leap, spring," ضفر, whence

צָפִיר "he goat," צְפִירָא, ܨܦܝܪܐ:

(4) צפר, ظفر, whence

צִפֹּרֶן "nail," ظُفْر, ጽፍር: Ass. *ṣupru*, ܛܦܪܐ.

Perhaps we may add in Aramaic, by interchange of צ and שׁ,

(5) צַפְרָא, ܨܦܪܐ, "dawn" = שַׁפְרָא from radical שׁפר.

V. The labials ב *b* and פ *p* interchange freely with one another; as also ב *b* and *m*.

1. *b* and *p*: בַּרְזֶל, ܦܪܙܠܐ, Ass. *parzillu*, Ar. فِرْزِل *fetter, forceps*[1].

בִּקְעָה, بقعة, ܦܩܥܬܐ

גָּפְרִית, ܟܒܪܝܬܐ, كِبْرِيت[2]

עֹפֶרֶת, ܐܒܪܐ

פַּגִּין, ܦܓܐ

Particularly when the letter *t* ת follows; as ܢܒܚܬܐ or ܢܦܚܬܐ,

[1] [This last according to Guidi, *Sede*, p. 18, Fränkel, p. 153, is a loanword from the Aramaic.]

[2] [Loanword from the Aramaic according to Fränkel, p. 153.]

زِفْتٌ "pitch"[1]; ܟܘܦܣܬܐ for ܟܘܒܣܬܐ; ܡܦܣܬܐ for ܡܒܣܬܐ; even when a vowel intervenes, as Mand. פת for בַּת, פתולא for בְּתוּלָא.

2. *b* and *m*: בָּחַן, مَحَنَ.

זְמָן, زَمَنٌ or زَمَانٌ, ዘመን: ܙܒܢܐ.

The Arab grammarians mention such cases as بَكَّة for مَكَّة, بَا اسْمُكَ for مَا اسْمُكَ; and the like. In Ḥimyaritic בן stands for מַן, *who*, and בן for מִן, *from*.

A slight aspiration of ב *b* and פ *p* modifies these sounds into *v* and *f*. Hebrew and Aramaic have both sounds, the latter after a vowel, and indicate the difference merely by points. Arabic and Ethiopic have only *b* and *f*; Assyrian only *b* and *p*. The sound of *p* is one of extreme difficulty to an Arab. The Ethiopic ጰ *p̣* and ፐ *p* (or *ps*) are in native words usually modifications of an original *b*, sometimes of an *f*.

(1) בָּכָה, יִבְכֶּה; ܒܟܐ, ܢܒܟܐ;

بَكَي يَبْكِي; በከየ: ይበኪ:

(2) פָּרָה, יִפְרֶה;

فَدَي يَفْدِي; ፈረየ: ይፈሪ:

In modern Syriac, I may remark, *f* is generally hardened into *p*, as ܡܰܠܦܳܢܳܐ *malpānā* for ܡܰܠܦ݂ܳܢܳܐ. The modern Ethiopic dialects, on the contrary, such as Tigriña and Amharic, possess the aspirated *b*, or *v*.

In Assyrian an original *m* passes into aspirated *b*, or *v*, as in *argamānu* or *argavānu*, "purple," Heb. אַרְגָּמָן, Aram. אַרְגְּוָן; *surmēnu* or *survēnu*, "a sort of cypress," Aram. שַׁרְבִּינָא, שְׁרוִינָא, modern Arabic شَرْبِين; *arakh-šamnu* (*samnu*), "eighth month,"

[1] [The Arabic is a loanword, Fränkel p. 151.]

or *šavnu* (*savnu*), Heb. מַרְחֶשְׁוָן. These two letters, *m* and *v*, are not distinguished from each other in Assyrian writing.

The aspirated *b* and *p*, that is to say *v* and *f*, are liable to undergo a further change, viz. into *w* (ܘ, و). Examples of this are comparatively rare in the older dialects; e.g. כּוֹכָב, ܟܘܟܒܐ, كَوْكَب, for כַּבְכָּב; ܪܘܒܐ, ܪܘܒܒܐ, רוּבְּא, for רִבְּרְבָא, רַבְרְבָנִין; פָּשַׁט, بَسَطَ, but Hiph. ܐܘܫܛ, הוֹשִׁיט. In some of the modern dialects, on the contrary, this change is common. We find it, for instance, in Amharic, e.g. ሰው: *saw*, "man," for ሰብእ: *sabĕ'*; ነበረ: *navára* and ኖረ: *nōra* (for *navra*, *naura*). But especially is it common in modern Syriac, where aspirated *b* is constantly treated as = ܘ, *w*, and often wholly disappears; e.g. ܙܒܢܐ *zōnā*, "time"; ܓܒܪܐ *gōrā*, "husband"; ܕܒܫܐ *diūshā*, "honey"; ܬܒܢܐ *tiūnā*, "straw"; ܚܘܠܐ for ܚܘܒܠܐ, *khūlā*, "debt"; ܚܘܝܐ for ܚܫܘܟܐ, *khūyā*, "darkness"; ܫܘܩ for ܫܒܘܩ, *shūḳ*, "let alone," "pardon." The same remarks apply to *f*, in the few cases in which it is not hardened into *p*; e.g. ܢܘܫܐ *nōshā*, for ܢܦܫܐ; ܪܘܫܬܐ *rūshtā*, "winnowing shovel," for ܪܦܫܐ.

A curious change in Arabic is that of ث *th* into *f*; e.g. ثُمَّ, "then," فُمَّ; ثُومٌ, "garlic," فُومٌ; ثُرْغٌ, "interstice" (between the crosshandles of a bucket), فُرْغٌ; ثَدَمٌ, فَدَمٌ, "stuttering, stammering"; ثِدَامٌ, فِدَامٌ, "a cloth used as a strainer"; عَاثُورٌ, عَافُورٌ, "calamity"; مُغْثُورٌ and مُغْفُورٌ, "sweet sap" or "gum" issuing from certain plants; جَدَثٌ, جَدَفٌ, "a tomb" (connected with גָּדִישׁ "a stook"). Compare the substitution of *f* in Russian for the Greek *θ*; e.g. *Feodor* for *Theodore*, *Afinui* for *Athens*, etc.

VI. The liquids ל, נ, ר, and the letter מ, interchange freely.

(1) ל with נ, and vice versâ: לחש and נחש[1]; לִשְׁכָּה and נִשְׁכָּה; נֵדֶן, Aramaic נְדַן and לְדַן[2]; לֶהֱוֵא and ܢܶܗܘܶܐ; Talmud. נקט for לקט, נהמא for לחמא, הני for הלין, ܗܳܠܶܝܢ.

(2) ל with ר, and vice versâ: אַלְמָנָה, ܐܰܪܡܠܬܳܐ, أَرْمَلَةٌ; שַׁרְשְׁרָה, שַׁלְשֶׁלֶת, سِلْسِلَةٌ, Ethiopic plur. ሰናስል:, ܫܰܪܫܠܬܳܐ (for ܫܰܠܫܠܬܳܐ); Mand. תארמידא for ܬܰܠܡܝܕܳܐ, and כאלחא for ܟܪܽܘܚܳܐ; חֲלָצַיִם, Mand. האלצא, but Aram. חַרְצָא, ܚܰܨܳܐ.

(3) נ with ר, and vice versâ: נָהַר and اِنْجَهَمَ; טָמַן and ܛܡܰܪ; זָרַח and دَنَحَ.

(4) מ with נ; as מוֹרַג *tribulum* (threshing-machine), نَوْرَج (Syriac ܢܰܪܓܳܐ "axe"); ܡܫܫܠܳܐ and נַחְשׁוֹלָא. Especially at the end of words; e.g. בֹּהֶן, בְּהוֹנוֹת, Arab. إِبْهَامٌ; בָּטְנִים, بُطْمٌ, ܒܶܛܡܬܳܐ; דָּשֵׁן, دَسِمَ; אִם, "if," إِنْ, أَنْ. So in the pronouns, أَنْتُمْ, אַתֶּם, but ܐܰܢ̈ܬܽܘܢ; كُمْ, כֶם, כוֹם, ܟܽܘܢ; هُمْ, הֵם, ܗܽܘܢ. So in the plural terminations of the noun, Arab. ـُونَ, ـِينَ, Aram. ـִין, ـܝܢ, Heb. ־ִים; in the dual, Arab. ـَانِ, ـَيْنِ; Aram. ־ַיִן, ـܝܢ, Heb. ־ַיִם.

Final ם and ן are apt to fall away:—

(1) In the *construct* state of nouns dual and plural.

(2) In the *absolute* plural of nouns, not only in Talmudic, Mandaitic, and modern Syriac, but also in Assyrian, where we have such plurals as *malkî* "kings," *ilî* "gods," *pagrî* "bodies"[3].

[1] [But see *Journ. of Phil.* xiv. 115.]

[2] [Probably from a Persian word *niddna*; Nöld. in *G. G. A.* 1884, p. 1022.]

[3] [Or also, according to Haupt and Delitzsch, *malkē* etc.]

In Hebrew a few cases may perhaps be found, both in the plural and dual, but they are doubtful.

(3) In the 2nd and 3rd pers. plural imperfect masc. and fem. of the verb; e.g. Arab. يَقْتُلُونَ, يَقْتُلْنَ; Heb. יִקְטְלוּן, יִקְטֹלְנָה (תִּ); Syr. ܢܶܩܛܠܽܘܢ, ܢܶܩܛܠܳܢ; but in vulgar Arabic, and more commonly in Hebrew, يِقْتِلُوا, יִקְטְלוּ; and in Ethiopic, ይቀትሉ ፡ ይቀትላ ። So also in Assyrian we find the termination *ūnu* or *ūni*, as well as the shorter *ū*.

(4) In various other instances. For example, ם in the 2nd pers. plural perf. of the verb; קְטַלְתּוּהוּ compared with קְטַלְתֶּם, vulg. Arab. قَتَلْتُوا for قَتَلْتُمْ. Again, Talmud. קָאֵי or קָא, for קָאִים; נֵיקוּ or לֵיקוּ, fem. תֵּיקוּ, for ניקום, תיקום; מִידֵּי for מידים (ܡܶܕܶܡ, מִדַּעַם, Mand. מינדאם and מינדא)—ן in such Hebrew words as מְגִדּוֹן and מְגִדּוֹ; שִׁילֹה and גִּלֹה for שילון, גילון, as proved by the adjectives שִׁילֹנִי, גִּלֹנִי; etc. Much more frequently in the later dialects; as Talm. בֵּי for בֵּין, הני for הלין, ܗܳܠܶܝܢ; האי and מאי for הָאדֵין and מָאדֵין; Mand. דאינילון for דאינין להון; אמארתולי for אמארתון לי; ניהדוביה for ניהדון ביה (ܢܶܣܩܽܘ ܒܶܗ).

Initial *n*, when pronounced with the shortest vowel, is liable to be dropped in Hebrew and Aramaic, particularly in the imperative of verbs פ״ן (תֵּן, גַּשׁ, ܦܽܘܩ), of which more hereafter. Initial *m* too, according to some scholars, is occasionally rejected in Hebrew, in the participle Pu"al, לֻקַּח, יוּלַּד; whence we can explain the modern Syriac form ܩܘܒܠܢܐ ܠܒ as standing for ܡܩܘܒܠ ܐܢܐ ܠܒ.

Lastly, medial ל, נ, ר are exceedingly apt to be assimilated to a following letter; and conversely נ and ר are frequently employed, especially in the younger dialects, for the purpose of dissimilating the component elements of a double consonant.

(1) Assimilation: in verbs פ״ן; further, ܡܶܥܰܠܬܳܐ (ܡܰܥܠܠܬܳܐ), ܡܶܥܠܬܳܐ (ܡܰܥܠܠܬܳܐ), ܓܶܓܠܬܳܐ (ܓܰܠܓܠܬܳܐ, cp. גַּלְגַּל and גִּלְגָּל); ܓܓܘܠܬܳܐ, גֻּלְגֹּלֶת; ܓܓܪܬܳܐ, גַּרְגְּרוֹת; ܟܰܟܪܳܐ, כִּכָּר, for כרכר; אִשָּׁה for אִנְשָׁה; אַפַּיִם for אַנְפַּיִם; בָּתֵּי for בַּנְתֵּי; אֲמָתוֹ for אֲמַנְתּוֹ; ܡܕܺܝܢ̄ܬܳܐ, ܫܶܢܬܳܐ, ܓܽܦܬܳܐ, ܓܰܒܬܳܐ, ܐܰܢ̄ܬܬܳܐ (ܐܢܬܬܐ and ܐܢ̄ܬܐ). Forms like אִישׁ (rare pl. אִישִׁים, gen. אֲנָשִׁים), ܡܺܥܠܬܳܐ, ܓܺܓܠܬܐ, are easily explained, the long vowel being merely a compensation for the lost doubling.

(2) Dissimilation: ܓܰܢܒܳܪܳܐ, גִּבּוֹר, جَبَّار; יַנְדַּע, מַנְדַּע, for יַדַּע, מַדַּע; מִנְדָּה for מִדָּה (tribute); Mand. מינדאם, מינדא, for מידאם, מידא; Mand. מינילתא, pl. מיניליא, for ܡܶܠܬܳܐ, ܡܶܠܶܐ (interm. ܡܶܢܠܬܳܐ); דַּמֶּשֶׂק and דַּרְמֶשֶׂק, ܕܰܪܡܣܘܩ; כִּסֵּא, כָּרְסְיָא, ܟܽܘܪܣܝܳܐ, كُرْسِيّ.

VII. The weak letters י *y* and ו *w* would easily furnish me with material for more than one lecture, if I entered into a minute account of all their changes and vicissitudes. At present, however, I intend to dwell only upon a few points of primary importance.

Initial י *y* runs through all the dialects, though in comparatively few words; e.g.

يَبِسَ	የብሰ:	יָבֵשׁ	יְבֵישׁ	ܝܶܒܫ
يَوْم	ዮም:	יוֹם	יוֹמָא	ܝܰܘܡܳܐ
يَقِظَ		יָקַץ		

More usually an initial *w* in Arabic and Ethiopic has been changed into *y* in Hebrew and Aramaic. The priority of the *w* is proved by its reappearance in various derived forms of the verb and noun, as we shall see hereafter.

وَلَدَ	ወለደ፡	יְלַד	יְלִיד	ܝܶܠܶܕ
وَهَبَ	ወሀበ፡	יְהַב	יְהַב, יַב	ܝܺܗܶܒ and ܢܶܗܒ
وَيْن	ወይን፡	יַיִן		
وَجِلَ وَجِرَ		יָגֹר		
	ወገረ፡		יְגַר	ܝܰܓܪܳܐ

The original initial *w* rarely appears in Hebrew and Aramaic, as וָלָד or וְלָד (if correct); [post-Biblical] וַדַּאי, וְכַתָּה; ܘܳܠܶܐ, ܘܰܪܕܳܐ, ܘܰܪܕܳܐ [Ϝρόδον]; and in some cases where it has been protected by a preceding consonant, as in the Hithpa"ēl forms הִתְוַדָּה, הִתְוַדַּע, הִתְוַכַּח.

The fate of the initial י in Aramaic is worthy of further notice. In Biblical Aramaic and some other dialects we find י, as יְלִיד, יְתִיב. In Syriac this letter is vocalised and becomes *ī*, written in older times אי, more recently י only, as ܐܺܝܠܶܕ, ܝܺܠܶܕ (whence ܝܰܠܕܳܐ, ܝܺܩܳܪܳܐ). Modern Syriac, however, simply drops the initial י; as ܬܝܳܒܳܐ *tīwā*, "sitting"; ܩܺܝܕܠܗ, "they burned." Mandaitic follows the ancient Syriac in the Pĕ'al form of the verb and similar cases; as עתיב[1] = ܝܺܬܶܒ, עתבית = ܬܶܒܳܬ̈ܐ; עית or עת = ܐܺܝܬ, עקארא = ܝܺܩܳܪܳܐ; but drops the י in the Ethpe'ēl, as עתהיב = ܐܶܬܝܺܗܶܒ, עתליד = ܐܶܬܝܺܠܶܕ.

In Assyrian the initial י of Hebrew and Aramaic is displaced, we are told, by א. We find, for example, *ûmu*, "day"; *idu*,

[1] [ע in Mandaitic is a mere vowel-letter and represents initial *e* or *i*.]

"hand," Eth. አድ፡; *arkhu*, "month," יָרֵחַ, ܝܲܪܚܵܐ, ወርኅ፡; *âšib* "he dwells, dwelling," יֹשֵׁב; *âṣû*, "going out," יֹצֵא; *âlidtu, âlittu*, "bearing," יֹולֶדֶת, وَالِدَةٌ; *akru*, "costly," יָקָר. Nor is this dislike of the sound of initial *y* or *w* confined to Assyrian. Even the Arabs were prone to change initial وُ *wu* and وِ *wi* into أُ *'u* and إِ *'i*; and the combination *wawâ* is always modified at the beginning of a word into *'awâ*. So in the Ḳor'ân we find أُقِّتَتْ for وُقِّتَتْ; further, إِسَادٌ for وِسَادٌ, "cushion"; إِشَاحٌ for وِشَاحٌ, "belt"; أَوَاصِلُ for وَوَاصِلُ, plural of وَاصِلَةٌ, "connecting link, proximate cause"; أَوَاقٍ for وَوَاقٍ, plural of وَاقِيَةٌ, whether in the sense of "guard" or of "ounce." Hence we see at once the connexion, on the one hand, between أَرَّخَ, "to date," and Eth. ወርኅ፡ "month"; אַצִּיל "joint," and وَصْلٌ, where the *w* is original; and, on the other hand, between ܝܶܠܰܦ and אָלַף, "learn"; ܝܺܪܰܟ and אָרַךְ, "be long," where the א claims the priority.

Of the disappearance of initial *w* in some verbal and nominal forms, I shall treat hereafter, when we come to the verbs פ"י in the Hebrew Grammar.

Medial *w* and *y* are chiefly liable to change under the influence of a preceding and following vowel, which lead to their vocalisation, and in some cases to their entire disappearance. E.g.

Perf.	قَامَ	ቆመ፡	קָם	ܩܳܡ	for *ḳawama*,
		ሠየመ፡	שָׂם	ܣܳܡ	for *sayama*;
Imperf.	يَقُومُ	ይቄውም፡	יָקוּם	ܢܩܽܘܡ	for *yaḳwumu*,
		ይሠይም፡	יָשִׂים	ܢܣܺܝܡ	for *yasyimu*.

Compare also مَاتَ, מֵת, ܡܺܝܬ, for *mawita*; and طَالَ, for *ṭawula*, with בּוֹשׁ and אוֹר, for בָּוֹשׁ and אָוֹר. Uncontracted examples are, however, to be found; as عَوِرَ "be blind of one eye," حَوِلَ "squint," هَيِفَ "have a slender waist," גָּוַע, חָוַר, רָוַח, ܙܘܰܥ, ܗܘܰܪ; and the contraction does not take place when the 3rd radical is likewise a *w* or *y*, as رَوِيَ, רוה, ܪܘܶܐ; שָׁוָה, ܫܘܳܐ; etc.

Medial *w* passes into *y* chiefly under the influence of an accompanying *i*, as قِيَامَة. ܩܝܳܡܬܳܐ, "resurrection" (where the Arabic *i* has become a mere *shĕvā* in Syriac), for قِوَامَة. Instances like הָיָה, Aram. הֲוָא, ܗܘܳܐ, Arab. هَوِيَ, are rare. In the Hebrew Pi"ēl and Aramaic Pa"ēl the change is more frequent; as קִיֵּם, חִיֵּב, ܩܰܝܶܡ, ܚܰܝܶܒ, ܙܰܝܶܢ; but examples to the contrary are not wanting, as עִוֵּד, "surround," עִוֵּר, עִוֵּת, ܙܰܘܶܓ, ܚܰܘܶܪ, ܥܰܘܶܠ, ܛܰܘܶܦ, ܩܰܘܶܡ. As the original form is the Arabic *ḳawwama*, the change perhaps began with the 2nd *w*, which passed into *y*, *ḳawyama*; this worked upon the preceding *w*, so as to cause assimilation, *ḳayyama*; and hence arose the Aramaic form *ḳayyēm*, and finally the Hebrew *ḳiyyēm*, as we shall afterwards see in more detail.

Final *w*, when it appears at all as a consonant, is generally found in the shape of *y*; e.g. in Hebrew גָּלְיוּ, יְכַסְיֻמוּ, "they cover them." Its retention in such forms as שָׁלֵו, "be quiet," is rare; for even the Arabic, which tolerates حَلُوَ, requires رَضِيَ and سَلِيَ for رَضُوَ and سَلُوَ. In שָׁלֵו, כִּסְלֵו, גֵּו, וָו, and the like, we should probably pronounce the final ו nearly as *ū*; as also in the forms with pronom. suffixes, like פִּיו *pīū* (for פִּיהוּ), דְּבָרָיו or דְּבָרָו *dĕbhārāū* (for דְּבָרֵיהוּ). This view derives some confirmation from ancient Hebrew seals, on which we read such inscriptions as:

לשבניו עבד עזיו i.e. לְשְׁבַנְיָהוּ עֶבֶד עֻזִּיָּהוּ

לאביו עבד עזיו i.e. לַאֲבִיָּהוּ עֶבֶד עֻזִּיָּהוּ

In the perfect of the verb the Ethiopic alone retains the distinction of the final radicals, e.g. ተለወ: *talâwa*, "follow," በከየ: *bakâya*, "weep." In the other languages the *w* has been changed into *y*, and the combination *aya* contracted into *â*. In Arabic the grammarians have introduced an arbitrary distinction, and write تَلَا for *talawa* and بَكَي for *bakaya*, but the sound is the same in both cases, *talâ*, *bakâ*; and hence the Aramean has ܬܠܐ, ܒܟܐ, with ܐ, א. In Hebrew a ה is substituted for this א, תָּלָה, בָּכָה; but this does not warrant us in speaking of them as verbs ל״ה. The only real verbs ל״ה in Hebrew are such as תָּמַהּ, גָּבַהּ, in Syriac ܬܡܗ, ܒܗܬ, and the like. Upon the whole subject of the weak letters و and ي I shall find it necessary to enter into fuller details, when we come to the classes of verbs in which they appear as first, second and third radicals.

Having thus gone through the various classes of letters in the Semitic alphabet, and enumerated the principal changes to which they are liable in the different Semitic languages, I will conclude this branch of my subject by briefly recapitulating those permutations which are of primary importance, any deviation from which must be regarded with a careful scrutiny before we accept the relationship of the words in question. In so doing, I shall follow the order of the Hebrew alphabet.

1. ה = *h* in all the languages; but also

   ה init. = Assyr. א, Arab. أ, Eth. አ, Aram. א, ܐ.

2. ז = *z* in all the languages; but also

   ז = Assyr. *z*, Eth. ዘ, Arab. ذ, Aram. ד, ܕ.

3. ח = Aram. ח, ܚ, Eth. ሐ, Arab. ح, Assyr. א (as *imêru*); but also

   ח = Aram. ח, ܚ, Eth. ኀ, Arab. خ, Assyr. *kh* ($\underset{\smile}{h}$).

4. י init. = *y* in all the languages except Assyrian, where it is א; but also

 י init. = Aram. י, Eth. ወ, Arab. و, Assyr. א.

5. ס = Aram. ס, ܣ, Eth. ሰ, Arab. س, Assyr. *s* (*sh*).

6. ע = Aram. ע, ܥ, Eth. ዐ, Arab. ع, Assyr. א; but also

 ע = Aram. ע, ܥ, Eth. ዐ, Arab. غ, Assyr. א.

7. צ = *ṣ* in all the languages; but also

 צ = Eth. ጸ, Arab. ظ, Aram. ט, ܛ, Assyr. *ṣ*;

 צ = Eth. ፀ, Arab. ض, Aram. ע, ܥ, ק, Assyr. *ṣ*;

 צ = Eth. ፀ (ጸ), Arab. ض, Aram. צ, ܨ, Assyr. *ṣ*.

8. שׂ = Aram. ס [שׂ[1]], ܣ, Eth. ሠ, Arab. ش, Assyr. *š* (*s*).

9. שׁ = Aram. ܫ, Eth. ሰ, Arab. س, Assyr. *š* (*s*); but also

 שׁ = Eth. ሰ, Arab. ث, Aram. ת, ܬ, Assyr. *š*.

[1] [Biblical Aramaic and the oldest Aramaic monuments have ש = שׂ. In Palmyrene this ש interchanges with ס, e.g. שׂניאן and סניאן.]

CHAPTER V.

THE VOWELS AND THEIR PERMUTATIONS.

We now go on to treat of the vowels and their permutations, a topic which I must, however, handle in a somewhat superficial manner; as time forbids me to enter into more than the most necessary details. In fact, a mere outline of the subject is all that I can pretend to lay before you. Your own reading and reflection must do the rest; and I recommend to you, at present, the Grammars of Olshausen, Bickell (translated by Curtiss), and Stade, as being, on the whole, the most suggestive and the best adapted to your present purpose.

The vowel-system of the Semitic languages, like that of the Indo-European[1], was at first very simple. There were only three primitive vowel-sounds, *a, i, u*, which might naturally be either short or long, thus giving rise to six vowels:

ă ā, ĭ ī, ŭ ū.

Of real primitive diphthongs, like the Indo-European *ai* and *au*, we can hardly speak in Semitic; for a careful examination will, I think, shew us that in every case the second element in a Semitic *ai* or *au* was originally the consonant *y* or *w*. Still, it is convenient in this place to treat *ai* and *au* as being practically diphthongs, and I shall therefore so regard them, with the reservation already mentioned. It may perhaps be well to use in writing *ay* and *aw* instead of *ai* and *au*.

No one of the Semitic languages, however, is exactly restricted to this limited number of vowel-sounds, in the state in which we

[1] [This passage appears to have been written before the general acceptance, among comparative philologists, of the new doctrine of the Indo-European vowels which recognises primitive *e* and *o*.]

are acquainted with it, save perhaps the Assyrian, which seems to designate in writing only the six vowels above mentioned. The Arabic, it is true, also exhibits in writing only the same six vowels, but we know that the actual range of the spoken language is far wider; and probably the same held good in regard to the Assyrian, which is unfortunately, as a spoken tongue, wholly beyond our ken.

Beginning, then, with the Arabic, we find that the ancient *ă ĭ ŭ* are capable of modification in sound, chiefly according to the nature of the consonants with which they are in juxtaposition.

In connexion with one of the gutturals, ح خ ع غ, or with the letter ر, *ă* retains its broad sound, as حَدّ *hadd*, خَمْر *khămr*, لَعِب *lă'b*, مَبْلَغ *mablagh*, رَبّ *rabb*, فَرَس *faras*; whilst with one of the emphatic or harsh consonants, ص ض ط ظ ق, it inclines to a duller, more obscure sound, somewhat like that of the broad Scotch *a* (*å*) or the English *u* in *but*; e.g. بَقِيَ *båkiya*, طَلَبَ *tålaba*, مَطَر *måtår*, ضَرَبَ *dåraba*, صَدْر *sadr* (*su*), بَطْن *batn* (*bu*). Also with *w*, as وَلَد *wåläd*, أَوَّل *auwal* (nearly *auwul*). Under the same circumstances *ĭ* has likewise a duller sound, with the gutturals, especially ع and ح, inclining more to *e* pronounced far back in the mouth, and with ص ض ط ظ ق to that of the deep Turkish *y* or English *i* in *bird*, as عِلْم *'elm*, سِحْر *sehr*, حِبْر *hebr*, قِشْر *kyshr*, قِصَّة *kyssah*, طِبّ *tybb*, اِضْرِب *ydrib*; whilst *ŭ* inclines to *ŏ*, or with ح and ع to *ö*, as ظُفْر *dŭfr*, لَطُفَ *latofa*, لُطْف *lotf*, حُسْن *hosn* or *hösn*, رُعْب *ro'b*, عُمْر *'ömr*, حُكِيَ *hökiya*. The same influences operate upon the long vowels: as طَاهِر *tåhir*, صَاحِب *såhib*, نَظَّارَة *naddåra* (spectacles), *wågib*; صَحِيح *sahīh*, حِيلَة *hīle*, طِين *tīn*, طُور *tūr*.

Again, in connexion with the other consonants, whether in a shut or open syllable, *ă* takes a weaker sound, like that of the common English *ă* (in *hat, cap*), or it becomes *ä, e* (as in *Männer, pet*); whilst *ĭ* and *ŭ* are pronounced with their natural sounds, as in *pin* and *bull*, or nearly so. E.g. كَتَبْتَ *katabta*, مَرْكَب *markeb*, سَمَك *semek*, شَمْس *shems*, ذِكْر *dhikr*, كُلّ *kull*. The sound of *ü* was also heard dialectically in old Arabic, as شُدَّ *shüdda*, رُدَّ *rüdda*, for *shŭdda, rŭdda*; سِيقَ *sûka*, قِيلَ *ḳûla*; and is found occasionally in the vulgar dialects, as *küll* for *kŭll*; in this latter case perhaps under the influence of the Turkish. In a short open syllable, followed by a long one, the short vowels are liable to be modified and reduced almost to the compass of the Hebrew *shĕvâ*; e.g. سَمِين *sĕmîn*, جَلِيل *jĕlîl*, مَدِينَة *mĕdîneh*, مُبَارَك *mŭbârăk*, of which the first two are sometimes vocalised *sĭmîn*, *jĭlîl*, whilst the last is vulgarly pronounced *m'bârăk* or, with a prosthetic vowel, *ĕmbârăk*. In modern dialects, e.g. that of Egypt, *a* becomes *i* even in a shut syllable, e.g. مِن, *mîn*, for مَن "who?" اِسوِد for أَسوَد "black," إِسلِم for أَسلَم "became a muslim," *igzâ* for *agzâ*, أَجزاء "parts." It is also liable to be changed into *u*, under the influence of a proximate *b, f, m* or *w*, e.g. *mŭḥabbe*, *mŭwedde* for مَحَبَّة، مَوَدَّة، *guwâr* for جَوَار *female slaves*; similarly, *muftâḥ* for مِفتاح، *Ḥumṣ* for حِمص.

Just as *ă* was thus modified into *ä ĕ ĭ*, so did *â* pass into *ê* and even into *î*. A word like خَاتَم or غَافِل suffered no change; but the weaker sound in كِتَاب *kĭtâb*, رِكَاب *rĭkâb*, لَاكِن *lâkĭn*, underwent a modification into *kĭtêb*, *rikêb*, *lêkĭn*, and among the Arabs of Africa and Spain into *î*, so that لِسَان *lĭsân* and بَاب *bâb* became *lisîn* and *bîb*. Hence the Spanish names *Jaen* and

Caniles are written by the Arabs جَيَّان and قَنَالَش. This is also the usual pronunciation in modern Maltese, as رَمَاد *r'mîd*, نَازِل *nîzil*.

The diphthongs *ay* and *aw* retain their original sound after the guttural and emphatic letters, as صَيْف *ṣayf*, خَوْف *khawf*. Otherwise they are pronounced almost like *ē* and *ō*; e.g. سَيْف *se'f* (almost *sēf*), مَوْت *m°ot* (almost *mōt*). In the spoken dialects the original sounds *aw* and *ay* or *ey* are still heard, especially when a *w* or *y* follows, as *awwal* أَوَّل, *ṭaiyib* طَيِّب, *seiyed* سَيِّد, *aiwa* أَيْوَهْ. Otherwise they are pronounced *ô* and *ê*, as *sôda* سَوْدَاء, *ḳos* قَوْس, *khôf* خَوْف; *bêḍa* بَيْضَاء, *dêr* دَيْر, *sêf* سَيْف, *ṣêf* صَيْف.

You see then that the Arabic, instead of being limited to the six primitive vowels and two diphthongs, has in reality as wide a range of vowel-sounds as the Hebrew.

On the Hebrew and Aramaic we must dwell at greater length, because in these languages the vowels have undergone considerable modifications, and it is important for an understanding of many grammatical forms that we should be able to trace them back to their original sounds, in doing which the Arabic, ancient and modern, will be of signal service to us.

We start then in Hebrew from the same position as before:

3 short vowels, *ă ĭ ŭ*;
3 long vowels, *ā ī ū*;
2 diphthongs, *ay aw*.

Short *ă* is liable in Hebrew to undergo changes analogous to those which it experiences in Arabic, that is to say to be modified into *ĕ* (ֶ) and *ĭ* (ִ). Compare, for instance, שָׁאַלְתִּי with שְׁאֶלְתֶּם and שְׁאִלְתִּידוּ; בַּת with בִּתִּי; סַף with סִפִּים; קִרְיָה with قَرْيَة; דִּמְעָה with دَمْعَة; מִזְבֵּחַ with مَذْبَح; מִגְדָּלָה with مَهْرَة; מֶרְכָּב with مَرْكَب; נֶחְבָּא with נַחְבֵּאת; נַעֲשָׂה and fem.

נַעֲשְׂתָה with נִגְלָה and fem. נִגְלְתָה; יַד, يَد, with יֶדְכֶם (يَدُكُمْ); דַּם, دَم, with דִּמְכֶם (دَمُكُمْ); דִּבְרֵי, for דַּבְרֵי, from דָּבָר (for *dăbăr*); הֶרָה from הַר. These examples are taken, you will observe, almost exclusively from shut syllables, or half-shut syllables before the tone. In such cases the Syriac often ranges itself on the side of the Arabic: ܡܰܪܟܰܒ݂ܬܳܐ, ܡܰܪܓܰܠܬܳܐ, etc.; whilst at other times it is the Arabic which exhibits the weakening of the vowel, as Heb. צַדִּיק, Arab. صِدِّيق; Syr. ܫܰܒܺܝܩ, ܦܰܩܺܝܕ, Arab. سِكِّير, شِرِّيب; Heb. and Syr. תַּלְמִיד, ܬܰܠܡܺܝܕ݂ܳܐ, Arab. تِلْمِيذ. This change has spread extensively in the later dialects, as compared with the classical Syriac and Arabic. In Hebrew two conspicuous cases are exemplified by segolate nouns of the form גֶּבֶר and by the perfect Piel of the verb. That words like אֶרֶץ, גֶּפֶן and קֶרֶן, were originally pronounced אַרְץ, גַּפְן and קַרְן, might be inferred from the Arabic forms أَرْض, جَفْن and قَرْن; it is rendered certain by the pausal forms אָרֶץ, גָּפֶן, קָרֶן, and by the suffixed forms אַרְצִי, גַּפְנִי, קַרְנוֹ. Besides, we can cite the authority of the LXX., who write Ἄβελ for הֶבֶל, Γασιων Γαβέρ (1 Kings ix. 26) for עֶצְיוֹן גֶּבֶר, and the like. In many other words of the same class the root-vowel has been farther modified into *ĭ*; as קֶבֶר, קָבֶר, קִבְרִי, Arab. قَبْر; שֶׁמֶשׁ, שָׁמֶשׁ, שִׁמְשֵׁךְ, Arab. شَمْس. In all such words the vowel of the 2nd syllable is merely supplementary, and has nothing to do with the original form, but merely lightens the pronunciation of the two final consonants. Again, as to the verbal form Piel, that קִטֵּל stands for קַטֵּל is obvious from the following considerations. (1) The Arabic form is قَتَّلَ *kattala*, with a *fetḥa* in each syllable.

(2) The *ă* of the 1st syllable appears in the Aramaic ܩܛܰܠ, and in Hebrew itself in the imperat. and imperfect קְטֹל and יִקְטֹל. (3) The *ă* of the 2nd syllable is seen in the 2nd pers. sing. קָטַלְתָּ and analogous forms, as well as in numerous examples of the 3rd person, e.g. בִּשַּׂר, חִזַּק, יִסַּר, גִּדַּל, where the vocalisation depends partly upon the accentuation and partly upon other considerations. Sometimes the *ă* of the 2nd syllable is modified into *ĕ*, as in כִּבֵּס, כִּפֶּר, דִּבֶּר; and this weakening, combined with the influence of the *ĭ* in the 1st syllable, has led to the form with *ē*, גִּדֵּל, דִּבֵּר. In the Hiphîl, as we shall afterwards see, the process goes yet a step farther, *ă* being changed into *î* by the successive steps *haḳṭal, hiḳṭal, hiḳṭĕl, hiḳṭêl, hiḳṭîl.*

On short *ĭ* we may content ourselves with noting that in Hebrew it is often modified in unaccented shut syllables into *ĕ* (ֶ), as חֶפְצִי, עֶגְלֵךְ; and that in western Syriac it usually appears as *ĕ* (ܶ), e.g. ܣܶܦܪܶܗ for סִפְרוֹ, סִפְרָהּ, سِفْرُهُ.

As for short *ŭ*, it chiefly appears in Hebrew in a shut syllable with dagesh forte, as חֻקִּי, עֻזּוֹ, and the verbal form קֻטַּל. In an unaccented shut or half-shut syllable it generally becomes *ŏ*, as קָדְשׁוֹ (for קֻדְשׁוֹ, قُدْسُهُ), חָקְכֶם; but also קְצָרְכֶם, גָּדְלוֹ. In Syriac this vowel is usually written *plene* with ܘ, as ܩܽܘܕܫܶܗ, ܙܽܘܚܳܠܳܐ, but you must not therefore imagine it to be long in these and similar words.

An original short *ŭ* or *ŏ* has sometimes been modified in Hebrew into *ĕ*, which may appear in pausal forms as *ē*. This remark applies especially to the pronouns of the 2nd and 3rd pers. pl. and to the word אֶת־. For instance, אַתֶּם stands for *'ăntŭm*, as is shewn by the Arabic أَنْتُمْ and the Syriac ܐܰܢ̱ܬܽܘܢ. Similarly, the suffixes כֶם and הֶם were originally *kŭm* and *hŭm*, as proved by the Arabic كُمْ and هُمْ, the latter of which becomes in certain cases هِمْ. The word אֶת־ stands for אֹת־ *ŏth*, as shewn by the suffixed forms אִתִּי, אִתּוֹ, אִתְּכֶם and אוֹתְכֶם, אִתְּהֶם and אוֹתְהֶם. The interchange in these cases between these two dull vowels ŏ and ĭ will be less surprising to you, if you call to mind such forms as חָצְנִי and חִצְנוֹ from חֹצֶן, i.e. *ḥŏṣn*, but Arabic حِضْن; further, נִכְחוֹ from נֹכַח; and the frequent interchange of ĭ and ŭ in such words as قِضْبَان and قُضْبَان; دُبّ, דֹּב, Syriac ܕܶܒܳܐ; ظُفْر and ظِفْر, Syriac ܛܶܦܪܳܐ; أُنْس, אִישׁ, ܐܢܫܐ; שֹׁרֶשׁ, Syriac ܫܶܪܫܳܐ; in modern Syriac, ܨܶܒܥܳܐ for ܨܶܒܥܳܐ, ܟܶܦܬܳܐ for ܟܽܘܦܬܳܐ, etc.

Let me next call your attention to a set of phenomena which are common in Hebrew to all three short vowels: a weakening and a heightening.

The utmost weakening or (as Bickell calls it) volatilizing of these vowels takes place in Hebrew more especially in the 2nd open syllable before the tone, but also (though less frequently) in the open syllable immediately preceding the tone. As examples of the first case, I may give צְדָקָה for *ṣădăḳăh*, Arab. صَدَقَة; מְדִינָה for *mă*, مَدِينَة; רְדָפוּנִי for *ră*, from רָדַף; דְּבָרִים for *dă*, from דָּבָר; סְפָרִים for *si*, from סֵפֶר; בְּקָרִים for *bŭ* (*bŏ*), from בֹּקֶר; יְזַמְּרוּ for *yŭsammĭru*, as shewn by the Arabic. As examples of the second case take: צִדְקַת י״י *ṣĭdʻkath* for *ṣădăḳăt*, from צְדָקָה; כַּנְפֵי רוּחַ *kănʻphē* for *kănăphē*, from כָּנָף; דְּבַר for *dăbăr*, from דָּבָר; the verbal forms קָטְלָה and קָטְלוּ; the plural participle קוֹטְלִים for *ḳāṭĭlīm*, قَاتِلِين; כְּתָב for *kĭ*, كِتَاب; זְרוֹעַ for *zĭ*, ذِرَاع. Sometimes this short vowel is more distinctly indicated by one of the compound shĕvās; thus: עֲבָדִים for *ʻă*, from עֶבֶד (for *ʻăbd*); עֲגָלִים for *ʻĭ*, from עֵגֶל, عِجْل; עֲנָבִים for *ʻĭ*, from עֵנָב, عِنَب; חֳרָשִׁים for *ḥŏ*, from חֹרֶשׁ; חֲדָשִׁים for *ḥă*, from חָדָשׁ, حَدَث; אֶכְתְּבֶנָּה from אֶכְתֹּב, יִרְדְּפֶךָ

from יִרְדֹּף; צִפֳּרִים from צִפֹּר; חֲצִי, with suffix חֶצְיוֹ, in pause חֵצִי, for *ḥiṣi*. More rarely still a fuller vowel is employed, as in קֳדָשִׁים (also קֳ) from קֹדֶשׁ, שֳׁרָשִׁים from שֹׁרֶשׁ, אֳהָלִים (and אֳהָ) from אֹהֶל. I call your attention to these last forms in particular, as Delitzsch and Baer have recently sought to revive the erroneous pronunciation *ḳâdâshîm* and *shârâshîm*.

The Aramaic, I may remark in passing, shares the tendency of the Hebrew to weaken or volatilize its short vowels, though it often proceeds by different rules. For instance, ܩܛܰܠܬ, ܢܦܰܫܳܐ, ܡܕܺܝܢܬܳܐ, are weakened in exactly the same way as in Hebrew; but ܢܶܫܡܬܳܐ, ܢܶܫܡܳܬܳܐ, and ܩܛܰܠܬܽܘܢܝ follow different rules from נְשָׁמָה and קְטַלְתּוּנִי.

The heightening or elevation of the three short vowels *ă ĭ ŭ* takes place in Hebrew, generally speaking, either in the tone-syllable of a word, or in the open syllable immediately preceding the tone. Short *ă* is heightened into *â*; short *ĭ* into *ê*; and short *ŭ* or *ŏ* into *ô*. Bickell, following Olshausen, speaks of this heightening (§ 42, note 1) as being "merely a mechanical strengthening of the vowel through an *a*, which is placed before it, and which finds its complete analogy in the Indo-Germanic *guna* and the pronunciation of vowels in new high German and modern English[1]." I am not quite sure that I understand this explanation; but it is at all events clear that Olshausen[2] and Bickell regard the heightened vowels *â ê ô* as arising by contraction from *ă + ă*, *ă + i*, and *ă + ŭ*; and they believe this heightening to have been produced by the solemn reading or chanting of the Scriptures, and not to have existed in the language of ordinary life. As to the latter proposition, I myself believe that the slow and solemn recitation of the Scriptures in the synagogue has exercised a considerable effect upon the punctuation as exhibited to us in the Masoretic text of our Bible; but, on the other hand, I feel sure that even in the speech of everyday life such differences at least as exist between the pausal and the common forms of words must have been

[1] With this compare his explanatory observation at p. 140 [of the Eng. Tr.].

[2] [*Lehrb.* p. 110, § 57 a.]

more or less perceptible. The Egyptian fellâḥ says *mĕn hāda* ("who is this?"), but if you knock at his door, he calls out *mīn* ("who's there?"). You ask a shopkeeper *bi-kem er-raṭl*, "how much a pound?"; but if you use the first word only, you say *bi-kām* "how much?" If we consider, further, that the vowels *ĭ* and *ĕ*, *ŏ* and *ŭ*, frequently interchange in Hebrew, without our being able to assign any satisfactory reason; and that even in Arabic the sound of *kesr* is not, according to the best authorities, so sharp and distinct as that of our *ĭ* in *pin*, but rather inclines towards *ĕ*; we shall I think find little difficulty in believing that the heightened vowels *ā* (ָ), *ē* (ֵ), *ō* (ֹ), may, as Noeldeke holds, have arisen in Hebrew from the short *ă ĭ ŭ*, without the addition of any other element.

Of the three vowels, *ĭ* and *ŭ* are almost always heightened in the tone-syllable; as זָקֵן for *săkĭn*, כֹּהֵן for *kăhĭn*, יְדַבֵּר for *yădăbbĭr*, סֵפֶר for *sĭfr*; כֹּל for *kŭll*, יָקֹם for *yăkŭm*, קֹדֶשׁ for *kŭdsh*. But *ă* often remains in the tone-syllable; as in דָּבָר, מִשְׁפָּט; נַחַל, בַּיִת; קָטַל. In fact, *ā* chiefly appears in the closed tone-syllable of the absolute state of nouns, as in דָּבָר, מִשְׁפָּט; and in the open syllable before the tone, as in קָטֹן, לָבֵשׁ, קָטַל, דָּבָר. *ĭ* is also often heightened into *ē* in the open syllable before the tone, as לֵבָב for *lĭbăb*, עֵנָב for عِنَب. The second syllable before the tone is less frequently heightened; as in קָטְלָה and קָטְלוּ, וְקָטַלְתָּ, הָעֲבַרְתָּ (for הֶעֱבַרְתָּ), אֹהָלִים, etc.

It may have struck you as curious that, in many of the Hebrew words which I have lately cited, the short vowel *ŏ* and the heightened vowel *ā* should be represented to the eye by the same sign ָ. This admits, however, of an easy explanation. Just as the pure *ă* of the Sanskrit is pronounced *ŏ* in Bengālī, so the heightened *ā* of the Hebrew gradually passed in the mouths of many of the Jews (not of all) into *â*, and then into *o*. Consequently the punctuators were fairly justified, from a certain point of view, in representing it and *ŏ* by the same sign, even though there was a difference in the quantity of the two vowels. The same thing happened in the case of ָ, which represents

vowels of such different quantities as ֶ in גֶּבֶר and in יֶלֶד.
In the former instance, however, some confusion of sounds may actually arise. For instance, the plural of בַּיִת is written בָּתִּים, which must be read *bátīm*, and not *bottīm*, as is proved by Jewish tradition, by the accentuation, and by the evidence of the cognate Syriac form ܒܳܬܺܝܢ *bātīn*. If *bottīm* had been right, the Syriac form would certainly have been ܒܶܬܺܝܢ. Another example is afforded by רָזִי־לִי (Isaiah xxiv. 16), which, as I believe, is rightly read by Böttcher *rōzī-lī* (from a noun רֹזִי), and not *rázī-lī*.

In treating of this heightening of the vowels, I have taken no account of the Aramaic dialects, because in them it is neither so widely spread nor so readily perceived, owing to the defects of the vowel-system. I think, however, that the vowel of the tone-syllable in such verbal forms as ܢܶܣܰܒ, ܢܶܚܰܡ, ܢܶܓܠܶܐ, ܢܶܩܛܶܠ, must have differed in sound from that of the first syllable almost, if not quite, as much as in the Hebrew יִתֵּן. As for *ó* in place of *ŭ*, it occurs, according to the eastern dialect of Syriac, in many verbal and nominal forms; for example, the imperfect and imperative ܢܶܩܛܘܿܠ *nĕḳṭól* (*niḳṭŭl*), ܩܛܘܿܠ *ḳĕṭól*; and in the personal pronouns ܐܰܢ̱ܬܘܿܢ, ܐܶܢܘܿܢ, with the suffixes ܟܘܿܢ, ܗܘܿܢ, and the verbal form ܩܛܰܠܬܘܿܢ. In these latter cases, as we have seen above, the Hebrew has modified the original *ŭ* into *ĕ*, אַתֶּם, כֶם, הֶם, קְטַלְתֶּם. The western Syrians weakened this *ó* again into *u*, saying ܢܶܩܛܘܽܠ, ܐܰܢ̱ܬܘܽܢ, but no doubt the quantity of this vowel much exceeded in length that of the original short *ŭ* in *niḳṭŭl*.

I now proceed to speak briefly of the long vowels, *ā*, *ī*, *ū*.

Long *ā* has, we may say, almost disappeared from the Hebrew. Just as the long *ā* of the Sanskrit was modified in Greek into η and ω, so the long *ā* of the Arabic passed in Hebrew into *ō*. As *dadāmi* became δίδωμι, or *āmas*, ὠμός[1], so

[1] [The priority of *ā* in these cases is not now admitted.]

did *kāṭala* become קוֹטֵל (Poel); *kāṭil^un*, קוֹטֵל (participle); حَمَار, חֲמוֹר; etc. Exceptions to this rule are exceedingly rare. כְּתָב, كتاب, can scarcely be reckoned a pure Hebrew word; and פְּרָת, فُرَات, is foreign to both languages [Assyrian *Purăt* (*Burat*), Accadian *Pura-nunu*, "the great river"]. מְעָרָה corresponds to the Arabic مَغَارَة, but the Syriac form has *pathach*, ܡܥܰܪܬܳܐ, and not ܡܥܳܪܬܳܐ. The most conspicuous of apparent exceptions is that which is presented to us by the perfect of verbs ע״ו, as קָם, שָׁר, corresponding to the Arabic قَامَ, بَانَ. Next are adjectives of the form קַטָּל, like צַיָּד, טַבָּח, עַוָּל, כַּחָשׁ, אִכָּר, if they really correspond to such Arabic words as صَيَّاد, طَبَّاخ, أَكَّار, etc. This identification, however, is, as we shall afterwards see, somewhat doubtful; the Arabic forms just cited find their precise equivalents in such words as גִּבּוֹר = جَبَّار, שִׁכּוֹר = سَكَّار (in sense سِكِّير), קִפּוֹד = قَفَّاز, יִסּוֹר, and, with a rare retention of the original *pathach* in the first syllable, קַנּוֹא = קַנָּא. The Aramaic vowel corresponding to the Arabic *ā* and Hebrew *ō* is the *zĕḳāfā*, ܳ, pronounced by the eastern Syrians even at the present day *ā*, by the western *ā* or *ō*, whence the latter represent it in writing by the Greek *omikron*, ܳ. Compare with the above cited words the Syriac forms ܩܳܛܶܠ, ܚܡܳܪܳܐ; ܟܬܳܒܳܐ, ܦܪܳܬ, ܡܥܰܪܬܳܐ, ܐܟܳܪܳܐ, ܢܰܓܳܪܳܐ (with dissimilation); ܩܳܡ, ܫܳܡ.

This vowel is sometimes weakened, both in Hebrew and Syriac, into *ū*; e.g. נָקוֹם, נְקוּמוֹת; קַשְּׁאִים, from a sing. קִשּׁוּא, Arab. قِثَّاء; תַּפּוּחַ, Arab. تُفَّاح; מָתוֹק, fem. מְתוּקָה, pl. מְתוּקִים; מָנוֹס, מְנוּסִי; מָעוֹן, מְעוּנִים; ܬܰܢܽܘܪܳܐ or ܬܰܢܽܘܪܳܐ, for ܬܰܢܳܪܳܐ, ܐܶܣܛܽܘܡܟܳܐ for ܐܶܣܛܳܡܟܳܐ, ܡܽܘܚ for ܡܳܚ. As a parallel I may mention that in some parts of Persia long *ā* is pronounced *ū*, e.g. نان *nūn*, for *nān* or *nân*, "bread"; بيا *biyū*, for *biyā* or *biyâ*, "come." But indeed I need go no farther than our own language, where such words as *bone*, *stone* represent an Old English *bân*, *stân*, whilst *moon* stands for *mōna*, which was in its turn preceded by a form *māna*. In the Hebrew words just cited you will observe that this weakening depends upon the removal of the tone to the following syllable; but in the Syriac words it seems to be due to the influence of the letter *n*. The Phœnicians appear to have gone beyond the Hebrews in this respect, pronouncing for instance *shūfēṭ* instead of שׁוֹפֵט (sufes, -ētis), *rūfê* for רוֹפֵא, *shâlūsh* (salus) for שָׁלֹשׁ, *rūsh* (rus) for רֹאשׁ, and in the plur. fem. *alōnūth* for אֱלֹנוֹת. In a shut syllable such an *ū* might even be shortened into *ŭ*, *ŏ*; thus נְחֻשְׁתָּם and נְחֻשְׁתִּי from נְחֹשֶׁת, ܢܚܫܐ, نحاس; שְׁלָשְׁתָּם from שְׁלֹשֶׁת, ܬܠܬܐ, ثلاثة. I may add that in a few cases, in Aramaic, long *ā* has passed into *ē* and *ī*, just as the Sanskrit *ā* of *dadhāmi* became *ē* in Greek τίθημι, or the Arabic *ā* successively *ē* and *ī*. Thus the Arabic رأس *rā's* first became راس *rās*, which the Hebrews modified into רֹאשׁ, *rōsh*, whilst the Arameans preferred רֵישָׁא, ܪܝܫܐ.

The long vowel *ī* I may here dismiss with the remark that in the few cases where it has been shortened into *ĭ*, *ĕ*, this vowel is reheightened by the accent into *é*. Thus, יָבִין = يَبِينُ, but יָבֵן and וַיָּבֶן = يَبِنْ.

So also long *ū* may in certain instances be shortened into *ŭ*, *ŏ*, and then this vowel be reheightened into *ó*; as יָשׁוּב = يَتُوبُ, but יָשֹׁב and וַיָּשָׁב = يَتُبْ.

Whether long *ū* can in Hebrew be differentiated into *ō* seems a doubtful matter. יִלּוֹד seems to be identical in form with the

Syriac ܡܠܰܩܦܳܢܳܐ; and ܡܰܛܡܳܢ, with its construct plur. מַטְמֻנֵי, may perhaps be only a variation upon מַטְמוֹן, according to the form מַלְבּוּשׁ; but both words admit of other explanations. In Aramaic, however, a distinction of this sort existed, and actually forms one of the main distinctions in pronunciation between the eastern and western dialects of Syriac. The modern Syrians still retain *ō* in many forms where *ū* prevailed in the west. The vowel is represented by the letter ܘ; a point above this letter indicates the sound *ō*, beneath it the sound *ū*. The Western Syrians, who use the Greek vowels, write ܘ݂, i.e. the Greek diphthong *ου*. Some of the principal forms in which the Eastern Syrians pronounced *ō* are the following: the pronominal forms ܐܢ̱ܬܘܿܢ, ܗܢ̱ܘܿܢ, ܗܘܿܢ, ܐܢܘܿܢ, ܟܘܿܢ, ܗܘܿܢ, ܡܩܛܠܘܿܢ; the verbal forms ܢܩܛܘܿܠ, ܐܬܩܛܘܿܠ, ܩܛܘܿܠ; the nominal forms ܩܛܘܿܠܐ (ܩܕܘܿܫܐ, ܡܠܟܘܿܬܐ); and the diminutive terminations ܘܿܢܐ and ܘܿܬܐ (ܐܣܩܘܿܦܐ, ܨܘܪܘܿܢܐ, ܠܚܡܘܿܬܐ).

We next enter upon the examination of the so-called diphthongs *ay* (*ai*) and *aw* (*au*).

I have already told you that their sound has been weakened in Arabic to that of *ē* and *ō*. Compare in other languages *θαῦμα* and *θῶμα*, *παιδίον*, vulgar *παιδί*, *plaustrum* and *plostrum*, *causa* and *chose*; German *Auge* and Dutch *oog*, German *Stein* and Dutch *steen*; etc. In North Africa, however, a further weakening has taken place into *ū* and *ī*. Thus يَوْم *yawm* has gradually become first *yōm* and then *yūm*; بَيْت *bayt*, first *bēt* and then *bīt*.

Now mark the same progression in the other Semitic languages.

In Assyrian I find that our authorities write *ûmu*, *bîtu*, *înu* (عين), *bîṣu* (egg) without apparently the slightest trace of the older forms, which must necessarily have preceded them.

In Hebrew *ay* and *aw* are of somewhat rare occurrence in a perfectly pure form; for example, גַּי, שַׁי, מַיְמִינִים, קַו, צַו, שַׁלְוְתִי,

עֲוְלָה, חַוְרָן (حَوْرَان); in the suffixed form דְּבָרַי; and when the letters ו and י are doubled, as כַּוָּן ("cake"), דַּיָּן, or with suffixes חַיַּי, גַּוָּם, גַּוֶּךָ. More generally *ay* and *aw* are modified in various ways.

At the end of a word ַי usually becomes ֶ or ֵ. We find סִינַי, שַׂדַי, שָׂרַי, and the like; but far more frequently ֶ, as שָׂדֶה (in the construct state שְׂדֵה), מַרְאֶה, יִגְלֶה, יִבְנֶה, imper. גְּלֵה. The intermediate step is marked by the pronunciation of the LXX., Σινᾶ, Σάρα, corresponding to the Arabic termination ـَي in مِنًى, رَمَى, *Minā, ramā*, which some pronounce with the 'imālah, *Minē, ramē*. In other cases, the *ă* element in the diphthong prevailed in Hebrew, and the termination became *ā*, ָ, as in גָּלָה. On these points I shall have more to say when I come to treat of the verbs ל״ה.

In the body of a word *ay* and *aw* exhibit several modifications. Sometimes a supplementary vowel is introduced, to lighten the pronunciation; as בַּיִת for בַּיְת, מָוֶת for מַוְת. This latter form, in which the *ă* is heightened to *á* is rare: אָוֶן, מָוֶת, תָּוֶךְ; but שָׁוְא, like גַּיְא. The same supplementary vowel is found in the termination of the dual, ַיִם standing for ַיְם, Arabic ـَيْن. At other times the *ă* sound in the diphthong predominates, yielding *á* instead of *ay*. So אָן, אָנָה, מֵאָן, for אַיִן, Arabic أَيْن; דָּתָן for דָּתַיִן, עֵינָם for עֵינַיִם; בָּתִּים *bātīm* for בַּיְתִּים, from בַּיִת; the suffixed form דְּבָרָיו, also written דְּבָרָו, for דְּבָרַיְהוּ. You will find a similar substitution of *á* for *ai* in the older stages of our own language. The Gothic *ai* in *hails, hlaibs*, and *aigan*, became in Anglosaxon *hāl, hlāf*, and *āgan*, in English *whole, loaf* and *own*.

[1] If so, בַּיִת follows the form of תּוֹר, תּוֹרִים; זַיִת, זֵיתִים; אַיִל, אֵילִים; לַיִל, לֵילוֹת; not that of שׁוֹר, שְׁוָרִים; עַיִר, עֲיָרִים; תַּיִשׁ, תְּיָשִׁים; חַיִל, חֲיָלִים; עַיִן, עֲיָנוֹת. Noeldeke however pronounces the word *bâttîm*.

Generally speaking, however, *ay* and *aw* are modified as in vulgar Arabic into *ē* and *ō*, the *ē* being represented by ֵי, and sometimes by ֶי, the *ō* by וֹ. So in אֵי for אַי (with suffix, אַיֵּן), אוֹ for אַו (أَو, أَوْ); in segolate nouns צוֹם, שׁוֹר, and in the construct state בֵּית, מוֹת; in the Niphal and Hiphil of verbs פ״י, as נוֹלַד for נַוְלַד, הוֹלִיד for הַוְלִד, הֵיטִיב for הַיְטִב; and in several forms of verbs ל״ה, as גִּלֵּיתָ for גִּלַּיְתָ, הִגְלֵיתָ for הִגְלַיְתָ, תִּגְלֶינָה for תִּגְלַיְנָה. This *ē* is frequently attenuated into *ī*, and more rarely *ō* into *ū*. Thus גִּלִּיתָ for גִּלֵּיתָ, גִּלַּיְתָ, as in the vulgar Arabic of North Africa رميت *r'mīt* for *r'mēt* (*ramaita*). Perhaps also the proper name אֲמִינוֹן, instead of אַמְנוֹן (2 Sam. xiii. 20), if we regard it as a contemptuous diminutive, "that wretch of an Amnon." אֲמִינוֹן would then stand for אֲמֵינוֹן i.e. *'umainān*, just as, in vulgar Arabic, *k'fīfah* for *kufaifah*, as the diminutive of قُفَّة *kuffah*, "a basket." As examples of *ō* becoming *ū*, I may mention לוּ for לוֹ, Arabic لَوْ; יוּכַל for יוֹכַל, יֻכַל, imperf. of יָכֹל; and נוּגֵי, part. plur. Niphal of יָגָה, for נוֹגֵי, נַוְגֵי. Here again we find a parallel in the vulgar Arabic forms of the imperfect of verbs פ״ו, يُوصَل, يُوقَف, يُوعَد, for يَوْصَل, يَوْقَف, يَوْعَد.

In Aramaic the position of matters is on the whole, *mutatis mutandis*, much the same as in Hebrew. In Syriac the original diphthongs appear, however, more frequently than in Hebrew; for example in the emphatic form of the segolates ܚܰܝܠܳܐ, ܒܰܝܬܳܐ, ܝܰܘܡܳܐ; in the construct plural ܡܰܠܟܰܝ̈, where the Bibl. Aramaic, like the Hebrew, has ֵי; in the plural suffixed forms ܡܰܠܟܰܝ̈ܟ, ܡܰܠܟܰܝ̈ܗܝ, ܡܰܠܟܰܝ̈ܟܘܢ, ܡܰܠܟܰܝ̈ܗܘܢ (Ch. מַלְכוֹהִי); in the Aphel of verbs פ״י, as ܐܰܘܟܶܠ, ܐܰܘܬܶܒ, ܐܰܝܢܶܩ (Ch. אוֹלֵד, אוֹתֵב); and in such words as the diminutives ܢܽܘܗܪܳܐ and ܥܠܰܝܡܳܐ (Ch. עוּלֵימָא).

At the end of a word we find forms similar to those of the Hebrew; e.g. with *ē*, ܚܢܳܢܶܐ ܡܟܣܳܢܶܐ, ܢܳܡܘܣܶܐ ܡܰܪܓܳܢܶܐ, ܬܰܠܝܶܐ; with *ā*, ܬܰܠܝܳܐ.

In the body of a word, Syriac *ay* sometimes becomes *ē*, as in the construct ܒܶܝܬ, and in the duals ܬܪܶܝܢ, ܡܳܐܬܶܝܢ, ܡܰܪܬܶܝܢ; in Biblical Aramaic תַּרְתֵּין, but מָאתַיִן.

The *ă*-sound predominates, for example, in Targumic מָאתָן (200) and תְּמָנָן [תְּמָנַן] (80, for תְּמָנֵין, ܬܡܳܢܝܢ, as well as תְּמָנִין, ܬܡܳܢܶܝܢ); in the plural ܒܳܬܶܝܢ; in the adverb ܐܰܝܟ, pronounced *ăkh* (Ch. אֵיךְ, הֵיךְ); in the plural suffixed forms of the Jewish Aramaic עַבְדָךְ or עַבְדָּיךְ, "thy servants," [Targumic] עַבְדָהָא or [Biblical] עַבְדַהּ [*ḳĕrī* עַבְדָיהּ] "her servants," עַבְדָינָא *ḳĕrī* עַבְדָנָא "our servants," as contrasted with עַבְדַי, עַבְדֵיכוֹן and עַבְדֵיהוֹן.

Further, *ē* sinks into *ī*, according to the western pronunciation, in the simple forms of the segolates ܓܶܒܪ, ܢܶܦܠ; also in the forms ܟܬܶܒܬ (construct), ܟܬܶܒܬܗܘܢ, ܟܬܶܒܬܶܗ, ܟܬܶܒܬܳܟ; in many forms of the 1st and 2nd pers. in the perf. of verbs ל"א, as perf. Peal ܓܠܶܝܬ (but Nestorian ܪܡܶܝܬ), Pael ܓܰܠܶܝܬ and ܓܠܶܝܬ, ܓܠܶܝܬܘܢ, etc. Similarly, *ō* sinks into *ū*, in ܐܶܠܘ "if" (= ܠܘ + ܐܶܢ); and, at least according to the western pronunciation, in the simple state of the segolates ܢܽܘܗܪ, ܣܽܘܦ ("end").

In the later Aramaic dialects there is a strong tendency to get rid of the diphthongs. Already in old Syriac we find ܐܶܝܟ *ăkh*, with short *ă*, for ܐܰܝܟ; ܠܺܠܝܳܐ *lilyā*, for *lēlyā*, *lailyā* (ܠܶܠܝܳܐ); and another example of the same kind is ܐܶܡܰܬܝ (for אֵי מָתַי); but the modern Syrian says *līt* for ܠܰܝܬ; *ikā* or *īkā* (ܐܺܟܳܐ) for ܐܰܝܟܳܐ; *īdh* (ܐܝܕ) for אֵידָן and אֵידָא, ܐܰܝܕܳܐ and ܐܰܝܢܳܐ; ܒܳܬܘܳܬܶܐ *bāthwā(th)ē*, "houses," ܒܳܬܘܳܬܰܢ "our houses"; and even *tyēkhvā* for ܩܘܼܒܚܐ. So also, though to a less extent, in Mandaitic, where we find לית as well as לאיית (לַיְת), and קרית for ܩܪܝܬ as well as ܩܪܺܝܬ.

I will now say a few words on the different classes of supplementary vowels, especially in Hebrew. These, as is indicated by the term which I have just employed, do not belong to the original vocalisation of the word, but have been introduced at subsequent periods, to make the pronunciation of it easier by facilitating the utterance of a harsh consonant or of a combination of consonants.

(1) The so-called *furtive pathach*, which is inserted between a long or heightened vowel and the final gutturals ה ח ע; as אֱלוֹהַּ for *ĕlōh*, Aram. אֱלָהָא, ܐܠܗܐ, Arab. إِلٰه; זְרוֹעַ for *zĕrō'*, Aram. דְּרָעָא, ܕܪܳܥܳܐ, Arab. ذِرَاع; תַּפּוּחַ for *tappūḥ*, Arab. تُفَّاح; רוּחַ for *rūḥ*, رُوح, ܪܽܘܚܳܐ; מֹחַ for *mōḥ*, מוֹחָא, مُخّ; מְשַׁלֵּחַ for *mĕshallēḥ*, i.e. *mushallĭḥ*; רֵעַ for *rē'*, *rī'*. This sound is heard in the spoken Arabic of the present day, in such words as صَاحِبِيح, مَلِيح, سَطُوح *suṭŭᵃh*, بَطِّيخ, مَنْفُوخ *mamfŭᵃkh*, رِيح, رُوح, but it is not, and never has been, written in this language or in Syriac, where we find only ܠܡܫܬܡܚܬܐ ܪܘܚܐ and the like.

(2) The auxiliary *pathach* which is sometimes inserted between ע or ח and ך or ת at the end of a word. It is so slight in sound as not even to effect the aspiration of the ך or ת. For example: שָׁמַעַתְּ, שָׁכַחַתְּ, הַמְלַחַתְּ, as well as שָׁכַחְתְּ, לָקַחְתְּ; וַיִּחַדְּ for וַיִּחַדְּ, as compared with וַיֵּרְדְּ, יֵרְדְּ, יֵפְתְּ, וַיִּפְתְּ.

(3) The auxiliary vowel ֶ, ַ, ָ, in various nominal and verbal forms, which is very little stronger than no. 2. For example, in segolate nouns: סֵפֶר, פֶּרֶא, זֶרַע, יֶלֶד, תַּחַת, נַעַר, נֵצַח, קֹדֶשׁ, פֹּעַל, מָוֶת, בַּיִת, and in the dual termination ַיִם. The auxiliary is actually wanting in such words as נֵרְדְּ, קֹשְׁטְ

(also קֹשְׁטְ), חֵטְא, גַּיְא, שָׁוְא. And again, in the shortened imperfect or jussive of verbs ל״ה: וַיִּרֶב, וַיִּרֶף, יִגֶל, וַתֵּבֶל, וַתַּעַשׂ, יִרֶא, יֵרַע, יִחַר; contrasted with וַיֵּבְךְּ, יֵשְׁתְּ, וַיֵּשְׁתְּ, וַיֵּרְדְּ, וַיִּפְתְּ, וַיֵּשְׁבְּ, וַיַּשְׁקְ, and וַיַּרְא, where perhaps the final shĕvā may have once been slightly moveable, *wayyiftĕ*, *wĕ-yérdĕ*, etc. A somewhat similar insertion of a short *ă* takes place in Mandaitic in the word איאך for أيك, and in the plural suffix of the 1st pers. איאן for ـينا, as כאפאיאן *our hands*, עדאיאן *our hands*. Perhaps also in the pronoun of the 2nd pers. masc. אנאת, אנאתון. The vulgar Arabic has this auxiliary vowel, for example, in the segolates, صُبْح, *subᵃh*, رُمْح, *rumᵃh*, سَطْح, *saṭᵃh*, نَسْخ, *näsᵉkh*, نَفْخ *nafᵉkh*.

(4) A guttural letter at the end of a toneless syllable often takes a very short vowel, when an ordinary consonant would remain vowelless. This vowel, which is represented in writing by a *compound shĕvā*, conforms in character to the preceding vowel. Thus: יַעֲמֹד and יֶחֱזַק, for יַעְמֹד and יֶחְזַק, of the form יִקְטֹל; הֶחֱרִים, יַחֲרִים and יָחֳרַם, for הֶחְרִים, יַחְרִים and יָחְרַם, of the forms הִקְטִיל, יַקְטִיל and יָקְטַל; נַעֲרוֹ, פָּעֳלוֹ, for נַעְרוֹ and פָּעְלוֹ. Examples to the contrary are: יֶאְסֹר, יֶאְשַׁם, אֶהְפֹּךְ and נֶהְפַּךְ, יַחְשֹׁב, נֶחְבָּא, יֶעְשַׁן, תַּעְלִים, וַעְמִי, טַעְמוֹ.

(5) The compound shĕvā spoken of under no. 4 frequently becomes a *full short vowel*, when the guttural is followed by a consonant with the shortest vowel (*shĕvā mobile*). Thus

with	יַעֲמֹד	compare	יַעַמְדוּ,	for	יַעְמְדוּ
„	יֶחֱזַק	„	יֶחֶזְקוּ	„	יֶחְזְקוּ
„	וַיֵּאָסֵף	„	וַיֵּאָסְפוּ	„	וַיֵּאסְפוּ
„	נֶאֱסַף	„	נֶאֶסְפוּ	„	נֶאְסְפוּ
„	נַעֲרוֹ	„	נַעַרְךָ	„	נַעְרְךָ
„	פָּעֳלוֹ	„	פָּעָלְךָ	„	פָּעְלְךָ

but on the contrary observe such forms as וַיַּחְלְקוּ, מַחְשְׁבוֹתַי.

Of this supplementary vowel a far wider use is made in Aramaic. Thus in the Targums we find מְרִינְחָא for מַדְנְחָא, מְשִׁירְיָיתָא for מַשְׁרְיָתָא; whilst in Syriac we may say ܡܰܕܢܚܳܐ, ܡܰܫܪܝܬܳܐ, ܢܶܫܡܥܬܳܐ, ܬܶܫܡܫܬܳܐ, ܙܰܪܥܳܐ and ܡܰܗܒܳܐ, for ܡܰܕܢܚܳܐ, ܡܰܫܪܝܬܳܐ, ܢܶܫܡܥܬܳܐ, ܬܶܫܡܫܬܳܐ, ܙܰܪܥܳܐ and ܡܰܗܒܳܐ; ܢܰܦܫܰܩ, ܐܶܬܢܣܶܒ, ܐܰܬܓܶܒ and ܡܰܥܙܶܠ, for ܢܰܦܫܰܩ, ܐܶܬܢܣܶܒ, ܐܰܬܓܶܒ and ܡܰܥܙܶܠ. In Mandaitic this insertion is very general, the vowel *u* being also occasionally employed, as הוכומתא and היכומתא (ܚܶܟܡܬܳܐ, חָכְמָה), ניצובתא and ניצבתא (ܢܶܨܒܬܳܐ); in the conjugation Ethpe'ēl, the normal form is עתינסיב = ܐܶܬܢܣܶܒ.

(6) Here, too, may find its place the *prosthetic vowel*, which is prefixed to a word to facilitate the pronunciation of an initial consonant which has weakened or lost its original vowel. Compare in Greek χθές and ἐχθές, ἀσπαίρω and σπαίρω; Spanish *escudo, escuela*; French *espère, esprit*; Italian *con iscienza, in Ispagna*. In ancient Arabic this vowel is usually *ĭ* or *ŭ*, as in the imperative اُفْرُقْ, اِجْلِسْ, اُقْتُلْ; in the verbal conjugations اِنْقَتَلَ, اِقْتَتَلَ, and اِسْتَقْتَلَ; in اِبْنٌ (for بَنَيٌ), *son*, اِثْنَانِ, *two*, اِسْمٌ or اُسْمٌ, *name*, etc. In the vulgar dialects examples are far more numerous; e.g. اِتْقَتَلَ and اِتْقَاتَلَ, for تَقَتَّلَ and تَقَاتَلَ, اِمْبَارَك for مُبَارَك, etc. In Hebrew we find *ĕ*, ־ָ, as in אֶזְרוֹעַ for זְרוֹעַ, אֶצְעָדָה for צְעָדָה, and perhaps a few more, such as אֶתְמוֹל and תְּמוֹל, אֶתְנַן, אֶשְׁפָּר "measure." In שְׁתַּיִם the prosthetic אֶ, though pronounced by many of the Jews, has not been written. In Aramaic occur both ܐܰ and ܐܶ. Already in Biblical Aramaic we have אַרְכֻבָּה "knee," in the Palestinian dialect ܐܶܪܟܘܒܬܐ. In Syriac we find ܐܰܣܢܳܐ for ܣܢܳܐ, ܐܶܣܛܶܟܣܳܐ for

ܐܣܦܝܩܠܐ, ܐܕܩܠܐ and ܐܕܢܐ, for ܕܩܠܐ, ܕܢܐ, ܐܫܘܩܐ for ܫܘܩܐ "street," ܐܫܬܐ and ܐܫܬܝܢ for ܫܬܐ and ܫܬܝܢ, ܐܫܬܝܬ for ܫܬܝܬ or ܫܬܐ, etc. In ܐܘܪܩܥܬܐ the prosthetic vowel has been influenced by the original vowel of the ܪ, as shewn in the Arabic رُقْعَة. In the later dialects of Aramaic, examples of the prosthetic vowels become more and more numerous.

(7) Different from this vowel is the likewise very short vowel which is occasionally prefixed in Hebrew and Aramaic to words beginning with a consonant and a full vowel. This addition may sometimes find its explanation in the harshness of the initial consonant, as when it is ק, ט, or even ר; but in other cases even this reason is wanting. Examples in Hebrew are: אֲבַטִּיחִים "melons" (بَطِّيخ, ܦܛܝܚܐ), אֲבַעְבֻּעֹת "blains" or "small blisters" (ܒܥܒܘܥܬܐ "bubbles" of water), אֲגַפִּים "wings" of an army, אֲזִקִּים "fetters," אֲגַרְטְלִים probably the same as *κάρταλος*, *κάρταλλος*, which is also found in Arabic and Syriac; אֲדַרְכֹּן a Persian coin, called by the Greeks *δαρεικός*[1]; אֱגוֹז "a nut," Arab. جَوْز, Syr. ܓܘܙܐ, probably from the Persian گوز *gôz*; in Syriac ܐܪܙܐ for ܪܙܐ (Pers. راز), where the ܐ was doubtless once sounded, *ărāzā*; in later dialects אֶדָּם for דַּם "blood," אִטְּרַפָּא "leaf," for טַרְפָּא; Mand. עשומיא for שומיא "heaven," אראמאתא for ראמאתא "heights," אקאמרא "wool," אקאפרא "dust," for the older ܥܡܪܐ and ܥܦܪܐ.

This concludes what I have to say for the present upon the consonants and vowels of the languages with which we are dealing—Arabic, Hebrew and Syriac. I now proceed to treat of the different parts of speech, beginning with the pronouns.

[1] [In a Phoenician inscription of 96 B.C., recently found at the Piraeus, דרכנם and דרכמנם seem to stand for *δραχμαί*.]

CHAPTER VI.

THE PRONOUNS.

HERE let me call your attention, in the first place, to certain elements which enter into the formation of a great many of the pronouns, as well as of the demonstrative and other particles, of the Semitic languages. I can give these elements no better general or common name than that of *demonstrative* letters or syllables. Their origin and precise original force are in most cases unknown to me; or, at all events, I can only make such guesses at them as it is hardly worth while to lay before you just now, when you have need rather of facts than of speculations. The principal of these demonstrative letters, so far as regards the pronouns, are: א and ה, ד and ת, ש, כ, ל מ נ, ו and י. We shall notice each of them more particularly as occasion requires in our survey of the pronouns.

A. *The Personal Pronouns.*

In treating of the personal pronouns I shall begin, for reasons which will afterwards become apparent, with the suffixed forms which we find appended to substantives in the singular.

Of the 1st pers. sing. the fullest form in actual use is the Arabic ـِيَ *iya*, which is usually shortened, according to circumstances, into يَ *ya* or ـِي *ī*, as نَفْسِيَ, نَفْسِي, قَفَايَ. It is obviously identical with the Ethiopic የ: *ya*, in ነፍስየ: *nafsĕya*; and with the Assyrian *ya*, in *bīt-ya* "my house." This latter,

I am told, becomes *ī* and in certain cases *a*, as *bintī* "my daughter," *abūa* (for *abūya*), as well as *abī* and even *aba*, "my father"; with which last compare such Arabic forms as يَابْنَ عَمَّ *ya'bna 'amma*, يا رَبَّا *yā rabbā*. The Hebrew form is, as you all know, ִי, of which the *yūd*, though written, is no longer pronounced in Syriac: מַלְכִּי, ܡܰܠܟܝ. The intermediate step, no doubt, was the shortening of *ī* into *ĭ*, which we find sometimes in old Arabic, especially in vocative forms like يا رَبِّ, which in pause would be pronounced يا رَبْ *yā rabb*. The corresponding plural is in Arab. نَا *nā*, sometimes shortened into *nă*; in Eth. ነ: *nă*, in Assyrian *nī* or *nū*, Heb. נוּ, Aram. נָא, Syr. *n*, as מַלְכֵּנוּ, מַלְכָּנָא, ܡܰܠܟܰܢ. These plural forms serve also to designate the accusative after a verb, and we have here evidently the same *n* that appears in the suffix of the accusative sing., viz. Arab. نِي *niya* or *nī*, Eth. ኒ: *nī*, Assyr. *nī*, Heb. נִי, Aram. נִי, Syr. ܢܝ *n* (the *yūd* being suppressed).

In the 2nd person we find a necessary distinction of gender introduced by the differentiation of the final vowel; the masc. form was originally, as in Arabic, كَ *kă*, the fem. كِ *kĭ*. Identical with these are the Ethiopic ከ: *ka*, ኪ: *kī*, and the Assyrian *ka, kī*. The corresponding Hebrew forms are ךָ and כִי, the latter generally abbreviated into ךְ. The Aramaic forms are ךְ ܟ for the masc. and כִי ܟܝ for the fem., but the *yūd* has become silent, ܡܰܠܟܳܟ, ܡܰܠܟܶܟܝ; so that these forms are identical with those of the vulgar Arabic, masc. ـَكْ *ak*, or *k*, fem. *ek* or *kī*. The plurals were originally, as in Arabic, masc. كُمُ *kumū*, shortened into *kum*, fem. *kunna*; Ethiopic ክሙ: *kĕmū* and ክን: *kĕn*; Assyrian *kunu* or *kun*, of which the fem., according to analogy, should be *kina* or *kin*. The Hebrew forms are

כֶם for *kŭm*, fem. כֶן, but for the latter the fuller כֶנָה or כֵּנָה sometimes occurs. The Aramaic forms are כון ܟܘܢ, fem. ܟܝܢ, but כֹם is also found in Biblical Aramaic (Ezra).

In the 3rd person we have again a variation of vowels according to gender. The Arabic forms are, masc. هُ *hu* (with long vowel, though written defectively), which becomes هِ *hi* when preceded by an *i*, as *abū-hu*, *abī-hi*; fem. هَا. The corresponding forms in Ethiopic are ሁ: *hū*, ሃ: *hā*. In Hebrew the masc. is הוּ, but also הֹ, ו, which is nearly identical with the vulgar Arabic ـُه, pronounced *u* or *o*, as in كتابُه, also written كتابو. The Hebrew fem. is הָ and הָ. In Aramaic the masc. is הּ ܗ, fem. הּ ܗܿ. The corresponding plurals in Arabic are, masc. هُمُ *humū*, generally abbreviated *hum*, which may be changed by the influence of a preceding *i* into *himū* or *himī* and *him*; the fem. is هُنَّ *hunna* or *hinna*. The Ethiopic has ሆሙ: *hōmū* and ሆን: *hōn*. The Hebrew forms are, masc. הֶם and ם, or, with final vowel, מוֹ; fem. הֶן (rarely הֵן) and ן, or, with final vowel, נָה, נָּה, נָה. In Aramaic we find הוֹן, ܗܘܢ and ܗܝܢ, but in the Aramaic of Ezra also הוֹם הֹם. In contrast with these stand the Assyrian suffixes with initial *š*; sing. masc. *šu*, fem. *ša*, plur. masc. *šunu* or *šun*, fem. *šina* or *šin*. A similar form is found in one of the Ḥimyaritic dialects, where the sing. masc. is written סו or ס, pl. סם, whereas in the other we find הו and המו; and traces of it exist in the modern Mehrī, in which according to Maltzan, the sing. masc. is *he*, fem. *es*, plur. masc. *hum*, fem. *senn*.

From a comparison of these various forms we may fairly assume the oldest shape of the suffixed pronouns actually known to us to be:

1st	sing.	*iya*	plur.	*nā*		dual (only in Arabic)
2nd	„	m. *ka*	„	m. *kumū*	}	*kumā*
	„	f. *ki*	„	f. *kunna*	}	
3rd	„	m. *sū, hū*	„	m. *sūnu, humū*	}	*humā*
	„	f. *sā, hā*	„	f. *sīna, hunna*	}	

I have put *sū* and *hū* together in order to lay before you two alternatives; viz. (1) *hū* may be identical with *sū*, initial *s* having passed into *h*, just as in Sanskrit compared with Persian, or Greek compared with Latin; or (2) *sū* and *hū* may spring from different demonstrative letters *s* and *h*, a point to which we shall have to recur hereafter.

From these suffixed pronouns *iya*, *ka* and *hū*, we obtain, by prefixing the demonstrative syllable *an* (אן), the three pronouns *aniya*, *anka* and *anhū*. The syllable *an*,—itself a compound of א and נ,—we may regard as a sort of demonstrative particle or interjection, akin probably to the Arabic إِنَّ, إِنْ, Hebrew הֵן, הִנֵּה, Syriac ܗܳܐ, and Ethiopic እን: in እንከሙ: *ĕn'kĕmū*, "en vobis = accipite."

The third of these pronouns, *anhū*, appears but rarely as an independent word. I would instance the Talmudic אִיהוּ, fem. אִיהִי, possibly assimilated from אִנְהוּ, אִנְהִי, with the first vowel weakened from *a* to *i*. At any rate, the plural forms, which are without assimilation, are אִנְהוּ, אִנְהֵי, for אִנְהוּן, אִנְהֵין. In Syriac too we find ܐܶܢܽܘܢ, ܐܶܢܶܝܢ, assimilated for ܐܢܗܘܢ, ܐܢܗܝܢ. Otherwise these forms are used as suffixes; for example, in Hebrew, ־ֶנְהוּ, as יְבָרֲכֶנְהוּ, assimilated ־ֶנּוּ, fem. ־ֶנָּה; and also in the later Aramaic dialects, as Mand. ינהון or ינון, fem. ינהין, ינין; Talm. ינְהוּ, ינְהֵי.

The same is the case with the second of the above pronouns, *anka*, which appears in Hebrew only as a suffix, e.g. אֶתְּקֶנְךָּ (from נתק, Jerem. xxii. 24), usually with assimilation ־ֶךָּ; in Mand. ינכון, fem. ינכין.

The first of these three forms, *aniya*, is found, however, with slight modifications in most of the Semitic languages. What its origin may be, I can hardly pretend to explain, unless we connect it with a demonstrative root *i*, "this," also found in the Indo-European languages, in which case *an-iya* would literally mean *behold this one* or *this one here*, as a designation of the speaker. This would still, however, leave the final element *ya* or *a* unaccounted for.

In Hebrew the form *aniya* appears almost intact in אֲנִי, in pause, with fuller vowel, אָנִי. In the other languages the older form is more or less obscured: Arabic, أَنَا *ănă*, with short *a* in both syllables, dialectically *ānă*, in pause *ănā* and *ănăh*; Ethiopic likewise አነ: *ănă*; J. Aram. אֲנָא (אֲנָה Bibl.) or אֶנָא, Syriac ܐܶܢܳܐ *ĕnā* or *ĕnō*. Similarly in the younger dialects: Tigré አና: *anā*, Tigriña አነ: *anē* or አነ: *anä*, Amharic እኔ: *ĕnē*; Mand. אנא, modern Syriac ܐܳܢܳܐ. As the proper plural of אֲנִי we may regard אֲנוּ (Jerem. xlii. 6, *kĕthībh*), to which, among the later dialects, the Amharic offers a parallel in the form *ĕññā*. I may add that in Arabic, Ethiopic and Syriac this pronoun is liable to considerable mutilation. In Arabic we find أَنْ *an*, and likewise in Ethiopic, when followed by the particle ሰ: *sa*, አንሰ: *an-sa*. In Syriac the first syllable is liable to be elided under certain circumstances, whence arise such forms as ضحا أنا, ضحنا, ضحنا, ضحنا, and finally, dropping the last vowel, ضحن. Hence in modern Syriac the verbal form of the present, 1st pers. sing. ܦܳܪܶܡܢ *I end*, ܒܳܢܶܝܢ *I repair*.

There is, however, another form of the pronoun of the 1st pers. sing., which we must endeavour to explain, namely that which is found in Assyrian, Hebrew and Phoenician. Here the first demonstrative basis, *an*, has been strengthened by the addition of a second, *ak* or *āk*, which I take to be compounded of א and ך, and to be akin to such words as כָּא, ܟܳܐ, "here," כֹּה "thus, here, now," כִּי "that," הָכָא "here," אֵיכָה "how," etc. As the oldest form I venture to write *anākiya* or *anākī*, whence in Assyrian *anâku* (Haupt, *anakû*), in which the 2nd syllable must surely be long, as the corresponding Hebrew form is אָנֹכִי, in pause אָנֹכִי. The Hebrew has preserved the vowel of the last syllable in a purer state than the Assyrian. On the Moabite stone it appears as אנך, probably pronounced *ânōkh*; whilst in Phoenician inscriptions we also find אנך, which in the ears of Plautus sounded like *aněch*. I may remind you in passing that the Egyptian pronoun was also *anek*, *enek*, and the Coptic ⲁⲛⲟⲕ. The form *âku*, without the prefix *an*, is employed in Assyrian as an enclitic with the force of the substantive verb, e.g. *sarrâku* "I am king," *rabbâku* "I am great," *zikarâku* "I am manly"; thus corresponding to the use of ܐ̱ܢܐ for ܐܢܐ in Syriac.

The corresponding plural form is still more remarkable: Assyr. *anîni*, *nîni*, *nînu* for *anîḥni*, *anaḥni*, Heb. אֲנַחְנוּ, Phoen. אנחן. Here then כ of the singular has interchanged with ח (as in שָׁחַר, ܣܡܩܐ, compared with شَكَرَ, ܣܗܕܐ compared with אֲבַטִּיחִים), and the vowel has been shortened in the shut syllable. The last syllable of the word, נוּ, is probably shortened from אָנוּ, the plural form of אֲנִי, which we mentioned above. This plural אֲנַחְנוּ, abbreviated in Hebrew itself into נַחְנוּ, is found, in some shape or other, in nearly all the Semitic dialects. Arabic: نَحْنُ, vulgar نَحْنَ *neḥnè*, *neḥn*, أَحْنَا *aḥnâ* in Egypt *iḥna*. Ethiopic: ንሕነ: *nĕḥna*, Tigré *naḥna*, Tigriña *nĕḥnâ*. Syriac, with an additional demonstrative *n* at the end, ܐܢܚܢܢ, commonly ܚܢܢ, which is shortened in pronunciation into *nan*, as in ܐܡܝܪܝܢ ܢܢ. Also ܐܚܢܢ, with prosthetic vowel, whence in modern Syriac ܐܚܢܢ and ܐܚܢܢ, but also *äkhnôkhun* ܐܚܢܘܟܘܢ (with a curious assimilation to the pronoun of the 2nd pers. *äkhtôkhun* ܐܚܬܘܟܘܢ). In Samaritan we also find the form אנחנן, whilst in the Palestinian dialect of Syriac, ܐܢܢ,

and in the modern Syriac of Ma'lūla, ܐܢܚ *anaḥ*, the final *n* has vanished. Jewish Aramaic forms are אֲנַחְנָא and נַחְנָא; but in several dialects the guttural has been elided, whence in the Talmud אֲנַן, in Samaritan אנן, in Mandaitic אנין (*anēn* for *anān*), and in Palestinian Syriac ܐܢܢ and more commonly ܐܢܚ. Likewise in Assyrian, as above mentioned, *anīni*, *nīni* or *nīnu*.

On reviewing what I have said about the pronoun of the 1st pers. sing., you may think that much of it is very precarious and doubtful; in particular that the derivations which I have ventured to suggest of the forms אֲנִי and אָנֹכִי are very far-fetched; that אֲנִי can hardly be compounded with a demonstrative particle or interjection, י + (נ + א), and אָנֹכִי with two words of that class י + (כ + א) + (נ + א). In reply I can only point to the history of the pronominal forms in other languages, for instance the Romance. Whence comes the French *ce?* In some cases it appears in the modern language as *cet*, for which the older form is *cest*. But *cest* is identical with the Italian *questo*, which springs from *eccu isto*, i.e. *eccum istum*, i.e. *ecce eum istum*! Even the English *I* is but the last remnant of *ich* or *ik*, *ego*, ἐγώ, ἐγών, Sanskrit *aham*, all pointing to an original *agham* or *agam*, which has been supposed to be made up of three elements, *a* + *gha* (or *ga*) + *m*, the first of which is either the demonstrative root *a* "this," or else a mutilation of *ma*; whilst the second is a particle, identical with the Greek γε, and the third, in all probability, another demonstrative letter.

I pass on to the pronoun of the 2nd person in its independent form. Here the demonstrative syllable *an* is prefixed, not to the syllable *ka*, but to *ta*. Both these syllables are, it seems likely, also of a demonstrative character, and admit of being explained in one of two ways. Either (1) *ka* is a mere variety of *ta* (compare τίς τί with Sanskrit *nă-ki-s* "nemo," *ki-m* "what?" *quis*, *quid*); or (2) they spring from different demonstrative letters, *k* and *t*. The one of these we have already mentioned as lying at the root of כֹּה, כָּמָה, כִּי, and similar words; whilst the other gives birth to various forms, of some of which we shall have to treat presently. If so, the pronoun of the 2nd person designates the individual spoken to as a "this" or "here," in contradistinction to the more remote "that" or "there" of the 3rd person. In the Indo-European languages the same element seems to lie at the root of both pronouns, for Sanskrit *tvam*, i.e. *tu-am*, "thou," differs only in its vowel from *ta*, the base of the demonstrative pronoun *tat*, in Greek *τό*.

The oldest form of this pronoun known to us in Semitic is the Arabic أَنْتَ *anta*, with its fem. أَنْتِ *anti*, dual أَنْتُمَا, plur. masc. أَنْتُمُ *antumū*, shortened *antum*, and fem. أَنْتُنَّ *antunna*. The dual is found in Arabic only, and has disappeared from its vulgar dialects, in which the forms in use are *enta* or *ent* (Egypt. *inte*), *enti* or *entī* (Egypt. *inty*, *enty*), *entum* or *entū* (Egypt. *intū*). Almost identical with these are the Ethiopic አንተ፡ *anta, antī, antĕmū, antĕn*, which appear in Tigré as *anta, antī, antūm*, and in Amharic as *anta, antyī* or *anty*, plur. *antū*. But in Tigriña they have been displaced by the compound ንስኻ፡ *nĕss'khā*, fem. *nĕss'khī*, plur. *nĕssātkūm, nĕssātkĕn*, by assimilation for *nĕfs'khā*, etc.

In Assyrian and Hebrew *nt* have been assimilated into *tt*. The Assyrian forms are *attā, attī*, plur. masc. *attūnu*, (fem., according to analogy, *attīna*). In Hebrew the masc. sing. is אַתָּה, in pause אָתָּה or אָֽתָּה; but the shorter אַתְּ, *attĕ* or *att*, also occurs, Num. xi. 15; Deut. v. 24, and in some other passages in the Kĕthībh, e.g. Ps. vi. 4; Job i. 10; Eccles. vii. 22. Its fem. is אַתִּי, which occurs sometimes in the Kĕthībh, viz. Judges xvii. 2; 1 Kings xiv. 2; 2 Kings iv. 16, 23, and viii. 1; Jerem. iv. 30; Ezek. xxxvi. 13; but it has been almost supplanted by the shorter אַתְּ, *attĕ* or *att*, in pause אָתְּ. The plur. masc. is אַתֶּם, with *ĕ* for *ŭ*; the fem. is אַתֵּנָה, sometimes written אַתֵּנָּה and אַתֶּנָה; but the shorter אַתֶּן or אַתֵּן is found in Ezek. xxxiv. 31, and with assimilation of the *n* to a following *m*, in Ezek. xiii. 20, אֲשֶׁר אַתֵּם מְצֹדְדוֹת (observe Ezek. xxxiii. 26, עֲשִׂיתֶן תּוֹעֵבָה for עֲשִׂיתֶם, and Isaiah xxxv. 1, יְשֻׂשׂוּם מִדְבָּר for יְשֻׂשׂוּן).

In Biblical Aramaic and the Targūms we find both the primitive and the assimilated forms, אַנְתְּה, אַנְתְּ, אַתְּ, fem. אַתְּ, plur. masc. אַנְתּוּן, אַתּוּן, fem. אַנְתֵּין, אַתֵּין. In Syriac the *n*, though written, is never pronounced, and the final *t* of the fem. sing. has also been dropped, ܐܢ̄ܬ, ܐܢ̄ܬܝ, ܐܢ̄ܬܘܢ, ܐܢ̄ܬܝܢ. The forms of the later dialects are in some cases such as we should naturally expect; e.g. Samaritan אתה or את, fem. אתי, plur. אתון, אתין; Palestinian Syriac, ܐܬ, fem. ܐܬܝ, plur. ܐܬܘܢ and ܐܢܬܘܢ, ܐܬܝܢ. But in others there are points worthy of remark. For instance, in Mandaitic, instead of *n* and *t* being assimilated, a short *ă* is inserted between them, אנאת, plur. אנאתון. Again, in the vulgar Syriac of Ma'lūla, we find أچ *ach* or هچ *hach*, with the plur. أچخن *achkhun* or هچن *hachun*, where *t* has been softened into *ty*, *ch*, as in مدينچا (ܡܕܝܢܬܐ), ذارچا (ܙܪܬܐ), كاچبا (ܟܬܒܐ). The modern Nestorian or eastern forms are ܐܢ̄ܬ *at* or ܐܢ̄ܬܝ *attin*, the latter with a curious appendage; and not less strange are the plurals ܐܢ̄ܬܘܢ and ܐܢ̄ܬܘܟܘܢ, which can only be explained as having arisen under the influence of the 1st pers. ܐܢܚܢ or ܐܚܢܢ, whilst conversely the form of the 1st person ܐܚܢܘܟܘܢ must have owed its birth to this falsely formed ܐܢ̄ܬܘܟܘܢ.

The separate pronouns of the 1st and 2nd persons have, as we have seen, received a demonstrative increment at the beginning; with the pronoun of the 3rd pers. the reverse apparently is the case. The Assyrian *šû*, fem. *šî*, and the corresponding Syriac ܗܘ, fem. ܗܝ, may perhaps never have had any such increment; but it is, I think, otherwise with the Hebrew and Arabic singulars. In Hebrew these forms, with the ancient and necessary difference of vowels, are הוּא, fem. הִיא. Now some scholars believe that the *aleph* is a mere orthographic sign, like the Arabic *elif* in the 3rd pers. plur.

of the verb, قَتَلُوا, which is occasionally found even in Hebrew (הֶהָלְכוּא Josh. x. 24; אָבוּא Isaiah xxviii. 12). In this view I can hardly concur, because the words are written with this *aleph* in the oldest documents we possess, such as the Moabite stone (masc. ויאמר גם הא) and the sarcophagus of Eshmūn'āzār, king of Sidon (masc. אדם הא "that man," fem. הממלכת הא "this kingdom"). Had the original sounds been merely *hū* and *hī*, we should have found on such monuments הו and הי. I conclude, therefore, that the words must have sounded originally something like *hū-a* and *hī-a,* with the addition of a demonstrative *a* at the end. This will seem less improbable to you, when you are told that the modern Syrian forms from ܗܘ *ō* and ܗܝ *ē*, by the addition of ܗܳܐ, another demonstrative ܗܘ ܗܳܐ (ܗܘܳܐ) *ōā*, ܗܝ ܗܳܐ *ēā*, "that," "yonder." That Plautus heard the Phoenician word pronounced as *hy* only proves that the Carthaginians, like the Jews, had gradually let this additional sound drop, although they retained the symbol of it in writing.

I have said nothing to you as yet of the use of הוא for the fem. gender in Hebrew, because I do not believe in its existence. The distinction of the vowels in הוא and הִיא, *sū* and *sī*, is just as primitive and essential as in *anta, anti* and *ka, ki.* I am aware that הוא takes the place of היא in various passages of the Pentateuch; but in old Hebrew MSS. ו and י are very much alike, and the Masorets have done well to regard הוא as nothing but a clerical error, and to substitute for it the correct היא[1]. The same pretended archaism may be found in the famous Babylonian codex of the Prophets published by Strack, e.g. Hosea ii. 4, הוא (i.e. הִוא), Joel iv. 1, ההוא (i.e. הַהִוא).

To proceed. The same primitive difference of the vowels and the same affixed syllable are to be found in Arabic, although slightly obscured, since *hū-'a* and *hī-'a* have become *hŭwa* هُوَ and *hĭya* هِيَ. In Ethiopic these words have received a further

[1] [Cf. Kuenen, *Onderzoek,* 2nd ed. vol. i. (Leyden, 1887), § 16 and n. 7, who rightly refers the origin of the error to the old *scriptio defectiva* הא, for הוא and היא alike.]

increment at the end, and in consequence have suffered a slight curtailment at the beginning. The forms in actual use are ወእቱ: *wĕ'ĕtū*, fem. ይእቲ: *yĕ'ĕtī*, which have obviously lost an initial *hū* and *hī* on account of their having been lengthened by the syllable *tū* and *tī*. I find the same increment in the Assyrian demonstrative *šuatū*, "this," fem. *šaatī* or *šâtī* [Del. *šiati*], and in another form in *šâšū*, fem. *šâšī*, *šâša*, as also in *hagā-šū* (Del. *agāšu*), which last is found mainly in inscriptions of the Persian period. *Šū* seems to be only a weakening of *tū*, just as in Greek the pronoun *tu*, Doric τύ, became σύ; or τήμερον (to-day), τῆτες (this year) became σήμερον and σῆτες; or the nominal terminations τις, τιος, τια, τυνη, passed into σις, σιος, σια, συνη (πέψις, πλούσιος, γερουσία, δικαιοσύνη). Indeed it seems possible that *tū* is the oldest form of the pronoun of the 3rd pers. in Semitic, of which *sū* and *hū* are successive weakenings.

We have then the following forms of the pronoun of the 3rd person.

		singular	plural	dual
Assyr.	m.	*šū*	*šūnu, šūnu-tu, šūnut*	
	f.	*šī*	*šīna*	
Arab.	m.	هُوَ (vulg. Eg. *hūwä* هُوَّ)	هُمْ هُمُ (Eg. *hum* and *huma*)	هُمَا
	f.	هِيَ (vulg. Eg. *hīyä* هِيَّ)	هُنَّ	
Eth.	m.	ወእቱ: *wĕ'ĕtū*	እሙንቱ: *ĕmūntû* or ወእቶሙ: *wĕ'ĕtômū*	
	f.	ይእቲ: *yĕ'ĕtī*	እማንቱ: *ĕmāntū* or ወእቶን: *wĕ'ĕtôn*	
Heb.	m.	הוּא (Ph. הא)	הֵם, הֵמָּה	
	f.	הִיא (Ph. הא)	הֵנָּה	
J. Ar.	m.	הוּא	אִנּוּן; הִמּוֹן, הִמּוֹ	
	f.	הִיא	אִנִּין	

		singular	plural
Syr.	m.	ܗܽܘ	ܐܶܢܽܘܢ ܗܶܢܽܘܢ
	f.	ܗܺܝ	ܐܶܢܶܝܢ ܗܶܢܶܝܢ
Talm.	m.	אִיהוּ	אִינְהוּ
	f.	אִיהִי	אִינְהִי
Mand.	m.	הו	הינון
	f.	הע	הינין

After what I have already said, in this and former lectures, very few of these forms call for any further remark. I need only add, I think, that هُمْ, هُمَا, vulgar Egypt. *hum*, *huma*, הֵמָּה, הֵם, and הֵמּוֹ, הֵמּוֹן, are really identical, the last being strengthened by an additional demonstrative element, as is also the case with እሙንቱ: and እማንቱ:: The Talmudic forms אִינְהוּ and אִינְהִי (for אִינְהוֹן and אִינְהֵין) shew us that the double *n* of the Chaldee, Syriac and Mandaitic is an assimilation of *nh*, the syllable *in*, *en*, *hen* being, as I formerly stated, an interjectional or demonstrative element prefixed to the pronoun. The simple ܗܽܘ and ܗܺܝ of the old Syriac have entirely disappeared in the modern language; and in the modern dialects of Ethiopia the place of this pronoun has been usurped by later compounds. Thus in Tigriña, *nĕssū*, fem. *nĕssā*, plur. masc. *nĕssātōm*, fem. *nĕssātōn*, for *nĕfsū*, etc.; and in Amharic, እርሱ: *ĕrsū*, fem. እርስዋ: *ĕrsĕwā*, plur. እርሳቸው: *ĕrsātyaw*, or with a further assimilation እሱ: *ĕssū*, etc., from ርእስ: *rĕ'ĕs*, "head."

On the formation of the plurals of the personal pronouns, I shall make some additional remarks when I come to treat of that subject in relation to the noun and verb. Meantime I pass on to the other classes of pronouns.

B. *The Demonstrative Pronouns.*

From the pronoun of the 3rd person, by prefixing the demonstrative particle or interjection *hâ*, in vulgar Arabic *â*, we get the compound pronoun *hā-hū*. This appears in the

Talmūd as הָהוּא, fem. הָהִיא, plur. הָנְהוֹ (for הָאִנְהוֹן). The word is often wrongly pointed הַהוּא, הַהִיא, whereby it is confounded with the Hebrew הַהוּא, הַהִיא, which is of a totally different origin, viz. by assimilation for הַלְהוּא. In Mandaitic the same word exists in the singular, האהו, האהע, without any corresponding plural. In Syriac the second *h* was elided, and the syllables *hā-ū*, *hā-ī*, contracted into ܗܿܘ *haw*, ܗܿܝ *hāy* or *hōy*, plur. ܗܿܢܘܢ *hānnūn*, ܗܿܢܝܢ *hānnēn* (for *hā-ēn-hūn*, *hā-ēn-hēn*). In the Palestinian dialect we also find the singular forms ܗܐܘ, ܗܘ; fem. ܗܐܝ, ܗܝ, but not the plural. In modern Syriac the corresponding words are ܗܿܘ *aw*, ܗܿܝ *ay*, often written and pronounced ܐܘ̇, ܐܘ, ܐܝ, *ō* and *ē*, with the plur. ܐܢܝ *ānī* (from the old fem. ܗܿܢܝܢ), shortened into ܐܢ *ān* and ܐܢ *an*. From this is formed another pronoun by the addition of the particle ܗܐ at the end, to designate a more remote object; "that," "yonder," viz. ܗܿܘ ܗܐ (ܐܘ̇ ܗܐ), *ō'ā*, fem. ܗܿܝ ܗܐ, *ē'ā*. The *n* which we have found in the plurals ܗܿܢܘܢ, הָנְהוֹ, etc., seems to appear in the singular in the Assyrian *annu*, "this," whether we regard it as merely = *an* + *hū*, or as = *ā* + *in* + *hū*. The forms given by the grammarians are:

sing. masc. *annu* (fem. *annat*), (*annit*)
plur. masc. *annūtu* fem. *annātu*, *annītu*,

with another plural form, perhaps of both genders, *annī* or *annē*.

In vulgar Arabic of Egypt the forms corresponding to הָהוּא, הָהִיא, הָנְהוֹ, are still used with the original interjectional force: *āhō*, "there he is," *āhī*, "there she is," *āhūm* or *āhōm*, "there they are."

A very large number of demonstrative pronouns have their source in the cognate letters *d* and *t*, in juxtaposition with which we often find *k*, *l* and *n*. You will remember that Aram. ד *d* = Arab. ذ *dh*, ז = Eth. Heb. Assyr. *z*; and that Aram. ת *t* = Arab. ث *th*, þ = Eth. ሰ: *s*, Assyr. *š*, Heb. ש *sh*.

One of the simplest of these pronouns is the Arabic ذَا, fem. ذِي, ذِهْ, تِي, تَا, plur. أُلَى or أُلَاءِ, often written *plene* أُولَى, أُولَاءِ. The corresponding forms in vulgar Arabic are *dā* or *dē*, fem. *dī*, plur. دول *daul* or *dōl, dōla, dōlī* (which seems to arise from a combination of the singular with the ancient plural). In Ethiopic we have the same word in the form ዘ፡ *zĕ*, fem. ዛ፡ *zâ*, plur. እሉ፡ *ĕllû*, fem. እላ፡ *ĕllâ*. Its Hebrew equivalent is זֶה, fem. זֹאת, for *zât*, shortened into זֹה and זוֹ, plur. אֵל (1 Chron. xx. 8, generally with the art. הָאֵל[1]), אֵלֶּה. The Phoenician forms are, as might be expected, very similar; viz. ז for both genders (perhaps with a difference of pronunciation, *zĕ, zū*); fem. also זת, in Plautus *syth*; plur. אל, in Plautus *ily*. The form אז, which also occurs in Phoenician, has been regarded as equivalent to the Hebrew הַזֶּה; but the article in Phoenician is the same as in Hebrew, and ז does not take the article in Phoenician even when the preceding substantive is defined (מִשְׁכָּב ז and הַשַּׁעַר ז). I prefer therefore to consider the *aleph* in אז as merely prosthetic. The very curt form of the word ז might readily lead to such a vowel being prefixed; and we find some support for this idea in the modern Ethiopic or Tigriña form እዚ፡ fem. እዛ፡፡ In the later Hebrew of the Mishnah we have masc. זֶה, fem. זוֹ (*zō* or *zū*), plur. אֵלּוּ. In Assyrian it is curious to find the form with *l* in the singular as well as the plur.;

sing. masc. *ullu*	fem. *ullat*
plur. masc. *ullūtu*	fem. *ullītu*[2].

By appending a demonstrative *n* to the masculine, we obtain the common J. Aram. form דֵּין, דֵּן, emphatic דְּנָה, דְּנָא, with its simple fem. דָּה, דָּא, and its plur. אִלֵּין. The corresponding

[1] [The latter only in the Pentateuch, where it is probably to be viewed as a mere *scriptio defectiva* (הָאֵל) as in Phoenician. Cf. Kuenen *ut supra*. In any case הָאֵל is younger than הָאֵלֶּה, final ה being readily lost in Hebrew, as in רֵעַ=רֵעֶה.]

[2] [The feminines are not recognised by Delitzsch.]

Phoenician forms are זן and זא; and in certain Aramaic dialects (Egypto-Aram., Nabathean) these words appear as זנא and זא. An Ethiopic form, with further demonstrative increment, is ዝንቱ: *zĕntū*, fem. ዛቲ: *zātī*, plur. እሉንቱ: *ellōntū*, fem. እላንቱ: *ellāntū*.

For the sake of still greater emphasis, *hā* is prefixed to these forms, giving in Arabic هٰذَا, fem. هٰذِهِ or هٰذِي, هَاتِي, هَاتَا, plur. هٰؤُلَا or هٰؤُلَاءِ; and vulgarly *hādā*, fem. *hādī*, plur. *hādaul*, and in Africa *hādūm*. In Egypt, with somewhat of the original interjectional force, *ādī*, "this here." The corresponding Aramaic words vary considerably in form according to the dialects. In the Targūms and the Talmūd we find הָדֵין, fem. הָדָא (or עָדָא), plur. הָאִלֵּין and הָלֵּין (less correctly pronounced הַאִלֵּין and הָלֵין); and similarly in the Palestinian dialect ܗܕܝܢ or ܗܕܝ, fem. ܗܕܐ (*hādē* for *hādā*), plur. ܗܠܝܢ. In Mandaitic ז has generally taken the place of ד: האזין, fem. האזא, plur. האלין. הארא however occurs, as also the compound הארינו = Talmud. הדינו, i.e. הדין הו. The ordinary Syriac forms are ܗܢܐ, fem. ܗܕܐ, plur. ܗܠܝܢ. Of these, ܗܢܐ stands for הָדְנָא, and ܗܕܐ is weakened from ܗܕܐ, which occurs in the combination ܗܕܐܗܘ (for ܗܕܐ ܗܘ). Shorter forms are ܗܢ, for הָדֵן, and ܗܕ. Here too must be placed the Talmudic הָהֵן or אָהֵן, which latter is also found in Samaritan. Here א has taken the place of ה, whilst the aspirated ד *dh* is represented only by the aspiration *h*. This gradual elision of the *d*, combined with the ordinary dropping of the final *n*, enables us to explain the common Talmudic forms הָאי, fem. הָא, plur. הָנֵי or הַנֵּי, as corruptions of הָדֵין, הָדָא, and הָלֵּין. The modern Syriac words are very similar, viz. ܐܗܐ *āhā* or ܐ *ā*, plur. ܐܢܝ *annē*. ܐܗܐ springs from the fem. ܗܕܐ, the original aspirated *d* (*dh*) being represented, as in אָהֵן, by an *h*; *h* having been gradually dropped, *ā'ā* has been contracted into *ā*. Dialectically the forms ܐܳܙܶܒ, ܐܳܕܶܒ, are also used, both from הָדֵין.

Now if to these series of pronouns we append the letter ךְ, we obtain another series, generally designating more distant objects.

The simplest of these is the J. Aram. דֵּךְ or דֵּיכִי, fem. דָּךְ, plur. אִלֵּךְ, which are formed from דֵּן, דָּא and אִלֵּין. The Palestinian dialect exhibits the plural in the form ܗܶܠܶܝܟ. By prefixing *hā* we arrive at the Talmudic הָאִיךְ, fem. הָךְ, plur. הָנֵךְ or הַנֵּךְ, and the Mandaitic האך (masc. and fem.), plur. האניך, which are contractions for הרינך, הראך, and הלינך. Here too the Syriac varieties ܗܠܟܘܢ, fem. ܗܠܟܝܢ, find their place; the former of which may perhaps be compounded with a form corresponding to the Mishnaic אִלּוּ. As for ܗܘܟܡ (ܗܟܡ), which is always masc., it is probably not a mere variation of ܗܠܟܘܢ, but a different compound, viz. from ܗܳܟܰܢ and ܡ. In Arabic the corresponding pronoun is ذَاكَ, fem. تَاكَ, تِيكَ, plur. أُولَاكَ or أُولَائِكَ. The Arabs have, however, regarded the suffixed كَ as being the pronoun of the 2nd person, and hence, though ذَاكَ is commonly used in speaking to two or more persons of both sexes, it is also permitted to use ذَاكِ in addressing a woman, ذَاكُمَا in speaking to two, and ذَاكُمْ or ذَاكُنَّ in speaking to several, according to their sex. The vulgar forms, at least in North Africa, are ذَاك *dāk*, fem. ذِيك *dīk*, plur. ذُوك *dūk*. In Egypt we find, with the addition of *hā*, the forms *dikhā* (masc. fem.) and *dukhā* (masc.); and these may be still further strengthened by appending the pronoun of the 3rd pers., masc. *dukhauwā*, masc. fem. *dikhaiya*, plur. masc. fem. *dukhamma*. The Ethiopic presents us with this augmented pronoun in the form ዝኩ: *zĕkū*, fem. እንትኩ: *ĕntĕkū*, plur. እልኩ: *ĕllĕkū*. Here the fem. is remarkable, but we shall speak of it when we come to the simple relative form እንተ: *ĕnta*.

These pronouns again may be heightened by the accession of a fresh demonstrative syllable. Thus in Chaldee we find דִּכֵּן for both genders, with additional *n*. The Ethiopic presents us with a form with additional *tū*, viz. ዝኩቱ: *zĕkwĕtū* or ዝክቱ: *zĕktū*, fem. እንታክቲ: *ĕntākti*, plur. እልኩቱ: *ĕllĕkwĕtū* or እልክቱ: *ĕllĕktū*. The Arabic prefixes *hā* in the form هَاذَاكَ, fem. هَاتَاكَ, هَاتِيكَ, plur. هَآؤُلَائِكَ; which are much used in the vulgar dialects, هذاك *hādāk*, هذيك *hādīk*, plur. هولائك *hāulāʾik*, or in North Africa هذوك *hādūk*. From *hādāk* seems to arise, by elision of the *d*, the form هَك *hak*, used by the Bedouins; just as هذا *hādā*, in combination with the article *'al*, becomes *hal*, which is used for all numbers and genders, as هَلْكِتَاب, هَلْبِنْت, هَالشَّيخ, هَالرَّجُل, هَلْكِلَاب. Another strengthened form in old Arabic is ذٰلِكَ, where the letter *l* has been inserted between ذَا and كَ; its fem. is تِلْكَ, by contraction for تِيلِكَ. Peculiar to the Mandaitic is the word האנאתה (masc. and fem.), plur. masc. האנאתון, fem. האנאתין. Here it seems tolerably clear that we have again the prefixes הא and אין, contracted into האן, and the suffixes of the 3rd person; but it is not so easy to say what is represented by the letters את, unless we admit Noeldeke's suggestion that they are identical with יָת, the Aramaic form of את.

Finally, under this head, we have a few demonstratives that are formed by means of the prefix אִי *ĭ*. Here I mention first, though somewhat doubtfully, the Talmudic pronoun אִיהוּ, fem.

אִידְהִי; doubtfully, I say, because it may also be explained, as I did above, by assimilation from אִינְהִי, אִינְהוּ. This latter view is countenanced by the plurals אִינְהִי, אִינְהוֹ. The forms נִידְהוּ and נִינְהוֹ, representing the substantive verb, seem to be fresh compounds of the demonstrative *n* and אִידְהוּ, אִינְהוֹ; e.g. מַאי נִידְהוּ "what it is," אנא נידהו "it is I," צַדִּיקֵי גְּמוּרֵי נִינְהוֹ "they are perfectly righteous men." More certain examples of this formation with prefixed *ī* are אִידֵי (for אִידֵין), fem. אִידָא; and אִידָךְ, plur. אִינָךְ.

To designate a definite pronominal accusative, especially of a somewhat emphatic kind, we find in the Semitic languages a peculiar word joined with the pronominal suffixes. In Ethiopic this is ኪያ: *kīyá*, a word regarding the origin of which various conjectures have been hazarded, but which I am inclined to think finds its source in the demonstrative *k*, to which we have so often referred. From this are formed, with the usual pronominal suffixes, *kīyá-ya, kīyá-ka*, etc. By the weakening of כ into ה (of which I gave some examples in a former lecture), we obtain the Arabic dialectic form هِيَّا. From this it is but a step to the common Arabic إِيَّا *īyā*, which is used precisely like its Ethiopic equivalent, and appears in Tigriña in the contracted form of ኢ: *ī*, denoting *self*, as ኢዩ: *īyē*, ኢኻ: *īkhā*, ኢዩ: *īyū*. In the other Semitic languages this word takes the feminine termination *at* or *t*, probably appended to it in order to bring out more strongly the abstract idea of *hoccitas* (if I may use such a word); and in these languages its range of use is considerably wider than in Arabic and Ethiopic. Hence we get, in the first place, the Phoenician אית, which was doubtless pronounced in the earlier stages of the language *īyāth* or *īyath*; for otherwise the י would not have been inserted in writing, as is almost invariably the case in the older inscriptions. In the inscriptions of later date, however, we find את, and Plautus heard the word pronounced *yth*. The Aramaic forms seem to be shortened from the Phoen., viz. Syr. ܝܳܬ, Chald. יָת, less correctly יַת. These are used not only as a sign of the definite accus., ܒܪܫܝܬ ܒܪܐ ܐܠܗܐ ܝܬ ܫܡܝܐ ܘܝܬ ܐܪܥܐ; but also as a substantive, signifying *self*, e. g. ܗܘ ܕܝܕܥ ܠܝܬܗ "he who knows himself," ܡܫܠܛܘܬ ܝܬܐ "free-will"; and likewise in the Palestinian dialects and in Samaritan to form demonstratives, as in the phrases בְּיָתֵהּ יוֹמָא "on that same day," בְּיָתֵהּ שַׁתָּא "in that same year," ܒܝܬܗ ܕܙܒܢܐ "at that same time," ܠܝܬܗ ܕܓܒܪܐ ܓܢܒܐ ܗܘ "that man is a thief," דֵּין הֲנַיִין לִי יָתְהוֹן לָא הֲנַיִין לִי "this is of use to me, those are not." In this way we may best explain the Mandaitic demonstrative spoken of above, האנאתה (masc. and fem.), האנאתין, האנאתון, where את is probably = יָת. Similarly in Hebrew *yâth* was further altered into *âth*, whence, by the usual change of *â* into *ō*, resulted the common form *ōth*, אוֹת. In close connection with a following word this *ōth* was shortened into *ŏth*, just as from נְחֹשֶׁת and שָׁלֹשֶׁת we get נְחֻשְׁתִּי and שְׁלָשְׁתְּכֶם. Next, *ŏth* was changed into *ĕth* ־אֶת, as in אֶתְכֶם for *attŭm*; and finally this ־אֶת was heightened by the tone into *ēth*, אֵת. In later Hebrew, perhaps under the influence of the surrounding Aramaic dialects, אות came to be used, like יָת, as a demonstrative: באותו היום, באותָהּ שָׁעָה, יָשַׁב לו אותו "that one sat down," זָכוּר אותו הָאִישׁ לְטוֹב. In Assyrian I find a word *attu*, which seems to be nearly connected with *yāth* and *ōth*, for example in such phrases as *attūa abūa* "my father" ("mon père à moi"), *sirya attūa* "my family" (זרע), *dīnāta attūa* "my laws" (דין), *bīta attūnu* "our house," *ša la iptallaḥū abīya wa attua* "who revere (פלח) not my father and me." Schrader also regards as cognate with *yāth* the words *yātī* and *āšī*, in such phrases as *yātī Nabūnahīd šuzibanni*, "as for me, Nabunit, save (שיזב) thou me"; and again, *ša lā iplaḥū abūtīya u āšī lā iṣbatū nīr sarrūtīya*, "who did not fear my fathers, and, as regards me, did not take up the yoke of my rule." These words *yātī* and *āšī* he explains as made up of *ya* + *a* + *ti* or *šī*, i.e. *ya* for *yath*, *a* suffix of the 1st pers., and a further demonstrative *ti* or *šī*. Sayce, however, gives a different explanation of both words, so that we are evidently on unsafe ground. Even the Hebrew אֹת has been explained in a manner different from that which I have just suggested to you, for some scholars have regarded it as a substantive, nearly equivalent in form and meaning to the Arabic آيَة "sign" or "mark," "form" or "body," thus identifying it with the word אוֹת (for אֹוֶת or אֹוִית), or else assuming a form אִוָּה or אִיָּה, from the construct state of which (אִיַּת or אִוַּת) אֹת might be derived by contraction.

Before quitting the demonstrative pronouns, I will say a few words regarding the definite article, which really belongs to this class of words. Its original form was, in all probability, הַל, a compound of *hā* and *l*, nearly in the sense of the Latin *ille*, connected with the adverbs הָלְאָה "away," "beyond," and הֲלֹם "here," "hither." In Hebrew the *l* was assimilated to all following letters; and when the doubling wholly ceased to be audible, the loss of it was compensated by the heightening of the vowel into *ā* ָ, as in הָאִישׁ, הָהָר, הָעִיר, הָרֹאשׁ, on which and other modifications of the article see your Hebrew grammars. In Phoenician its form is the same as in Hebrew, but it is not so frequently used as in the latter language, e.g. משכב ז for המשכב הזה, השער ז for השער הזה, אדם הא for האדם ההוא, הממלכת הא for הממלכת ההיא.

The Arabs ordinarily weakened the initial ה to א, but restricted the assimilation of the final *l* to a following dental, sibilant or liquid (the so-called *solar letters* ت ث د ذ ر ز س ش ص ض ط ظ ل ن); e.g. الإنسان, الجبل, المدينة, but النُّور (הַשּׁוֹר), الشَّمس (הַשֶּׁמֶשׁ), النَّهر (הַנָּהָר). In Egypt this assimilation is nowadays extended to ج and ك, as *eg-gazzār*, *eg-gum'a* "Friday," *ek-kull*, *ek-kenīse* "church." The letter *l*, however, though assimilated in pronunciation, is always written. The Arabian Bedouins are still said to retain the old pronunciation *hal*, saying *has-sanah* instead of *as-sanah*, הַשָּׁנָה[1]. Generally speaking, however, the initial *elif* is regarded as so weak in sound that it suffers elision whenever another word precedes, e. g. أَبُو ٱلْمَلِكِ *abu 'l-maliki*, not *abū al-maliki*, فِي ٱلنَّاسِ *fi 'n-nāsi*, not *fī an-nāsi*, قَالَ ٱلرَّجُلُ *ḳāla 'r-rajulu*, not *ḳāla ar-rajulu*, قَالَتِ ٱلْمَرْأَةُ *ḳālati 'l-mar'atu*, not *ḳālat al-mar'atu*. Indeed it was at times dropped altogether and only the *l* sounded, and this is common at the present day, e. g. *laḥmar* "red," *liswid* "black," *lazhar*, the "*Azhar*" mosque, *letnēn* "the two."

In Ethiopic there is no definite article, and the same appears to be the case in Assyrian. The Aramaic dialects labour under the same deficiency, but make up for it by appending to the noun the demonstrative *hā* or *ā*, which appears in writing as an *aleph*; thus גַּבְרָא, ܓܒܪܐ; סְפִינְתָא, ܣܦܝܢܬܐ. With this we may compare the postpositive *en* and *et* of the Scandinavian tongues, derived from an older *inn* and *it* (e. g. Danish *Mand*, *Manden*; *Hus*, *Huset*), of which we shall have to make mention again hereafter. More to our present purpose, however, is the Ḥimyaritic suffixed *n*, e.g. in מונרן "this monument" or "tablet," | שעדלה | ובנהו | בנו | מרתדם | הקניו | אלמקה | דהרן | מונרן |; or in משלמן "this stone," | שמהעלי | עדב | ובן | בן | חמעתת | הקני | עתתר | משלמן |. The words מונרן and משלמן are apparently contractions of מונרהן and משלמהן, as seems to result from such forms as | בין | מחפדניהן | "between these two towers" or "castles," | אבעל | ביתנהן | "the lords of these two houses," ביתנהן "this house of ours" (where the נ is the suffix of the 1st pers. plur.[2]). Often the demonstrative pronoun דן, fem. דת, is prefixed to such words, as דן מונרן.

[1] [This statement rests on a misconception: هالسنه stands for هاذي السنه. Nöld.]

[2] Other examples are: דן מטרן, "this inscription"; דן ותנן, "this idol"; דן פתחן, "this door"; דן מבנין, "this building"; צלמן, "this statue"; ואבלנהן, "and these two camels."

C. *The Relative Pronouns.*

The relative in its simplest form is, it may be said, identical with the demonstrative pronoun. As the Germans use *der* instead of *welcher*, and we English *that* instead of *who*, so did the Semites employ closely cognate or identical words as demonstratives and relatives.

The simplest of the relative forms is the דִּי of the Biblical Aramaic, shortened in the Targums and in Syriac into דְּ, ܕ *dĕ*. One or other of these forms appears in all the Aramaic dialects except the Egyptian and that of some ancient inscriptions, which have זי. The Mandaites say *ĕd* as well as *dĕ*, and the same form ࠀࠃ is occasionally found in Samaritan. I need only remark in addition that in Mandaitic ט is used in a few cases instead of the common ד, as טאביד טאב "he who does good," טאביד סניא "he who does evil" (where טאביד = דְּעָבֵד); רוחא טאבאהאתאן "spirit of our fathers." The word זי, which is mentioned by Gesenius and others as the Mandaitic form of the relative, has no existence, being merely a false reading of the somewhat abbreviated character of the word ד. In modern Syriac ܠ or ܕܠ is frequently employed for ܕ, as ܦܪܘܩܐ ܕܥܠܡܐ (for ܦܪܘܩܐ ܕܥܠܡܐ) "the Saviour of the world," ܫܘܒܩܐ ܕܚܛܗ̈ܐ (for ܫܘܒܩܢܐ ܕܚܛܗ̈ܐ) "forgiveness of sins," ܚܫܐ ܕܡܪܢ (for ܚܫܗ ܕܡܪܢ) "the passion of our Lord," *bārit īshū*, i.e. ܒܬܪܗ ܕܝܫܘܥ, "after Jesus."

Identical with this דִּי or דְּ is the Arabic ذُو, generally employed in this one form for both genders and all numbers; as أَتَانِي ذُو قَالَ ذَلِكَ "he who said that came to me," بِئْرِي ذُو حَفَرْتُ "my well which I dug." The use of this word is, however, only dialectic. In S. Arabia the Ḥimyaritic furnishes us with similar forms: masc. ד (𐩹), fem. דת, plur. אלי or אל.

In Ethiopic we find ዘ: *zá*, with a fem. እንተ: *ĕnta*, and a plur. *ĕlla*, all bearing a striking resemblance to the corresponding forms of the demonstratives. H: *zd* may be used, like דִּי and ذُو, for both genders and numbers. The fem. እንት: we must trace back to the demonstrative particle *en*, or the letter *n*, *plus* the fem. termination *t*; and the plur. እለ: to the demonstrative letter *l*. In Hebrew occurs the cognate form זוּ, likewise invariable.

In Arabic and Hebrew the simple article أَلْ, הַ, is sometimes employed as a relative; e.g. مِنَ ٱلْقَوْمِ ٱلرَّسُولُ ٱللّٰهِ مِنْهُمْ "of the people of whom is the Apostle of God," for ٱلَّذِينَ رَسُولُ ٱللّٰهِ مِنْهُمْ; Joshua x. 24, הֶהָלְכוּא אִתּוֹ "who went with him"; 1 Sam. ix. 24, אֶת־הַשּׁוֹק וְהֶעָלֶיהָ; 1 Chron. xxvi. 28, וְכֹל הַהִקְדִּישׁ שְׁמוּאֵל.

Hence, from a combination of these two words, with the insertion of the demonstrative letter *l* (as in ذَٰلِكَ), arises the ordinary Arabic relative ٱلَّذِي, with its fem. ٱلَّتِي, for the full inflection of which see the Arabic grammar. Its form in the vulgar dialects is إِلِّي *ellī*, in Maltese even shortened into لِي *lī*, for all the genders and numbers. Identical with ٱلَّذِي in form, though not exactly in meaning, is the Hebrew demonstrative הַלָּזֶה, shortened into הַלָּז, just as ٱلَّذِي is sometimes found in the form ٱلَّذْ. הַלָּז is used as fem. in 2 Kings iv. 25, הִנֵּה הַשּׁוּנַמִּית הַלָּז, and another form, הַלֵּזוּ *hallēzū*, also occurs as fem. in Ezekiel xxxvi. 35, הָאָרֶץ הַלֵּזוּ הַנְּשַׁמָּה. This last seems to be weakened from הַלָּזוּ, and to exhibit this pronoun in even a purer form than הַלָּזֶה and ٱلَّذِي.

The relative pronoun in Assyrian is *ša* or *šā*, which admits of no variation, but is evidently connected with the simple pronoun *šū*, "he," and the demonstrative *ša-šu*.

The Hebrew word אֲשֶׁר, though familiar to us all, is difficult to analyse. Some, as for instance Fleischer, Mühlau and Sayce, following an older scholar named Tsepregi, regard אֲשֶׁר as the Hebrew representative of the Aramaic אֲתַר, ܐܬܪ, "place," in Syriac also "trace," "track," "footstep," as in ܒܳܬܰܪ (for *ba-athar*) "after," "behind," Arab. أَثَر and إِثْر, "trace," "track," "footstep," Eth. አሠር:: In support of this view they appeal to analogies in other languages, e. g. the Chinese, where *so* means both "place" and "which," and to the vulgar use of *wo* in German, for example, "Der Mann, *wo* ich gesehen habe," instead of *welchen*, or again, "Der Fremde, wo du mit ihm gegessen hast," instead of "mit welchem du gegessen hast." Gesenius, in his immortal work, the *Thesaurus Linguae Hebraeae*, sought to connect אֲשֶׁר with the Hebrew radical אָשַׁר: "Modo in tali vocabulo de etymo quaerendum est, אֲשֶׁר pr. *rectum* valuisse conjecerim ab אָשַׁר *rectus fuit*, deinde *recte*, *ita*, i. q. כֵּן et Germ. *so*, idque in antiquiore lingua in pron. relat. abiisse. Cf. כֹּה *ita*, et relativum כִּי, et contra Germ. *so*, i.e. propr. relat. fem. Simonis relationem ita exprimi censet, quod ad sequentia rectâ tendat." Ewald, whose opinions I would always mention with the respect due to so great a scholar,—Ewald's latest view seems to have been that אֲשֶׁר stands for אֲשֶׁל, and is compounded of two demonstratives, שׁ = ת, ד, ז and ל, *plus* the prosthetic אֱ. Finally, Friedrich Böttcher looks upon אֲשֶׁר as standing for אֲשֶׁל, and as made up of a merely prosthetic אֱ, and a word שֶׁל, which he regards as an older form of the article הַל (just as *su* seemed to be an older form of הוּא, or the verbal conj. שַׁקְטֵל = הִקְטִל, אַקְטֵל). As the matter at present stands, we have to choose, I think, between Fleischer's view on the one hand, and Ewald's or Böttcher's on the other; and, on the whole, I incline to the latter, in so far as I would seek the origin of the relative pronoun somewhere in the region of the demonstratives. For the interchange of ל and ר, even in this region, compare the Syriac ܗܪܟܐ, "here," with the Chaldee הָלְכָּא. In Hebrew the longest form of the word is אֲשֶׁר, but there are several shorter forms, without א and usually with assimilation of the final *r* or *l* to the following letter; viz. שַׁ·, שֶׁ, שָׁ·, but also שְׁ (in שְׁהֵם־, Eccles. iii. 18, and according to one reading in שְׁהוּא for שֶׁהוּא, Eccles. ii. 22). In Phoenician the word is written אש, but that the ש may originally have had a vowel is at least suggested by the transcription of words handed down to us by Latin and Greek authors, such as *Nesso esse sade* (capillus Veneris), i. e. נֵצָּה אֵשׁ שָׂדֶה. More frequent, however, are the shorter forms *as*, *es*, *ys*, *is*, and also *si*, *su*, which last correspond to the Hebrew שֶׁ·; e. g. in the Poenulus, *assamar binam*, אשאָמַר בְּנַעַם "what he says is friendly"; *ys siddobrim*, *thyfel yth chyl ys chon them liful*, i. e. (probably), אִישׁ שֶׁדִּבְרִים תִּפְעַל אֶת־כָּל־אשׁ־כֵּן תַּם לְפָעַל, in Latin *eum fecisse aiunt, sibi quod faciundum fuit*; or, to quote another line, *yth alonim valonuth sicorathi simacom syth*, i. e. אֶת־אֱלֹנִים וְאֱלוֹנוֹת שֶׁקָּרָאתִי שֶׁמָּקוֹם זֹאת.

The use of the relative as a conjunction, and as a sign of the genitive relation between two substantives, belongs rather to the department of Syntax than of Etymology. These phenomena need cause you no surprise, if you reflect, on the one hand, that the Greek particle ὡς is only a case of the relative pronoun ὅς; and, on the other, that the Persian *iẓāfat* or connective vowel *i* in such constructions as نامِ پدرِ من *nām-i pidar-i man*, "the name of my father," is merely a corruption of what was the relative pronoun in the older stages of the language.

I may therefore conclude my remarks on the relative by referring briefly to certain *possessive* pronouns, which are formed from it in several of the Semitic languages. In Ethiopic we find ዚአ፡, fem. እንቲአ፡, plur. እሊአ፡, combined with suffixes as follows: *zī'á-ya*, *zī'á-ka*, *zī'a-hū*, *zī'á-na*, *zī'a-kémū*, *zī'a-hómū*, etc. Here we may perhaps discern the relative ዘ፡ *za*, in combination with the pronoun *kīyā*, or rather its Arabic form *īyā*, of which I spoke in a former lecture. In Aramaic we meet with two forms, דְּיד and דִּיל. The former is found in the Talmūd, e.g. אֲנַן בְּדִידָן וְאִינְהוּ בִּדִידְהוּ "we (occupy ourselves) with our affairs, and they with theirs." This arises, as Luzzatto has suggested, from a combination of דִּי with יַד, "hand." It also occurs in modern Syriac in the forms ܕܝܝ, ܕܝܘܟ, ܕܝܢ, *dīyī, dīyukh, dīyan*, etc., with elision of the *d* between two vowels. The other form דִּיל, i.e. דִּי plus the prep. לְ, is found in Biblical Aramaic, e.g. Dan. ii. 20—דִּי חָכְמְתָא וּגְבוּרְתָא דִּי־לֵהּ הִיא; and prevails in the Targūms and in Syriac[1]. The equivalent שֶׁל, from אֲשֶׁר לְ, occurs in later Hebrew, as well as in Phoenician. Already in Jonah i. 7 we read בְּשֶׁלְּמִי "for whose cause?" and in ver. 12, בְּשֶׁלִּי "for my sake"; and similarly in the Poenulus *ulic silli*, הוֹלֵךְ שֶׁלִּי, "my guest" (lit. "wanderer"); *amma silli*, אַמָּא שֶׁלִּי, "my mother"; *bene silli*, בְּנִי שֶׁלִּי, "my son." A fuller form seems to occur on a Tyrian signet ring, viz. לְבַעַלְיָתֹן אִשׁ אֵלֹם אֲשֶׁלְמְלְקַרְתְּ רצף "(belonging) to Ba'al-yathon, a priest (lit. a gods'-man) of Melḳart Rṣph."

D. *The Interrogative Pronouns.*

The first of these to which I would direct your attention is the Arabic أَيٌّ *ayy*, fem. أَيَّةٌ *ayyah*, fully inflected, meaning "who, which, what?" It governs a genitive, as أَيُّ أَرْضٍ or أَيَّةُ أَرْضٍ, "which land?" أَيُّ ٱلرَّجُلَيْنِ "which of the two men?" أَيُّ ٱلرِّجَالِ "which of the men?" أَيُّهُمَا, أَيُّهُمْ "which of them[2]?"

[1] Compare the African ذيال = الذي ل.

[2] In vulgar Arabic it has become *ē*, or in combination with شَيّ (thing) *ēsh*; لي

This word seems to me to have its ultimate source in the interrogative particle أ, Heb. הֲ. It is found in Ethiopic too in the sing. አይ፡ *ây*, plur. አያት፡ *ayyât*, for both genders; and in the modern Tigriña it appears as አይን፡ አየን፡ እየን፡ አያን፡ or እያን፡, which are probably compounds of አይ፡ and the Ethiopic interrogative ኑ፡፡ In the other Semitic languages this word has more of an adverbial force, being prefixed to other words to convert them into interrogatives, and entering into the composition of a great many interrogative adverbs. In Hebrew, for example, it appears as אֵי (*ê* for *ay*) in אֵי זֶה, "who, which?" אֵי מִזֶּה "from which?" אֵי לָזֹאת "wherefore, why?" But also as an independent word in the sense of "where?" with pronom. suffixes, אַיֶּכָּה, אַיּוֹ, אַיָּם; and in a longer form without suffix, אַיֵּה. Of compound words the most ordinary examples are: אַיִן (for אַיִן, Arabic أَيْنَ) "where?" contracted אָן, and as an accusative אָנָה "whither?" אֵיךְ, אֵיכָה, and אֵיכָכָה, "how?" אֵיפֹה "where? how?" Similar formations in Ethiopic are አይቴ፡ "where?" and, with a shortening of አይ፡ into እ፡ *ĕ*, እፎ፡ *ĕfô*, "how? how!" reduplicated እፎፎ፡ *ĕfôfô*, እፋፎ፡ *ĕfâfô*, or እፈፎ፡ *ĕfăfô*; and እስፍንቱ፡ "how much? how many?" from ስፍን፡ *sĕfn*, which is properly a noun meaning "number," "quantity." In Aramaic we have two forms of this word, for just as the Arabic أ is in Hebrew הֲ, so in Aramaic we find both אֵי and הֵי. The latter, הֵי, is the ordinary form in the Talmûd Bâblî and in the Syriac dialect of Palestine. For instance, in the Talmûd, הֵי דֵּין or הֵידֵין, fem. הֵיְדָא or הֵידָא "who?" "which?"; in Palestinian Syriac likewise ܗܝܢ, fem.

lê, "why?" In Egypt, *ênhû*, *ênhî*, *enhûm*, as *min ênhû gins*, "of what kind," but separately *enhû*, *enhî*, *enhûm*, "who?" "which?", where *en* is probably for *ên* = أَيْنَ. [So Spitta, p. 80. But Nöldeke explains the *n* as a remnant of the old Tanwîn, مِن أَيٍّ هو, and so forth.]

ܗܘܢ. Further, in the Talmūd, הַיְי דֵנוּ or הֵידֵנוּ "who," "which," "what is—?" for הַיידין הו; הֵיךְ "how?" הֵיכָה "where?" אַהֵיָּיא "in respect of which?" "in reference to which?" for עַל־הַיָּיא; לֵיָּיא "to which?" "whither?" for לְהַיָּיא. In the Aramaic of the Targūms both forms occur; אֵיךְ and הֵיךְ "how?" אֵידֵין and הֵידֵין, fem. אֵידָא and הֵידָא, "who, which?" אֵיכָא and הֵיכָא, "where?" אֵיכְדֵין and הֵיכְדֵין, "how?" In Syriac we have only the forms with *aleph*, but in great abundance; for instance: ܐܝܟ (*ăkh*) "how," "as," with its derivatives ܐܝܟܘܬ "as," "like," ܐܟܚܕܐ "together," "at once," ܐܝܟܡܢ "as one who," "as if," ܐܝܟܡܐ, "as"; further, ܐܝܟܐ "where?" from ܟܐ "here"; ܐܝܟܢ, ܐܝܟܢܐ, "how?" for ܐܝܟ ܗܢ and ܐܝܟ ܗܢܐ; ܐܝܡܟܐ "whence?" for ܐܝ ܡܢ ܟܐ; ܐܝܢܐ for ܐܝ ܗܢܐ, "who?" with its fem. ܐܝܕܐ, and plur. ܐܝܠܝܢ for אַי אִלֵּין; and finally, with a shortening of ܐܝ into ܐ, ܐܡܬܝ "when?" in the Targūms אֵימָתַי and אֵימַת, from the Heb. מָתַי, Arab. مَتَى. In modern Syriac there are similar forms, though of course more or less corrupted. Such are: ܐܝܟܐ *ikā* or ܐܟܐ *ĭkā*, "where?" ܐܝ ܕܥܢܐ *ēdānā*, for אַי עִדָּנָא, "when?" *iminē* or *imnē*, "which of them?" ܐܝ ܡܢܝܗܝ or ܐܡܢܝܗܝ, in Talmudic הַי מִנַּיְיהוּ; further, ܐܢܝ "who?" from אי דנא and אי דא, with another form ܐܝܢܝ *ēnī*, which is, strictly speaking, derived from the old plural ܐܝܠܝܢ. In Mandaitic the same interrogative exists in מנא *m'nā*, "whence?" which is also a Talmudic form, for מִנָּא or מִנַּן, i.e. מִן אַיִן; מיני לאך *minnē lākh*, in the Talmud מנא לך, *undenam tibi?* Also in ליא or לע, *lē*, for לְאַי, "whither?" מיליא *millē*, "whence?" עמאת or לעמאת "when?" עכא and אכא or האכא, "where?" from הֵיכָא, אֵיכָא, with suffix כַּארוּ "where is—?" in which form the real interrogative has wholly disappeared, just as in the modern Syriac

ܐܟܐ ܠܗ "where is he?" from ܐܝܟܐ *ikā*, "where?" Here too I should mention the Mandaitic forms האמניא and האמנו, probably standing for הַאי מִנַּהּ and הַאי מִנְּהוֹן, e.g. בהאמניא תיהילפון "in which will ye cross over?" כורסיא דיליא האמנו הו "which (of them) is my throne?"

Another interrogative pronoun in the Semitic languages is that which is characterised by the initial letter *m*. Its oldest forms appear to me to be *man* for the masc., and *mant* for the fem.; but in practice *man* is used as the interrogation for persons of both sexes, "who?" whilst *mant* is employed in speaking of things, "what?"

In Ethiopic we actually find these oldest forms in use; መኑ፡ *mdnū*, acc. መነ፡ *mdna*, "who?" and ምንት፡ *mĕnt*, acc. ምንተ፡ *mĕnta*, "what?" The Himyar. form is also מן, but more usually בן, with the substitution of ב for מ. In Arabic we have ordinarily مَنْ *man* for persons, but a distinction of gender is made in the rare case of the word standing alone, when it is fully inflected, the masc. sing. being مَنُو *manū*, and the fem. مَنَهْ *manah* (with aspirated *h*, for مَنْتَ) and sometimes مَنْتْ *mant*. The Assyrian forms are said to be *mannu* or *manu* and *man*, which last is identical with the Aramaic מַן, ܡܰܢ. Hence arise in the Aramaic dialects, by the addition of the pronoun *hū*, such forms as Syriac ܡܰܢܘ; Talmudic מַנּוּ, fem. מַנִּי, for מַן הוּ, מַן הִי; Mandaitic מאנו; modern Syriac ܡܰܢܝܼܒ, ܡܰܢܝܼܒ, ܡܶܢܝܼܒ, which is strictly speaking derived from the old feminine. The forms in the vulgar dialects of Abyssinia are not dissimilar to those of the ancient Ethiopic, viz. Tigriña መን፡ "who?" and ምንታይ፡ *mĕntāy*, rarely ምንታ፡ and እንታይ፡ "what?" This latter is compounded of ምንት፡ and the other interrogative አይ፡፡ In Amharic the commonest forms are ማን፡ "who?" and ምን፡ "what," shortened from ምንት፡፡

Vulgar Arabic forms of مَنْ are مَن and مِن. The change of vowel in the former case is due to the influence of the labial *m*;

in the latter, it is the natural weakening of *ă* in the shut syllable, and is pronounced in pause *mīn* مِينْ. From a form resembling this last must have arisen, by the rejection of the final *n*, the Hebrew מִי "who?" It is also found in Ethiopic, but as a neuter, "what?" or else as an adverb "how!" e.g. ሚ፡አደመ፡ "how pleasant!" ሚ፡የዐቢ፡ "how great is—!" ሚመጠን፡ "how great?" "how much?" (from መጠን፡ "measure, quantity"). The Phoenician form of the personal interrogative seems also, from some phrases in the *Poenulus*, to have been *mi*.

The neuter form *mā* is common to the Arabic, Hebrew, Phoenician, and the Aramaic dialects, مَا, מָה, מָא, ܡܳܐ; and we also find abundant traces of it in Assyrian, as I shall show you presently. This form I would venture to explain, with Fr. Böttcher, as follows. The original *mant* became by assimilation *matt*; the doubling was gradually dropped, because hardly audible, at the end of the word, leaving *mat*. This would gradually lead to the aspiration of the final *t*, *math*. The aspirated letter would first pass into *h*, מַהּ, *mah*, and finally disappear altogether in pronunciation, the vowel being lengthened in the now open syllable, מָה, *māh*. Compare the different stages of such words as אִנְף, אַף, אָף "anger" (Arab. أَنْف "nose"), or תֵּת, with suffix תִּתִּי, from תִּתְּ, תִּנְת, תִּנְתְ or תְּנִתְ, תֶּנֶת (for נְתֶנֶת); and the series of changes which produced the ordinary feminine termination of nouns ָה, ָא, out of the original *at*, viz. (1) *at*, (2) *ath*, ַת, (3) *ah*, with aspirated *h* (found in Arabic in rhyme), and finally (4) *ā*, ָה, ָא. In this way too we are enabled to give an easy explanation of the *daghesh forte* which so constantly follows this word, and of the forms מַה־, מָה, מֶה, as compared with those of the article הַ, הָ, הֶ, from הַל.

From מָא by the addition of הוּ we obtain in Talmudic and Mandaitic the forms מָהוּ, מאהו, "what is it?" מאהו is contracted in Mandaitic into מו in the word אמו "why?" i.e. על מארו-אל מארו. By adding דֵּין to מָא there arises in Talmudic the word מָאי "what?" in composition אַמַּאי "wherefore?" "why?" = עַל מָאדֵין. In ancient Syriac the same combination of מָא with דְּנָא and דֵּין finally resulted in the contracted forms ܡܢܳܐ and ܡܢܶܐ, the latter of which was farther weakened into ܡܢܘ. Hence in combination with הוּ arose the form ܡܢܘ "what is it?" = ܡܢܳܐ ܗܘ. In modern Syriac this same *mā-dēn* has been contracted into ܡܕܝܢ, with a rather unusual weakening of the vowel in this dialect; and this is farther shortened into ܡܕܝ, ܡܕܝ, and even ܡܘ, as in ܡܘ ܥܒܕܝܢ "what shall we do?"

With regard to the neutral مَا in Arabic, I may observe that it is not unfrequently shortened into مَ *mă*, especially in connection with prepositions, as عَلَامَ, إِلَامَ, عَمَّ for عَنْ مَ, مِمَّ, for مِنْ مَ. فِيمَ. بِمَ. لِمَ. These last two words are still further abbreviated in poetry into بِمْ and لِمْ, which shows us the origin of the word كَمْ "how much?" standing for كَمَ or كَمَا, Syriac ܟܡܐ, Hebrew כַּמָּה. In Ethiopic this abbreviated *mă* is frequently appended to other interrogatives, with somewhat the same force as the Latin *nam*; e.g. መኑ:መ: (*mănū-mă*) አንተ: "who art thou, pray?" ምንትኑመ: *měnt-nū-mă*, አይቴመ: *aytē-mă*, እፎመ: *ĕfŏ-mă*, ማእዜኑመ: *mă'ĕzē-nū-mă*.

That these interrogative pronouns should pass into indefinites, with the sense of "who, whoever, what, whatever," is only what might be naturally expected, and the consideration of this point belongs rather to comparative syntax than to our present subject. Sundry forms must, however, for the sake of completeness, be noticed here. And firstly, the Assyrian words *mannū-ma*, *mannā-ma*, *man-man*, by assimilation *mamman*, and *man-mā*, "whoever," "any one"; *mimma*, "whatever." Of these, ***manman*** or ***mamman*** is merely a reduplication of ***man***; ***manúma***, ***mandma***, and ***manma***, are formed by the addition of ***ma*** to ***mannu*** or ***man***; and ***mimma*** arises from a neuter ***mi***, like the Ethiopic ሚ: *mî*. Similar words may be found in the modern dialects of Abyssinia. For instance, Tigriña has ሚንም: or መንም: "whoever," "any one"; and in Amharic there occurs ሚንም:, with the neuters ምንም: and ምንምን::

The indefinite *mā* is often attached in Arabic as an enclitic to another word, to give it a certain vagueness, as قَلِيلٌ مَّا "a small quantity"; أَعْطِنِي كِتَابًا مَّا "give me some book or other." At other times it conveys something of an intensifying force, as جِئْتَ لِأَمْرٍ مَّا "thou art come for some matter" (of importance); whence فَتًى مَّا is often nearly equivalent to أَيُّ فَتًى "what a youth!" "what a man!" Hence we obtain an easy explanation of such a word as the Chaldee מַדַּעַם "something," which is in reality a contraction of מַדַּע מָה "*scibile quid.*" All the other forms of this word are only more or less corrupted; e.g. Chald. מִנְדַּעַם (like מַנְדַּע for מַדַּע), Mand. מינדאם, Syr. ܡܶܕܶܡ, Talmud. מִידִּי, modern Syriac ܡܸܕܸܡ. In later times the word began to be treated in some of the dialects as a simple substantive, and to form a plural; e.g. in old Syriac ܡܶܕ̈ܡܶܐ, and in modern Syriac ܡܸܕܡ̈ܢܹܐ, whilst the Mandaitic forms a new substantive מינדא, "a thing," plur. מינדיא.

To return to the Arabic مَا: we also find it used, especially with prepositions, without its apparently adding anything to the sense; e.g. فِي كُلِّ مَا عَامٍ "in every year," مِنْ غَيْرِ مَا جُرْمٍ "without any offence," مِمَّا خَطِيئَاتِهِمْ "because of their sins,"

عَمَّا قَلِيلٍ "after a little," بِمَا رَحْمَةٍ مِنَ ٱللّٰهِ "by God's mercy." The same is the case in Hebrew, only that מָה has in this case been modified into מוֹ. Hence בְּמוֹ־שָׁלֶג, Job ix. 30, *ḳĕrē*; בְּמוֹ־אֹפֶל, Ps. xi. 2; לְמוֹ־חָרֶב, Job xxvii. 14; and כְּמוֹ־אָבֶן, Exod. xv. 5. So also before pronominal suffixes כָּמוֹנִי, כָּמוֹךָ, כָּמוֹהוּ. Here the Ethiopic at once shows the old form in its ከመ : *kĕma*, "as," "like," but with suffixes ከማየ : *kamā-ya, kamā-ka, kamā-hū, kamā-hōmū*. You will, I think, find the same weakening of *mā* to *mō* in a word which appears in the Chaldee lexicons as מוֹדְלָא or מוֹלָא "wealth," "property," with the variants מִידְלָא and מוּלָא, the former of which is certainly a mere error. מוֹלָא seems to me to be identical with the Arabic مَالٌ, which is in reality a compound of مَا "what" and لِ "to," literally, "what belongs to one." In מוֹדְלָא the compound has been strengthened by the relative דְּ; that is to say מוֹדְלִי "my property," or מוֹדְלֵיהּ "his property," is really מוֹ + דְ + לִי or לֵיהּ, literally "that which is to me" or "to him."

E. *The Reflexive Pronouns.*

Finally, it may be as well to say a few words regarding the mode of expressing the reflex pronouns in the Semitic languages, though this pertains rather to the subject of comparative syntax than to our present topic.

In some cases, as you are aware, the reflex idea is conveyed by means of a peculiar form of the verb, for instance in Hebrew the Niph'al or Hithpa"el.

In other cases, the ordinary pronouns of the 3rd person have to do duty for the reflex pronouns as well; e.g. וַיִּקַּח אֶת־שְׁנֵי נְעָרָיו אִתּוֹ, where we also say "he took two of his young men with *him*," whilst the German more accurately expresses it by "und er nahm zween (zwei) seiner Knechte mit *sich.*" I may remark, however, in passing, that even in German, so late as Luther's time, *ihm*, *ihr*, and *ihnen*, could be employed for *sich*, just as *sein* and *ihr* serve at the present day both for *suus* and *eius* or *eorum*.

In other cases still, where it was positively necessary to make a distinction, recourse was had to a compound pronoun, such as ኪያሁ፡, אֹתוֹ, ܝܳܬܶܗ; or—and this is the point to which I more particularly wish to direct your attention just now,—a substantive, most frequently one expressing some part of the human frame, was employed with the appropriate pronominal suffix, e.g. נַפְשִׁי "my soul," for "myself."

In Arabic the words frequently used for this purpose are نَفْس "soul," plur. أَنْفُس, and عَيْن "eye, essence," plur. أَعْيَان; but in the later stages of the language we also find رُوح "spirit," حَال "state," and ذَات "essence"; e.g. تَجِي بِرُوحَك "thou wilt come thyself" (or "in person"), قَتَل حَالَه "he has killed himself," رَاح هُو بِذَاتِه "he is gone himself" (or "in person").

In Ethiopic ለሊ፡ is employed for the nominative in the forms ለሊየ፡ *lalī-ya* or ለሊየ፡ *lalĕ-ya*, ለሊከ፡ *lalī-ka*, ለሊሁ፡ *lalī-hū*, etc. This ለሊ፡ Dillmann maintains to be nothing more than a reduplication of the demonstrative syllable *la*, which we have already found in so many pronominal forms. Praetorius has suggested another derivation, viz. from the verb ሌለየ፡ "to separate," whence the Amharic ሌላ፡ "another"; and for this no doubt analogies might be produced from other languages; but for the present I prefer to abide by Dillmann's view as the simpler. For other cases than the nominative the Ethiopic employs the word ርእስ፡ "head," as መኑ፡ ትሬሲ፡ ርእሰከ፡ "whom dost thou make thyself (to be)?" ላዕለ፡ ርእስክሙ፡ "against yourselves." ነፍስ፡ is of comparatively rare occurrence in this sense, as መጠወ፡ ነፍሶ፡ ለሞት፡ "he gave himself up to death." In the vulgar dialects, Tigriña and Amharic, there seems to be a still greater variety of expression. In Tigriña we find ባዕሉ፡

or ብዓል፡ "lord, master," as ባዕልየ፡ ርኢኩ፡ "I myself have seen," እኒሆ፡ አኒ፡ ብዓልዬ፡ ለዩ፡ "behold, it is I myself." More rare is the use of ብዓልቤት፡ "master of the house," e.g. ምድርሰ፡ ብዓልቤታ፡ ተፈሪ፡ "for the earth brings forth fruit (of) itself." These two are generally used for the nominative, whilst for the other cases is commonly employed ርእሰ፡ "head"; less frequently ነፍስ፡ "soul," and ሥጋ፡ "flesh," "body." From ነፍስ፡ are formed, as I said before, the personal pronouns ንስከ፡ *nessĕ-khā*, "thou," and ንሱ፡ *nessū* "he," as well as the reduplicated ንስንስ፡ "one another," as ተባሀሉ፡ ንስንሳቲሆሙ፡ "they spoke to one another," or "among themselves." The word ብሕት፡ *solitudo*, is also used in the sense of *self*, apparently for any case; and similarly ሰብነት፡ "humanity"; though these two may perhaps be restricted to the third person. In Amharic nearly the same words occur in their appropriate dialectic forms, viz. ባለቤት፡, ራስ፡, ነፍስ፡ and ሰውነት፡፡ From ራስ፡ has been derived the pronoun of the 3rd person, እርሱ፡, farther contracted into እሱ፡ *ĕssū*.

In Assyrian the common reflexive is *rāman*, which seems to stand for *raḥman*, just as *rūḳ* for *raḥuḳ*, רָחוֹק. It is therefore equivalent to the Heb. רֶחֶם, or rather רַחֲמִים, τὰ σπλάγχνα, and forms with suffixes *rāmanīya*, *rāmanīka*, *ramanīšu*, etc. One might have imagined this, after the analogy of the Hebrew, to be a plural in *ān*, against which the form *ramannīšu*, with double *n*, would perhaps not have militated; but the form *ramnīšu* seems to show that the vowel of the second syllable, even though accented, was short, and might in some cases be elided.

In Biblical Hebrew the most usual word as a reflexive is נֶפֶשׁ, though פָּנִים, "face, presence," is also employed, e.g. Exod. xxxiii. 14, פָּנַי יֵלֵכוּ, 2 Sam. xvii. 11. עֶצֶם, "bone," is used in the Bible in speaking of things only, as כְּעֶצֶם הַשָּׁמַיִם, בְּעֶצֶם הַיּוֹם הַזֶּה; but in later Hebrew it is applied to persons, לְעַצְמִי "for myself"; as are also גֶּרֶם "bone" and גּוּף "body," with which last you may compare the old German phrases *mīn līp*, *dīn līp*, for *ich* and *du*.

Among the Aramaic dialects there is some variety of usage.

In the Targūms נפש is common; in later writings גרם, which we also find in Samaritan and in the Palestinian dialect of Syriac. In Syriac ܢܰܦܫܳܐ and ܩܢܽܘܡܳܐ are the dominant words, ܝܳܬܳܐ being very rare. In Mandaitic נאפשא is used; whilst ܩܢܽܘܡܳܐ is found in Samaritan, in the forms קנום and קלום, and may possibly also occur in Phoenician[1]. I regret my inability as yet to give any satisfactory etymology of this word. Modern Syriac still makes use of ܢܘܿܫܳܐ *nōshā*, but far more frequently employs the word ܓܝܳܢܳܐ, which is merely the Persian جان *jān*, "soul"; as ܕܟܹܡ ܗ̄ܘܳܐ ܟܢܳܐ ܐܘܼܪܚܝ ܡܪܝܼܪܬܳܐ ܠܓܝܳܢܝ "who was making my way bitter to me," ܠܢܘܿܦܘܿܨܹܐ ܓܝܳܢܹܗ "to shake himself."

[1] [Viz., in the inscription of Eshmūn'āzār, *C. I. S.*, No. 3, l. 4, 20. Cf. G. Hoffmann, *Ueber einige Phoen. Inschrr.* (4° Gött. 1889) p. 37.]

CHAPTER VII.

THE NOUN.

FROM the pronoun we naturally proceed to the *Noun*, in treating of which it will be most convenient for our present practical purpose to speak first of the distinction of gender, and then of the distinctions of number and case. With respect to gender and number, it may be desirable to consider the verbal forms to a slight extent along with the nominal, because there is in the Semitic languages a close resemblance in the flexion of the noun and verb, for which we look in vain in the Indo-European languages.

I. *Gender.*

The vivid imagination of the Semite conceived all objects, even those that are apparently lifeless, as endowed with life and personality. Hence for him there are but *two genders*, as there exist in nature but two sexes. All that we are accustomed to look upon as indifferent and neuter, was of necessity classed by him as either masculine or feminine, though the latter predominated, as we may see from the formation of abstract nouns, from the employment of the fem. as the impersonal form of the verb, and from other phenomena in Semitic speech The Mandaite only pushes this use to its utmost limit, when he construes as fem. such words and expressions as מינדאם "something," כול ד "all that," and מא ד or מאהו ד "what," "whatever." Even the word مَا, מָא, מָה, the nearest approach in the Semitic languages to a neuter, is only, as I tried to show you in a former lecture, a corruption of *mant*, which is actually the fem. of مَنْ, מַן, מִי.

There are, of course, a great many cases in which the Semitic languages, as well as others, do not mark the difference of gender by any difference of termination, both in respect of living and of inanimate objects. אֵם "mother," רָחֵל "ewe," עַיִן "eye," עִיר "city," are not designated as fem. by any external mark. But in the greater number of cases it was found convenient, if not absolutely necessary, to indicate the fem. gender by an external sign; and for this purpose the letter *t* was commonly employed as an affix.

In this simple form of affixed *t* the fem. termination is rare in Arabic, as بِنْتٌ "daughter," أُخْتٌ "sister"; but common in Ethiopic, especially in adjectives and participles, as ልሂቅ፡ *lĕhîḳ*, "old," ልህቅት፡ *lĕhĕḳt*; ፍቁር፡ *fĕḳûr*, "beloved," ፍቅርት፡ *fĕḳĕrt*; ጻድቅ፡ *ṣâdĕḳ*, "just," ጻድቅት፡ *ṣâdĕḳt*; መስተምሕር፡ *mastâmḥĕr*, "asking mercy," መስተምሕርት፡ *mastamḥĕrt*. We find it, however, in substantives too, as ንጉሥ፡ *nĕgûs*, "king," ንግሥት፡ *nĕgĕst*, "queen"; አንስት፡ *anĕst*, "woman"; ወለት፡ *waldtt*, "daughter," for ወለድት፡፡ In Hebrew the simple *t* is found in some cases where the masc. ends in a single consonant, as יֹלַדְתְּ "bearing," Gen. xvi. 11, Judges xiii. 5, 7; לַת "to bear," for לַדְתְּ, 1 Sam. iv. 19; אַחַת "one," for אַחַדְתְּ; but more commonly a short supplementary vowel is inserted between the last two letters, resulting in the vocalisation ֶ ֶ, or, if there be a guttural at the end of the word, ַ ַ, and the like; thus, יוֹלֶדֶת, לֶדֶת, חֹתֶמֶת for חֹתַמְתְּ, מִשְׁעֶנֶת for מִשְׁעַנְתְּ, מוֹדַעַת for מוֹדַעְתְּ, נְחֹשֶׁת for נְחֻשְׁתְּ or נְחֹשְׁתְּ, מַאֲכֶלֶת for מַאֲכַלְתְּ or מַאֲכָלְתְּ.

Instead of the simple *t*, however, we more usually find *at*, with a connective short *ă*. This is by far the most common form in Arabic, as اِمْرَءٌ "man," اِمْرَأَةٌ "woman"; جَدٌّ "grandfather,"

جدّة "grandmother"; عظيم "great," عظيمة; قاتل "killing," قاتلة. In Ethiopic it is less frequent than *t*, though by no means uncommon; e.g. ርደት፡ "descent," ሶምት፡ "garlic" (שׁוּם, ثوم, ܬܘܡܐ), ናቀት፡ "she-camel" (ناقة), በረከት፡ *barákat* "blessing" (בְּרָכָה, بركة), ኀጢአት፡ "sin" (خطيئة), መጸለት፡ "tent" (مظلّة, ܡܛܠܬܐ). In Hebrew this termination is rare in the simple form of nouns; as examples take בָּרֶקֶת (a precious stone), גִּבְעַת, אֵילַת, דָּבְרַת, צָרְפַת (places), בָּשְׂמַת, מָחֲלַת (women); also with *kāmes*, הַקָּאַת "the pelican," בַּעֲלַת (a place), פֹּרָת (Gen. xlix. 22), חַטָּאת "sin," מְנָת for *manayat*, "portion"; also אָחוֹת, חָמוֹת, for *aḥawat*, *ḥamawat*. But we find it everywhere in the so-called construct state, and also before the pronominal suffixes, as נַחֲלַת, נַחֲלָתִי.

Now observe the history of these forms, from which you will perceive the absurdity of saying that the fem. termination in Hebrew is ָה, and that it becomes ַת in the construct state. The reverse is the fact. The original form is the ַת of the construct, and it becomes ָה. The Ethiopic presents us with the original form *t* or *at*. The Hebrew retained this termination in the construct state, before pronominal suffixes, and in a few other cases. But in the simple form of the noun the aspirated ת̄ passed into aspirated ה, and finally, when this *h* was dropped, nothing remained but the vowel, which was heightened in the open syllable into *ā*, ָה, as נַחֲלָה[1]. So also in Arabic; the original *t* is retained in بنت, اخت, and in the Ḳor'ān in a few other words, e.g. Sūra xi. 76, رحمت ٱللّه; as also before suffixes, رحمته, رحمتي. The next step was to the aspirated *h*, which

[1] Cf. what has been said above, p. 124, of the pronoun ما, מָא, מָה.

form is used by the Arabic poets in rhyme, as, for example, when الْعَذَلَهْ (for الْعَذَلَةْ) is rhymed with أَبِلَهْ (for أَبِلَةْ) and with وَوَلَهْ (for وَوَلَةْ); or السَّلَامَهْ (for السَّلَامَةْ) with أَمَامَهْ (for أَمَامَةْ). The last step is to drop the *h*, as is done in the vulgar pronunciation, الْعَذَلَه, السَّلَامَه, الرَّحْمَه. The spelling with the dotted ة is merely a compromise of the grammarians between the old ـَتْ and the vulgar ـَهْ; if I write سَنَةْ, I indicate at once the old pronunciation سَنَتْ, שְׁנַת, and the more recent سَنَهْ, שָׁנָה. If you ask for analogies in other languages for such changes as this of *at* into ת_, *ath*, then into ה_, *ah*, and finally into *á*, ה_, I can give you several. The final aspirated *d* of the Spaniard, for example in the word *ciudad*, has a very faint sound to an English ear, and the consonant has altogether vanished in the corresponding Italian *città* for *civitad* (i.e. *civitatem*). So also in French, in the verb, *il aima*, from *ille amât* (for *amavit*), but interrogatively *aima-t-il?* from *amât ille?* Indeed aspirated letters, in all positions, are apt to disappear entirely or else to leave no trace behind them save the mere aspiration. Compare the Talmudic אָהֵן for הָהֵן, and the modern Syriac ܗܳܘܳܐ for הָדָא, ܗܳܢܳܐ; or, to go a little farther afield, consider the Armenian *hayr* and the Irish *athir*, both the regular equivalents in these languages of the Latin *pater*. In *hayr* an aspirated *p* remains as *h*, and an aspirated *t* has vanished (as in *père*); in *athir* an aspirated *p* has vanished, whilst an aspirated *t* remains only in writing, for the word is actually pronounced *ahir*.

Having thus, by the help of Arabic, Ethiopic and Hebrew, established the fact that the principal fem. termination in these languages is *t* or *at*, let us trace this form in the remaining Semitic tongues.

In Assyrian we find such forms as *bint* "daughter," *iḥit* "one" (for *iḥidt*), and the like, with simple *t*; but the usual shape of this affix is *at*, weakened into *it*, e. g. *šarrat* "princess," *malikat* "queen," *nâkat* "she-camel," *šanat* "year," *âšibat* "inhabiting" (יֹשֶׁבֶת), *bilat* or *bilit* "mistress, lady," *riš'at* or *riš'it* "wickedness," *irṣit* "earth."

In Phoenician the noun ends in ת, whether it be in the simple or the construct state, as in the usual dedication of the Carthaginian *ex voto* tablets לרבת לתנת, "to the goddess Tanith," or in the words from the sarcophagus of king Eshmunazar, וְאִמִּי אֲמַעַשְׁתֹּרֶת כֹּהֶנֶת עַשְׁתֹּרֶת רַבָּתַן הַמַּלְכַּת, or again וְשֹׁכֵב אָנֹךְ בְּחַלַּת זֶ. We find however traces of a younger form in א *ô*, corresponding to the Hebrew ָה, very rarely in inscriptions, more frequently in the words handed down to us by classical authors; e.g. κιττώ, Heb. קְדָּה, "cassia" or "cinnamon"; *nesso*, Heb. נִצָּה, "flower"; *Dido*, either for נְדִידָא, according to the explanation of the *Etymol. Magnum* πλανῆτις, or for יְדִידָא; Καρχηδών, *Carthago*, corruption of קרת חדשא. In the Aramaic dialects the forms run exactly parallel to the Hebrew; e.g. in Syriac the construct state ends in *ath*; the *t* is retained in the emphatic form and before suffixes; but it disappears in the simple form of the noun, and is represented in writing by an *aleph*. Thus: ܡܠܟܐ, ܡܠܟܬ, ܡܠܟܬܐ, ܡܠܟܬܗ.

Here I may be allowed to remark that this original fem. in *t* has been retained in another instance in several of the Semitic languages, viz. as an adverb. Examples are: Hebrew, רַבַּת, Ps. lxv. 10, cxx. 6, cxxiii. 4; Aramaic, טְוָת "fasting," Dan. vi. 19; Syriac, ܪܒܬ, ܬܘܒ; ܚܝܬ "alive," ܦܐܝܬ "well," ܥܪܛܠܝܬ "naked," ܡܣܘܣܓܒ "gratis, for nothing"; ܐܚܪܝܬ "last," ܩܕܡܝܬ or ܩܕܡܐܝܬ "first," where *ith* is merely, as Noeldeke has remarked, a weakening of the older *yath*; ܦܓܪܢܐܝܬ "carnally," ܪܘܚܢܐܝܬ "spiritually," from ܦܓܪܢܐ and ܪܘܚܢܐ; ܚܝܘܬܢܐܝܬ "like a wild beast," from ܚܰܝܘܬܳܢܳܐ; and hence, in Syriac and the Palestinian dialect, as an adverbial termination, even where an adjective in ـܳܝ, ـܳܝܳܐ, is not in use, as ܫܰܦܺܝܪܳܐܺܝܬ "well," ܢܺܝܚܳܐܺܝܬ "gently," ܫܰܪܺܝܪܳܐܺܝܬ "truly." Such adverbs, being really feminine adjectives in the old form of the *status absolutus*, may be construed with a preposition, as ܒܝܰܘܢܳܐܺܝܬ "in Greek," ܒܣܘܪܝܳܐܺܝܬ "in Syriac"; and still more freely in Mandaitic, בסארהבאיית "in haste," בניהאיית "gently." Sometimes the abstract termination ות is used in the same way in both languages, as ܬܢܝܳܢܘܬ "a second time, again," ܬܠܺܝܬܳܝܘܬ "a third time"; in the dialect of Palestine, ܝܐܘܬ "rightly, well"; in Mandaitic ראבות "grandly"; and among the later Jews יָאוּת, טָבוּת.

I may next remark that this fem. in ת has in some cases received a curious increment in Mandaitic and the Talmudic dialect. Here namely we find some feminine adjectives ending in תי, Mand. תיא, instead of תא. The correct pronunciation of this termination is held by Noeldeke to be most probably תֵּי. With the Hebrew רַבָּתִי in Lament. i. 1, הָעִיר רַבָּתִי עָם, it can have nothing to do; that form is to be classed with גְּנֻבְתִי יוֹם, אֹסְרִי לַגֶּפֶן עִירֹה, etc., which I shall try to explain when we speak of the cases. Examples of this fem. in תי from the Talmud and Targūms are: אֶצְבְּעֵיה זוּטַרְתֵּי "his little finger," שַׁתָּא חֲדַתֵּי "the new year," אוּכַּמְתֵּי, חִוַּרְתֵּי, מִילְּתָא אַחֲרִיתֵּי, רַבְּתֵי. So in Mandaitic, ראבתיא, צטארתיא "small," האדיתיא "new," הורינתיא "another," היוארתיא "white," כארירתיא "heavy," האתיקתיא "ancient," שאפירתיא "beautiful," etc.

I would now call your attention to the parallel form in the flexion of the verb, viz. the 3rd pers. sing. fem. of the perfect, in Hebrew קָטְלָה. Here too the original termination was *at*, as is proved not only by the Arabic قَتَلَتْ *ḳatalat*, the Ethiopic

ቀተለት: *ḳatálat*, and the Syriac ܩܛܠܬ *ḳĕṭláth*, but also by the following evidence derived from Hebrew itself. (1) The form with final *t* is actually found in Deut. xxxii. 36, אָזְלַת יָד (for אָזְלַת), Ezek. xlvi. 17, וְשָׁבַת; possibly too Isaiah xxiii. 15, וְנִשְׁכַּחַת צֹר (for וְנִשְׁכַּחַת); as also in the whole class of verbs ל״ה so-called, e.g. עָשָׂת for עָשְׂיַת, הִרְצָת for הִרְצְיַת, הָגְלָת for הָגְלִית. This is exactly the Arabic جَلَتْ, by contraction for جَلَيَتْ; and the uncontracted גָּלְיָה is actually found once in Hebrew in the pausal חָסָיָה נַפְשִׁי, Ps. lvii. 2, whereas the ordinary pausal form is עָשָׂתָה. The ordinary non-pausal form עָשְׂתָה, גָּלְתָה, etc., is a secondary formation, in which the fem. suffix is repeated in the form ָה, thus aiming at uniformity with the ordinary קָטְלָה. (2) The form with final *t* invariably occurs in connexion with pronominal suffixes; e.g. יְלָדַתְנִי; גְּמָלַתְהוּ, or with assimilation יְלָדַתּוּ, אֲחָזָתְהוּ; בָּאַתְנוּ; יְלָדַתְךָ, רְאָתְךָ, אֲהֵבַתְךָ; אֲכָלָתַם, גְּנָבָתַם. Into this subject I shall have to enter more fully in treating of the verb; here it must suffice to have thus indicated the identity of the fem. termination in the singular noun and in the 3rd pers. sing. of the perfect tense.

The feminine termination ָה is occasionally written in Hebrew with א in place of ה, according to the usual practice in Aramaic; e.g. חָגָּא Isaiah xix. 17, קָרְחָא Ezek. xxvii. 31, שֵׁנָא Ps. cxxvii. 2, מַטָּרָא Lament. iii. 12; and even in the verb, גָּבְהָא Ezek. xxxi. 5. We also find the vowel of this syllable weakened, though very rarely, into ֶ, as in the noun הַזּוּרֶה for הַזּוּרָה, Isaiah lix. 5, and in the verb לָנֶה for לָנָה, Zechar. v. 4.

Besides the feminine termination in ـَتْ or ـَةٌ, the Arabic language possesses two others, viz. ـَى *ā* and ـَاءُ *āu*, both, as it would seem, originally of abstract signification. Examples of the former are بُشْرَى "good news," حُمَّى "a fever," دَعْوَى "a claim," رُؤْيَا "a vision"; of the latter, صَحْرَاءُ or بَيْدَاءُ "a desert," كِبْرِيَاءُ "glory, pride." The one, viz. ـَى *ā*, forms the feminine of adjectives ending in ـَانُ, as شَبْعَانُ "sated, not hungry," f. شَبْعَى; and of the form أَفْعَلُ used as a superlative, e.g. الأَصْغَرُ "the smallest," f. الصُّغْرَى. The other, ـَاءُ, forms the feminine of أَفْعَلُ, when it is not a comparative or superlative, as أَحْمَرُ "red," حَمْرَاءُ; أَحْمَقُ "foolish," حَمْقَاءُ. These terminations seem to find their representatives in Ethiopic in nouns ending in *ā*, as ሕንጻ: "building," ፍሥሓ: "joy," መሐላ: "oath," ዐመፃ: "wrong," መከራ: "temptation," ጻማ: or ፃማ: "toil," ጾታ: "order, row"; and in *ē*, as ሠረዊ: "beam, mast," ሰረዊ: "army," ፀፄ: "moth," ጊዜ: "time," ዐድሜ: "appointed time." The rules of gender are, however, very loosely observed in Ethiopic, and most of the words just cited may also be construed as masculine.

The Arabic termination ـَى is represented in Syriac by the form *ai*, as in [illegible], [illegible], [illegible], [illegible], [illegible], [illegible], and a few more. In Hebrew this termination can hardly be said to exist, unless we reckon as examples of it the proper name שָׂרַי, of which the later form is שָׂרָה, and the numeral עֶשְׂרֵה, in the compounds אַחַת עֶשְׂרֵה, etc., which may stand for an original עֶשְׂרַי. Of the other ending ـَاءُ I can find at present no certain trace in Aramaic and Hebrew, for Hebrew words in וֹ or ־ֹה, mostly proper names, seem, without exception, to have lost a final *n*, וֹן—. גִּלֹה and שִׁילֹה, for example, form the adjectives גִּילֹנִי and שִׁילֹנִי. Since, however, in Arabic, we find

صَنْعَانِيٌّ derived from صَنْعَاءُ, بَهْرَانِيٌّ from the name of the tribe بَهْرَآءُ, رَوْحَانِيٌّ from رَوْحَآءُ, it may be that גִּלֹּה and שִׁילֹה, as well as the Moabite קרחה, represent an original *Gailâ'u*, *Shailâ'u*, and *Ḳarḥâ'u*.

Finally, I may say a few words regarding a curious feminine form in Ethiopic, which consists entirely in an internal change of vowels. This is found in adjectives of the form *ḳatîl*, which take in the feminine *ḳatâl*; e.g. ሐዲስ: "new," ሐዳስ:; ጠቢብ: "learned, wise," ጠባብ:; ዐቢይ: "great," ዐባይ:; ረሒብ: (for *raḥîb*) "wide, spacious," ረሓብ:; ቀይሕ: (for *ḳayiḥ*) "red," ቀያሕ:: Of this formation Ewald has discovered a trace in Arabic in حَصَانٌ "chaste," applied to a woman, as compared with حَصِينٌ "inaccessible, unapproachable"; and in رَزَانٌ "grave, staid," also used of a woman, whereas the masculine is رَزِينٌ.

II. *Numbers and Cases.*

In treating of the *Numbers* and *Cases* of nouns in the Semitic languages I shall begin with the latter, for reasons which will become apparent as we proceed.

Of what we are accustomed to call *cases*—those varieties of termination which express the relations to one another of a noun and verb or of two nouns—the Semitic languages possess but three: the *casus rectus*, nominative or subject, and two *casus obliqui*, the one indicating the accusative or direct object, and also serving in a variety of ways as a *casus adverbialis*, the other corresponding most closely to the Indo-European genitive.

In the *singular* number these three cases are distinguished in ancient Arabic, in the great majority of nouns, by three terminations, *ŭ* for the subject or nominative, *ă* for the object or accusative, and *ĭ* for the genitive, as we may appropriately designate the second oblique form. In certain classes of nouns, however, the accusative has at an early period supplanted the genitive, so that these have only two terminations, *ŭ* for the nominative, and *ă* for the accusative and genitive. Examples of the triptote declension:—

بَيْتٌ   بَيْتٍ   بَيْتًا

جَنَّةٌ   جَنَّةٍ   جَنَّةً

The usage of the Arabic restricts these simple terminations to the definite and construct states of the noun. The noun must be defined by the article,

اَلْبَيْتُ;   اَلْبَيْتِ   اَلْبَيْتَ

or it must be followed by a genitive, which is also a species of definition,

بَيْتُ يُوسُفَ   بَيْتِ يُوسُفَ   بَيْتَ يُوسُفَ

بَيْتُهُ   بَيْتِهِ   بَيْتَهُ

In no other Semitic language has this inflexion been retained in such fullness and purity as in the ancient Arabic, the Arabic of the prae-Mohammedan poets and of the Ḳor'ān. In the modern language, as spoken at the present day, the case-terminations are either confounded with one another or entirely lost. In the Sinaitic peninsula, for example, one hears *'ammuk*, عَمُّك, which is really the nominative, used for all three cases.

In Ethiopic we can distinguish only one of these cases by an external mark; the accusative, with the termination *ă*. The vowel-endings of the nominative and genitive have disappeared; and the accusative *ă* takes the place of the others in the construct state, without any regard to the real case of the governing noun. E.g., አፍቀረ፡ ብእሲተ፡ "he loved a woman," ንጉሠ፡ ኢትዮጵያ፡ "the king of Ethiopia." In the case of proper names, the accusative termination is ሃ፡ *hā*, to which form I shall call your attention more particularly hereafter; e.g. ቃየንሃ: "Cain," ይሁዳሃ: "Judah."

In Assyrian, so far as I can understand the statements of the grammarians, these terminations are, as a general rule, appended to the noun when it is not in the construct state, but apparently without any regard to the actual relation of case. Thus, according to Schrader, the Assyrian writes *ina lisân mât Aḥarri*, "in the language of the country of Phoenicia," without any case-sign in *lisân* and *mât*; *šar Babîlu*, "king of Babel"; *malku bânušun*, "the king their builder"; *âšib libbišun*, "dwelling in their midst"; *'iribu ša šanši* or *'irib šanši*, "the setting of the sun"; *Dariyavus šarri*, "Darius the king." Here, therefore, the state of matters seems to be much the same as in modern Arabic; the case-endings, when employed, are used without any strict regard to their proper signification.

In Hebrew traces of all three terminations may be found. The accusative indeed is not uncommon, particularly in its adverbial sense, indicating direction or motion towards. E.g., אַ֫רְצָה "to the ground," בַּ֫יְתָה "homewards," "inwards," הַבַּ֫יְתָה "into the house," הָעַ֫יְנָה "to the well," הָ֫רָה "uphill," הֶהָ֫רָה "to the mountains," שְׁכֶ֫מָה "to Shechem," לְשָׁכָּ֫תָה "into a chamber," הַבָּמָ֫תָה "to the highplace," בְּאֵ֫רָה שֶׁ֫בַע, אַ֫רְצָה גֹּשֶׁן, יָ֫מָּה סּוּף, בֵּ֫יתָה יוֹסֵף. As real objective accusatives I may cite הֵקַל אַ֫רְצָה זְבֻלוּן וְאַ֫רְצָה נַפְתָּלִי "he abased, etc." Isaiah viii. 23; מִי פָקַד עָלָיו אַ֫רְצָה "who hath committed to his charge the earth?" Job xxxiv. 13. Here you may remark that the vowel *a* is expressed in writing by the letter ה. This does not, however, justify us in speaking of a "ה *locale*," as if the ה were anything more than the mere indication of the final vowel.

The terminations of the nominative and genitive are far rarer, and seem indeed to be used now and then only as archaistic forms, just as our poets occasionally indulge in such archaisms as *yode*, *whilom*, *yclept*, *ywis*, and the like. We need not therefore expect them to be employed with more regard to grammatical accuracy than in Assyrian or in modern Arabic. The nominative termination is וֹ, in such phrases as וְחַיְתוֹ־אֶרֶץ Gen. i. 24, כָּל־חַיְתוֹ־יָעַר Ps. l. 10, לְחַיְתוֹ־אָרֶץ Ps. lxxix. 2, בְּנוֹ צִפֹּר "O son of Ṣippôr," Num. xxiii. 18, נְאֻם בִּלְעָם בְּנוֹ בְעֹר Num. xxiv. 3, 15, לְמַעְיְנוֹ־מָיִם Ps. cxiv. 8. The purer form וּ I can discover only in a few compound nouns, e.g., פְּנוּאֵל, אֲחוּמַי, מְתוּשָׁאֵל, and מְתוּשֶׁלַח. The genitive termination is ִי, as in עַל־דִּבְרָתִי מַלְכִּי־צֶדֶק Ps. cx. 4, רַבָּתִי עָם Lament. i. 1, מְלֵאֲתִי מִשְׁפָּט Isaiah i. 21, בְּנִי אֲתֹנוֹ (acc.) Gen. xlix. 11. It appears also in many compound proper names, as מַלְכִּי־צֶדֶק, גַּבְרִיאֵל, חַנִּיאֵל, עָזְרִיאֵל.

All these three forms, no doubt, existed likewise in the Phoenician language, though the defective orthography of the monuments does not enable us to recognise them. In the inscription of Eshmûn'azar, for example [*C. I. S.*, No. 3, l. 11, 12], the words למט and למעל are no doubt to be pronounced לְמַטָּה and לְמַעְלָה, just as in Hebrew. In other cases the classical writers come to our aid. *Hannibal*, for instance, is חַנִּיבַעַל (genit.), but *Asdrubal* is עַזְרוּבַעַל (nomin.).

In Syriac we look in vain for any trace of these case-endings, save in two or three nouns regarding which I may be allowed to say a few words. I mean the words ܐܒ "father," ܐܚ "brother," and ܚܡܐ "father-in-law"; in Arabic, أَب, أَخ, حَم; in Hebrew, אָב, אָח, חָם. These have all lost their third radical, which was a *w*, and which reappears in Arabic in the construct state thus:—

N.	أَبُو	for	أَبَوُ
G.	أَبِي	for	أَبَوِ
A.	أَبَا	for	أَبَوَ

Of these three forms the Ethiopic has preserved before pronominal suffixes the nom. አቡ:, as አቡከ: "thy father," and the accus. አባ:, as አባከ: "thy father," though አቡከ: is also used for the accusative. The Hebrew has chosen the genitive for all its three cases, אֲבִי "father of —," אָבִיךָ; whereas the Syriac has preferred the nom., ܐܰܒܽܘܟ݂, and similarly ܐܰܚܽܘܟ݂ and ܚܰܡܽܘܟ݂.

Let us now return once more to the Arabic, and examine its three flexional forms, *ŭ*, *ĭ*, *ă*. What may the origin of these be? With regard to the accusative the answer seems to be tolerably certain. It is a pronominal element, of a demonstrative nature, appended to the object noun to indicate the direction of the action of the governing verb. It is in fact nothing but the demonstrative *hā*, with which we are already acquainted in all the Semitic languages. In Ethiopic the full form ሃ: is employed, as I already mentioned, to form the accusative of proper names. ቆየኒሃ: etc. The gradual weakening of the *h* gives us such adverbial forms as አፍአ: *af'ā*, or አፍአ: *af'a*, "out, outside" (*forās, foris*), ገሙራ: "at all, ever"; but ordinarily the particle is shortened to the utmost, and appears as final *ă*. The Hebrew ָה preserves somewhat of the original lengthening of the vowel, for a primitive short *ă* would certainly have disappeared *in toto*.

The origin of the nominative *ŭ* is more obscure; but we may possibly venture to see in it the pronominal element *hū*, as designating the subject. Finally, the genitive *ĭ*, ִי, may perhaps be connected with the termination of the so-called relative adjectives in ִי (Arabic ـِىٌّ, vulgarly ـِي), the origin of which is, however, not yet clear to me.

I said at the commencement of this discussion that the use of the singular terminations *ŭ*, *ĭ*, *ă* in Arabic was restricted to the defined noun, whether the definition was by the article or by a following genitive. I now remark that the undefined noun is inflected with the same terminations *plus* the sound of *n*, viz. *ŭn*, *ĭn*, *ăn*. E.g.

بَيْتٌ	بَيْتٍ	بَيْتًا
جَنَّةٌ	جَنَّةٍ	جَنَّةً

In the accus. form بَيْتًا the letter *'alif* may perhaps serve to mark the pausal pronunciation, *baitâ*, or it may be a mere indication of the *a*-sound, to distinguish this case more clearly in writing from the other two. This addition of the *n*-sound in Arabic is technically called the *tanwîn* or "nunation," from the name of the letter *nûn*.

If we look around us for a similar appearance in the other Semitic languages, we find its counterpart in the *mîmation* of the Assyrian, which is not, however, according to the grammarians, restricted to the undefined noun, but also irregularly used with that which is defined. The forms are usually written *uv*, *iv*, *av*, but as *v* and *m* are not distinguished in writing, we are justified by analogy in pronouncing them *um, im, am*.

The same *mîmation* is found in the Ḥimyaritic inscriptions of South Arabia in the form ם for all three cases, its use nearly corresponding with that of the Arabic *nûnation*; e.g., שמשם شَمْسٌ, אדנם أُذُنٌ, שנאם شَانِئٌ; כלבתם كَلْبَةٌ, עגלתם عِجْلَةٌ; עבדם عَبْدٌ, but עבד שמשם عَبْدُ شَمْسٍ.

In Hebrew the *mîmation* seems to me to present itself in such words as אָמְנָם or אָמְנָם, חִנָּם, רֵיקָם, which I consider as the accusatives of אָמֵן, חֵן and רֵיק. יוֹמָם is doubtful, as it may be connected with ܐܺܝܡܳܡ rather than with יוֹם. In Ethiopic we may perhaps find a trace of it in the word ትማልም፡, Heb. תְּמוֹל, אֶתְמוֹל.

Now what is the origin of these terminations *un, in, an*, and *um, im, am*? And are they identical, or different? These questions are hard to answer; but I incline on the whole to consider them as identical, and to derive them both from an appended, indefinite מָה, مَا. That *n* and *m* readily interchange is known to us; and it is quite conceivable that some of the Semitic languages may have substituted *n* for original *m* in certain grammatical forms, whilst others carried out the change through the whole of them. That the word מָה, مَا might have been used at an early period in the way suggested, can only be inferred from the recurrence of the phenomenon at a later period. History is apt to repeat itself, especially linguistic history. Now we find this use of مَا as an indefinite affix in Arabic in the so-called مَا ٱلْإِبْهَامِيَّة, i.e. مَا appended to an indefinite noun with a vague, often intensifying, force; e.g., أَعْطِنَا كِتَابًا مَا "give us some book (or other)"; قَلِيلٌ مَا "some (small) quantity"; جِئْتَ لِأَمْرٍ مَا "thou art come for some matter (of importance)." Similar is the origin of the Aramaic word מִדַּעַם, מינדאם, מִנְּדַע, מִידַּי, a contraction of מִדַּע מַה "scibile quid." For the rest, how readily مَا may be shortened into *mă* and *m* appears from such Arabic forms as كَمْ "how much?" عَلَامَ, حَتَّامَ, بِمَ, لِمَ, shortened into بِمْ, لِمْ.

We have thus far established the following scheme of inflexion by cases in the Semitic languages for the *singular* number.

	Arabic	Assyr., Ḥimyar., Hebrew
N.	*u, un*	*u, um*
G.	*i, in*	*i, im*
Acc.	*a, an*	*a, am*

Let us next examine the formation of the *plural*.

To express the idea of plurality in the inflexion of the noun the Semitic languages had recourse to the simple expedient of lengthening the vowel-ending of the singular. The lengthening of the sound, the dwelling upon the utterance, sufficed to convey the idea of indefinite number. Consequently in Arabic the undefined plural of masculine nouns must originally have been—

N. *ûn*, G. *în*, Acc. *ân*.

But as the Arabs seem to have objected to terminate a long syllable with a consonant (save in pause), a short final vowel was added, giving the forms—

N. *ûna*, G. *îna*, Acc. *âna*.

These forms were also employed in the plural when defined by the article; but in the construct state, as we should naturally expect, the final vowels of the singular were merely lengthened—

N. *û*, G. *î*, Acc. *â*.

In the actual language, however, as known to us from the old poets and the Ḳor'ān, the accusative *â*, *âna*, has become obsolete, so that we have in real use only two cases—

N. *û*, *ûna*; G. Acc. *î*, *îna*.

The vulgar dialects of the present day have gone yet one step farther, and have discarded the nominative from ordinary use, retaining only the form *în*. In Ethiopic, on the contrary, the accusative *ân* has supplanted the other cases, and forms the ordinary plural of adjectives and participles; as ሕያው፡ "alive," "living," ሕያዋን። ሐዲስ፡ "new," ሐዲሳን። ክሡት፡ "revealed," "manifest," ክሡታን። Forgetful however of the real origin of this form, the language forms for itself an accusative and a construct state by appending to it the vowel *â*, as in the singular; and the real construct plural in *â* is found only in the numerals for 20, 30, etc., which are ዕሥራ፡ ሠላሳ፡ አርብዓ፡ ኀምሳ፡ etc. In all this the Assyrian runs curiously parallel to the Ethiopic. According to Schrader, the plural in *ân* appears in the forms *ânu*, *âni*, *âna*, with an appended vowel (obviously borrowed from the singular); as *ṣalmânu*, "statues" (צֶלֶם, صَنَم); *ḥursâni*, "woods" (חֹרֶשׁ); *šûrâni*, "walls" (שׁוּר); *šarrâni*, "princes" (שַׂר); whilst the numerals, 20, 30, etc., are *'ĭšrâ*, *šilašâ*, *irbâ*, *ḫanšâ*.

The Aramaic dialects make use, not of the accusative, but of the other oblique form, the genitive, for their plural. Hence we find the forms ־ִין in the Biblical Aramaic, ـܝܢ in Syriac, and in Mandaitic both ־ין and ־יא (*î*).

The same choice was made by the Hebrews and Phoenicians. They discarded both the nom. *ûm* and the accus. *âm*, retaining only the gen. *îm* in ordinary use[1]. In later stages of the language the *m* was dropped, a form of which there are two or three doubtful examples in the Bible; but curiously enough

[1] But the Moabites took the form ־ִן, e.g., המלכן. ארבען שת. גברן. חמת הישרן. etc.

this form in *ī* is said to be not uncommon in Assyrian, as in *ilī*, "gods"; *malkī* or *malikī*, "kings"; *ūmī*, "days"; *pagrī*, "dead bodies"; with suffixes *karḫīšu* "its towers"; *ašrī-šunu*, "their places." The full form in *īm* is rare and archaistic, as in the proper names *Ašur-rīš-ilīm*, *Sumīrīm* and *Akkadīm*. Haupt finds traces of the form *ām*, representing the old accusative, in the Assyrian *šamāmu*, *šamāmi*, "heaven," *māmi*, "water," and the adverbial *akhāmiš*, "with one another, mutually (*lit.* like brothers)." It seems probable, as he suggests, that the plural *ān* is only a later form of this *ām*. And indeed he goes so far as to deny the existence of the termination *ī*, which he pronounces *ē*, and considers to be only a deflection of *ā*, from *ān*, *ām*.

You must not suppose that there is anything singular in this apparently capricious choice of a single case-ending to take the place of all its fellows, in the later stages of a language. It is precisely what has happened elsewhere than on Semitic ground. I need hardly remind you that Greek nouns appear in Syriac mostly in the *accusative*, simply because that was the one form with which the Syrians were familiar in the mouths of the Greeks; e.g. ܠܡܦܐܕܐ (*λαμπάδα*), ܩܪܩܝܕܐ (*κερκίδα*), ܐܢܕܪܝܐܢܛܐ (*ἀνδριάντα*), ܐܪܟܣ (*ἀρχάς*), etc. The Latin *accusative* too has supplied the ordinary nominal forms of the different Romance languages. In modern Persian the plural ان *ān* is regarded by the best authorities as derived from an ancient *genitive* in *ām* (*añm*).

Turning to the plural of *feminine* nouns, we find the same principle in force, only applied in a different way. The weight of utterance was thrown in this case not upon the case-endings, but upon the feminine termination *ăt*, which accordingly became *āt*, and took the case-endings as the singular.

Sing.	N.	*atu, atun*	Plur.	*ātu, ātun*
	G.	*ati, atin*		*āti, ātin*
	Ac.	*ata, atan*		*āta, ātan.*

In Arabic these forms are all in common use, except the accusative plural, which has disappeared even in the oldest stages of the language. The Ethiopic has *āt*, with its accusative and construct *āta*. In Aramaic we find, as we should naturally expect, the termination ָת, ܵܬ݂, *âth, ôth*; in Hebrew, with the usual vowel-change, וֹת, which sinks in the later Phoenician into *ûth*, as in Plautus's *yth alonim valonuth.* In Assyrian *âtu, âti, âta*, are common; but there is also (if the grammarians may be trusted) a termination *ût*, corresponding perhaps to the Hebrew and Phoenician *ôth, ûth*; and a third form in *ît* (or as Haupt pronounces it *ēt*), restricted to such words as have already weakened *at* into *it* in the singular. E.g., *ina šanâti dannâti*, "in long (*lit.* strong) years"; *tabbanûtu*, "buildings," from *tabbanu*; *'ibšîti*, "deeds," from *'ibšit* (עבשת), according to Haupt *ēpšētī*; *išrîti* (*ēšrēti*) "temples."

Of the so-called *broken plurals* of the Arabic I cannot speak at any length in this place. You will find these various forms enumerated in any Arabic Grammar, and many of them occur likewise in Ḥimyaritic and Ethiopic. In the northern dialects examples are either wanting or of rare occurrence. Böttcher has endeavoured to point out several in Hebrew; see his *Ausführliches Lehrbuch*, vol. i. p. 458–9. In Syriac we may perhaps refer to this class such words as ܩܘܼܪ̈ܝܵܐ from ܩܪܝܼܬ݂ܵܐ (Arabic قَرْيَة, plur. قُرًى), and ܚܡܵܪ̈ܵܐ from ܚܡܵܪܵܐ (Arabic حِمَار, plur. حُمْر). These so-called broken plurals are, however, in all probability without exception, singular abstract forms, which gradually came to be used in a concrete and collective sense, and hence pass for plurals. We are told, for example, that نَصْر is a plural of نَاصِر, "helper," or عَدْل of عَادِل, "just"; but in reality these are nothing but the infinitives of نَصَرَ and عَدَلَ, meaning "help," and "justice," and may be applied alike to one or more, man or woman; for we can say رَجُلٌ عَدْلٌ, اِمْرَأَةٌ عَدْلٌ, and قَوْمٌ عَدْلٌ. Another plural of قَاتِل, viz. قُتَّال, is an example of the same sort, being really an intensive infinitive, to be compared with the Syriac ܩܘܼܛܠܵܬ݂ܵܐ, ܩܘܼܛܵܠܵܐ, ܢܘܼܗܪܵܐ, etc.

In addition to the singular and plural, the Semitic languages employed from their earliest period a third form to designate a pair or two of any objects. The principle of formation of this *dual* would naturally resemble that of the plural; that is to say, the vowel of the singular would be lengthened in some way, so as to indicate the increase of number. But as the simple lengthening was appropriated to the plural, in the case of the dual recourse was had to the heightening of the singular terminations by the insertion of a short *ă*. Hence result the forms—

N. *ă* + *ŭn* = *aun*
G. *ă* + *ĭn* = *ain*
Ac. *ă* + *ăn* = *ân*.

For the same reason as in the plural, the Arabs added here also a final vowel; but on account of the greater weight of the dual endings, or perhaps merely for the sake of variety, they selected in this case the weaker vowel *ĭ*; whence the forms

N. *auni* G. *aini* Ac. *âni*.

These forms were used, like the corresponding plurals, when the noun was defined by the article; but in the construct state the syllable *ni* is of course absent, and we have merely the vowel-endings

N. *au* G. *ai* Ac. *â*.

Of these terminations the nominative must have fallen into disuse at a very early period, and its place was usurped by the accus.; so that we actually meet in Arabic only the two forms

N. *â*, *âni*
G. Ac. *ai*, *aini*.

In modern Arabic the first of these has now disappeared from ordinary use, leaving only the form *ain*, *ên*, for all the cases. In S. Arabian or Ḥimyaritic the termination is also ן, as צלמן ואבלנהן (acc.), ולביתנהן "and their two houses (castles)," מאתן אסדם "two hundred warriors" (nom.), צמלנהן "these two statues" (acc.). In Ethiopic scarcely a trace of the dual can be detected. In Assyrian Schrader gives as examples *idâ*, "two hands"; *uznâ*, "two ears"; *šipa-ai* (for *šipâ-ya*), "my feet"; *birka-ai*, "my knees"; *ḳata-ai*, "my hands." Here the final *n* seems to have been cast off, according to the analogy of the plural in *î* for *îm*.

The Aramaic form is ַ־ֵין, with slight supplemental vowel, for ַ־ְין *ain*, corresponding to the ordinary Arabic oblique form ـَيْنِ، ـَيْنِ. This was contracted into ָ־ן, as in מָאתָן for מָאתַיִן, "two hundred"; or into ֵ־ין, as in תְּרֵין for תְּרַיִן, "two." In Syriac it survives in only two or three words, in the form *ên*, viz. ܬܪܶܝܢ, f. ܬܰܪܬܶܝܢ, ܡܳܐܬܶܝܢ, and ܬܪܶܝܢ; further weakened into *în*, in ܦܰܕܰܢ ܢܰܗܪܺܝܢ, "Mesopotamia," ܐܝܟ ܦܕܢܐ ܡܐܬܝܢ ܙܪܥܐ (1 Kings xviii. 32), Heb. כְּבֵית סָאתַיִם זֶרַע, and even ܐܝܕܝܢ = יָדַיִם, ܐܦܝܢ = אַפַּיִם; just as in Latin the sole representatives of the dual are the words *ambo*, *duo*, and *octo*. The Hebrew form is ַ־ִים, for ַ־ְים *aim*, with *m* for *n*, as in the plural; e.g., יוֹמַיִם, שְׁנָתַיִם, כִּכָּרַיִם, מָאתַיִם, אַלְפַּיִם; and often in proper names, as הָעֵינַיִם, חֲפָרַיִם, חֹרֹנַיִם, קִרְיָתַיִם, עֵין עֶגְלַיִם, בֵּית דִּבְלָתַיִם. Rarer forms are the contracted ָ־ם, as הָעֵינָם (Josh. xv. 34), קִרְיָתָמָה (Ezek. xxv. 9, *kethîbh*); and ֵ־ים in שְׁנֵים עָשָׂר, f. שְׁתֵּים עֶשְׂרֵה. Further, ַ־ִן, contracted ָ־ן; e.g. דֹּתַיִן, דֹּתָן, and קַרְתָּן (Josh. xxi. 32). On the Moabite stone both forms appear, ם and ן; e.g., הצהרם (הַצָּהֳרַיִם), l. 15, but מאתן, בית דבלתן, קריתן, חורנן.

And here I may intercalate the remark that the words מַיִם and שָׁמַיִם are not duals, but plurals, from obsolete singulars מַי and שָׁמַי. The original forms must have been *mayîm* and *shamayîm*, which were contracted into *maym* and *shamaym*, just as in Arabic خَيِّير، لَيِّين، مَوِيت، and هَوِين، gradually pass into خَيْر، لَيْن، مَيْت، and هَيْن. But since forms like *maym* and *shamaym* were intolerable to the ear of the later Hebrews, a short vowel was inserted to lighten the pronunciation, resulting in the forms מַיִם and שָׁמַיִם, the latter of which was pronounced in Phoenician *shamêm*, as in Plautus's *gune balsamem*, i.e., גאוני בעל שמים.

I shall conclude this survey of the declension of the noun with a few remarks on some forms which we have not as yet noticed.

(1) The construct state of the dual and plural in Hebrew and Aramaic, viz., ֵי, ܝ̈.

In Arabic the forms of the dual in actual use are, as we have seen,

Simple,	N. *âni*,	Construct,	*â*
	G. Ac. *aini*		*ai*

and of the plural,

Simple,	N. *ûna*	Construct,	*û*
	G. Ac. *îna*		*î*.

In Assyrian in like manner the construct dual ended in *â*, as *birka-ai* (for *birkâ-ya*), "my knees"; the plural in *î* [or *ê*], as *šarrî-šunu*, "their kings." Consequently we should expect the Hebrew and Aramaic dual to have the construct form *ai*, *ê*, but the plural in both languages *î*; יְדֵיהֶם, ܐܝ̈ܕܝܗܘܢ, from יָדַיִם, ܐܝ̈ܕܝܢ; but from מְלָכִים, ܡܠܟ̈ܝܢ, we should look for מַלְכִּיהֶם, ܡܠܟ̈ܝܗܘܢ, which however do not exist. The actually existing forms are מַלְכֵיהֶם, ܡܠܟ̈ܝܗܘܢ; and these can, I think, be explained only on the supposition that the dual forms have supplanted those of the plural number. I find additional evidence for this notion in the forms מְלָכַי, ܡܠܟ̈ܝ, "my kings," for *malakai-ya*, corresponding with יָדַי, "my hands," for *yadai-ya*; and מְלָכָיו, מַלְכוֹהִי, ܡܠܟ̈ܘܗܝ, "his kings," corresponding with יָדָיו, ܐܝ̈ܕܘܗܝ, standing for *malakai-hû*, *yadai-hû*, and *malakau-hû*, *yadau-hû*, in which latter I descry a vestige of the long obsolete nominative dual in *aun*, construct *au*.

(2) The form ܵܢ, ـن, used as the simple plural of feminine nouns in Aramaic; e.g., ܩܛܠܢ, ܡܕܝܢܢ, as contrasted with the construct ܩܛܠܬ, ܡܕܝܢܬ, which correspond with the Arabic plural in *ât* and the Hebrew in *ôth*. This form in *ân*, *ôn*, which also plays an important rôle in the verbal inflection, I regard as a variation of the masculine *ûn*, under the influence of the ordinary fem. *ât*. The language felt the want of an additional feminine termination in the plural, and framed it from existing material after the analogy of an established form.

(3) The so-called *status emphaticus* of the Aramaic; גַּבְרָא "the man," גַּבְרַיָּא; מְדִינְתָּא "the city," מְדִינָתָא. The essence of this form is the postposition of a demonstrative particle. The Swedes and Danes say *mand-en*, "the man," *hus-et*, "the house," where *en* and *et* are corruptions of *inn* or *hinn* and *itt* or *hitt*. And just so the Aramean added to his noun in its simplest form the demonstrative *hâ*, gradually weakened into *â*. גְּבַר + הָא became גַּבְרָא; מְדִינָת + הָא, מְדִינָתָא. Other forms underwent greater alteration. מְדִינַת + הָא was contracted into מְדִינְתָּא (instead of מְדִינְתָּא). גַּבְרַיָּא, on the other hand, is another example of the transference of a dual form to the plural, since it arises by assimilation from גַּבְרַי + הָא. In Syriac and Mandaitic the termination ـַיָּא is shortened into ܹܐ, ـיא (*ê*), though the full form is retained in some cases; for example, in Syriac, in the plural of many words derived from radicals ל״א, and in a few other instances, such as ܐܠܦܝܐ, "thousands." This contraction naturally commenced with a weakening of the final syllable into *ê*, as in ܗܟܢ for הָדָא, הֵא as interjection for הָא, and the like.

Having thus treated briefly of the personal pronouns and of the noun, I must next speak of the pronouns as they appear when appended to nouns substantive in the form of genitive suffixes. In doing so I shall confine myself chiefly to Arabic, Hebrew and Aramaic, as represented by Biblical Aramaic, the Targūms and the old Syriac.

In classical Arabic these suffixes are appended to the different cases of the noun in the construct form, i. e. without the tanwīn or nūnation. E. g.

2. كِتَابُكَ f. كِتَابُكِ, "thy book" (nom.)

كِتَابَكَ f. كِتَابَكِ, "thy book" (acc.)

كِتَابِكَ f. كِتَابِكِ, "of thy book" (gen.)

3. كِتَابُهُ f. كِتَابُهَا, "his, her book" (nom.)

كِتَابَهُ f. كِتَابَهَا, "his, her book" (acc.)

كِتَابِهِ f. كِتَابِهَا, "of his, her book" (gen.)

and so on. Only the suffix of the 1st pers. sing. absorbs the vowels of the case-endings, so that "my book," "of my book," is كِتَابِي or كِتَابِيَ in all the three cases.

The forms of the spoken Arabic of the present day are such as we should naturally expect, when we take into account the loss of the case-terminations and other final vowels. "My book" is كِتَابِي, "my father" أَبِي or أَبُوي; "thy father" is أَبُوك, fem. أَبُوكِ or أَبُوكِي. But the final vowel of the fem. pronoun also disappears in most cases, and the difference of gender is marked by a transposition, as it were, of the final vowels; instead of كِتَابَكْ and كِتَابِكْ we have كِتَابَكْ *kitābak* and كِتَابِكْ *kitābik*. The 3rd pers. sing. masc. is properly *kitāb-hu*, كِتَابُهُ, but this is almost always written and pronounced كِتَابُهْ *kitābuh* or *kitāboh*, or else كتابُو *kitābō*. The fem. is كِتابَها *kitāb-hā*, more commonly with shortening of the vowel, *kitab-hā*. From أب the corresponding forms would be أبُوهُ *abūh* and أبُوها *abū-hā*. The plurals are كِتابنا, كِتابكُم and كِتابهُم; the fem. forms كِتابكُنّ and كِتابهُنّ being very rarely used. The long vowel is either shortened in pronunciation, *kitab-nā, kitab-hum*, or a slight vowel (*shĕvā*) is interposed, *kitābŭkum*. Should the noun end in two consonants, as عبد *'abd*, this *shĕvā* is necessarily inserted, *'abdăhā* or *'abdĭhā, 'abdŭkum, 'abdŭhum, 'abdĭnā*.

Let us now take a Hebrew and Aramaic noun with its suffixes, and examine them by the light we receive from the Arabic, ancient and modern. For example, מֶלֶךְ, corresponding to the Arabic مَلْكٌ, مَلِك, and the Aramaic ܡܠܟܐ.

1st pers. sing. in old Arabic مَلْكِي or مَلِكِي, vulg. مَلِكِي; Hebrew מַלְכִּי; Chald. also מַלְכִּי, Syr. ܡܠܟܝ, dropping the final vowel.

2nd pers. sing. masc. Arabic مَلْكُكَ, vulg. مَلْكَك. The Hebrew form is מַלְכְּךָ, in pause מַלְכֶּךָ, with a trace of the original case-endings in the moveable *shĕvā* and the *sĕgōl*. The Aramaic forms are, Chald. מַלְכָּךְ, Syr. ܡܠܟܟ, with long *ā, ō*, whereas we should have expected *a* short. Probably *mal-kākh* stands for *malkă-ăkh*, and that for *malka-ka*, the old accusative with suffix.

2nd pers. sing. fem. Arabic مَلْكُكِ, vulg. مَلْكِك. In Hebrew the usual form is ךְ◌ֵ, e.g. מַלְכֵּךְ, which may be either merely tone-lengthening of *malk-ik*, or may spring from the coalition of the two vowels in *malkă-ik*. In Aramaic two forms are found, כִי ַ and ךְ ָ. The Syrian writes ܡܰܠܟܶܟܝ, but does not pronounce the final *ī*. The *ī* in these forms is apparently tone-lengthening of the old genitive termination, *maliki-ki*, which must have received the accent, like the corresponding Ethiopic forms *nĕgŭsē-kī*, acc. *nĕgŭsá-kī*. Hebrew parallels are רָעָתֵכִי, Jerem. xi. 15; עֲוֹנֵכִי, Ps. ciii. 3.

3rd pers. sing. masc. Ar. مَلِكُهُ, gen. مَلِكِهِ; vulg. مَلِكُه، مَلْكُو. The Hebrew forms very nearly resemble those of the vulgar Arabic, viz. מַלְכֹּה, generally מַלְכּוֹ. These seem to find their origin in the old accus. *malka-hu*, with elision of the *h*, *malka-u*. Quite different is the Aramaic הּ ֵ, as in ܡܰܠܟܶܗ, which I trace to the ancient genitive *malki-hu* or *malki-hi*. Parallel forms to this in Hebrew are לְמִינֵהוּ, Gen. i. 21; אוֹרֵהוּ, Job xxv. 3. Instead of הּ ֵ we occasionally find in Aramaic א ֵ, the *h* having apparently become silent; and this form appears in the Phoen. suffix א, more commonly written י, as in קלא and בני. Hebrew forms like אָבִיו (*abhīu*), פִּיו (*pīu*), also spring from the old genitive, with elision of the *h*, for אָבִיהוּ, פִּיהוּ, which likewise occur.

3rd pers. sing. fem. Ar. مَلِكُهَا, vulg. مَلِكْهَا. In Hebrew we have הָ, as in אָבִיהָ, but more commonly הּ ָ, agreeing with the Aramaic הּ ָ (הּ ַ), ܗ̇ ܳ, as in מַלְכָּהּ, ܡܰܠܟܳܗ̇, which we may derive from *malkă-āh*, for *malkă-hā*.

1st pers. plur. Ar. مَلِكُنَا, vulg. مَلِكْنَا. In Hebrew מַלְכֵּנוּ, from the old genitive *malki-nū*. The rare forms with נוּ ָ, such as קִימָנוּ "our adversary," Job xxii. 20, מֹדַעְתָּנוּ, Ruth iii. 2, may perhaps represent the old accus. *malka-nū*. They stand therefore nearer to the Aramaic ־ָנָא, ـَنَا, as מַלְכָּנָא (ﺍﻮ), ܡܰܠܟܰܢ. The Jewish Aramaic form has a tone-long vowel in the penult owing to the accent, (as in the Ethiopic *nĕgūsá-na*). The Syriac has lost the final vowel of the pronoun, under the influence of the same accentuation (compare ܚܢܰܢ for ܚܢܰܢܳܐ, ܚܢܰܢ ܐܢܳܐ.

2nd pers. plur. masc. Ar. مَلِكُكُمْ, vulg. مَلِكْكُم. Hebr. מַלְכְּכֶם, probably from the old accus. *malka-kum*; Aramaic similarly ܡܰܠܟܟ݂ܽܘܢ, with a purer form of the suffix.

2nd pers. plur. fem. Ar. مَلِكُكُنَّ, vulg. مَلِكْكُن. Hebr. מַלְכְּכֶן, Aram. ܡܰܠܟܟ݂ܶܝܢ, probably from the old accus. *malka-kunna*.

3rd pers. plur. masc. Ar. مَلِكُهُمْ, مَلِكُهُمُو; مَلِكِهِمْ, مَلِكِهِمُو; vulg. مَلِكْهُم. In Hebrew the simplest form of the suffix is *hĕm* for *hum*, as in פִּיהֶם, אֲבִיהֶם, really old genitives. Most of the forms in use, however, are to be explained from an old accus., such as I descry in the rare form כֻּלָּהֵם, 2 Sam. xxiii. 6, in pause for *kulla-hĕm*; whence, by elision of the *h* and contraction, arises the common כֻּלָּם. A still fuller form is represented by the suffixes ־ָמוֹ, מוֹ, as in חֶלְבָּמוֹ, עָזְמוֹ, פְּרִימוֹ, פִּימוֹ, contracted from *ḥĕlba-hĕmū*, etc. מַלְכָּם stands therefore for original *malka-humū*. The Aramaic forms need no further explanation, ܡܰܠܟܗܽܘܢ, etc.

3rd pers. plur. fem. Ar. مَلِكُهُنَّ, مَلِكِهِنَّ, vulg. مَلِكْهُن. Here again the oldest Hebrew form is the rare ־ָהֵנָּה; as in לְכֻלָּהֵנָּה, 1 Kings vii. 37, בְּתוֹכְהֵנָּה, Ezek. xvi. 53, for *kulla-hĕnna* and *tōkha-hĕnna.* Contracted from this are the forms in ־ָ֫נָה and ־ֶ֫נָה, as קִרְבֶּ֫נָה, לְבַדֶּ֫נָה, כֻּלֶּ֫נָה, כָּאֵ֫נָה, לְדָתֶ֫נָה. Still shorter is the common הֶן, as in חֶלְבְּהֶן, לְבַדְּהֶן, and ־ֶן, as in לְבֶּן. The successive Hebrew forms appear then to have been *malka-hĕnna, malka-hĕn*, contracted *malkāhĕna, malkāna, malkān.* The Aramaic form ܡܰܠܟܰܝܗܶܝܢ calls for no further remark.

In the dual number the Arabic appends the suffixes to the construct forms in *ā* and *ai*; in the plural, to those in *ū* and *ī*; as

Dual nom. عَبْدَايَ "my two servants," عَبْدَاكَ, etc.

gen. عَبْدَيَّ, عَبْدَيْكَ, etc.

Plur. nom. بَنُوهُ "his sons," بَنُوكَ, etc.

gen. بَنِيهِ, بَنِيكَ, etc.

But "my sons" is expressed by بَنِيَّ for both nom. بَنُويَ and gen. بَنِيَ. In Hebrew and Aramaic this difference between the dual and plur. has disappeared; because, as it seems to me, the dual terminations in the suffixes have wholly supplanted the plural. The Assyrian said *šipa-ai* "my two feet" [Del. *šepāa*], *birka-ai* "my knees," *ḳata-ai*, "my hands," for *šipā-ya, birkā-ya, ḳatā-ya*, just as the Arab said رِجْلَايَ, رُكْبَتَايَ, يَدَايَ; but the Assyrian had also the plural forms *šarrī-šunu* [*šarrē-šunu*], "their kings," *ašrī-šunu* [*ašrē-šunu*], "their places." The Hebrew on the other hand used only one form for both numbers. יָדַ֫יִם for *yadaim* (Arab. يَدَيْنِ, vulg. يَدَيْنْ) would naturally give in the construct form *yadai* (Ar. يَدَيْ), which became יְדֵי; but קֹטְלִים for *ḳātilīm* (Ar. قَاتِلِينَ, vulg. قَاتِلِينْ) should equally yield קֹטְלֵי

= Ar. قَاتِلِيَّ. As a matter of fact, however, it is not so. The forms in use are קֹטְלַי, מַלְכַּי, which I maintain to be strictly speaking duals, standing for *ḳāṭilai* and *malakai*. Herewith all the forms of the Hebrew and Aramaic become intelligible.

1st pers. sing. Arab. يَدَيَّ، مَلَكَيَّ. Heb. יָדַי, מְלָכַי stand for *yadai-ya* and *malakai-ya*; but the language has dropped the final vowel, and with it the doubling of the final *y*. Similarly in Aramaic, מַלְכַּי, ܡܰܠܟܰܝ.

2nd pers. sing. Arab. يَدَيْكَ، مَلَكَيْكَ. Heb. יָדֶיךָ and יָדַיִךְ for *yadai-ka* and *yadai-ki*, shortened *yadai-k*, מְלָכֶיךָ for *malakai-ka*. The fuller form of the fem. also occurs, e.g. חַיָּיְכִי and נְעוּרָיְכִי in Ps. ciii., for חַיַּיִךְ and נְעוּרָיִךְ. This leads us to the Syriac forms ܡܰܠܟܰܝܟ and ܡܰܠܟܰܝܟܝ, with silent *yūd*. In Biblical Aramaic the diphthong has been weakened into *ā*, just as in Hebrew אַיִן became אָן, or in Aramaic itself מָאתַיִן became מָאתָן. Hence the masc. מלכיך, for *malkai-ka*, is according to the *ḳ'rē* to be pronounced מַלְכָךְ; whereas the fem. is usually pointed מַלְכַּיִךְ [in the Targums], though מַלְכָךְ is also found.

3rd pers. sing. masc. Arab. يَدَيْهِ، مَلَكَيْهِ (for ـهُ). In Hebrew the fullest form is יָדֵיהוּ, עֵינֵיהוּ, גְּבוּרֵיהוּ, for *yadai-hu*, etc., with weakening of *ai* to *ē*. The more common form, however, is יָדָיו, מְלָכָיו, with elision of the *h* and weakening of *ai* to *ā*. We also find a form without *yud*, as דְּבָרָו; and the question arises whether this is identical with דְּבָרָיו, or not. If identical, then דְּבָרָו is only incorrectly written, according to ear, for דְּבָרָיו. But it may also be that דְּבָרָו stands for the old nominative dual דְּבָרָוְהִי *dabarau-hu*, by elision of the *h*, *dabarau-u*, and then *dabarau*, דְּבָרָו; just as the 1st pers. *dabarai-ya* became *dabarai*, דְּבָרַי. Such at any rate must be the origin of the Aramaic forms מַלְכוֹהִי, ܡܰܠܟ݁ܰܘܗ݈ܝ, the latter with silent ܘܗܝ, for *malkau-hu*. The form מַלְכוֹי, with elision of the ה, also occurs; and this appears to be the Phoenician form in such phrases as בְּעַגְל אַשְׁ קַרְנֵי לֵם, כִּ שָׁמַע כָּל־דְּבָרַי, though we may perhaps also read דְּבָרַי and קַרְנָי, in closer accordance with the Hebrew forms.

3rd sing. fem. Arab. يَدَيْهَا, مَلَكَيْهَا; Heb. יָדֶיהָ, מְלָכֶיהָ, for *yadai-hā*, *malakai-hā*. The corresponding Aramaic forms are, מַלְכָּהָא (rarely מַלְכֵּיהָא), Biblical, מלכיה, *k'rē* מַלְכַּהּ; Syriac ܡܰܠܟ݁ܶܝܗ̇, both standing for *malkai-hā*.

1st pers. plur. Arab. يَدَيْنَا, مَلَكَيْنَا. Heb. יָדֵינוּ, מְלָכֵינוּ, for *yadai-nū*, *malakai-nū*. Aramaic, מַלְכָּנָא (*k'rē*, מַלְכַּנָא), ܡܰܠܟ݁ܰܝܢ, for *malkai-nā*.

2nd pers. plur. masc. Arab. يَدَيْكُمْ, مَلَكَيْكُمْ. Heb. יְדֵיכֶם, מַלְכֵיכֶם, for *yadai-kum*, *malakai-kum*. Aramaic ܡܰܠܟ݁ܰܝܟ݁ܽܘܢ, מַלְכֵיכוֹן.—The corresponding *fem.* forms are: Arab. يَدَيْكُنَّ, Heb. יְדֵיכֶן, Aram. ܡܰܠܟ݁ܰܝܟ݁ܶܝܢ. The fuller form כֶנָה is found in Hebrew in Ezekiel xiii. 20, כִּסְּתוֹתֵיכֶנָה ("pillows").

3rd pers. plur. masc. Arab. يَدَيْهِمْ, مَلَكَيْهِمْ, shortened from يَدَيْهُمْ, مَلَكَيْهُمْ. In Hebrew the oldest form was of course *yadai-humū*, *malakai-humū*. Hence, on the one hand, the ordinary

יְדֵיהֶם, מַלְכֵיהֶם; and, on the other, the more poetic שִׁנֵּימוֹ, זִבְחֵימוֹ. Archaistic is the form in Ezekiel xl. 16, אֵלֵיהֵמָּה, from אַיִל as an architectural term. The Aramaic forms are ܡܰܠܟܰܝܗܘܢ, מַלְכֵיהוֹן.—The corresponding *fem.* is in Arab. يَدَيْهِنَّ; Heb. יְדֵיהֶן, מַלְכֵיהֶן; Aram. ܡܰܠܟܰܝܗܶܝܢ, מַלְכֵיהֵן. Ezekiel indulges in the archaistic form גְּוִיֹּתֵיהֶנָה, ch. i. 11.

As to the forms of feminine nouns with pronominal suffixes, I would merely call your attention at this time to one point in which Hebrew differs most markedly from Arabic and Syriac. The Arab adds the simple suffixes to the plural substantive, for example, جَنَّاتِي, جَنَّاتُكَ, جَنَّاتُهُ, جَنَّاتُهُمْ. So also the Syrian: ܡܕ̈ܝܢܳܬܝ, ܡܕ̈ܝܢܳܬܟ, ܡܕ̈ܝܢܳܬܗ, ܡܕ̈ܝܢܳܬܗܘܢ. But the Hebrew almost invariably employs what is really an incorrect form. He does not say חֻקּוֹתִי, חֻקּוֹתְךָ, חֻקּוֹתוֹ, etc., but he adds to the plural חֻקּוֹת the dual termination *ē*, borrowed from the masc., before appending the suffixes, and thus obtains the forms חֻקּוֹתַי, חֻקּוֹתֶיךָ, חֻקּוֹתָיו. Almost the only exception is in the forms of the 3rd pers. plur., where we find חֻקּוֹתָם as well as חֻקּוֹתֵיהֶם.

CHAPTER VIII.

THE VERB.

I NEXT proceed to treat of the *Verb*, in doing which I must direct your attention first, for reasons which will gradually become apparent, to certain *nominal* forms, partly adjectives and partly substantives.

Among the commonest nominal forms in the Semitic languages are those which I may represent by the types *ḳatal*, *ḳatil* and *ḳatul*, especially as concrete substantives and as adjectives. It is in the latter function that we notice them here. Examples of the form *ḳatal* in Arabic are تَبَعٌ "following," "a follower," بَطَلٌ "brave," حَسَنٌ "handsome"; in Hebrew, חָכָם "wise," יָשָׁר "upright," רָשָׁע "wicked." The form *ḳatil* may be exemplified in the one language by بَطِرٌ "proud," دَنِسٌ "dirty," عَجِلٌ "quick"; in the other, by כָּבֵד "heavy," זָקֵן "old," טָמֵא "unclean." As instances of the form *ḳatul* I will cite in Arabic فَطُنٌ "clever," يَقُظٌ "awake," حَذُرٌ "timid"; in Hebrew, יָגֹר "afraid," קָטֹן "small," גָּבֹהַּ "high."

In seeking to modify these simple forms, so as to make them express greater extension or greater energy, the Semites adopted one of two methods; they either *lengthened a vowel*, or they *doubled a consonant*. The former process might affect either the first or second vowel; the latter affected chiefly the middle consonant.

The heightening of the first vowel of *ḳatal* would yield the form *ḳâtal*, which is of comparatively rare occurrence, as in طابَع and خاتَم, "a stamp," "a seal," Heb. חוֹתָם, and in the participles of Hebrew verbs ל״ה, as חוֹזֶה for חוֹזַי (i.e. *ḥâzai*). The vowel of the second syllable has generally been weakened into *i*, thus rendering it indistinguishable from the heightening of *ḳatil*, viz. *ḳâtil*. Hence, in the words just cited, the forms طابِع, خاتِم, as well as the great bulk of the participles of the form قاتِل, Heb. קוֹטֵל. Here the lengthening of the first vowel seems to express the continuity or duration of the action.

The heightening of the 2nd vowel yields us the common intensives of the form *ḳatâl*, *ḳatîl* and *ḳatûl*. (1) *Ḳatâl*, as in Arabic شَجَاع "brave," جَبَان "cowardly," كَهَام "blunt"; Heb. גָּדוֹל "great," עָשׁוֹק "an oppressor," קָדוֹשׁ "holy." (2) *Ḳatîl*, as in Arabic رَحِيم "merciful," كَرِيم "noble," ثَقِيل "heavy"; جَرِيح "wounded," قَتِيل "slain," أَسِير "bound, a prisoner"; Heb. נָבִיא "a prophet," חָסִיד "gracious, pious"; אָסִיר "bound, a prisoner," מָשִׁיחַ "anointed." (3) *Ḳatûl*, as in Arabic أَكُول "gluttonous," كَذُوب "lying," جَسُور "daring"; Heb. עָצוּם "strong," חָרוּץ "sharp," נָחוּשׁ "brazen," and the ordinary participle passive קָטוּל.

The Aramaic furnishes us with an example of the heightening of *both* vowels in the form *ḳâtôl*, as כָּרוֹזָא, ܟܳܪܽܘܙܳܐ; נָטוֹרָא, ܢܳܛܽܘܪܳܐ.

The doubling of the 2nd consonant appears in Hebrew in the common form *ḳattal*, intensive of *ḳatal*; e.g. גַּנָּב "thief," טַבָּח "cook," "executioner," חָרָשׁ "cutter," קַנָּא "jealous," and with weakening of the first vowel in the shut syllable אִכָּר "husbandman." Also in the form *ḳattil*, intensive of *ḳatil*, with weakening of the 1st vowel to *i* in the shut syllable and tone-lengthening of the 2nd into *ē*, *ḳittēl*, as גִּבֵּן "humpbacked," עִוֵּר "blind," פִּקֵּחַ "openeyed, seeing," חֵרֵשׁ "deaf."

The intensives of the first grade, *ḳatâl*, *ḳatîl*, and *ḳatûl*, are all capable of being heightened in the same way, thus yielding the forms *ḳattâl*, *ḳattîl*, and *ḳattûl*. (1) *Kattâl* is very common in Arabic and Aramaic, e.g. طَبَّاخ, نَجَّار, صَيَّاد, ܚܰܛܳܦܳܐ, ܢܰܓܳܪܳܐ, ܩܰܛܳܠܳܐ. In Hebrew we find קַנּוֹא "jealous," with *ô* for *â*, but more usually the vowel of the 1st syllable is weakened into *i*, e.g. גִּבּוֹר = ܓܰܢܳܒܳܐ, جَبَّار, שִׁכּוֹר "drunken," יִסּוֹר "one who reprehends" or "finds fault" (Job xl. 2 or xxxix. 32). (2) *Kattîl* is very common in Hebrew and Aramaic, e.g. אַבִּיר "strong," צַדִּיק "just," עַלִּיז "exulting," "rejoicing," עָרִיץ "oppressor," "tyrant," אַסִּיר "bound"; ܚܰܟܺܝܡܳܐ "wise," ܙܰܕܺܝܩܳܐ "just," ܚܰܬܺܝܬܳܐ "exact." In Arabic the first vowel is weakened into *i*, e.g. سِكِّير "drunken," صِدِّيق "very truthful," عِرِّيض "very fond of meddling." (3) *Kattûl*, as Heb. רַחוּם "merciful," חַנּוּן "gracious," שַׁכּוּל "deprived, bereft of young," אַלּוּף "tame, domesticated, intimate"; Arab. فَرُّوق "very timid," قَيُّوم "abiding, everlasting," قَدُّوس "most holy." In Arabic the vowel of the 1st syllable is sometimes assimilated to that of the 2nd, as قُدُّوس, سُبُّوح or سُبُّوح "all pure" or "all glorious."

Another important class of nouns in the Semitic languages is the so-called *Segolates*, of which the normal form is *ḳatl*, *ḳitl*, *ḳutl*, still retained in Arabic, e.g. أَرْض "earth," عِجْل "calf," أُذْن "ear." They are also used as adjectives, e.g. صَعْب "difficult," عَذْب "sweet"; طِفْل "small, young," جِلّ "large, coarse"; صُلْب "hard," حُلْو "sweet," مُرّ "bitter." The corresponding Aramaic forms are *ḳ'tal, ḳ'til, ḳ'tul,* with transposition of the vowels, which however resume their normal place in the emphatic state, e.g. ܥܒܕ ܥܒ̈ܕܐ, ܟܢܫ ܟܢܫܐ, ܟܡܘܪ ܟܘܡܪܐ. The ordinary Hebrew forms are identical with the Arabic, for the 2nd vowel in Hebrew is merely supplementary, and disappears before a suffix; e.g. אֶרֶץ for אַרְץ, with suffix אַרְצוֹ; סֵפֶר for סִפְר, with suffix סִפְרְךָ; אֹזֶן for אֻזְן or אֻזֻן, with suffix אָזְנִי. But the Aramaic forms are also found in our Hebrew text, though more sparingly, in the construct state; e.g. גְּבַר תָּמִים Ps. xviii. 26; כִּזְרַע־גַּד Num. xi. 7; נְטַע שַׁעֲשׁוּעָיו Isa. v. 7; מִסְּחַר כָּסֶף Prov. iii. 14; and the like.

I have dwelt for a little while on these classes of nouns, because I believe that they really lie at the root of the inflection of the verb in the Semitic languages. In one of the most recent Hebrew Grammars, that of Prof. Bernh. Stade (1879), you will find plainly stated, what I have long believed, that the verbal forms of the Semites are really nominal forms, mostly in combination with pronouns. Each person of the verb is, so to say, a sentence, consisting of a noun and a pronoun, which has gradually been contracted or shrivelled up into a single word. The same view was enunciated some years before by Philippi, in an article on the Semitic verb in the volume entitled *Morgenländische Forschungen*, 1875, and by Sayce in the JRAS. 1877 and in his lectures on Assyrian Grammar.

With this idea in our minds, let us submit the different forms of the Semitic verb to a careful analysis, selecting for the purpose the first or simplest form, and commencing, according to ancient custom, with the perfect state[2].

[1] [The absolute state and construct of nouns of this class usually appear with ֶ instead of ַ except before gutturals or *rīsh*.]

[2] [Cf. Nöldeke's article "Die Endungen des Perfects" in *ZDMG.* vol. xxxviii (1884), p. 407 sqq.]

I. *The Perfect.*

In Arabic, the 3rd pers. sing. masc. exhibits three forms, *ḳátala*, *ḳátila*, *ḳátula*, precisely corresponding to the three nominal or adjectival forms mentioned above. The form *ḳátala* is, generally speaking, transitive; whilst *ḳátila* and *ḳátula* are intransitive, the latter being the stronger form of the two. Here then we are face to face with the oldest and simplest form of this state and person; and here we at once encounter one of our greatest difficulties, the explanation of the final vowel *a*. On the whole I am inclined, after careful consideration, to acquiesce for the present in Stade's view, that we have here a simple noun, without any pronominal affix, and that the final *a* is really the oldest termination of the Semitic noun. If so, *ḳátala* would be an ancient adjective signifying "killing," or, as a verbal form, "he killed"; حَزِنَ would signify "sorrowing" or "he sorrowed"; ثَقُلَ, "being heavy" or "it was heavy." It is possible however that *ḳatala* may already be a contraction for *ḳatal-ya*, with the pronominal element *ya* postfixed, like *ta*, *na*, etc. That the final vowel existed anterior to the separation of the Semitic stock, is apparent from the following considerations. (1) The Ethiopic has also the forms *ḳatála* and *ḳĕtla*. (2) The Hebrew and Aramaic, which (like the vulgar Arabic) drop the final vowel under ordinary circumstances, retain it when a pronominal suffix follows; e.g. Heb. קָטַל, but קְטָלַנִי *k'ṭálá-nî* = Arab. *ḳatala-nî*; Aram. ܩܛܠ *ḳ'ṭal*, but with suffix ܩܛܠܢ *ḳaṭlá-n* for *ḳaṭlá-nî*, *ḳaṭala-nî*.

The Arabic has, as we have seen, three forms of the perfect state, distinguished by the vowels *a*, *i*, *u*. The same distinctions are maintained, to a greater or less extent, in the modern dialects, e.g. in Egypt, *katab*, "he wrote," فضل *fiḍil*, "it was over and above," كثر *kitir*, *kutur*, "it was much," سكت *sikit*, *sukut*, "he was silent." The existence of the same forms in the other Semitic languages can easily be proved. In Ethiopic the transitive form is identical with the Arabic, ቀተለ: *katala* = قَتَلَ. In the intransitive forms the vowels *i* and *u* were both weakened to *ĕ*, and finally dropped, whence resulted such words as የብሰ: *yabsa*, "to be dry," ጸድቀ: "to be just," ረውየ: "to be satisfied with drink," ቀርበ: "to be near," exactly corresponding to rare Arabic forms like عَلْمَ for عَلِمَ, رَضْيَ for رَضِيَ, حَسْنَ for حَسُنَ, قَرْبَ for قَرُبَ. If the 2nd radical was a guttural, an assimilation of the first vowel to the 2nd took place, giving us the series *kátĕla, kĕtĕla, kĕtla*, e.g. መሐረ: "to pity," ሰሐነ: "to be hot," = رَحِمَ سَخِنَ. Similar forms also exist in classical Arabic, e.g. شِهِدَ for شَهِدَ, نِهِبَ for نَهِبَ "to be dazzled with the sight of gold," نِعِمَ or نَعِمَ, بِئِسَ or بَئِسَ. In Hebrew we find in like manner all three vowels, although the forms in *i* and *u* are disappearing, as in vulgar Arabic. For example, with *i*, זָקֵן "to be old," טָהֵר "to be pure," כָּבֵד "to be heavy," יָרֵא "to fear"; with *u*, יָכֹל "to be able," שָׁכֹל "to be bereft," יָגֹר "to be afraid." On the other hand, שָׁמַע, but שָׁמֵעַ, as in vulgar Arabic سِمِعَ for the classical سَمِعَ (שָׁמַע); גָּבַר, but גָּבֵרוּ; דָּבַק, but דָּבְקָה and דָּבֵקוּ; שָׁכַח, but שְׁכֵחָנִי; גָּדַל, but גְּדֵלַנִי; and many more. In Aramaic, verbs with *u* are nearly as rare as in Hebrew; e.g. דְּמוּךְ "he slept"; חֲרוּב "it was dried up, waste, desolate"; תְּכוֹל "he was bereft." In Syriac only one such seems to be certain, viz. ܩܦܘܼܣ "to be shrivelled," as in Job vii. 5, ܩܦܘܼܣ ܡܫܟܝ ܘܐܬܦܫܚ; Ps. cxviii. 120, ܩܦܘܼܣ ܒܣܪܝ. Another may perhaps be found in ܐܣܘܼܪ, Nahum ii. 10, if that stand for ܐܬܩܘܿܡܘ, in the phrase ܘܐܩܘܿܡ

ܟܠܗܘܢ ܐܬܦܩܕ. ܐܝܟ ܦܘܩܕܢܐ ܕܡܪܝܐ. Verbs of the form *ḳaṭila* are, on the contrary, very common in Aramaic; as סְלֵק, ܣܠܩ; קְרֵב, ܩܪܒ; יְתֵב, ܝܬܒ; ܕܚܠ. Regarding Assyrian I find it difficult to say anything, owing to the conflict among the grammarians as to the real nature of certain forms. Schrader quotes a word *mîti*, "he is dead," which would correspond to the Heb. מֵת, Syr. ܡܝܬ, except in its rather perplexing final vowel[1].

I proceed to the 3rd pers. sing. fem.

If we have rightly regarded *ḳatala*, etc., as being originally nouns, without any pronominal affix, we should naturally expect the existence of a feminine formed in the same way as in the noun. And this is actually the case. The fem. of *ḳatala* is formed, as in the noun, by the addition of *t*. The Arabic has *ḳátalat*; the Ethiopic, *ḳatálat*, *yábsat* for *yábisat*, *mĕḥrat* for *máḥirat*. In vulgar Arabic, e.g. in Egypt, we have the forms *katabet*, *fiḍlet*, *suktet*. In Aramaic the same form occurs, with the further weakening of the 1st vowel, in the now shut syllable, into *i*, viz. קְטַלַת, ܩܛܠܬ, for *ḳaṭlat*, *ḳaṭ'lat*, *ḳaṭalat*. In Hebrew the usual form is *ḳāṭ'lā*, קָֽטְלָה, with the same termination *ā* as in the noun; but as in the one case so in the other, *ā* is only a weakened form of *at*, the successive steps being *at*, *ath*, *ah*, *ā*. The proof lies in the following facts[2]. (1) The termination *at* actually occurs, e.g. in אָֽזְלַת Deut. xxxii. 36, חָטָאת (for חָֽטְאַת) Exod. v. 16, קָרָאת (for קָֽרְאַת) Deut. xxxi. 29, שָׁבַת Ezek. xlvi. 17, עָשָׂת (for עָֽשְׂיַת) Levit. xxv. 21; etc. (2) The termination *at* has always been retained before pronominal suffixes, in which case we find the forms גְּמָלַתְהוּ, אֲהֵבַתְהוּ, אֲהֵבָתְךָ, and the like. The difference of vocalisation depends upon the difference of accentuation, a point on which I shall offer a few remarks by

[1] [Delitzsch writes *mît*, and recognises a permansive form *ḳaṭil* as common to most verbal themes, to express the idea of prolonged or completed activity as well as that of a permanent state or affection; *Ass. Gr.* p. 235, sq.]

[2] [Cf. p. 133, supra.]

and by, after we have treated of the 3rd pers. plur. masc. and fem. The final *t* is also lost in Phoenician, e.g. יטנא (prob. יִטְנָא) in a Cyprian inscr. of B.C. 254 [*C.I.S.* 93]; in Carthag. inscrr. נדרא or נדרע, "she vowed" (also נדרעא), שמע "she (Tanith) heard," for שמעא, etc. I will only add that the final *t* disappears also in Mandaitic before enclitic ב and ל with suffixes, e.g. נפאלאלה, "she fell," for נפאלאתלה, instead of ניפלאת. So also in the dialect of the Talmūd Bablī, עריקת "she fled," אזלת "she went," side by side with שלחה ליה, אמרה ליה, and in derived conjugations אִינְסִיבָא "she was married," אִיקַּדְּשָׁה ליה "she was betrothed to him." In such Talmudic forms as הֲוַאי for הֲוָת, and אֲתַאי אֲחָתֵיהּ "his sister came" for אֲתָת, we may perhaps discover a lingering trace of the original 3rd radical *yūd*.

If we be right in regarding *ḳatala*, etc., as originally nouns without pronom. affix, we shall again expect to find their plural agreeing in form with that of the nouns. This is also really the case. We shall not be far wrong in assuming *ḳatalûna* as the oldest form of the 3rd pers. plur. masc., which is still preserved to us in יֵדְעוּן Deut. viii. 3, 16, and perhaps in צָקוּן "poured forth" Isa. xxvi. 16; as also in the Aramaic forms קְטַלוּן, ܩܛܠܘܢ, and the Assyrian *katlūni*, side by side with *katlū*. Usually, however, the final *n* has been dropped, as in the construct state of the noun; whence we obtain the ordinary Arabic *ḳátalū*[1], the Ethiopic *ḳatálū*, *lábsū*, *mĕḥrū*; the Heb. קָטְלוּ; and the Aramaic קְטַלוּ. In the Aramaic dialects the process of corruption has gone yet farther. The Syriac pronounces *ḳ'ṭal*, and hence we find in old MSS. ܩܛܠ as well as the more accurate ܩܛܠܘ. In Mandaitic too the ordinary form is נפאק, סגיד, though the termination *ū* is sometimes restored before enclitics, as נצאבולאך

[1] Arabic قَتَلُو and قَتَلُوا, as in Hebrew occasionally קָטְלוּא, e.g. הָהָלְכוּא Josh. x. 24, אָבוּא Isa. xxviii. 12, if the text be correct. Sayce makes a strange blunder in considering the quiescent *alif* of the Arabic to be a trace of the original *n*.

"they planted for thee." I may add that in Mandaitic the full form in *ûn* is usually preceded by a *yûd*, for the insertion of which I find it hard to account; e.g. רהיטיון, סליקיון, נפאקיון "they ran." In the dialect of the Talmûd Babli we find the same rejection of the termination *û*, but it seems to leave its mark in an assimilation of the vowel of the preceding syllable; thus, אֲסוּר "they have bound" or "banned," for אֲסַרוּ; עֲבוּד for עֲבַדוּ; נְפוּק for נְפַקוּ.

The feminine of *ḳatalûna* we should naturally expect, in accordance with the nominal flexion, to be *ḳatalâna*; and though this form has entirely disappeared in Hebrew, it exists in the other languages. In the Aramaic dialects we find the final *n* retained, in the termination *ān*, or, with a weakening of the vowel, *ēn*. So in the Targûms there occur such words as אֲמַרָן, אִתְנַהֲרָן "were made clear"; in Mandaitic, with inserted *yûd*, פראשיאן "they understood," רגאזיאן "they were angry"; in Syriac, ܩܛܰܠܶܝܢ for *ḳ'ṭalān*. The Arabic exhibits the form *ḳatálna*, which I cannot as yet make up my mind to regard as anything else than a strong contraction of *ḳatalāna*[1]. It has almost gone out of use in the vulgar dialects. Several of the ancient Semitic languages, however, reject the final *n*. The Ethiopic is *nagdrā*, *lábsā*, *mĕḥrā*; the J. Aram. קְטַלָא. The Syriac must of course have once had the form *ḳ'ṭálē*, but dropped the final vowel, whence we find in MSS. both ܩܛܰܠܶܝ and ܩܛܰܠ. In the Christian Palestinian dialect we find קטלי, and so also in Samaritan; but the Mandaitic writes נפאק, סליק, like the Syriac. The older form with the final vowel *ā* appears in Syriac only before some of the pronominal suffixes, e.g. ܩܛܰܠܳܢܝ "they have killed me," ܩܛܰܠܳܟ, ܩܛܰܠܳܗܝ, corresponding with the Jewish Aramaic קַטְלָנִי, קַטְלָךְ, קַטְלָהִי.

In what I have said of the 3rd pers. plur. masc. and fem. I

[1] [It would seem from a deletion in the MS., that Prof. Wright had hesitated between this view and that of Nöldeke (*ZDMG.* xxxviii. 412) who regards the Arabic *ḳatalna* as formed on the analogy of the corresponding imperfect form *yaḳtulna*.]

have gone on the assumption that the original forms are *ḳata-lūna* and *ḳatalāna*. I must tell you however that this is altogether denied by such scholars as Noeldeke and G. Hoffmann[1], who maintain the originals to be *ḳatalū* and *ḳatalā*, and explain the forms in *ūn* and *ān* or *ēn* as later pronominal additions, comparing in particular the vulg. Arab. *katabum* for *katabū*, i.e. *katabū* + *hum* (see Noeldeke in *ZDMG.* xxxviii. p. 410), or else as analogical formations to ܩܛܠܘܢ, ܩܛܠܝܢ; ܐܢܘܢ, ܐܢܝܢ; ܗܘܢ, ܗܝܢ; ܗܢܘܢ, ܗܢܝܢ.

Here I will make, as promised, a few remarks on the accentuation of certain of these verbal forms and the changes in vocalisation which result therefrom.

The original accentuation of the 3rd pers. I believe to have been that of the old Arabic, *ḳátala, ḳátalat, ḳátalū*. The Ethiopic, Hebrew and Aramaic carried the accent onward to the next syllable, thus obtaining the forms *ḳatála, ḳatálat, ḳatálū* ; *ḳāṭál*; and *ḳ'ṭál, ḳ'ṭálū*. The vulgar dialects of the Arabic vary, I believe, between *ḳátal* and *ḳatál*. But in the intransitive forms the Ethiopic left the accent unshifted, and dropped the vowel of the middle syllable, *yábsa, sĕ́klua*. That the Hebrew accentuation too was once the same as in the old Arabic is clear, as it seems to me, from the vocalisation in particular of the fem. קָֽטְלָה and the plur. קָֽטְלוּ, which have now the accent on the last syllable. Had the accent originally fallen on that syllable in the verb, as it does in the noun, we should have had the forms קְטָלָה and קְטָלוּ, as in the noun we have חֲכָמָה from חָכָם. But this is not the case. On the contrary, we find the Ethiopic accentuation of the 2nd syllable in the so-called pausal forms, e.g. נָתָֽנָה, דָּבֵֽקָה, יָכֹֽלוּ; and it is only when pronom. suffixes are appended, and the tone is consequently thrown forwards towards the end of the word, that we get in Hebrew the forms קְטָלַת and קְטָלוּ, e.g. אֲכָלַתְהוּ, אֲכָלֻהוּ, and אֲכָלוּם; just as in Ethiopic we have *nagardtō, nagarū́-nī, nagarĕ́wō*, and in Arabic itself *ḳataldt-hu, ḳatalū́-hu*. The Aramaic 3rd pers. sing. fem.

[1] [See *ZDMG.* xxxii. 747.]

קְטָלַת, ܩܛܠܬ, also favours this view, for the suppression of the 2nd vowel of the original *ḳaṭalat* must have been due to the accentuation of the 1st syllable, as in the modern Arabic of Egypt, *ḳátalet, wíldet, kútret.* With suffixes the form approximates more to the Hebrew, e.g. קְטָלַתְּהָ, ܩܛܠܬܗ; Mand. לא כאלתאן "she has not devoured me," אכאלתה "she devoured him." The Mand. form with enclitics, e.g. נפאלאלה "she fell," is almost identical with the Heb. אֲכָלַתְהוּ.

Passing on to the 2nd person, we find that the Semitic languages split into two divisions, the one exhibiting *t* as the characteristic letter of the pronominal ending, the other *k*. On the one side are the Hebrew, Aramaic, Arabic, and Assyrian; on the other, the Ethiopic, and most likely the Ḥimyaritic. At least we are told that the South Arabian of the present day says كُنْكْ *kunk* for كُنْتْ *kunt* "thou wast"; and the form with ك for ت is vouched for in other parts of Arabia[1]. It is hard to say which is the more ancient form, if either. More probably the two existed side by side from remote antiquity, as we find in all of these languages the separate form with *t, anta,* etc., as well as the accus. and genit. suffixes with *k*. In quite modern times the *k* appears where we should not have expected it, as in the Samaritan hymns, גליך for גְּלִית "thou hast revealed," and in a dialect of Syria أَنْكُو for أَنْتُو or أَنْتُمْ. It should further be noted that in the 2nd person no variation is made as to the verbal part of the word, for the purpose of indicating the sex and number of the person or persons addressed. The whole weight of these distinctions has to be borne by the pronominal part. It appeared perhaps to be a waste of energy to point out these differences in both parts, and if one was to be selected, the pronoun seemed to be the better adapted for the purpose.

The 2nd pers. sing. masc. is in classical Arabic قَتَلْتَ, in

[1] See Noeldeke, *ZDMG.* xxxviii. 413; Halévy, *Études Sabéennes*, p. 46.

vulg. Arab. *katábt, misíkt, kutúrt.* In Hebrew the final vowel is often indicated by the addition of the letter ה, קָטַלְתָּ or קָטַלְתָּה. The Ethiopic equivalent is *ḳatálka.* The other dialects, like the vulgar Arabic, have dropped the final vowel. Hence in Bibl. Aramaic קְטַלְתָּ and קְטַלְתְּ; in the Targūms קְטַלְתָּא and קְטַלְתְּ, in Syriac ܩܛܰܠܬ.

In Arabic and Ethiopic the accent naturally rests on the 2nd syllable, *ḳatálta, ḳatálka*; but when an accus. suffix is added, the Ethiopic throws forward the tone, *ḳatalká-nī, ḳatalká-na,* and lengthens the vowel before the uncontracted forms of the suffixes of the 3rd pers., *ḳatalkā-hū* or *ḳatalkó, ḳatalkāhā,* etc. In Hebrew the tone is thrown forward not only with pronom. suffixes, but also when the so-called vāv conversive precedes; וְקָטַלְתָּ, קְטַלְתַּנִי, but קְטַלְתָּהוּ or קְטַלְתּוֹ, etc. Similarly in Jewish Aramaic, with suffixes, קְטַלְתַּנִי, קְטַלְתֵּהּ, but in Syriac ܩܛܰܠܬܳܢܝ, ܩܛܰܠܬܳܗܝ, in Mand. שבאקתאן, and in the Talmūd מְנַעְתַּן "hast hindered me," אַדְכַּרְתַּן "hast reminded me." I do not regard the vowel of the Ethiopic and Syriac forms as proving that the termination *ta* had originally a long vowel, *tá,* which is Noeldeke's view; on the contrary, I believe that the lengthening of the vowel is here due partly to the weight of the accent, but still more to an effort to distinguish this form from the almost identical one of the 3rd sing. fem., ܩܛܰܠܰܬܢܝ "she has killed me." Others would explain it as a contraction of the final vowel of *ta* with a supposed connective vowel *a*, as if ܩܛܰܠܬܳܢܝ stood for *ḳatalta-anī.*

To the masc. form of the 2nd pers. *anta* corresponds the fem. *anti*; and hence we should expect to find the 2nd pers. sing. fem. of the verb the form *ḳatalti,* which is actually the case. The Arabic has قَتَلْتِ, and the *i* is often lengthened before suffixes, كَسَرْتِهِ or كَسَرْتِيهِ. The vulg. form of the present day is

قَتَلْتِي *ḳataltī*. The corresponding Ethiopic form is *ḳatálkī*, written, according to the exigencies of the Geez syllabary, with long *ī*, which passes before suffixes into *ĕ* or *ĕy*, as *nagarkĕ-nī*, *nagarkĕyō*, *nagarkĕyōmū*. In Hebrew the ordinary form is קָטַלְתְּ with the loss of the final vowel; but קָטַלְתִּי is sufficiently common, though usually altered by the Massorites into קָטַלְתְּ; e.g. יָרַדְתִּי and שָׁכַבְתִּי, Ruth iii. 3, 4; לִמַּדְתִּי Jerem. ii. 33; דִּבַּרְתִּי Jerem. iii. 5. Sometimes the full form seems to have been left through a misunderstanding; e.g. Jerem. ii. 20, where שָׁבַרְתִּי and נִתַּקְתִּי seem to be 2nd pers. sing. fem. rather than 1st pers.; so also Micah iv. 13, וְהַחֲרַמְתִּי. Similarly before suffixes, קְטַלְתִּינִי, קְטַלְתִּיהוּ or קְטַלְתִּיו, etc. Forms like יְלִדְתָּנוּ, Jerem. ii. 27 (*Kĕth.* ילדתני), or וַהֲבֵאתוֹ, 2 Sam. xiv. 10, are very rare. In Aramaic the same phenomena present themselves. In Jewish Aramaic we have קְטַלְתְּ side by side with קְטַלְתִּינִי; whilst the Syriac has preserved the older termination, at least in writing, ܩܛܰܠܬܝ, with suffixes ܩܛܰܠܬܺܝܢܝ, ܩܛܰܠܬܺܝܗܝ. Here again I regard the vowel of the syllable *ti* as being originally short, whilst Noeldeke regards it as long. To me the lengthening seems to be due to the shifting of the accent.

The plural of *anta*, as you may remember, we found to be in its oldest form *antumū*; and consequently we expect in the verb for the 2nd pers. plur. masc. the form *ḳatáltumū*, which actually occurs in Arabic poetry and before suffixes, قَتَلْتُمُو, قَتَلْتُمُونِي. Generally however the final vowel is dropped, *antum*, قَتَلْتُمْ; and the common form in the vulgar language is قَتَلْتُوا with the loss of the final *m*. Parallel to these run the Ethiopic forms with *k*, viz. *ḳatalkĕmmū*, with suffixes *ḳatalkĕmmū-nī*, *ḳatalkĕmmĕwō*, *ḳatalkĕmmĕwōmū*. The corresponding form in the modern Tigré and Tigriña is *ḳatalkūm* or *ḳatalātkūm*, which latter appears in Amharic as *ḳatalāchhū*, ቀተላችሁ፡. In S. Arabia these forms with *k* are heard at the present day, e.g. سمعكم *samiʿkum* (Halévy, *Études Sab.* p. 46). As *antum* becomes in Heb. אַתֶּם, so *ḳatáltum* appears in the shape of קְטַלְתֶּם, the accent being thrown forward upon the pronoun, as in Ethiopic. The original vowel appears however, in the rather rare form קְטַלְתּוּ (corresponding to the vulgar Arabic قَتَلْتُوا), used in connexion with accusative suffixes (Num. xx. 5, xxi. 5, Zech. vii. 5). In Aramaic *n* takes the place of *m* in pronoun and verb. Thus in Syriac ܩܛܰܠܬܽܘܢ; in Mand. נצאבתון "ye planted." In the latter dialect the final *n* disappears before enclitics, as נצאבתוליא "ye have planted me," שאדארתוליא "ye have sent me"; and also before accusative suffixes, as נסאבתון "ye took me," שאדארתון "ye sent me," which is contrary to Syriac usage, but in accordance with Hebrew and Chaldee, where we find קְטַלְתּוּנִי, קְטַלְתּוּנָא, beside קְטַלְתּוּנָה, קְטַלְתּוּנוּן. In the Talmūd such forms as בְּעִיתוּ, ספיתו, occur even without suffixes, as in vulgar Arabic.

The feminine of *antumū* we found to be in its fullest form *antunna*, whence the fem. of *ḳataltum* should be *ḳataltunna*. This actually occurs in old Arabic, though it has disappeared from the vulgar dialects. The Ethiopic form is analogous to the Arabic, but has lost the final syllable, *ḳatalkĕn*; the final vowel appears, however, in the form with suffixes *ḳatalkĕnāhū* (Cornill, *das Buch der weisen Philosophen*, p. 51). But, on the other hand, the form is also liable to a further mutilation before suffixes into *ḳatalkā* (Dillmann, p. 274). The Hebrew form is almost identical with the Ethiopic, viz., קְטַלְתֶּן. The existence of a longer form in תֶּנָה, exemplified by הִשְׁלַכְתֶּנָה, Amos iv. 3, is very doubtful; and no example with accus. suffixes occurs. The Aramaic forms are such as we might expect, קְטַלְתֵּין, ܩܛܰܠܬܶܝܢ.

In Mandaitic however the feminine is a rarity, its place being mostly usurped by the masculine.

Proceeding to the 1st pers. sing., I would remind you that the root form of the pronoun of the 1st pers. we found to be *iya* or *î*, giving, in combination with the demonstrative *an*, the form *aniya* or *anî*. We found also that some of the Semitic languages inserted a second demonstrative, *ak*, whence the Assyrian *anâku*, the Hebrew אָנֹכִי, the Moabite אנך, and the Phoenician אנכי and אנך *anech*. It is this latter form that has given rise to the verbal affix in the Ethiopic *ḳatalkû*, which is also said to be the form in use in S. Arabia, كُنْتُ, اعتفرتُ, etc. (comp. Halévy, *Études Sabéennes*, p. 46). In the other Semitic languages we encounter an affix form with *t* instead of *k*, which demands explanation. It may be that *t* has interchanged with *k*, as in the 2nd person we find *ta* and *ka*; but more probably, I think, *tu* has been substituted for *ku* in the 1st person under the influence of the forms of the 2nd person. The solitary *ḳatalku* gave way before the greater number of *t*-forms, and was gradually changed into *ḳataltu*, except, as we have seen, in Ethiopic (which was destitute of *t*-forms in the 2nd person).

While the Assyrian pronoun *anâkû* (Haupt *anakû*) is indisputably older, in respect of its *â*, than the Hebrew *ânôkhî*, the latter would appear to have preserved the termination in a purer form. We may therefore fairly assume that the Arabic *ḳatáltu* and the Ethiopic *ḳatálkû* represent, in respect of the final vowel, a somewhat later stage than the corresponding Hebrew קָטַלְתִּי, with vāv conversive וְקָטַלְתִּי, with suffixes קְטַלְתִּיהוּ or קְטַלְתִּיו, etc. Whether the *scriptio defectiva* in such forms as יָדַעְתָּ Job xlii. 2, בָּנִיתָ 1 Kings viii. 48, is merely accidental, or really indicates a tendency to dull the final vowel or to drop it altogether, it is hard to say. The Moabite and Phoenician forms were doubtless identical with the Hebrew. King Mesha' writes מלכתי, בנתי, etc., and in one Phoen. inscr. we find בנתי (Umm 'Awāmid, *C.I.S.* nr. 7), though the usual spelling is בנת. Plautus too has *corathi* for קראתי. In Aramaic the suffix sometimes appears in full, especially in the case of verbs 3rd י, as קְנֵיתִי, אסגיתי; but more frequently the suffix has lost its vowel, the usual form being קִטְלֵת, ܩܛܠܬ, which stands for *ḳaṭlat*, by transposition from *ḳaṭalt*, which is the form used in vulg. Arab., *ḳatalt, misikt, kuturt.* The transposition probably took place to distinguish it from the 2nd pers. קְטַלְתְּ, ܩܛܠܬ; and the alteration of the vowel in the last syllable may be ascribed, either to the lingering influence of the lost termination *t*, or to an effort to differentiate this form from the 3rd pers. sing. fem. קִטְלַת, ܩܛܠܬ (for *ḳaṭlat*, out of *ḳaṭalat*). Remark however a difference between the Biblical Aramaic and the Syriac. The former has *movable shĕwā*, עַבְדֵת Dan. iii. 15, vi. 25, קִרְבֵת Dan. vii. 16; the latter silent shĕwā, ܢܦܩܬ, ܩܛܠܬ. The older form *ḳaṭalt* appears with the accus. suffixes, ܩܛܠܬܗ, ܩܛܠܬܟܘܢ. The Mandaitic form is ordinarily the same as the Syriac, ניפקית, לינטית; but with the enclitics the *t* disappears, and we have the vocalisation *ḳ'ṭalē* for *ḳ'ṭalēth*, e.g. נטארילה "I tied to him," סליקיבה "I went up on it." In the Targūms we find the fully vocalised form אֲכָלִית, דְּחֵילִית, etc., which is indeed older than the Biblical forms just cited. In the Talmūd Bāblī both the forms which we have noted in the Mandaitic occur independently of enclitics; כְּבַשִׁית "I subdued," שְׁמַעִית "I heard," אַרְגֵּישִׁית side by side with אֲמַרִי "I said," נְפַקִי "I went out," חזאי "I have seen," קראי "I called." The final vowel is merely tone-long, and hence can be shortened when the tone is thrown back, as הֲקֵימֶת, Dan. iii. 14; and with suffixes, as פְּרַעְתֵּיהּ, ܩܛܠܬܗ.

You will remark that in the first person, as in the second, the sex or number of the speaker or speakers is not marked in the verbal part of the word; whilst no variation was thought necessary in the pronominal part, any more than in the actual pronoun אָנֹכִי or أَنَا, אֲנָ.

As to the plural, the original form of the pronom. affix was probably *nû*, from אֲנַחְנוּ or אֲנוּ; but it underwent various modifications in the several languages, as we shall presently see.

The Hebrew has preserved the old form in קָטַלְנוּ, with suffix קְטַלְנוּהוּ. The Arabic form is *ḳatalnâ*, قَتَلْنَا, with long *â*, which is however sometimes shortened in poetry, *ḳatalnă*. On the other hand, the Ethiopic has *ḳatalna*, with short *ă*, which is lengthened before suffixes: *nagárna*, but *nagarnâ-ka*, *nagarnâ-kĕmmû*. Similar is the Chaldee form קְטַלְנָא, with suffixes קְטַלְנָכוֹן, קְטַלְנָךְ. In Syriac *nâ* is shortened into *n*, ܩܛܠܢ, but the fuller termination appears with pronominal suffixes, as ܩܛܠܢܢܗܝ, etc. The abbreviated form also prevails in the Talmûd Bâblî, אַשְׁכַּחַן, אֲמַרַן. Frequently however the Syriac form is lengthened, by a repetition of the pronoun, into ܩܛܠܢܢ (sometimes written ܩܛܠܢ ܢܢ). This, in the weakened shape of נין, is the usual termination in Mandaitic, e.g. נפאקנין, סהידנין; but with enclitics the older נא is restored, e.g. נפאקנאבה "we went out therein," שאדארנאלון "we sent them." The accusative suffixes are added to the shorter form in *n*, as רחימנאך "we loved thee," פתאחנה "we opened it."

I have reserved the *dual* for the last place in our view, because it occurs in only two or three of the Semitic languages, the Arabic and Ḥimyaritic, and possibly the Assyrian. The rest,—Ethiopic, Hebrew, and Aramaic,—lost it in the verb before they reached the stage at which we become acquainted with them.

The Arabic forms are precisely such as we should expect, that is to say, almost identical with those of the noun and pronoun. The 3rd pers. masc. is *ḳátalâ*, like the noun in *âni*, construct *â*, e.g. *raǵulâni*, *raǵulâ*. Similarly in the feminine we find in Arabic *ḳatálatâ*, formed like *ǵannatâni*, *ǵannatâ*, from *ǵannat*.

In Ḥimyaritic the final *â* seems to have been weakened into *ē*. The pronoun هُمَا is written המי *humē*, and similarly in the verb חמרי, בניי, עהדי, החדתי (أَحْدَثَا), fem. שמתי (shēmatē, شَامَتَا), "they two set up." The dual of the pronoun of the 2nd person being in Arabic *anṭumâ*, the corresponding form of the perfect is naturally *ḳatáltumâ*. The 1st person, as in the case of the pronoun, has no dual.

Herewith I finish my survey of the perfect state of the verb. You may remember that I regarded it, in most of its forms, as made up of a nominal and a pronominal element; as being in fact a sentence which gradually shrivelled up and contracted into a word. Only the 3rd pers. seemed to be a noun without any pronominal adjunct. Perhaps you are inclined to demur to this view, on the ground of intrinsic improbability. If so, I would remind you that history is apt to repeat itself, and nowhere more so than in language. The formation of the Romance tongues out of Latin, or of the modern Indian dialects out of Sanskrit, illustrates many points in the early history of the Indo-European group. And so the later formations of the Semitic dialects may help us largely to understand the older ones. The ancient Syrian pronounced, and sometimes wrote, ܩܳܛܠܢܳܐ for ܩܳܛܶܠ ܐܢܳܐ, "I am killing"; ܒܳܥܶܝܢܳܐ, and even ܒܳܥܶܢ, "I am seeking." In the Talmūd we find such words as ידענא "I know," אזלינא "I am going." The Mandaite could say not only לאניטנא, "I take," but also לאניטנאך, "I take thee." But above all the modern Syrian forms his present tense solely in this way. Where can you find a more complete parallel to the formation of the Hebrew perfect, as I have explained it, than in the Nestorian present, according to the following paradigm?

sing.	3 p. m.	ܦܳܪܶܩ	*pârik*, "he comes to an end."
	f.	ܦܰܪܩܳܐ	*parḳâ*[1].
	2 p. m.	ܦܰܪܩܺܝܬ	*parḳit*.
	f.	ܦܰܪܩܰܬ	*parḳat*.

[1] [The *â* is shortened in the closed syllable *par*.]

	1 p. m.	ܦܪܩܝܢ	*parḳîn.*
	f.	ܦܪܩܢ	*parḳân.*
plur.	3 p. c.	ܦܪܩܝ	*parḳî.*
	2 p. c.	ܦܪܩܝܬܘܢ	*parḳîtôn.*
	1 p. c.	ܦܪܩܢ	*parḳâkh* (*ḳûkh*),

also ܦܪܩܝܢ (ܦܪܩܝ + ܐܢܚܢ).

II. *The Imperfect.*

Having thus discussed the various forms of the perfect state of the verb, I proceed to the consideration of the imperfect.

Here the first thing that strikes us is the different collocation of the parts which go to the constitution of the verbal form. In the perfect the verbal element preceded, and was followed by the pronominal element. The action, as completed, seemed apparently to be more prominent than the agent. In the imperfect, on the contrary, the pronominal element takes precedence of the verbal; the agent seems to be more conspicuous in relation to the still unfinished act. The whole arrangement may of course be, as some have thought, merely accidental; but if we are to seek a reason for it, that just given seems to be the most natural.

Another point of difference between the two verbal states is that the 3rd pers. sing. masc. of the perfect appears to be destitute of any pronominal affix, whereas the corresponding person of the imperfect is furnished with a peculiar pronominal prefix. The reason of this probably also lies in the greater prominence of the pronominal element in the imperfect state. It may of course be said, with Dietrich and Stade, that the 3rd pers. sing. masc. of the imperfect is a noun of the form *yaḳtul*, יִקְטֹל, etc., without any pronominal element. But surely the preformative *ya* demands some explanation; and if so, what explanation is more probable than that it is pronominal in its nature? Rödiger connected it with the Amharic ይኸ: or ይህ:

"this," and የ "who, which," but of these Praetorius has attempted a different explanation in his Amharic Grammar, as we shall see hereafter.

A third difference between the two states lies in the variety of the vocalisation of the 2nd syllable; and herein we descry another effort of the language to mark the contrast in their signification. Given in Arabic the perfect with *a* in the 2nd syllable, then the corresponding imperfect has either *u* or *i*; *ḳátala* has *yaḳtulu*, but *gálasa*, *yaglisu*. So in Hebrew, יִפְקֹד, but יִתֵּן; in Syriac, ܢܶܚܬܽܘܡ, but ܢܶܬܶܠ. But if the perfect has *i* in the 2nd syllable, the vowel of the imperfect is usually *a*; e.g. Arab., *fáriḳa*, *yáfraḳu*; Heb. כָּבֵד, יִכְבַּד; Syr. ܪܚܶܡ, ܢܶܪܚܰܡ. If the 2nd, and still more frequently if the 3rd radical be guttural, ا ه ح ع the favorite vowel is *a*, as فَتَحَ. يَفْتَحُ; دَفَعَ، يَدْفَعُ; ذَهَبَ، يَذْهَبُ; سَحَبَ، يَسْحَبُ; and similarly in Hebrew and Syriac[1]. If the perfect has *u* in the 2nd syllable, this vowel is ordinarily retained in Arabic in the imperfect, as *tháḳula*, *yáthḳulu*; but in Hebrew and Syriac the few verbs of this form seem to take *a*, as יָכֹל, יוּכַל [if this is not Hof'al]; קָטֹן, יִקְטַן; שָׁכֹל, יִשְׁכַּל; ܙܥܽܘܪ, ܢܶܙܥܰܪ. Exceptions to these rules are comparatively rare; occasionally, for example, we find the perfect in *i* connected with an imperfect in *u*, e.g. שָׁכֵן, יִשְׁכֹּן; נָבֵל, יִבּוֹל; ܣܓܶܕ, ܢܶܣܓܽܘܕ; ܩܪܶܒ, ܢܶܩܪܽܘܒ; ܫܬܶܬ, ܢܶܫܬܽܘܬ; מֵת, יָמוּת, ܡܺܝܬ, ܢܡܽܘܬ, and even مِتُّ، أَمُوتُ.

The Semitic languages seem in their earliest stage to have formed imperfects from two nominal roots. The one of these was *ḳatil*, which we found above as one of the forms of the perfect; the other the shorter *ḳ'tal*, *ḳ'til*, *ḳ'tul*. The former has survived in only two of these languages, both of which have preserved to us many archaisms, the Ethiopic and the

[1] [In Syriac the influence of the guttural is less marked; indeed most transitive verbs 3rd gutt. have the imperfect in *o*.]

Assyrian. The original shape of the 3rd pers. sing. masc. we may assume in this case to have been *yaḳátilu*. In Ethiopic it appears under the normal form of *yĕḳátĕl*, and corresponds in its general use with the imperfect indicative of the Arabic; whereas the other form *yĕngĕr* answers to the Arabic imperfect subjunctive and jussive. In Assyrian its form, according to Sayce, is *isákinu* or *isákin* [Delitzsch *išákan*], the signification of which is "he makes" or "he will make"; whereas the form *iskun* takes, according to the same authority, the aoristic sense of "he made."

We need not at present dwell longer on this form *yĕḳátĕl*, because its prefixes and flexion are identical with those of the other form *yĕḳtĕl*, which is common to all the Semitic languages, and therefore better adapted for the purpose of a comparative survey.

Of the different moods,—subjunctive, jussive, and energetic or cohortative,—we will not treat just now, but confine our attention for the present exclusively to the indicative mood.

The 3rd pers. sing. masc. of the imperfect indicative is in classical Arabic *yáḳtulu*, with *ă* as the vowel of the prefix and a final *ŭ*. This we may accept as the archetype. The vulgar dialects drop the final vowel and weaken that of the first syllable, *yéḳtul*, *yíḳtul*, or *íḳtul*, *yimsik*, *yuskut*; thus giving us the same form which we find already in the Ethiopic *yĕngĕr*, the Assyr. *iskun* (יסכן, "he placed" [Del. ישכן]) or *iṣbat* (יצבת, "he seized"), and the Hebrew יִפְקֹד, יִכְבַּד. This too is the common form in the Aramaic dialects, e.g. Jewish Aram. יִקְטֹל, יִלְבַּשׁ, with some important exceptions, which we shall specify presently.

That the vowel of the preformative was originally *a* in Hebrew as well as in Arabic we may infer: (1) from verbs of which the first letter is a guttural, as יֶאְסֹר or יֶאֱסֹר, יַהֲרֹג, יַחְגֹּר, יַעֲבֹר; (2) from verbs ע"ע, as יָסֹב, יָעֹז, which stand for *yasbub*, *ya'zuz*; and (3) from verbs ע"ו, as יָקוּם, יָנוּחַ, which stand for *yaḳwum*, *yanwuḥ*. As we have often seen already, an original *pathach* may be gradually weakened into *segol* or *chireḳ*; but it is impossible that an original *chireḳ* should in such a case give rise to a *pathach*.

This person of the verb is identical in form, or nearly so, with a class of nouns in the older Semitic languages, which occur partly as proper names and partly as common nouns. Such are in Hebrew, יִצְחָק, יַעֲקֹב; יָרִיב "adversary," יִצְהָר "oil"; יַלְקוּט "bag," יַחְמוּר "kind of deer," יַנְשׁוּף "bittern" (?); in Arabic, يَغُوث "the Helper," يَعُوق "the Averter," يَنْبُع, يَثْرِب, يَحْيَي, يَعْلَي; يَحْمُور "oryx," يَحْبُور "male bustard," يَخْضُور "freshly cut branch," يَخْضُور and يَخْضِير "green," يَرْبُوع "jerboa," يَرْخَم and يَرْخُوم "male vulture," يَعْبُوب "rapid river, horse, etc.," يَعْسُوب "queen bee," يَعْفُور "gazelle," يَعْمُور "lamb, kid," يَنْبُوع "fountain," يَعْقِيد "thickened honey," يَعْضِيد "a kind of plant."

From all these cases it seems perfectly clear that the prefix *ya* must signify "one who, he who, that which"; but we do not find in the older Semitic languages any pronoun of this signification at all resembling *ya* in sound. In Amharic, one of the modern dialects sprung from the Ge'ez or Ethiopic, we find, it is true, a pronoun የ *ya*, used (exactly like דִּי, דְ, שֶׁ) both as the relative and as a sign of the genitive case. Praetorius seems however to have made it tolerably certain that this *ya* is only a modification of the Ethiopic ዘ *za*, which is still used in Hararī, the intermediate link being *zha* ዠ in one of the Tigriña dialects. The change of sound is the same as in the Amharic ይሀ:, ይኸ:, derived through ይኸ:, ዠኸ:, from an older ዚኒ, ዜኒ = ذَاكَ. This comparison therefore fails us. Neither does it seem likely that this *ya* can stand for *wa*, as an abbreviation of *huwa*; because, though initial *w* passes into *y* in Hebrew and Aramaic, the same change does not take place in Arabic and Ethiopic. I am obliged therefore to confess my ignorance of the derivation of this prefix.

Here I may add that some scholars have sought this same pronoun *ya* as a suffix in the perfect. According to them *ḳátala* and *ḳátalū* stand for *ḳatalya* and *ḳatalyū*. For this view I can find no support whatever save in the Mandaitic plural which I mentioned in a previous lecture, viz. רנאזיון, fem. רנאזיאן, instead of רנאן. It seems to me, however, very unlikely (1) that the *y* should have been simply elided, without leaving behind any trace of its existence; and (2) that, if it had wholly disappeared in Arabic, Ethiopic, Hebrew, and the older Aramaic, it should have been preserved in the comparatively late Mandaitic. I am compelled therefore to reject this view, though I cannot at present suggest any adequate explanation of the isolated Mandaitic forms just quoted.

I said before that there were some important exceptions to the formation of the 3rd pers. sing. masc. by *ya*. These I now proceed to enumerate.

Already in the Chaldee of the Old Testament we find the verb הֲוָא forming the 3rd pers. sing. masc. with ל instead of י; לֶהֱוֵא for יֶהֱוֵא in Ezra iv. 13, Dan. ii. 20, with the corresponding plur. masc לֶהֱוֹן Dan. ii. 43, and fem. לֶהֶוְיָן Dan. v. 17. The same form is common in the Talmūd Bablī, and occurs also in Mandaitic, in both cases side by side with the forms with *n*; e.g. לֵימָא "say," לְכְתוּב ,לֵיתֵי "bring"; לִיקוּם ,לִידְמִיא "be like," לִישְׁתְּרִיא "be dissolved." In Syriac the *n* alone is found, ܢܬܡܗܠ, ܢܟܬܘܒ, ܢܩܘܡ, ܢܗܘܐ. On the whole subject see Mr Lowe's note in his *Fragment of the Talmud Bablī Pĕsachim*. The identity of this *l* and *n* may perhaps be admitted; that either of them sprung from the *y* must be denied. De Goeje (in a review of Kautzsch's *Gr. des Biblisch-aramäischen*) supposes the form לֶהֱוֵא to be originally an infin. הֱוֵא compounded with the prep. לְ, "to be" taken in the sense of "is to be," "shall be"; and to this הֱוֵא he finds a parallel in the form לְבְּנֵא, Ezra v. 3, 13. To me it seems that the origin of the *l* may rather be sought in the demonstrative *l*, which is the essential element of the article أَلْ, הַל, and which appears in various pronouns and demonstrative adverbs such as الّذي, הַלָּזֶה, ذٰلكَ, אֵלֶּה, אִלֵּין, ܗܳܟܰܢ, הָלְאָה, הָלְכָה, هَلُمَّ, هُنالكَ, etc. The *n*, if it be anything more than a mere variation of the *l*, may also be explained from the demonstrative *n*, which appears for instance in דֵּן, ዝንቱ:, the pronominal base *an*, הֵן, הִנֵּה, إِنْ, أَنَّ, etc.

The 3rd pers. sing. fem. has for its prefix *ta*, that is, no doubt, the same mark of the fem. gender which we find at the end of the word in the perfect *ḳatalat*. The typical form is again the old Arabic تَقْتُلُ *taḳtulu*, vulgarly *taḳtul, teḳtul, tiktul, timsik, tuskut*, which latter coincide with the Assyrian *taskun, taṣbat*, and the Ethiopic *tĕngĕr, tĕlbas*. In Hebrew the *a* of the 1st syllable is ordinarily sunk to *i*, תִּקְטֹל, תִּכְבַּד; but *ĕ* and *ă* are found in the same cases as in the masc., e.g. תֶּאֱרֹב, תַּעֲבֹר, תַּעֲנֹג, תַּחְשֹׁב; תָּעֹז; תָּקוּם. Similarly in Aramaic, תִּקְטֹל, ܬܶܩܛܽܘܠ, תירגאז (Mandaitic).

Yaḳtulu being, as we have seen, essentially a nominal form, its plural is naturally obtained by the usual nominal inflexion, as in the perfect. The most ancient form is once more found in the Arabic *yaḳtulūna*, which is vulgarly shortened into *yaḳtúlū*, though *yaḳtulūn* is still heard. In Hebrew the fuller form יִקְטְלוּן is not uncommon, as יִדְרְכוּן, יֶהֶרְגוּן, יְקוּמוּן, יַעֲשׂוּן, in pause יִקְצֹרוּן, יֶחְפָּצוּן, יִבְכָּיוּן; but the shorter יִקְטְלוּ is far more frequent. The Ethiopic forms are *yĕngĕrū, yĕlbásū*, with which correspond in accentuation the Hebrew pausal forms יִפֹּלוּ, יִשְׁכָּבוּ, יֶחְדָּלוּ, יַעֲבֹרוּ, etc.; and the vulgar Arabic (Egypt) *yiḳtúlū, yimsíkū, yuskútū*. The Assyrian exhibits, as we might expect, the forms *iskunū, iṣbatū*. The old Aramaic dialects hold fast the final *n*, יִקְטְלוּן, לֶהֱוֹן, ܢܶܩܛܠܽܘܢ. So also in Mandaitic נישיתלון, ניליגטון "plant"; but before the enclitics the *n* disappears, נישביקולאך, נירשימובכון "register with you."

The feminine form corresponding to *yaḳtulūna* would naturally be *yaḳtulāna*. This is actually retained by the Aramaic dialects in the forms יִקְטְלָן, לֶהֶוְיָן, ܢܶܩܛܠܳܢ, Mand. נירימואן "wink." In Ethiopic and Assyrian we find the same forms with the loss of the final *n*; Eth. *yĕngĕrā, yĕlbăsā*; Assyr. *iskunā, iṣbatā*; and so also in Mandaitic, נירימוא, ניסינדרא, are more common than the fuller form in אן. The Arabic has contracted *yaḳtulāna* into *yaḳtúlna*, after the analogy of *ḳatálna* for *ḳatalána* in the perfect. The same form occurs in Hebrew; e.g. יֵחַמְנָה Gen. xxx. 38, וַיִּשַּׁרְנָה 1 Sam. vi. 12 (for וַיִּישַׁרְנָה), and יַעֲמֹדְנָה Dan. viii. 22; but more commonly the Hebrew employs a form with prefixed *t*, after the analogy of the singular, and says תִּקְטֹלְנָה, e.g. תִּפֹּלְנָה, תַּעֲבֹרְנָה, תִּלְבַּשְׁנָה, תִּשְׁכַּבְןָ. The same form occurs dialectically in Arabic, even among the various readings of the Ḳor'ān, e.g. Sūr. xlii. 3, تَنْفَطِرْنَ for يَتَفَطَّرْنَ. In the vulgar Arabic dialects the fem. seems to have vanished entirely.

The 2nd pers. is formed by prefixing to the verbal element the syllable *ta*, being, as we have already seen, the essential base of the pronoun *anta*. Hence we get in the sing. masc. the normal *táḳtulu*, which is the actual Arabic form; in the vulgar dialects, *taḳtul, tĕḳtul, tiḳtul, timsik, tuskut*. The Assyrian has retained the pure vowel in its *taskun, taṣbat*; whilst the Ethiopic exhibits the weaker *tĕngĕr, tĕlbas*. The Hebrew offers exactly the same variations as the 3rd pers.; we find תִּזְכֹּר, תִּקְרַב, but תֶּאֱסֹף, תַּעֲבֹר, תַּהֲרֹג, תַּחְמֹל; תָּחֹג; תָּקוּם. The Aramaic forms, תִּקְטֻל, ܬܶܩܛܽܘܠ, Mand. תישבוק, תירגאו, call for no remark.

The 2nd pers. sing. fem. is differentiated from the masc. not by any change in the pronominal prefix, but by the addition of the termination *īna*, the origin of which seems quite obscure. The normal form is again the Arabic تَقْتُلِينَ, *taḳtulīna*, which has survived in Hebrew in such forms as תִּדְבָּקִין Ruth ii. 8, 21 תַּעֲשִׂין iii. 4; תֵּדְעִין iii. 18. So also in Aramaic, תִּקְטְלִין,

ܬܩܛܠܝܢ. In other cases, the final *n* has altogether disappeared, as in the vulgar Arabic تقتلي *tiḳtúlī, timsíkī, tuskútī*; Assyr. *taskunī, taṣbatī*; Eth. *tĕngĕrī, tĕlbásī*; Heb. תִּזְכְּרִי, in pause תִּשְׁקֹטִי, תִּלְבָּשִׁי, תִּירָאִי. In Mandaitic this fem. form seems to have gone out of use. In what I have said I regard *īna* as being the original termination of this person, and *ī* as a shortening thereof. Other scholars take *ī* to be the original termination, and consider *īn, īna* to be a later formation after the analogy of the plur. *ūn, ūna*.

The formation of the plural in the 2nd pers. is identical with that in the 3rd. The normal form in the masc. is, as usual, the Arabic تَقْتُلُونَ. The final *n* is preserved in Hebrew in such words as תִּשְׁמְרוּן, תַּחְקְרוּן, תַּעַמְדוּן; or with fuller vowels in pause, תַּעֲבֹדוּן, תִּשְׁכָּבוּן, תֶּאֱהָבוּן. So also in Aramaic. תִּקְטְלוּן, ܬܩܛܠܘܢ, Mand. תירמזון or more frequently תירימזון. In vulgar Arabic the final syllable has been rejected, leaving تقتلوا *tiḳtúlu, timsíkū, tuskútū*; with which correspond the Assyrian *taskunū, taṣbatū*, the Ethiopic *tĕngĕrū, tĕlbásū*, and the Hebrew תִּזְכְּרוּ, תַּעַזְבוּ, תַּחְמְלוּ; in pause, with fuller vowels, תִּשְׁמֹרוּ, תַּעֲזֹבוּ, תִּזְבָּחוּ, תֶּאֱהָבוּ, תֶּאְשָׁמוּ. In Mandaitic too the *n* disappears before the enclitics, as in the 3rd person.

The fem. corresponding with *taḳtulūna* ought to be *taḳtulāna*; and this form is preserved, with the loss of only the final vowel, in the Aramaic תִּקְטְלָן, ܬܩܛܠܢ. In Mandaitic, however, it seems to have fallen into disuse. The Assyrian and Ethiopic exhibit forms with the loss of the final *n*; Assyr. *taskunā, taṣbatā*; Eth. *tĕngĕrā, tĕlbásā*. In Arabic *taḳtulāna* is contracted as I take it, after the same manner as the 3rd pers. fem., into *taḳtúlna*, a form which is lost in the vulgar dialects, but has been preserved in some examples in Hebrew, e.g. תְּקַסֵּמְנָה, Ezek. xiii. 23, תִּשֶּׂאינָה, Ezek. xxiii. 49, and a very few more.

An example like תִּרְאֻנִי, Song of Songs i. 6, shows that here, as well as in other cases, in Hebrew the masc. was gradually supplanting the fem.

The prefix of the 1st pers. sing. א is apparently derived from the corresponding pronoun אֲנִי, أَنَا. In Arabic it is أَقْتُلُ (vulg. *aktul, amsik, askut*), which appears in Assyrian, with the loss of the final vowel, as *askun, aṣbat*. In Ethiopic the vowel is weakened, *ěngěr, ělbas*; and so also in Aramaic, אֶקְטֹל, ܐܶܩܛܘܿܠ, Mand. עשבוק. Similarly in Hebrew, אֶשְׁמֹר, אֶחְמֹל, אֶעֱבֹר, אֶאֱסֹף; but אָחֹן, אָשׁוּב, with the original *a*.

The corresponding plural takes its prefix *na* from אֲנַחְנוּ, נַחְנוּ, نَحْنُ. In Arabic it is نَقْتُلُ, vulgarly *neḳtul, niḳtul, nimsik, nuskut*. In most of the other languages the vowel of the first syllable is weakened; e.g. Eth. *něngěr, nělbas*; Assyr. *niskun, niṣbat*; Aram. נִקְטֹל, ܢܶܩܛܘܿܠ, Mand. נישבוק. The Hebrew alone retains the original *a* with gutturals and in verbs ע"ע and ע"ו, e.g. נִשְׁמֹר, but נֶאֱסֹף, נַעֲבֹר, נָסֹב, נָקוּם.

The *dual* number is found, as in the perfect, only in old Arabic and Assyrian; and only in the 3rd and 2nd persons, not in the first. The 3rd pers. masc. in Arabic is يَقْتُلَانِ, with the same termination as in the perfect and in substantives. It is represented in Assyrian, according to Sayce, by the form *iskunā, iṣbatā*, with the loss of the final syllable[1]. The corresponding fem. in Arabic is تَقْتُلَانِ, to which the Assyrian inscriptions seem to offer no counterpart. The 2nd pers. is likewise تَقْتُلَانِ, which form serves for both genders, and is found in Arabic alone.

In conclusion, let me call your attention to the gradual shifting of the accent here, as in the perfect, at least in certain

[1] [Delitzsch regards these forms as plurals.]

forms. The original accentuation appears to me to be that of the classical Arabic, viz. on the first syllable of the 3rd pers. sing. *yáḳtulu*, in Eth. *yĕngĕr*. In the lengthened forms of the 2nd sing. fem. and the 3rd and 2nd plur., the Ethiopic threw forward the accent one place, *tĕngĕrī*, *yĕngĕrū -rā*, *tĕngĕrū -rā*, as compared with the corresponding Arabic *táḳtulī*, *yáḳtulū*, *táḳtulū*; and this accentuation we find in Hebrew in the so-called pausal forms, תַּעֲבֹרִי, תִּלְבָּשִׁי, תֵּלֵכִי; תַּחְשֹׁבוּ, תִּשְׁמָעוּ, תִּתֵּנוּ; יִמְשֹׁלוּ, יְחַדְּלוּ, יֵשֵׁבוּ; and also in the vulgar Arabic *tiktúlī*, *timsíkī*, *tusḳútī*; *tiḳtúlū*, *timsíkū*, *tuskútū*. Generally speaking, however, the Hebrew, like the Aramaic, shifts the accent to the last syllable, יִקְטֹל, תִּקְטְלִי, יִקְטְלוּ, תִּקְטְלוּ. The forms ending in *īna*, *ūna*, are already accented in Arabic on the penult, and the accent remains on the same syllable when it becomes final in Hebrew and Aramaic, תִּקְטְלִין, יִקְטְלוּן; ܬܩܛܠܘܢ. So also the Aramaic feminines in *ān*, יִקְטְלָן, ܬܩܛܠܢ; whereas the Arabic forms يَقْتُلْنَ, تَقْتُلْنَ, with the corresponding Hebrew ones, are accented on the penult.

III. *The Imperative.*

Passing on to the imperative mood, I would point out to you its perfect identity in the masc. sing. with the nominal form that constitutes the base of the Arabic imperfect. With substantially the same vowels as in the imperfect, the original forms are *ḳ'tul*, *ḳ'tal* and *ḳ'til*. Nearest to this postulated original stand the Aramaic forms ܩܛܘܠ, ܠܒܫ, ܐܦܩ; and the Hebrew זְכֹר, לְבַשׁ, תֵּן (for נְתֵן); in which latter the vowels *u* and *i* are heightened by the tone, as in the imperfect. The Ethiopic *nĕgĕr*, *lĕbas*, show by the accent that more weight was given to the first syllable than in Aramaic and Hebrew; and the same appears to have been the case in Assyrian, where we find the vowel of the first syllable assimilated to that of the second, *šukun*, *ṣabat*, *riḳiṣ*. The Arabic attained the same intonation by means of a prosthetic *'alif*, with partial assimilation of its vowel to that of the 2nd syllable. Thus, for *ḳ'tul*, the Arab wrote and spoke *'úḳtul*, اُقْتُلْ; for *g'lis*, *'íglis*, اِجْلِسْ; but for *fraḳ*, he said اِفْرَقْ, *'ifraḳ*, not *'áfraḳ*, because the vowel *a* appeared to him to be too heavy for a merely prosthetic syllable.

As the fem. of *ḳ'tul* we should naturally expect *ḳ'tulîna*, after the analogy of *taḳtul, taḳtulîna*, in the imperfect; but this full form has been nowhere preserved, except in such rare Syriac forms as ܩܛܘܠܝܢܝ or ܩܛܘܠܝܢܝܢ, e.g. ܐܬܕܟܪܝܢܝ, "remember thou me," ܕܟܪܝܢܝܢ, ܩܘܡܝܢܝܢ, ܐܙܠܝܢܝܢ. As in the imperfect, so here, the final *n* has usually been dropped, e.g. Chald. קְטֻלִי; and then the *i* has disappeared also, as in the Syriac ܩܛܘܠܝ, ܐܙܠܝ; Mand. סגוד, בהאר. In the Talmūd the final י is retained, at any rate in writing, e.g. שקולי, תברי, זילי. The Ethiopic form is *nĕgĕrî, lĕbásî*, with shifting of the accent, as we might expect. In the Assyrian forms *šukinî* or *šuknî, riḥiṣî* or *riḥṣî, ṣabtî*, the elision of the vowel seems to indicate that the accent remained on the first syllable. The classical Arabic too retains the accent on the prosthetic vowel, *'úḳtulî, 'íglisî*; whereas in vulgar Arabic (Egypt) it is shifted, *uḳtúlî, imsíkî*. In Hebrew the forms *ḳ'ṭúlî, ḳ'ṭálî*, are found in pause, e.g. עֲבֹרִי, וּשְׂמָחִי, תֵּנִי; but also out of pause, according to the *k'thîbh*, in מלוכי Judg. ix. 12, קסומי 1 Sam. xxviii. 8. Out of pause, however, the word is commonly modelled somewhat after the form of segolate nouns, and becomes *ḳuṭ'lî, ḳaṭ'lî*; e.g. מָלְכִי, עָלְזִי, קָרְחִי, וָעֲקִי, רַחֲקִי; but the vowel of the first syllable is mostly weakened to *i*, or even, in certain cases, to *shĕvâ*; e.g. עִמְרִי, עִבְרִי, לִבְשִׁי, שִׂמְחִי, רְאִי, עֲשִׂי.

The plural of *ḳ'tul* we should naturally expect, after the analogy of the imperfect, to be *ḳ'tulûna*; and this form is actually found in Syriac, ܩܛܘܠܘܢ. Usually, however, the *n* is dropped, as in the Chaldee קְטֻלוּ; and lastly the final *u* disappears, as in the perfect, leaving in Syriac the form ܩܛܘܠ, ܐܡܪܘ, written in Mandaitic without the *w*, פרוש. בהאר. The Mandaitic however exhibits a few examples of the full termination *ûn*, or even, as in the perfect, *yûn*, e.g. ארדוביון (with prosthetic א), "lay waste." The final *û* is also retained before the enclitics, e.g. שביקולה, סגודולה. In Talmudic the *u* is often retained, at any rate in writing, as עבודו, כתבו. If dropped, it seems in some cases to affect the vowel of the previous syllable, as אימור (for אימְרו) or the interjectional אֵשַׁר ("quick!"). The Ethiopic form is, as we might expect, *nĕgĕrû*, *lĕbásû*, with shifting of the accent; the Assyrian, *sukinû* or *suknû*, *riḥiṣû* or *riḥsû*, *ṣabtû*, were perhaps accentuated on the first syllable, as the elision of the vowel seems to indicate. The old Arabic retains the accent on the prosthetic syllable, *'úḳtulû*, *'iglisû*; but the vulgar dialect (Egypt) shifts it, *uḳtúlû*, *imsíkû*. In Hebrew the forms *ḳ'ṭúlû*, *ḳ'ṭálû*, appear in pause, as זְכֹרוּ, עֲבֹדוּ, אֱכֹלוּ, שְׁמָעוּ, אֱהָבוּ, שֵׁבוּ (for יְשֵׁבוּ). Out of pause, the word is modelled somewhat after the form of segolate nouns, and becomes *ḳuṭ'lû*, *ḳaṭ'lû*, as מָשְׁכוּ, זַעֲקוּ, רַחֲצוּ. Mostly, however, the vowel of the first syllable is weakened to *i*, or even, in certain cases, to *shĕvâ*; e.g. זִכְרוּ, אִכְלוּ, עִבְדוּ, אִסְפוּ; אִמְצוּ, קִרְאוּ; רְאוּ, בְּכוּ, compared with the pausal בְּעָיוּ.

For the 2nd pers. plur. fem. the normal form ought to be *ḳ'tulâna*, which appears in Syriac, with weakening of the vowel in the last syllable, as ܩܛܘܠܝܢ. If the *u* be dropped, the vowel disappears with it, leaving ܩܛܘܠܝܢ *ḳ'ṭôl*. But with suffixes the original *â* is restored, as ܩܛܘܠܢܝܗ, ܩܛܘܠܢܝ. Similarly, the Ethiopic forms are *nĕgĕrâ*, *lĕbásâ*; and the Assyrian, *sukinâ* or *suknâ*, *riḥiṣâ* or *riḥṣâ*, *ṣabtâ*. The Arabic, on the contrary, follows the analogy of the imperfect. As *taḳtulâna* becomes *taḳtúlna*, so *ḳ'tulâna* becomes اُقْتُلْنَ *'uḳtúlna*. This too is the Hebrew form, רְאֶינָה, שְׁמַעְנָה, סְפֹּרְנָה. In a couple of instances the final נָה (also written ־ןָ) is shortened into *n*, viz. שְׁמַעַן Gen. iv. 23, and קְרֶאןָ Exod. ii. 20; which is in accordance with the vulgar pronunciation of a form like ضَرَبْنَ, as heard in Palestine by Robinson and Eli Smith, viz. *ḍurubn*.

The dual is to be found in ancient Arabic alone, and its form is analogous to that of the imperfect, viz., *'úḳtulâ*, for *'uḳtulâni*, *ḳ'tulâni*. It serves for both genders, like the imperf. *taḳtulâni*.

IV. *Variations of the Imperfect and Imperative.*

I now proceed to notice sundry variations of the imperfect and imperative, which are used in the Semitic languages to express different shades of meaning, and which correspond in part to the several moods of the Indo-European tongues. As regards the imperfect, it has four such forms, serving as indicative, subjunctive, jussive (cohortative, optative), and energetic; whilst the imperative has two, the simple and the energetic.

It is in the old Arabic alone that these forms appear in full vigour, clearly distinguished by their terminations. The imperfect indicative ends in *u*, *yáḳtulu*; the subjunctive in *a*, *yáḳtula*. The jussive has ordinarily no vowel, *yáḳtul*, but seems originally to have ended in *i*; at least the poets use *yáḳtuli* in rime. Furthermore, the shorter terminations *î*, *û*, and *â* are always substituted for the fuller *îna*, *ûna*, and *âni*, in the fem. sing., the masc. plur., and the dual; *táḳtulî*, *yáḳtulû*, *yáḳtulâ*, not *taḳtulîna*, *yaḳtulûna*, *yaḳtulâni*. The province of each form is also distinctly marked out. The subjunctive is used in dependent clauses after certain conjunctions, such as أَنْ "that," كَيْ "that," لِ "that, in order that," حَتَّى "until," and the like. The jussive serves as an imperative after لَا "not," as لَا تَقْتُلْ "do not kill," and after لِ, as لِيَقْتُلْ "let him kill" (commonly used in the 3rd pers. only). Preceded by لَمْ it designates the negative of the past, as لَمْ يَقْتُلْ, "he did not kill." It is also extensively employed in two correlative conditional clauses, whether actually introduced by the conditional particle إِنْ "if," or not; e.g. إِنْ تَعْجَلْ تَنْدَمْ "if thou art hasty, thou wilt repent"; مَنْ يَعْمَلْ سُوءًا يُجْزَ بِهِ "he who doth evil, shall be recompensed for it."

In such languages as have lost the final vowels, these distinctions are of course no longer clearly obvious. The Aramaic, for example, we may at once dismiss from our observation. In Ethiopic a special form *yĕnágĕr* is employed for the imperfect indicative; whilst the ordinary *yĕngĕr* represents the subjunctive and jussive, e.g. እግዚእ፡ ብሔር፡ ይዕቀብከ፡ (*yĕ'ḳábka*) "may God preserve thee," ለይኩን፡ ብርሃን፡ "let there be light." Similarly, in Assyrian, if the grammarians may be implicitly trusted, the imperfect indicative is *išákin*; whilst *iškun* has assumed an aoristic sense. Of this fact there appears to be no doubt. In the so-called precative, however, we see a form exactly corresponding to the Arabic jussive with لِ and the Ethiopic with ለ፡; e.g. 3rd pers. *liškun*, *liškunū*, 2nd pers. *lutaškun*, 1st pers. *luškun*.

In Hebrew there is a somewhat closer correspondence to the fullness of the Arabic. If we can no longer distinguish the subjunctive from the indicative, we can at any rate clearly discern the jussive, and perceive that it had originally the same form as in Arabic. This takes place most easily in the Hiph'îl of the regular verb, in the Ḳal and Hiph'îl of verbs ע״ע and ע״י, and in the various conjugations of verbs ל״ה; though there are equally clear cases in the Ḳal of some other classes, where the imperfect has *a* or *ē* for its characteristic vowel. The form is used as an optative or an imperative, especially after the negative אַל, or in the 3rd pers.; frequently too in correlative conditional clauses, as in Arabic; and lastly, with the so-called *vâv conversive.* On all these points see your Hebrew Grammar or Mr Driver's treatise on the tenses. Here I shall only seek to illustrate the different forms. If you compare אַל־תַּשְׁחֵת with תַּשְׁחִית, or אַל־יַאֲמֵן with יַאֲמִין, you perceive at once that you have before you two forms corresponding exactly to the Arabic يَقْتُلُ and يَقْتُلَ. תַּשְׁחִית or יַאֲמִין is, as I shall explain to you in a subsequent lecture, the equivalent of يُقْتِلُ with the loss of the final vowel; while תַּשְׁחֵת or יַאֲמֵן answers to the shorter يُقْتِلْ, *i* being heightened into *ē* in the tone-syllable. With *vāv conversive* this *ē* may even become *ĕ*, if the accent be thrown back, as וַיּוֹסֶף from יוֹסֵף. So also in verbs ע״ע, compare יָחֹן, יָסֹב, יָעֹז, with וַיָּחָן, וַיָּסָב, וַתָּעָז; Hiph'il יָגֵן, יָפֵר, with וַיָּרֶק, וַיָּפֶר. In verbs ע״ו, יָקוּם with יָקֹם and וַיָּקָם; Hiph'il, יָבִין with יָבֵן and וַיָּבֶן, יָסִיר with יָסֵר and וַיָּסַר. In verbs ל״ה the form is even more marked, if possible: יִשְׁבֶּה but וַיִּשְׁבְּ, יִרְאֶה but וַיַּרְא; with tone-lengthening, יִשְׁטֶה, יֵשְׁטְ; יִבְכֶּה, וַיֵּבְךְּ; יֵרְדְּ, וַיֵּרְדְּ, וַיֵּשְׁתְּ; with supplemental vowel, יְחַדֶּה, יְחַר, יָגֶל, יֵרָא, יַעַשׂ, יַעַל. In Pi''ēl, יְצַוֶּה, יְקַוֶּה, but יְצַו, יְקַו, וַיְגַל, וַיְכַם; in Hiph'il, יַפְתֶּה but יַפְתְּ, יַרְדֶּה but יַרְדְּ, יַשְׁקֶה but וַיַּשְׁק; with supplemental vowel, יֶרֶב, וַיִּחַר, וַיָּגֶל, וַיִּפֶן.

Once more; there exists in Arabic, as I have already told you, an *energetic* or *cohortative* in two shapes, the one with the fuller ending *anna*, the other with the shorter *an*, يَقْتُلَنَّ and يَقْتُلَنْ. If we seek after the origin of this termination, we shall perhaps discover it in that demonstrative *n*, which we have already found as a component part of so many pronouns and other demonstratives, such as הֵן; הֵן, הִנֵּה, إِنْ; أَنْ; and the like. I will not, however, pretend to decide as to the fuller form يَقْتُلَنَّ, whether it arises from an intensive doubling of the *n* of يَقْتُلَنْ, or whether, as Stade thinks, it is compounded of يَقْتُلَ and a particle, now lost in Arabic, equivalent in meaning to the Hebrew נָא and

Syriac ܢܳܐ. If the latter be the case, أَقُومَنْ would be exactly equivalent to אָקוּמָה נָּא. Similar is the form in the inscriptions of S. Arabia, as in the tablet: וליקמען עתתר דיתברנה.

These forms, or at any rate the shorter one of the two, have left distinct traces in Hebrew in two ways. (1) In all those forms of the imperfect with pronominal suffixes, where our grammars speak of an *epenthetic nūn* (Kautzsch's *nūn energicum* or *demonstrativum* is a better term). This *n* is sometimes preserved, as יַעַבְרֻנְהוּ Jerem. v. 22, יִצְּרֶנְהוּ Deut. xxxii. 10, יְבָרֲכֶנְהוּ Ps. lxxii. 5, אֶתְּקֶנְךָּ Jerem. xxii. 24, יְכַבְּדָנְנִי Ps. l. 23; but more usually assimilated, as יִשְׁמְעֶךָּ, יַעַזְבֶךָּ, יַעַזְבֶנָּה, יַחְקְרֶנּוּ. Similar forms are in constant use in the Aramaic dialects, though more widely in some than in others, and have even found their way into the perfect with plural suffixes in Mandaitic and Talmudic, as also perhaps in the Syriac form ܩܛܰܠ ܐܶܢܽܘܢ = Mand. לגאטינהון or לגאטינון, though ܐܶܢܽܘܢ may here be the independent pronoun = הִמּוֹ or הִמּוֹן in Biblical Aramaic. In Phoenician this demonstrative *n* occurs also in the suffixes appended to nouns. (2) In the separate forms in ־ָה. In Arabic أَقْتُلَنْ may also be written أَقْتُلَا, and is pronounced in pause أَقْتُلَا *'aḳtulā*. Hence is apparent its identity with the Hebrew אֶקְטְלָה. Observe, however, that whilst the form is fully inflected in Arabic, its use is almost restricted in Hebrew to the first person sing. and plur.: אֶחְבְּשָׁה, אֶעְבְּרָה, נַעַבְרָה; אֶעֱזְבָה, נַעַבְרֶךָּ, אֶפְּלָה, אֶצְּרָה; in pause, with older accent, אֶשְׁמֹרָה, אֶעֱבֹרָה, נַחְקֹרָה, אֶפֹּלָה, אֶצֹּרָה; אֶשְׁאֲלָה, אֶתְּנָה, אֶתְּנָה; אִישָׁנָה. Very rare are examples in the other persons; e.g., in the 3rd, Ps. xx. 4, Is. v. 19, Ezek. xxiii. 20, Prov. i. 20, viii. 3, Job xi. 17 (where some take תָּעֻפָה for the 2nd pers. masc.). Of a weakened form in ־ֶה we have two instances; יְדַשְּׁנֶה Ps. xx. 4, and וָאֶקְרָאֶה 1 Sam. xxviii. 15.

These same energetic forms are also used in the imperative, viz. in Arabic, اُقْتُلَنْ and اُقْتُلَنَّ. In Hebrew the form in ָה is restricted to the 2nd pers. sing. masc., but appears in two shapes. (1) With the older accentuation, קְטֹ֫לָה, קְטֹ֫לָה, from *ḳ'túlan*, *ḳ'tálan*; as פְּשֹׁטָה and חֲגֹרָה Is. xxxii. 11, מלוכה Judg. ix. 8 (*Kᵉthībh*), צרופה Ps. xxvi. 2 (*Do.*); שְׁמָ֫עָה, רְגָזָה, יְרָשָׁה; with suffixes שְׁמָעֶנָּה, קְרָאֶנָּה, תְּנֶנָּה. (2) More frequently the form is adapted to that of the augmented persons of the imperative, and the accent shifted to the last syllable; e.g. כְּרְתָה, עִזְבָה, זִכְרָה, שִׁמְרָה; or with weakening of the vowel, מִכְרָה, עָרְבָה, נִצְּרָה, שִׁמְעָה. With weakening of ָה into ֶה we find דְּעֶה in Prov. xxiv. 14, according to one reading, another being דְּעָה.

V. *The Infinitive.*

The *infinitive* of the Semitic languages is in reality nothing but a verbal noun, varying in form according to various modifying influences. In Arabic the grammarians enumerate some forty of these forms in the first conjugation only, though perhaps not more than a dozen or so of these are in common use. In the other languages the number is much smaller. In Ethiopic there are in the first conjugation only two, *nagîr* and *nagîrôt*; in Aramaic but one, מִקְטַל, ܡܩܛܠ. The Hebrew has likewise two infinitives, one of which, however, appears under several different forms.

Among the commonest infinitives in Arabic are the simple segolates قَتْل *ḳatl*, *ḳitl*, *ḳutl*, as ضَرْب, قَوْل; حِفْظ, ذِكْر; جُبْن, شُكْر; with their rarer feminines قَتْلَة *ḳatla*, *ḳitla*, *ḳutla*, as رَحْمَة, حِمْيَة, سُمْرَة. To these—or still more closely to their Aramaic equivalents [the nominal forms] *ḳ'ṭal*, *ḳ'ṭil*, *ḳ'ṭul*—correspond the forms of the ordinary Hebrew infinitive construct, קְטַל and קְטֹל, with their feminines קִטְלָה or קָטְלָה, and קְטָלָה or קְטֹלָה. Of these by far the most common is קְטֹל, with suffixes קָטְלִי and קָטְלֵנִי, קָטְלְךָ or קְטָלְךָ, קָטְלוֹ, etc. Of the rarer forms examples are: (1) שְׁכַב, שְׁפַל, חֲסַר, שְׁלַח; with suffixes, שִׁכְבָהּ Gen. xix. 33, בְּזַעְפּוֹ 2 Chron. xxvi. 19, בְּמַעֲלָם Ezek. xx. 27, זַעֲקֶךָ Is. xxx. 19. (2) אַהֲבָה Deut. vii. 8, חֶמְלָה Gen. xix. 16, יִרְאָה Is. xxix. 13; שִׂנְאָה Deut. i. 27. (3) עָצְמָה Is. xlvii. 9, גָּבְהָה Zeph. iii. 11, קָרְבָה Exod. xxxvi. 2, xl. 32, חֻמְלָה Ezek. xvi. 5, חֻמְצָה Hos. vii. 4.

The other Hebrew infinitive, the so-called infinitive absolute, has the form *ḳâṭôl*, as בָּנֹה, אָרוֹר, יָדוֹעַ, יָצוֹא, הָלוֹךְ, נָתֹן, גָּוֹעַ. Since *ô* in Hebrew ordinarily represents original *â*, this form seems to be identical with the interjectional or imperative form *ḳaṭâli* قَتَالِ in Arabic. As in Hebrew שָׁמוֹר means "keep, observe!" or זָכוֹר "remember!" so in Arabic نَزَالِ means "come down!" تَرَاكِ "let alone!"

VI. *The Participles.*

Of the active participle there would appear to have been originally three forms, corresponding to the three forms of the perfect, viz. *ḳaṭal*, *ḳaṭil*, and *ḳaṭul*. The first of these, however, is actually known to us only as a verbal adjective, e.g. חָכָם, יָשָׁר, חָדָשׁ; unless we except the fem. הָרָה, constr. הָרַת. The other two actually occur as participles: יָגוֹר Jerem. xxii. 25, xxxix. 17 (the only example of this form), רָעֵב, מָלֵא, גָּדֵל, יָשֵׁן, etc. The place of *ḳaṭal* has been usurped by an intensive form *ḳâṭal*, of which we find clear traces in the verbs ל״ה, e.g. חוֹזֶה,

for *ḥôzai* חֹזַי (which actually occurs as a proper name); and in the usual feminine *kôṭéleth*, for *kôṭalt*, as יֹשֶׁבֶת, יֹרֶדֶת, בֹּרַחַת, יֹדַעַת, in pause יֹשָׁבֶת, with suffixes יוֹלַדְתּוֹ, יוֹלַדְתְּכֶם; as well as, I think, in such construct forms as אֹבַד Deut. xxxii. 28, נֹטַע Ps. xciv. 9. Far more common however than *kâṭal* is the form *kâṭil*, which may be explained in one of two ways; either as a weakening of *kâṭal* by change of *a* in the second syllable into *i*; or as an intensive of the intransitive *kaṭil*, the use of which has been gradually extended so as to embrace all classes of verbs. Its oldest form is the Arabic *kâṭil*, fem. *kâtilat*, with which closely agree the Ethiopic *ṣâdĕḳ*, fem. *ṣâdĕkt*, and the Assyrian *sâkin*, *âsib*, fem. *sâkinat*, *âsibat*, as also the Aramaic קָטֵל, קָטְלָא, ܩܳܛܶܠ, ܩܳܛܠܳܐ. In the Biblical Aramaic this participle is pointed, at least in pause, קָטֵל, e.g. Dan. iv. 10, vi. 3, vii. 9, but also iii. 17, iv. 20, 34. In the same dialect the feminine and plurals have moveable *shĕvā*, e.g. בָּטְלָא Ezr. iv. 24, כָּתְבָה Dan. v. 5, יָתְבִין Ezr. iv. 17, סָלְקִין; whereas in Syriac the *shĕvā* is silent, ܩܳܛܠܺܝܢ, ܩܳܛܠܳܐ, whence it comes that in later Jewish Aramaic [and in some Hebrew Bibles] we often find *pathach* in the first syllable, though incorrectly. The moveable shĕvā is of course the older form, coinciding with the moveable shĕvā of the Hebrew, and the full vowel *i* of the Arabic *kâtilûna*, *kâtilatun*. The Hebrew form naturally substitutes *ô* for *â* in the 1st syllable, and heightens the vowel of the tone-syllable into *ē*, whence קוֹטֵל, fem. קוֹטְלָה, in certain cases with fuller vowel אוֹכֵלָה, בֹּגֵדָה.

In regard to the passive participle, the Semitic languages diverge from one another more than is usual. Of the passive voice generally I shall treat at another opportunity. At present it must suffice to say that the participial form ordinarily employed in Arabic is *maḳtûl*, with the prefix *ma*, of which I shall have more to say when we come to the derived conjugations of the verb. The Hebrew form *kaṭûl*, קָטוּל, is very common in Ethiopic, but with the first vowel weakened, *kĕtûl*, fem. *kĕtûlt*, e.g. *ṣĕḥûf* "written," *'ĕsúr* "bound," *mĕlû* "full," fem. *ṣĕḥêft, 'ĕsîrt, mĕlî'ĕt*. The Arabic form فَعُول is also sometimes used in a passive sense, e.g. رَكُوبَة "a she camel for riding," حَلُوبَة "a she camel for milking." In Syriac too there are a few examples of this kind, as ܪܚܘܡܐ, ܪܚܘܡܬܐ, "beloved," ܣܢܘܐ, ܣܢܝܬܐ, "hated," ܓܢܘܒܬܐ "a thing stolen," ܫܡܘܥܬܐ "a thing heard, a rumour." In Aramaic however the form קְטִיל, ܩܛܝܠ, is preferred, which is identical with the Arabic adjective *ḳatîl*; e.g. أَسِير, جَرِيح, قَتِيل. Of another verbally inflected *ḳĕṭîl* in Aramaic I shall attempt an explanation when we come to the passive voice.

VII. *The Derived Conjugations.*

A. *First Group.*

I next proceed to speak briefly of the more important of the derived conjugations.

These are divisible into groups, the members of which closely resemble one another in their inflexion. The first group consists of three: (*a*) an intensive and iterative or frequentative; (*b*) a form expressive of effort, with an implied idea of reciprocal effort; and (*c*) a factitive or causative.

1. The first of these, the intensive and iterative, finds its expression in the doubling of the second consonant of the root. You may remember that intensive nouns are formed in the same way; that a word of the form *ḳăṭăl*, like חָכָם or רָשָׁע, becomes *ḳăṭṭăl*, like גַּנָּב or טַבָּח. Now as the nominal *ḳăṭăl* lies at the root of the verbal form *ḳăṭălă*, so does the nominal *ḳăṭṭăl* at the root of the verbal *ḳăṭṭălă*.

The Arabic, as usual, exhibits this form in its primitive integrity, *ḳáttala*; قَتَّلَ "to kill many, to massacre"; كَسَّرَ "to break into many pieces"; بَكَّى "to weep much" or "constantly"; مَوَّتَ

"to die in great numbers"; طَوَّفَ "to go round and round." So in Ethiopic, ረሰየ: *rassăya*, "to do"; ፈነወ: *fannăwa*, "to send"; ጸውዐ: *ṣawwĕʻa*, "to call out" (where the vowel of the 2nd syllable is modified by the final guttural). In Hebrew the original form was, of course, *ḳaṭṭăl*; but as in the noun we find אִכָּר for אַכָּר, so in the verb *ḳiṭṭăl* for *ḳăṭṭăl*, as גִּדַּל, אִבַּד, שִׁבַּר, רִחַם, אֵרַשׂ "betroth to oneself." The *ă* of the 2nd syllable is sometimes weakened to *ĕ* ֶ, as in דִּבֶּר, כִּפֶּר, כִּבֶּס (with which compare the change of *ă* into *ĕ* in גֶּבֶר for גַּבְר); but far more usually into *ĭ*, more especially in pause, where it appears, owing to the force of the tone, as *ē* ֵ. This change is probably owing to the influence of the vowel of the same syllable in the imperfect and imperative (יְקַטֵּל, קַטֵּל). In the first and 2nd persons the original short *ă* is dominant, דִּבַּרְתָּ, דִּבַּרְתְּ, דִּבַּרְתֶּם, דִּבַּרְתִּי, דִּבַּרְנוּ. In the pausal forms of the 3rd pers. sing. fem., and the 3rd pers. plur., the weaker vowel predominates: לִקֵּטָה, גִּדֵּלָה, דִּבֵּרוּ, שִׁבֵּרוּ, though we also find קִבָּצָה, Micah i. 7. In the Aramaic dialects the weakened קַטֵּל, קַטֵּל, ܩܰܛܶܠ prevails, except where a guttural, or the letter *r*, as 3rd radical, may have protected the original vowel; e.g. ܫܰܒܰܚ, ܙܰܡܰܪ.

Glancing at the imperative, imperfect, and participle, we observe that in all the Semitic languages the vowels of the root-syllables are *a* in the first and *i* in the second, *ḳaṭṭil*. So the imperative in Arabic, قَتِّلْ *ḳăttil*; in Ethiopic, ፈጽም: *făṣṣĭm*; in Hebrew, דַּבֵּר, בַּקֵּשׁ; in Syriac, ܐܰܡܶܪ, ܟܰܬܶܒ. The nominal form *ḳăṭĭl*, intensified to *ḳăṭṭĭl*, lies at the root of the verbal form. Hence it appears that the use of *ă* in the case of radicals 3rd guttural, like בַּלַּע, שַׂמַּח, ܫܰܒܰܚ, ܙܰܡܰܪ, is due, not to the retention of the original vowel under the protection of the guttural, but to a later change of *ĭ*, *ē*, into *ă* under the influence of that guttural. Side by side with שַׂמַּח לִבִּי, Prov. xxvii. 11, we have שַׂמַּח נֶפֶשׁ עַבְדֶּךָ; and the pausal forms of the fem. and plur. are always דַּבֵּרִי, דַּבֵּרוּ, not דַּבָּרִי, דַּבָּרוּ.

The imperfect is formed and inflected on precisely the same principles as in the first or simple conjugation. The vowel of the preformatives was originally *ă*, yielding the forms *yaḳáṭṭilu, taḳáṭṭilu*, etc. This pure vowel I find, however, only in the Ethiopic subjunctive of verbs 1st guttural, e.g. የሐድስ: *yaḥáddĕs*. Otherwise it is weakened into *ĕ*, as *yĕfaṣṣĕm*, ይፈጽም:. In Arabic this dull obscure vowel appears in the classical language as *ŭ*, e.g. يُقَتِّلُ, تُقَتِّلُ; and the same is the case in Assyrian, where we have the forms *yušakkin, tušakkin*, etc. In vulgar Arabic Spitta gives the preformative the vowel *i*, whilst the vowel of the final syllable varies according to the nature of the last radical, *yiṣaddaḳ, yifattaḥ*, but *yikallim, yirattib*. In Hebrew and Aramaic the preformative vowel is also *ĕ*, יְקַטֵּל, ܢܩܰܛܶܠ, save that in the 1st pers. sing. ֲ appears in Hebrew and ֶ in Aramaic, אֲדַבֵּר, ܐܶܩܰܛܶܠ. As, in the 1st conj., the Ethiopic exhibits two varieties of the imperfect, one serving for the indicative, the other for the subjunctive and jussive, so here in the 2nd conj. In the 1st conj., however, the distinction was easily made, and effected by a mere change of the vocalisation; *yĕnágĕr* for the indicative, *yĕngĕr* for the subjunctive, corresponding in form at least to the Assyrian *išákin* and *iškun*. But here, in the 2nd conj., some further change is necessary, because of the double letter, which renders any mere vowel change almost impossible without entirely destroying the normal form. The Ethiopic therefore retained the normal *yĕfáṣṣĕm* for the subjunctive, and had recourse for the indicative to the form *yĕfēṣĕm*, ይፌጽም:, the origin of which is not perfectly clear. That the doubling of the 2nd radical has been dropped is certain; and therefore it seems most likely that the form *ḳaitála* has been resorted to, which would naturally appear in Ethiopic as *ḳētála*.

The active participle follows exactly the same vocalisation. Its preformative in Ethiopic is *ma*, e.g. መዐመፅ: *ma'ámmĕṣ*,

መኰንን: *makwdnnĕn.* The Hebrew and Aramaic weaken the vowel to *ĕ*, מְדַבֵּר, ܡܣܰܟܰܠ; and this dull vowel is represented in old Arabic and Assyrian by *u*, مُقَتِّل, *mušakkin*, in modern Arabic by *ĕ*, as *mĕfattaḥ*, *mĕṣaddaḳ*, *mĕkammil*, *mĕ'allim*.

The infinitive of this conj. also calls for a few remarks. Beginning with the Hebrew, we find the ordinary or construct infin. to be קַטֵּל, *ḳaṭṭēl*, from an original *ḳaṭṭil*. The weakening of the 1st vowel to *i* is a rarity, as חִלֵּץ Levit. xiv. 43, קִטֵּר Jerem. xliv. 21; שִׁלֵּם Deut. xxxii. 35[1]. Compare in the class of concretes such words as גִּבֵּן, עִוֵּר, from *gabbin*, *'avvir*. The same form *ḳaṭṭēl* serves for the infin. absolute (with weakening נִאֵץ 2 Sam. xii. 14); but with it occurs another, viz. קַטֹּל, e.g. קַנֹּא, יַסֹּר, רַפֹּא, בָּרוֹךְ. The corresponding concretes are exemplified by רַתּוֹק "chain," קַנּוֹא "zealous, jealous," or, with weakening of the 1st vowel, מִלּוֹא, גִּבּוֹר, שִׁכּוֹר, יִסּוֹר (Job xl. 2 = xxxix. 32), קִפּוֹז (قَفَّازَة). These all spring from an original *ḳaṭṭâl*, the intensive of قَتَال, קָטוֹל. The Arabic infin. قِتَّال is therefore weakened from قَتَّال, as in كِذَّاب, عِلَّام, حِمَّال, as compared with the concretes كَذَّاب, عَلَّام, حَمَّال.—The forms with prefixed *t*, which are generally assigned to this conjugation, تَقْتَال, تَقْتِيل, تَقْتِلَة, we shall explain elsewhere.—In Aramaic the forms of the infinitive diverge somewhat from one another. The Aramaic of the Bible and the Targūms generally has the form קַטָּלָא (קַטָּלָה); whilst the Talmūd Bablī, the Mandaitic, and the modern Syriac, exhibit קַטּוֹלֵי; e.g. Talm. B. שַׁבּוֹחֵי,

[1] [Kautzsch-Ges. (25th ed., p. 143) recognises only two certain examples of the infinitive const. with *i* in the first syllable, viz. Lev. xiv. 43 and 1 Chron. viii. 8, and in both the text is open to question; see *Journ. of Phil.* xvi. 72. In 2 Sam. xii. 14 the inf. abs. נִאֵץ seems to be influenced by the sound of the following word נִאַצְתָּ.]

אַפּוּיֵי, צְלוּיֵי; Mand. בארוכיא, נאטוריא, אסוייא, שאבוהיא; mod. Syr. ܢܛܘܪ̈ܬܐ, ܦܘܪܩܢܐ. This קַטּוּלֵי is not easy to explain, but most likely, as Noeldeke thinks, it is connected with such Hebrew forms as שְׁכּוּל (plur. שִׁכֻּלִים, Is. xlix. 20) and שִׁלּוּם, *plus* the originally fem. termination *ai*, which we find in Syriac in ܬܫܡܫܝ, ܬܢܘܚܝ, etc. In all these dialects an *m* is occasionally prefixed, Targ. מְקַטְּלָא, Mand. מפאקודיא, mod. Syr. ܡܦܩܘܕܐ, ܡܦܩܢܘܬܐ; and this is the ordinary form in old Syriac, but with a different termination, though also originally fem., viz. ܡܩܛܠܘ. The prefixing of the *m* may have been due to the influence of the participial forms, and of the infin. Pĕʻal, ܡܩܛܠ. — In Mandaitic and modern Syriac a fem. of קַטָּלָא is also in common use as a verbal noun or infinitive, viz. *kaṭṭâltā*, as פאקארתא "order," ראגאזתא "provocation," זאבאנתא "selling," זאהארתא "warning"; ܬܫܠܡܬܐ "completion," ܦܘܪܩܬܐ "deliverance." The most nearly corresponding forms in Hebrew are represented by such words as בַּקָּשָׁה "desiring," בַּקָּרָה "care," בַּלָּהָה "terror," בַּצָּרָה "cutting off (of rain), drought, distress," בַּקֹּרֶת "punishment," בַּצֹּרֶת "drought." These are intensives of the form ܩܛܠܬܐ *kĕṭâltā*, found in old Syriac and still more abundantly in mod. Syriac, ܦܘܫܩܬܐ, ܢܘܫܩܬܐ, ܡܘܢܚܬܐ; just as קַטָּלָא is the intensive of the Syr. and Mand. קְטָלָא, ܫܘܩܠܐ, ܦܘܩܕܢܐ, ܗܘܕܝܐ.

2. The second verbal form in this group is that which expresses an effort, with the implied idea of a counter-effort. Its expression lies in the lengthening of the vowel of the first syllable, *ḳâtala* instead of *ḳátala*. It is in general use in Arabic only, but examples occur in Ethiopic too, the form being identical in both languages, viz. بَارَكَ, ባረከ: "bless"; حَاكَمَ "go to law"; كَالَمَ "talk to"; نَافَقَ, ናፈቀ: "play the hypocrite."

In Hebrew its use is likewise restricted. It appears in this language under the shape of *ḳōṭēl*, for *ḳāṭāl*, and is most common in verbs ע״ע, e.g. פּוֹדֵר "cleave," חוֹלֵל "pierce, wound," חוֹנֵן "show mercy," סוֹבֵב "surround," הוֹלֵל "befool," רוֹצֵץ "crush to bits." In the ordinary triliteral verb examples are rare, but certain; e.g. שׁוֹפֵט (Job ix. 15, מְשֹׁפְטִי = مُحَاكِمِي), לוֹשֵׁן (Ps. ci. 5, מְלוֹשְׁנִי בַסֵּתֶר רֵעֵהוּ), סוֹעֵר (Hos. xiii. 3, יְסוֹעֵר "blows away"), שׁוֹרֵשׁ "to take root," הֹרוֹ וְהֹגוֹ "conceiving and uttering," Is. lix. 13. In Aramaic this form can hardly be said to occur, save in Biblical Aramaic, where we find מְסוֹבְלִין "set up," Ezra vi. 3. The inflexion runs entirely parallel to that of the intensive form, and therefore requires no special elucidation. I will merely remark as to the Arabic infinitive that the original form is قِيتَال *ḳîtāl*, of which the grammarians quote one or two examples, as ضِيرَاب and قِيتَال. Usually, however, it has been shortened into قِتَال, though some compensated for the loss of the long vowel by doubling the middle radical, قِتَّال, مِرَّآء, which must however have led to confusion with the infinitive of the intensive. The Hebrew infinitives הֹרוֹ and הֹגוֹ hold fast the original vowel *ā*, and would be represented in Arabic by some such words as قَاتَال and هَاجَآء, which do not actually exist.

As to the participle I would remark that an example without prefixed *m* seems to offer itself in the word עוֹיֵן 1 Sam. xviii. 9 (*Kĕthîbh* עוֹן), for the corresponding Arabic verb is عَايَنَ. We shall have occasion hereafter to notice other participial forms in Hebrew and modern Syriac without prefixed *m*.

And here I may call your attention in passing to another verbal form in Hebrew, which is in some cases identical in sound with this קוֹטֵל. I mean the form קְטַלֵּל, originally *kaṭalál, kaṭlál*, when derived from verbs ע״ו; e.g. כּוֹנֵן for כַּוְנֵן, עוֹרֵר for עַוְרֵר, and the like. Here too we find an active participle without prefixed *m*, שׁוֹרְרַי, "that lie in wait for me," Ps. v. 9, and elsewhere.

3. The factitive or causative conjugation of the verb seems originally to have been marked by a prefixed *ta, takáṭala*, contracted *táḳṭala*. Of this formation verbal examples are exceedingly rare in any dialect. תִּרְגַּלְתִּי, Hos. xi. 3, seems certain; perhaps also ترجم, ተርጐመ:, תִּרְגֵּם, ܬܰܪܓܶܡ, if connected, as seems probable, with the Assyrian root *ragâmu* "to speak," whence *rigmu*, "a word" (Delitzsch). For תְּתַחֲרֶה (Jer. xii. 5, xxii. 15) another explanation is possible. But in verbal nouns of the infinitive class it is exceedingly common, though in our Arabic grammars these are all ascribed to the intensive form, with which, strictly speaking, they have nothing to do. I mean the infinitives تَقْتِيل and تَقْتِلَة, تِقْتَال and تَقْتُول, with their Hebrew and Aramaic equivalents, such as Aram. and late Heb. תַּלְמִיד, תַּכְרִיךְ "shroud," "wrapper," תַּבְנִית "model," תַּרְבִּית "interest," תַּגְמוּל "benefit," תַּחְבּוּלוֹת "guidance"; Syr. ܬܰܟܣܺܝܬܳܐ, ܬܰܓܡܽܘܪܳܐ, ܬܫܰܠܚܽܘܦܳܐ "exchange," ܬܶܫܡܶܫܬܳܐ, ܬܰܘܕܺܝܬܳܐ, ܬܰܕܡܺܝܬܳܐ, ܬܰܘܪܺܝܬܳܐ.—This form with *t* appears to have had a sister form with prefixed *s* or *sh*. In Arabic this latter occurs in rare instances like سَقْلَبَ "dash to the ground," سَلْقَى "throw down flat on the back" (whence the triliteral سَلَقَ), and سَلْعَفَ "swallow," as well as in the exceedingly common reflexive اِسْتَقْتَلَ, of which, as well as of the corresponding Ethiopic forms we shall speak in a subsequent lecture. The Ḥimyaritic exhibits the *s* in one of its dialects, סחדת, סקני. In Amharic the

preformative ሰ, *sa*, more frequently አሰ, *as*, is an ordinary causative prefix, e.g. ክብረ፡ "be honoured," አስከብረ፡ "honour." In Assyrian such forms as *uškin*, "set up," *ušapriš*, "spread out," *ušaṣbit*, "let seize," seem to be common. In Biblical Hebrew, on the other hand, the prefix שׁ is found only in the derivative nouns שַׁלְהֶבֶת "flame," [from Aram. שַׁלְהֵב "kindle"], שְׁקַעֲרוּרוֹת (Levit. xiv. 37), "hollows, depressions," (rad. קער), and שַׁבְּלוּל "snail," (rad. בלל "moisten," بَلَّ). In the Aramaic dialects, on the contrary, there are numerous examples of it, such as שַׁכְלֵל, ܫܟܠܠ, שֵׁיזִב[1], ܫܘܕܥ, ܫܥܒܕ, ܫܠܗܒ, ܫܚܠܦ, ܫܘܬܦ. The form with ס is far more rare, e.g. סַקְבֵּל, סַרְהֵב; Syr. ܣܪܗܒ, ܣܟܠܠ, ܣܘܚܦ (rad. ܐܚܦ); Mand. סארהיב, סאסקיל "smooth."—This initial *s* underwent, however, in most cases, a further change into *h*. Hence some rare Arabic forms like هَرَاحَ "let rest," هَرَادَ "wish," هَرَاقَ "pour out," هَاتِ "give" (for آتِ, imperative of آتَى, from أَتَى "come"). This *h* does not occur in Ethiopic or Assyrian, but we find it in one of the Ḥimyaritic dialects, החדת, הקני. In Biblical Aramaic it is common, in the forms הַקְטֵל, הַקְטִל; and may also be found in the Targūms, at least in verbs פ"י and פ"ן. In Mandaitic there are likewise a few instances, e.g. האוליל "cry out, lament"; האשיט "despise"; האנפיק "lead out," and האנסיק "let ascend," as well as אפיק and אסיק. In Syriac it is unknown[2]; but it is the usual form in Hebrew. Here the original was *haḳṭal*, with *a* in both syllables. For the first syllable this is proved (1) by the vowel of the imperative and imperfect, and (2) by the forms of verbs פ"י, where הוֹרִישׁ, הוֹשִׁיב, can only

[1] [שכלל and שיזב appear to be of Assyrian origin. N.]

[2] [The solitary form ܗܝܡܢ, was regarded by Prof. Wright as a loan-word from the Hebrew.]

arise from הַוְרִישׁ, הַוְשִׁיב. For the second syllable the *a* is established (1) by the vowel of the 1st and 2nd persons, הִקְטַלְתָּ, הִקְטַלְתִּי, etc., and (2) by the form הִגְלָה for הִגְלִי, in verbs ל״ו or ל״י. The vowel of the first syllable was however mostly weakened into *i*, and that of the second into *ī*. In the second syllable we should naturally expect ֵ *ē*, but the language has in this case gone a step further and sunk *ē* into *ī*. Hence the normal הִקְטִיל, with its fem. הִקְטִילָה and plur. הִקְטִילוּ. The rest of the paradigm does not call for much remark. The imperfect יַקְטִיל is a contraction for יְהַקְטִיל, of which fuller form examples occur in Biblical Hebrew and Aramaic. The normal *ē* is retained in Hebrew in the jussive יַקְטֵל, the infinitive absolute הַקְטֵל, and the imperative הַקְטֵל and הַקְטֵלְנָה (הַאְזֵנָּה in Gen. iv. 23); but the long *ī* appears in the heavier forms of the imperfect יַקְטִיל, the energetic יַקְטִילֶנּוּ, הַקְטִילָה, the imperative הַקְטִילִי, הַקְטִילוּ, and the participle מַקְטִיל. The infinitive construct varies between הַקְטִיל and הַקְטֵל, though the former is much more common. A form like הַשְׁמִיד, Deut. vii. 24, xxviii. 48, is a rarity[1].

The last step in the history of the factitive or causative is the weakening of the initial *h* into the spiritus lenis. In Phoenician the perfect is written with initial י, but was probably pronounced *iḳṭîl*. Examples from the inscriptions are יטנא "he set up," and יקדש "he consecrated." This weakening is almost universal in Arabic, where the form is written أَقْتَلَ *'áḳtala*[2]. In Ethiopic too it is exceedingly common; and the prefix *'a* is used in this language to form causatives not merely from *ḳatála*, but also from *ḳattála*, and even from *ḳātála*; as መጽአ: "come," አምጽአ: "bring"; ሖረ: "go," አሖረ: "make to go"; ሠነየ: *sanáya*, "be beautiful," አሠነየ: *'asannáya*, "make beautiful"; አፈጸመ:

[1] [Indeed, the genuineness of such forms is doubtful; see *Journ. of Phil.* xvi. 72.]

[2] In vulgar Arabic one hears *islam* for *aslam*, "he has become a Muslim," but this is a rare exception.

"make one finish"; አለቀሰ: "condole with one." In Tigriña and Amharic too it is in ordinary use. In Hebrew it is very rare (אֶגְאָלְתִּי "I have defiled," Is. lxiii. 3; אַשְׁכֵּים, infin., Jerem. xxv. 3); but in the Aramaic dialects it is the almost universal form, ܐܩܛܠ. In one instance in Syr. the vowel of the 1st syllable is weakened to *ĕ*, viz. ܐܶܫܟܰܚ, as compared with אַשְׁכַּח, הַשְׁכַּח,—like the vulg. Arab. إِسْلِمْ mentioned above. With regard to the initial *a*, I may remark that it disappears after preformatives; e.g. in Arabic, يُقْتِلُ, part. مُقْتِلٌ; in Ethiopic, from አንገረ: "make speak," ያነግር: *yănăgĕr* and ያንግር: *yăngĕr*; Syr. ܢܩܛܠ, ܡܩܛܠ. The vulgar Arabic of Egypt has weakened the vowel of the 1st syllable to *i*, as *yikhbir* (يِخْبِر), *yimhil* (يِمْهِل). In the Aramaic dialects, the infinitive of Aph'ēl exhibits nearly the same varieties as that of Pa"ēl. The Biblical and Targumic form is הַקְטָלָה, אַקְטָלָא, corresponding very nearly to the Arabic إِقْتَالٌ; Talm. Babli and Mandaitic, אַקְטוֹלֵי, as אַפּוֹקֵי, אַחוֹיֵי; ארבוכיא "kneel," אגזוריא "condemn"; with prefixed *m*, מאסגוייא "go," מאיתוייא "bring"; Syriac, always with *m*, ܡܩܛܠܘ.

B. *Second Group.*

The 2nd group of derived conjugations consists of four members, serving originally as reflexives and reciprocals of the previous four, but often also as passives. The sign which is common to the whole of them is the prefixed syllable *ta*. This, whatever may have been its primitive form and derivation, must originally have been quite different from the causative prefix *ta*, of which we spoke above.

1. The reflexive of the first conjugation is *takătala*. Of this

we have two varieties in Ethiopic, ተከደነ: *takaddána*, and ተከድነ: *takádna*, "cover oneself, be covered"; ተዐቀበ: and ተዐቅበ: "guard oneself, abstain, beware, be guarded"; ተወልደ: "be born"; ተአኀዘ: "be taken"; ተመዐዐ: or ተምዐ: "be angry." In course of time the prefixed *ta* would lose its vowel, and take a prosthetic vowel instead, becoming firstly *t'*, and then *'it* or *'ith*. Hence the Aramaic form, אִתְקְטַל, more commonly, with weakening of the last vowel, אִתְקְטֵל, אִתְקְטִיל. In Syriac and Mandaitic we also find a supplementary vowel in frequent use, ܐܶܬܩܛܶܠ, עתיקטיל. The Biblical Aram. has the spiritus asper instead of the lenis, הִתְקְטֵל, e.g. הִתְרְחִצוּ Dan. iii. 28. In Hebrew this form is of very rare occurrence indeed. A possible example, without any prosthetic, may be תַּחֲרָה, of which the imperf. תְּתַחֲרֶה occurs in Jerem. xii. 5, and the participle מְתַחֲרֶה in xxii. 15. If so, this form is next of kin to the Syr. ܐܶܬܚܪܺܝ. More certain is a derivative from the rad. פקד, with the prosthetic spiritus asper, viz. הִתְפָּקֵד "to be numbered, mustered," e.g. Judges xx. 15, 17, xxi. 9, which is written without *daghesh* and with *ḳāmeṣ* wherever it occurs[1]. The Arabic form اِقْتَتَلَ, standing for تَقَتَّلَ, offers us the curious feature of a transposition of the preformative to the place after the first radical, قَتْتَلَ for تَقْتَلَ. This began no doubt with the verbs which commenced with a sibilant, as in Syr. ܐܶܣܛܰܡܰܟ, ܐܶܣܛܰܡܰܟ; ܐܶܙܕܰܟܺܝ, ܐܶܙܕܰܒܰܢ; ܐܶܫܬܰܡܰܥ, ܐܶܫܬܰܡܰܫ; and was gradually extended to all alike. The Arabic parallel to הִתְפָּקֵד is therefore اِفْتَقَدَ "to search for, inspect." Curiously enough the same transposition seems to have existed in Moabitic; at least in the inscription of king Mēsha' we find four times (ll. 11, 15, 19, 32) a form הלתחם, from the rad. לחם, in the

[1] The pronunciation as a passive הָתְפָּקְדוּ, Num. i. 47, ii. 33, xxvi. 62; 1 Kings xx. 27, is probably due to a misunderstanding of the Massoretes.

sense of the Heb. נִלְחַם "fight," Arab. اِلْتَحَمَ "join oneself to, adhere to," "rage" (of a battle). It is also found in Assyrian, as *ištakan* "he made," *iftikid* "he committed" or "entrusted"; and in Ḥimyaritic, without any prosthetic *alif*, e.g. שׁתטר from שׁטר, שׁתאל from שׁאל, נתדר from נדר. It would appear that forms without transposition of the *t*, as well as forms corresponding to those of classical Arabic, exist in the modern dialect of Egypt. At least Spitta distinguishes carefully verbs of the form *itfa'al* or *itfi'il* from the corresponding forms of the intensive with double radical. According to him *itfa'al* or *itfi'il* is usually passive of Conj. I, as *itḥabas, itkasar, itmisik, itfihim*; whereas the transposed *ifta'al* is more usually reflexive than passive, as *i'tamad, intaẓar, iṣṭalaḥ, istama'* ("be heard" and "obey").

2. The reflexive of the intensive and iterative is naturally *taḳáttala.* This form presents itself in Arabic, تَقَتَّلَ, and in Ethiopic, ተቀደሰ፡ *taḳaddása,* "be hallowed," ተፈጸመ፡ *tafaṣṣáma,* "be finished," ተአዘዘ፡ *ta'azzáza,* "obey," ተፈሥሐ፡ *tafasséḥa,* "rejoice" (because of the 3rd guttural). It would gradually be corrupted into اِتَّقَتَّلَ *itḳáttala,* of which we find examples even in classical Arabic, especially when the verb begins with a dental or sibilant, when assimilation takes place, as اِدَّثَّرَ "wrap oneself up in a garment," اِزَّيَّنَ "adorn oneself," اِسَّمَّعَ "hear, listen," اِصَّعَّدَ "ascend," اِصَّدَّقَ "give alms," اِطَّيَّرَ "regard as an evil omen." In this way تَنَفَّسَ would become اِتْنَفَّسَ, and so in vulg. Arabic اِتْعَلَّق *it'allaḳ,* "be suspended," اِتْنَظَّف *itnaḍḍaf,* "be cleansed," or with weakening of the 3rd vowel, اِتْعَمِّم, *it'ammim,* "put on a turban." Here we have the origin of the Aramaic אִתְקַטַּל, Syr. ܐܬܩܛܠ, in Bibl. Aram. הִתְקַטַּל, as הִתְנַדְּבוּ Ezra vii. 15,

v. 17, Dan. iv. 12, 20, 30, etc.; with weakening of the last vowel, הִזְדְּמִנְתּוּן, Dan. ii. 9 (*Kĕrî*); as well as of the Hebrew form הִתְקַטֵּל or הִתְקְטֵל. The assimilation of which I spoke above as occurring even in classical Arabic, is common in most of the dialects. In Arabic a word like اِدَّثَرَ makes in its imperfect يَدَّثِرُ for يَتَدَثَّرُ. Just so in Ethiopic, from verbs with initial dentals and sibilants, we have in this and in the preceding conjugation, such forms as ይጠመቅ፡ from ተጠመቀ፡ "be dipped, baptized"; ይደፈን፡ from ተደፈነ፡ "be covered, buried"; ይሰበር፡ from ተሰበረ፡ "be broken"; ይጸሐፍ፡ from ተጸሐፈ፡ "be written"; ይዜከር፡ from ተዘከረ፡ "remember"; ይጸደቅ፡ from ተጸደቀ፡ "pretend to be righteous." In Tigriña this assimilation extends to all verbs, ይገደፍ፡ "it will be forgiven," from ተገደፈ፡, ይመለስ፡ "he returns," from ተመለሰ፡, ይፈጸም፡ "it will be finished," from ተፈጸመ፡, ይቅበል፡ "he receives," from ተቀበለ፡፡ Indeed the doubling caused by the assimilation of the preformative seems to have been gradually dropped in pronunciation, and these words are now pronounced *yĕgĕdaf, yĕmĕlas, yĕfĕṣam, yĕḳĕbal.* Hence Hebrew forms like הִדַּכָּא, הִטַּהֵר, הִנַּבֵּא, are at once explained, as well as the similar הִכּוֹנֵן. In Mandaitic and the Talmūd this assimilation is as common in both conjugations as in Tigriña. E.g. in Mandaitic, not merely עדּנאר "were heaped up" (עתדנאר), עטּאמאם "were stopped up" (עתטאמאם), but also מיפּתא "opened" (מִתְפְּתַח), מיבּיא "wanted" (מִתְבְּעֵי), מיגּטיל "killed" (מִיתְקְטֵל); עגּאמאר "was fulfilled," עכּאנאש "was collected," מיכּאלאל "crowned"; in the Talmūd, מִיקְּטִיל, מִיגְּנִיב, מִבְּעֵי, מִפַּלְגִי for מִיתְפַּלְגִין, אִיכַּסָּאי "cover thyself" (fem.), and apparently with suppression of the doubling, איעסק "he gave himself the trouble," איעלמא "she hid herself," איעתרי "I am become rich." Similar phenomena occur in Samaritan; and even in Hebrew we have at least one similar instance in the word אֵרוֹמָם, Is. xxxiii. 10.

Yet again, the Ithpĕ'ēl and Ithpa"al forms have a peculiarity common to them in several of the dialects. This is, that when the first radical is a sibilant, the preformative is transposed and appears in the 2nd place, as is always the case with the Arabic اِفْتَعَلَ. Frequently too the ת is changed into a ט or a ד, according to the character of the initial consonant of the root. So in Hebrew, הִסְתַּבֵּל, הִשְׁתַּמֵּר, but הִצְטַדֵּק. So in Syriac, ܐܶܣܬܰܡܰܟ, ܐܶܣܬܰܟܰܠ, ܐܶܣܬܰܟܰܡ, but ܐܶܙܕܰܒܰܢ, ܐܶܙܕܰܗܰܪ, ܐܶܙܕܰܠܰܠ, ܐܶܙܕܰܥܰܩ. So in Arabic, in the conj. اِفْتَعَلَ, اِزْدَجَرَ from زَجَرَ, اِزْدَادَ from زَادَ, اِصْطَبَغَ from صَبَغَ, اِضْطَرَّ from ضَرَّ. In Arabic the assimilation of the two letters is the rule when the first radical is ث, د, ذ, or ظ, and it may take place either backwards or forwards; thus from ثَأَرَ Lane gives اِثَّأَرَ; from ثَرَدَ, اِتَّرَدَ and اِثَّرَدَ, "crumble bread"; from ثَغَرَ, اِتَّغَرَ and اِثَّغَرَ, "cut the front teeth"; from دَرَعَ, اِدَّرَعَ, "put on mail"; from دَلَجَ, اِدَّلَجَ, "journey by night"; from ذَخَرَ and ذَكَرَ, اِدَّخَرَ and اِدَّكَرَ, rather than اِذَّخَرَ and اِذَّكَرَ, but from ذَبَحَ and ذَرَى, اِذَّبَحَ and اِذَّرَى; اِظَّلَمَ or اِطَّلَمَ from ظَلَمَ, اِظَّعَنَ and اِظَّفَرَ from ظَعَنَ and ظَفَرَ. With initial ص and ض this assimilation is far less common, as اِصَّلَحَ, اِصَّبَرَ, اِضَّرَبَ, اِضَّجَعَ; and with س and ز it is very rare, as اِسَّمَعَ, اِزَّانَ. Bearing these facts in mind, we are, I think, justified in saying that a Hebrew form like הִזַּכּוּ (Is. i. 16) is assimilated from הִזְדַּכּוּ, just as the similar תִּשּׁוֹמֵם (Eccles. vii. 16) stands for תִּשְׁתּוֹמֵם, with backward assimilation. Similarly in Syriac, ܢܬܩܢܐ for ܢܬܩܢܐ, ܢܬܩܢܘܢ for ܢܬܩܢܘܢ, ܐܬܢܩܦ for ܐܬܢܩܦ. Here and there we find exceptions to the rule of transposition. In Aramaic the verb ﺍﺿ exhibits the forms יִתְזַבַּן (in Euting's *Nabatäische Inschriften aus Arabien*, no. 11) and מִתְזַבְּנָא in the great Tariff of Palmyra (*Journ. Asiat.* 1883, Aug. Sept., p. 165), A.D. 137 (last year of Hadrian). The solitary Hebrew example will be spoken of below (p. 213).

3. After all that I have said about the forms اِقْتَتَلَ and تَقَتَّلَ, the third member of this group requires but little notice. It is the reflexive and reciprocal of *ḳâtala*, viz. *taḳâtala*, which is the ordinary Arabic form, as تَرَامَى "to throw oneself down," تَمَارَضَ "to pretend to be sick," تَقَاتَلُوا "they fought with one another." So in Ethiopic, ተላጸየ: or ተላፀየ: "to shave oneself," ተሣሀለ: "to show oneself gentle to another, pardon," ተፋለጡ: "they parted from one another," ተሣቀየ: "he was tortured, afflicted." But تَقَاتَلَ gradually became اِتَّقَاتَلَ, and hence such forms in classical Arabic as اِثَّايَعَ "rush headlong," اِثَّاقَلَ "be heavy and troublesome," اِدَّارَأَ "repel one another," اِسَّاقَطَ. In the vulgar Arabic of Egypt the vowel of the 3rd syllable is weakened to *i* or to *shĕva*, as *itkāmil*, *it'ārik* "struggled with," *it'ârḍû*, *itnâsâbû*. In Biblical Aramaic occurs the form אֶשְׁתּוֹמַם, Dan. iv. 16. In Hebrew we may regard הִתְגָּעֵשׁ "stagger to and fro, toss itself," Jer. xxv. 16, xlvi. 7, 8; and מִנֹּאָץ, Is. lii. 5, for מִתְנֹאָץ, "blasphemed," as examples from the ordinary triliteral verb. From verbs ע"ע I may mention הִתְעוֹלֵל "perpetrate,

accomplish," Ps. cxli. 4; הִתְפּוֹרֵר Is. xxiv. 19; הִתְרוֹצֵץ Gen. xxv. 22; הִתְקוֹשֵׁשׁ Zeph. ii. 1; and הִתְהוֹלֵל. And here I will notice in passing one curious Hebrew form, though it does not belong to the conjugation تَقَاتَلَ, but to تَقَتْلَلَ. From the radical שׁוּט is derived the Pi'lēl שׁוֹטֵט, "wander about," and from this the Prophet Jeremiah has formed the Hithpa'lēl הִתְשׁוֹטֵט, in the imperat. plur. fem. הִתְשׁוֹטֵטְנָה, Jer. xlix. 3. It is the solitary instance that I know in Hebrew of the ת not being transposed with an initial sibilant; and the reason probably was to avoid the sequence of three *t*'s, הִשְׁתּוֹטֵטְנָה.

With regard to the moods and tenses of these three conjugations, there is but little to add to what has already been said regarding the simple *ḳátala, ḳáttala,* and *ḳâtala.* I will therefore merely make a remark upon the infinitives of the fifth and sixth conjugations in Arabic. As in the frequentative and iterative we found the form تِقْتَالٌ, for تَقْتَالٌ, though but little used, so we look here for a corresponding formation. This actually occurs in the rare تِقِتَّالٌ, with assimilation of the preformative vowel. Examples تِحِمَّالٌ, تِكِلَّامٌ, تِمِلَّاقٌ, تِنِقَّامٌ; to which we may add such concretes as تِلِقَّامٌ "glutton," تِلِقَّاعٌ "foolish chatterer," تِكِذَّابٌ "mendacious," and the like. A great many Hebrew and Aramaic words with prefixed *t*, especially of the form تَقْتِلَةٌ, belong by their signification to this conjugation, and not to the causative or factitive تَقْتِيلٌ. Such are in Syriac, ܬܫܡܫܬܐ, ܬܫܒܘܚܬܐ, ܬܘܕܝܬܐ, ܬܢܚܬܐ; in Hebrew, תְּחִנָּה, "entreaty, prayer," תְּפִלָּה "prayer," תַּעֲלֻמָה "secret," תַּעֲנוּגִים from הִתְעַנֵּג, תַּאֲוָה from הִתְאַוָּה, תִּגְרָה from הִתְגָּרָה, etc. The Arabic however generally uses another form of the infinitive, which is common to the 5th and 6th conjugations, viz. تَقَتُّل and تَقَاتُل, with *u* in the 3rd syllable. These seem to be closely connected with such Hebrew and Aramaic forms as שִׁלּוּם, שִׁלּוּחִים, שִׁבּוֹלִים, Bibl. Aram. אֶשְׁתַּדּוּר "rebellion," Mand. עתלאבּושיא, Talmud. אִימְּנוֹעֵי, for אִיתְמְנוֹעֵי, "withdraw from, abstain from." تَقَتُّل is almost exactly represented by the Hebrew concretes תְּבַלֻּל "having a white spot on the eye," תְּאַשּׁוּר "a kind of pine" or similar growing tree.

4. I pass on now to the last member of this group, the reflexive of the factitive or causative, which is represented by the 10th conjugation of the Arabic verb and the *Ettaf'al* of the Aramaic.

In Arabic the 10th conjugation is the reflexive or middle voice of the 4th; as اِسْتَسْلَمَ "to give oneself up," اِسْتَقَامَ "to hold oneself upright, stand upright," اِسْتَخْلَفَ "select one as a deputy for oneself," اِسْتَغْفَرَ "ask pardon for oneself," اِسْتَحَلَّ "deem something lawful" (for oneself to do). It is exceedingly common, and is derived, as I explained to you before, from the form *saḳtala*, by the prefixing of the syllable *ta*. This form *tasaḳtala* became *itsaḳtala*, and then, by the same transposition as is usual in Hebrew and Aramaic, *istáḳtala*. Hence its identity with the Aramaic אִשְׁתַּקְטַל from שַׁקְטֵל. It is found in Ḥimyaritic or S. Arabian, without a prosthetic letter, *sataf'al* from *saf'al*, as סתמלא, סתופי. It also occurs in Assyrian; as *ultíšib-šinât*, "I have set them" or "made them dwell," for *uštíšib* [or *uštéšib*], from אשב = יָשַׁב; *altabušu*, "I did," for *aštabušu*, from עבש (Haupt *epêšu*). In Ethiopic we had, you may remember, three forms of the causative, *'aḳtála*, *'aḳattála*, and *'aḳātála*; and so also we have three forms of the reflexive, *'astaḳatála* or *'astaḳtála*, *'astaḳattála* and *'astaḳātála*; e.g. ኣስተጋብአ:

"to draw breath, be refreshed," አስተበቍዐ: "to entreat," አስተአከየ: "to ill-treat"; ሰስተዐገሠ: "be patient," አስተፌሥሐ: "rejoice"; አስተማሰለ: "compare with one another," አስተጋብአ: "collect." On its inflexion it is unnecessary to make any remarks, as it runs parallel to that of *'iktatala*. The other causative form أَقْتَلَ *'aktala* forms in the Aramaic dialects a reflexive and passive by prefixing the syllable *eth*, as in the Palmyrene tariff יתאעל, מתאעלין, from ܐܰܥܶܠ, ܥܰܠ. In Samaritan, Syriac and Mandaitic the assimilation of the *t* with the following *alif* takes place, e.g. אתשקע (אִתַּשְׁכַּח, "be found"), אתסכם (אִתַּסְכַּם "be finished"), ܐܶܬ݁ܬ݁ܚܶܕ (ܐܚܕ), ܐܶܬ݁ܬ݁ܟܶܠ (ܐܟܠ), ܐܶܬ݁ܬ݁ܡܰܪ (ܐܡܪ), ܐܶܬ݁ܬ݁ܣܺܝܪ (ܐܣܪ), עתאפְראש, עתאשפאל, עתאגזאר.

C. *Third Group.*

Of the next group of derived conjugations the characteristic syllable is *na*.

1. The most prominent member of this group is a reflexive and passive of the simple form of the verb, in its original shape *na-katala*.

In Arabic this *nakátala* became first *nᵉkátala*, and then, with prosthetic vowel, *inkatala*, اِنْقَتَلَ; as اِنْشَقَّ "to split itself, open" (of a flower); اِنْهَزَمَ "to let oneself be put to flight, to flee"; اِنْقَادَ "to let oneself be led, to be docile *or* submissive"; اِنْكَسَرَ "to be broken"; اِنْقَطَعَ "to be cut off, to come to an end." In Hebrew the imperfect and imperative and two infinitives follow the same mode of formation as in Arabic. The Arabic imperfect is يَنْقَتِلُ; the Hebrew, יִקָּטֵל for יִנְקָטֵל, with constant assimilation of the preformative to the 1st radical. The Arabic imperative is اِنْقَتَلَ, the Hebrew הִקָּטֵל, with the usual substitution of ה for א in these preformative syllables. The Arabic infinitive is اِنْقِتَالٌ; the corresponding Hebrew form is הִקָּטֹל (with *ō* for *ā*), as הִנָּתֹן, הֵאָכֹל, beside which we have another form for the construct infinitive, viz. הִקָּטֵל, as הִלָּחֵם, הִפָּתַח, הֵעָזֵר. But in the formation of the perfect, the participle, and one form of the infinitive absolute, the Hebrew has taken a different line. In the perfect the Hebrew contracted the primitive *naḳaṭál* into *naḳṭál*, which was gradually weakened into *niḳṭál*. The original vowel of the 1st syllable is established by such words as נַחֲבֵאתָ, נַעֲשָׂה, נַעֲלָה, נוֹלַד (for נֻוְלַד), נָסַב (for נַסְבַב), נָסוֹג (for *nāsāg*, from נַסְוַג); whilst נֶעֶשְׂתָה, נֶחְבָּא, exhibit an intermediate state. The infinitive absolute is now נִקְטֹל, for *naḳṭāl*, as נַעְתּוֹר, נַהֲפוֹךְ [where the original vowel of the first syllable is protected by the guttural following], נִלְחֹם, נִקְרֹא. The Arabic participle, formed after the analogy of the imperfect, with prefixed *m*, is مُنْقَتِلٌ. The Hebrew, on the contrary, has no prefix, but exhibits the same form as the perfect, with a slight difference in the vowel of the 2nd syllable. As חָכָם is differentiated from חָכַם, so is *naḳṭâl, niḳṭâl*, from *naḳṭál, niḳṭál*; e.g. נַעֲרָץ, נֶחְתָּם, נֶאְזָר and נֶאֱזָר, נוֹלָד, נִבְהָל. We shall have occasion to notice a similar participial formation hereafter in the form *kuṭṭâl*, as אֻכָּל "eaten," יוּלָּד "born," לֻקָּח "taken." In a very few instances we seem to find an imperative after the form *niḳṭál* or *niḳṭél*, viz. נִקְבְּצוּ, in pause נִקְבָּצוּ, Is. xliii. 9; Joel iv. 11; נִלְווּ Jerem. l. 5. The Hebrew form of the Niph'al seems to extend to Phoenician and Assyrian. In Phoenician we find נתן as the perf. Niph'al of יתן "to give," which we pronounce either נִתַּן or נַתַּן, and also [ש]נענ, probably נַעֲנַשׁ.

In Assyrian Schrader gives such examples as *innabit* (נבת), "he fled," *innamir* (נמר), "was seen," *iššakin*, "was set up" or "restored," *iššibir*, "was broken," *ibbanû*, "were created." The imperative of *iššakin* is given as *naškin*, and the participle *muššakin*; the one resembling the rare Hebrew form נִקְבַּץ (mentioned above), and the other the common Arabic form مُنْقَتِل.

In Ḥimyaritic Halévy gives as an example the word הנגפש, with initial *h*.

2. Of the actual Niph'al of the Arabic and Hebrew there is no trace in Ethiopic, but a cognate form is preserved in the prefix *an*, which we find in quadriliterals, more especially reduplicated verbs of the form *ḳalḳala*, the Hebrew *Pilpēl*. The meaning of this formation in Ethiopic is not however so fixed as in Arabic and Hebrew. It generally implies motion, sometimes reflexive and reciprocal action; but sometimes too it is transitive, and admits of a passive being formed from it. Examples: አንሶሰወ: "to walk about," አንፈርዐጸ: "to leap, dance," አንጐድጐደ: "to thunder"; አንገለገ: "to come together, assemble"; አንቃዐደወ: properly "to lean forward, prostrate oneself," but generally used in the sense of "lift up the eyes *or* heart in prayer"; አንኰርኰረ: "roll" (intrans. or trans.); አንቀልቀለ: "totter" and "shake"; አንበሰበሰ: "to spread out" as a veil, which is only transitive. Dillmann explains this curious phenomenon on the supposition that the nominal forms with initial *na*, like ነጐድጓድ: "thunder," ነኰርኳር: "rolling, a whirlwind," ነቀልቃል: "shaking," gave rise to the notion that the prefixed አ might be identical with the causative or factitive prefix አ. Hence, according to him, the occasional change of meaning, and the formation in a few cases of a passive with ተ, e.g. ተንኰርኰረ: "to be rolled," ተንበሰበሰ: "to be spread out." This view may perhaps be correct; I am not in a position to affirm or deny it. It may however be well to inform you that the Assyrian grammarians speak of forms like *iftana"al* and *istanaf'al* [Del. *iftaneal* and *ittanafal*], in which an *n* is inserted, and yet the meaning of all the examples cited by Schrader is said to be transitive[1].

[1] [Those cited by Delitzsch, p. 233, are mostly intransitive or reflexive.]

3. Another member of this group is the Hebrew *Nithpa"el*, chiefly post-biblical. The Biblical examples are נִכַּפֵּר Deut. xxi. 8, for נִתְכַּפֵּר, "be atoned for, forgiven," and נִוַּסְּרוּ Ezek. xxiii. 48, for נִתְוַסְּרוּ, "let themselves be warned." In post-biblical Hebrew it is common, and has usurped the place of the perfect Hithpa"ēl, as נִטַּמָּא, נִזְדַּמֵּן, נִסְתַּבֵּל, נִשְׁתַּמֵּשׁ; and is then extended to other formations, as נִשְׁתַּעְבֵּד, נִתַּרְגֵּם, נִתְאַלְמְנָה "she is become a widow."

4. Lastly we may reckon here the third conjugation of the quadriliteral verb in Arabic, where the letter *n* is inserted after the 2nd radical; as اِبْرَنْشَقَ "to open" (of a flower), "to bloom"; اِحْرَنْجَمَ "to be gathered together in a mass *or* crowd"; اِسْلَنْقَى "to lie on one's back"; اِثْعَنْجَرَ "to flow."

D. *Fourth Group.*

I will next speak briefly of a group of *reduplicated* forms. This reduplication is of different kinds, but always takes place at the end of the root, not at the beginning. The chief varieties are, to use the Hebrew terms, *Pi'lēl*, *Pĕ'al'al*, and *Pilpēl.*

1. Starting from the root *ḳatala*, the simplest form of such a reduplication is the repetition of the 3rd radical, *ḳatalala*. But *ḳatalala* would naturally become *ḳaṭlál*, which would be weakened in Aramaic into *ḳaṭlēl*, and in Hebrew into *ḳiṭlēl*. Aramaic examples are not numerous; e.g. עַרְבֵּב "mix up, confuse"; ܦܪܟܣ "crumble," ܦܪܙܙ "separate," ܫܥܒܕ "practise, reduce to slavery," with its passive ܐܫܬܥܒܕ; ܡܪܡܪ "irritate," and ܐܬܡܪܡܪ "to become fierce"; ܐܬܗܘܢܢ "to be intelligent, sensible." In Hebrew this form has taken the place of Pi"ēl in verbs ע"ו, as נוֹדֵד (better from נוד than from נָדַד), כּוֹנֵן, עוֹרֵר, etc., and

forms a reflexive and passive with prefixed *ta*, הִתְפַּעְלֵל. In other classes of verbs it is rare, but we can refer to it שַׁאֲנַן "to be quiet, still," Jerem. xxx. 10; Job iii. 18; רַעֲנַן in the fem. רַעֲנָנָה Job xv. 33; further, with passive pronunciation, אֻמְלַל "to be withered, wither away, mourn"; and from verbs ל״ה, נַאֲוָה, contracted נָאוָה "to be seemly, beautiful"; מְטַחֲוֵי־קֶשֶׁת, from טַחֲוָה "to shoot," and the reflexive הִשְׁתַּחֲוָה, from שָׁחָה. As to the Arabic development of the original *katalala*, it generally took the following course; *katalala* became *kĕtalala, iktalala*, and finally *iktalla*. This form *iktalla* appears in the Arabic paradigm as the 9th conj. of the verb, with the cognate *iktâlla* as the 11th; e.g. اِزْوَرّ and اِزْوَارّ "turn away," اِرْبَثّ and اِرْبَاثّ "be scattered," اِرْقَدّ "run quickly," اِشْعَانّ "be dishevelled"; and constantly of colours and defects, as اِعْوَجّ, اِعْوَاجّ, "be crooked"; اِحْوَلّ, اِحْوَالّ, "squint"; اِصْفَرّ, اِصْفَارّ, "be yellow"; اِبْيَضّ, اِبْيَاضّ, "be white." The uncontracted form *iktalala* survives only in some examples from verbs 3rd rad. و or ي; as اِرْعَوَي "to abstain, refrain"; اِحْوَوَي "to become brownish," with its byform اِحْوَاوَي; اِجْنَوَي "to stand on tiptoe." A kind of reflexive or passive, with *n* inserted after the 2nd rad., may perhaps be discerned in the rare 14th conj. of the Arabic verb, اِقْتَنْلَلَ for تَتَنْلَلَ; as اِحْلَنْكَكَ "be jet black" (حَلَكَ), اِعْلَنْكَكَ "be long and thick" (of the hair), اِقْعَنْسَسَ "have a hump in front" (قَعِسَ).

2. A stronger form of the reduplication consists in the repetition of two radicals, the 2nd and 3rd. Hence the form

ḳataltala, appearing occasionally in Aramaic and Hebrew as *ḳĕṭalṭál*; e.g. סְחַרְחַר "to beat violently" (of the heart), Ps. xxxviii. 11; חֳמַרְמַר "to be red" with weeping, "to be agitated or troubled." Similar cases are Ps. xlv. 3, יָפְיָפִיתָ, which should probably be read יְפֵיפִיתָ; and אָהֲבוּ הֵבוּ, Hos. iv. 18, probably in the first instance a mere clerical error for אֲהַבְהֵבוּ, from אָהֵב. Aramaic examples in derived conjugations are ܐܬܚܠܡܠܡ "to dream," ܐܬܦܠܓܠܓ "to imagine."

3. The form *ḳalḳala*, Aram. *ḳalḳēl*, Heb. *ḳilḳēl*, is often produced by the repetition of an imitative syllable. E.g. خَشْخَشَ "to make things rattle or rustle," وَسْوَسَ "to whisper," حَمْحَمَ "to neigh," غَرْغَرَ "to gargle," צִפְצֵף "to chirp." Very frequently it is formed in Aramaic and Hebrew from verbs ע"ע and ע"ו by repeating the two chief letters of the root; e.g. in Aramaic, ܦܪܦܪ, ܛܠܛܠ, ܪܦܪܦ, ܓܠܓܠ; ܙܥܙܥ, ܪܡܪܡ, ܛܠܛܠ; with their reflexives; in Hebrew, גִּלְגֵּל, קִלְקֵל, שִׁעֲשַׁע "gladden, take delight in," כִּלְכֵּל, מְזַעְזֵעַ, מְטַלְטֵל "casting"; with their reflexives and passives.

4. Under this head I will next mention what is called in the Arabic Grammars the 12th conjugation of the verb, wherein the second radical is repeated, but separated from its fellow by the introduction of the diphthong *au*. The original form was فَعَوْعَلَ, which became in Arabic اِفْعَوْعَلَ, as اِحْدَوْدَبَ "be arched or curved, hump-backed" (حَدِبَ), اِعْصَوْصَبَ "be gathered together" (عَصَبَ), اِحْلَوْلَكَ "be jet black" (حَلِكَ), اِحْلَوْلَى "be sweet" (حَلُوَ), اِعْرَوْرَى "ride on a horse barebacked" (عَرِيَ).

I find a few similar forms in Syriac from verbs final ܘ and ܝ; e.g. ܐܶܫܬܰܥܠܘܺܝ "to boast or brag"; ܐܶܫܬܰܓܢܘܺܝ "to lie down, be hidden, be blamed"; ܐܶܫܬܰܛܠܘܺܝ "become young, be smeared over." In Hebrew it can hardly be said to exist, unless we take count of חֲצֹצֵר "to blow the trumpet" (מַחְצְצְרִים), from חֲצֹצְרָה. But the form is doubtful, the *ḳĕrê* being מַחְצְרִים; and even if we assume it to be correct, חֲצֹצֵר might stand for חֲצַרְצֵר, as יְעֹעֵרוּ in Is. xv. 5, if correct, stands for יְעַרְעֵרוּ.

5. The reduplication of the form *ḳatalala* or *ḳatlala* seems in some cases to have been softened into *ḳatlaya*, which would be represented in Arabic by *ḳatlā* قَتْلَي, and in Aramaic by קַטְלִי. Such words are in Mandaitic נאמביא "to bewail," נַאכְרִיא "to make an alien, estrange"; in Syr. ܫܰܠܗܶܒ "terrify," ܢܰܘܟܪܺܝ "estrange," ܫܰܪܘܺܝ "be deprived of, fail, perish," ܦܰܪܣܺܝ "expose," ܫܰܠܘܺܝ "deport," with their passives. In Arabic a passive of this form is found in the 15th conj. of the verb, اِفْعَنْلَي, with *n* inserted after the 2nd rad.; as اِحْبَنْطَي "to be swollen *or* inflated" (حَبِطَ), اِعْلَنْدَي "be stout and strong" (عَلِدَ "be hard"). Curiously enough, a few verbs of this form in Arabic have a transitive sense, e.g. اِسْرَنْدَي "to overcome" (سَرَنْدَي "strong, brave"), اِغْرَنْدَي "to assail, overcome"; and, still more strangely, the only Mandaitic parallel, עודראמביא, "to be shaken," is derived from an active זראמביא, which however does not occur in the extant literature.

E. *The Passive Forms.*

Lastly, in this enumeration of the verbal forms or conjugations, I would call your attention to the real passives, as distinguished from the reflexives and effectives, which so often discharge the functions of passives.

In Arabic nearly all the conjugations are capable of forming, and actually form, passives by means of internal modification of the vowels of the active voice. There are of course exceptions, which will readily suggest themselves to you. For instance, a verb like صَلُحَ "to be good *or* right," فَرِحَ "to be glad," or ثَقُلَ "to be heavy," cannot have a passive; nor one like اسوادّ, اسودّ, "to be black." The vowel-change in the passive voice consists, generally speaking, in the substitution of duller sounds for the clearer ones of the active, the vowel *u* almost always playing a prominent part.

In the other Semitic languages the use of these real passives is far less frequent. In Hebrew the largest survival is found; much less in Aramaic. In Ethiopic they have, to all appearance, utterly vanished. In Assyrian Sayce states that "a passive formed by means of the obscure vowel *u*" exists for Pa"ēl, Shaph'ēl, Aph'ēl, and Istaph'al; but I do not find that he is supported by Schrader or Oppert. From my own knowledge I cannot speak[1].

1. In Arabic the following are the principal passives:

	Perfect.		Imperfect.	
(1)	*ḳatala*	*ḳutila*	*yaḳtulu*	*yuḳtalu*
(2)	*ḳattala*	*ḳuttila*	*yuḳattilu*	*yuḳattalu*
(3)	*ḳâtala*	*ḳûtila*	*yuḳâtilu*	*yuḳâtalu*
(4)	*'aḳtala*	*'uḳtila*	*yuḳtilu*	*yuḳtalu*
(5)	*taḳattala*	*tuḳuttila*	*yataḳattalu*	*yutaḳattalu*
(6)	*taḳâtala*	*tuḳûtila*	*yataḳâtalu*	*yutaḳâtalu*
[(7)	*inḳatala*	*unḳutila*	*yanḳatilu*	*yunḳatalu*]
(8)	*iḳtatala*	*uḳtutila*	*yaḳtatilu*	*yuḳtatalu*
(10)	*istaḳtala*	*ustuḳtila*	*yastaḳtilu*	*yustaḳtalu*

[1] [According to Delitzsch, p. 249, the permansives II. 1 and III. 1 (Pa"el and Shaph'el) may be used either in active or passive sense, but without difference of form.]

2. In Hebrew the formation is similar, but not identical, the vowel *a* predominating throughout in the second syllable. The passives in use are:—

(*a*) Intensive and iterative, *kuṭṭal, koṭṭal*, imperf. *yĕkuṭṭal.* The infin. absolute has the form קֻטֹּל, as גֻּנֹּב, Gen. xl. 15. The participle appears in two shapes, the one with prefixed *m*, *mĕkuṭṭāl*; the other without it, as אֻכָּל, יוּלָּד, לֻקָּח, הֻלָּלָה, Ezek. xxvi. 17. And here it is curious to remark in what different ways the several Semitic languages have made use of the materials at their disposal. The Hebrew infinitive קֻטֹּל stands for *kuṭṭâl*; but the corresponding form in Aramaic is a verbal noun from the active Pa"ēl, e.g. ܓܘܢܒܐ "theft," ܙܘܗܪܐ "warning," ܫܘܡܠܝܐ "finishing"; whilst the Arabic *kuṭṭâl* is now the plural of the active participle of the simple verb *ḳatala*, as *ḳâtil*[un], a "murderer," *kuttâl*[un], "murderers." So again, the Hebrew participle אֻכָּל stands for *'ukkăl*, a sing. masc.; whereas the corresponding form in Arabic is another plural of the active participle of the simple *ḳatala*, as *sâǵid*, "worshipper," *suǵǵad*, "worshippers."

(*b*) The form expressive of effort, *ḳôṭal*, imperf. *yĕḳôṭal*, as יְשֹׁרָשׁוּ, Job xxxi. 8.

(*c*) The causative or factitive, *hoḳṭal, huḳṭal*, imperf. *yoḳṭal.*

Other forms are comparatively rare, but I may mention:—

(*d*) *Hothḳatal*, in the form הָתְפָּקְדוּ, Num. i. 47, ii. 33, xxvi. 62; 1 Kings xx. 27; instead of הִתְפָּקְדוּ.

(*e*) *Hothḳaṭṭal*, in הֻטַּמָּאָה, Deut. xxiv. 4; הֻדַּשְּׁנָה, for הִדַּשְּׁנָה, Is. xxxiv. 6; הֻכַּבֵּס infinitive, Levit. xiii. 55, 56.

In these two cases, if correctly pointed, observe that the Hebrew changes only the vowel of the preformative syllable; whereas in Arabic it is the vowel of the first radical syllable that is modified, and that of the preformative is assimilated to it. Compare اُفْتُقِدُوا with הָתְפָּקְדוּ, or تُتُبِّعَ with הֻדַּשְּׁנָה.

(*f*) A curious form is presented to us in the Hebrew נִגֹּאֲלוּ, Is. lix. 3; Lament. iv. 14. This is generally explained as a passive of Niph'al, נִגְאָלָה, Zeph. iii. 1. I should rather be inclined to regard it as a quasi-Niph'al formation from the Pi''el גֵּאֵל, Pu''al גֹּאַל. If you adopt the former view, you must regard נִגֹּאֲלוּ as = اُنْفُعِلُوا; if the latter, I can produce a parallel from the vulgar Arabic of Egypt, viz. اِتْضَيَّع "it is lost, forfeited" (Spitta, *Contes Arabes*, p. 9, l. 10), from ضَيَّع "to lose, forfeit." Here again perhaps the Massoretic punctuation may be erroneous (נִגְּאֲלוּ?).

(*g*) *Ḳuṭlal*, in אֻמְלַל.

(*h*) *Ḳolḳal*, in כָּלְכְּלוּ, 1 Kings xx. 27, and תְּשָׁעֳשָׁעוּ, Is. lxvi. 12.

3. Of the Aramaic passive the chief traces are the following.

(*a*) The passive of *Pĕ'al*, in a form which appears at first to be that of the passive participle *Pĕ'īl*, and is accordingly generally so treated, even by Kautzsch. In my opinion, however, the verbal flexion of this form forbids us to regard it as a participle, and Noeldeke is right in adopting the other view. The form was originally *ḳuṭil*, but the weight of the accent produced a lengthening of the vowel of the 2nd syllable, whilst that of the 1st syllable was weakened in the regular verb to simple shĕvā: טְרִיד Dan. iv. 30, יְהִיב Dan. vii. 4, 6, כְּתִיב Ezra v. 7, קְטִיל Dan. v. 30, רְשִׁים Dan. v. 24, שְׁלִם Ezra v. 16; 3rd fem. בְּטִלַת Ezra iv. 24, יְהִיבַת Dan. vii. 27, נְטִילַת Dan. vii. 4, פְּרִיסַת Dan. v. 28, קְטִילַת Dan. vii. 11; 2nd sing. masc. תְּקִלְתָּא Dan. v. 27; 3rd plur. masc. יְהִיבוּ Ezra v. 15, כְּפִתוּ Dan. iii. 21, טְרִיטוּ Dan. vii. 4, פְּתִיחוּ Dan. vii. 10. The distinction of form is clearer in the case of verbs ל״א, where the perfect passive is גְּלִי Dan. ii. 19, גְּלִי Dan. ii. 30, קְרִי Ezra iv. 18, 23; plur. רְמִיו Dan. iii. 21, vii. 9; whereas the form of the participle Pĕʻîl is בְּנֵה, מְנֵא, קְרֵי, שְׁרֵא, plur. שְׁרַיִן. Similarly in the Palmyrene tariff, גבי = Arab. جبي; see Sachau in *ZDMG.* xxxvii. pp. 564—5.

(*b*) The passive of *Hiph'îl*, viz. *Hoph'al*, in Biblical Aramaic and the Palmyrene dialect, viz. הָנְחַת Dan. v. 20, הוּבַד Dan. vii. 11, הֻסַּק Dan. vi. 24, הֻעַל Dan. v. 13, plur. הֻעַלּוּ Dan. v. 15; fem. sing. הָחָרְבַת Ezra iv. 15, הוּסְפַת לִי Dan. iv. 33, הֳקִימַת Dan. vii. 4 (cf. اُقيمت); 1st pers. הָתְקְנֵת (not ـنَت) Dan. iv. 33. Very peculiar are the forms הֵיתָיִת Dan. vi. 18, and הֵיתָיוּ Dan. iii. 13, the vocalisation of the 1st syllable of which is as yet unexplained. Similarly in the Palmyrene tariff, אֻשַּׁר (from שַׁר), e.g. ומדי אשר לאגורא; imperfect יֻכְּתַב, e.g. ויכתב למרעם מדעמא מכסה די מן עידא; part. מֻסַּק, e.g. מרעם די לא מסק בנמוסא; מְבַטַּל, e.g. ויהוא מבטל לארכוניא די הֲוֵן בזבן זבן; מְאֻפַּק, for מֻפַּק, e.g. מדי יהוא מ[תאעל] בר מן תחומא או מאפק.

(*c*) The passive of *Pi''ēl*, viz. *Pu''al*, in the Palmyrene tariff, יְזֻבַּן, e.g. [ומן כל] משך די יתאעל או יזבן למשכא אֻפְּרַיִן.

(*d*) The passive participles of *Pa''ēl*, *Aph'ēl* and *Shaph'ēl*, formed exactly as in Arabic. Thus in Biblical Aramaic מְהַלֵּךְ, מְמַלֵּל, but מְכַפְּתִין "bound," Dan. iii. 23, 24, from מְכַפַּת; מְסַתְּרָתָא "hidden things," Dan. ii. 22, from מְסַתַּר; מַשְׁפִּל Dan. v. 19, and מְהַנְזְקַת מַלְכִין Ezra iv. 15, but מְהַחְצְפָה Dan. ii. 15, or מְחַצְפָה Dan. iii. 22, from מְהַחְצַף, מַחְצַף. Also from *Pô'al*, מְסוֹבְלִין "set up, erected," Ezra vi. 3, from מְסוֹבַל.

Exactly so in Syriac, ܡܟܬܒ, ܡܟܬܒ; ܡܩܛܠ, ܡܩܛܠ; ܡܫܡܫ, ܡܫܡܫ; and in Mandaitic, מבארִיך "blessing," מבאראך "blessed"; מכאסִיא "covering," מכאסאי "covered"; מאפריש "teaching," מאפראש "taught," מאפִּיק "bringing out," מאפאק "brought out." The corresponding Arabic forms are مُقْتِل, مُقْتَل; مُقَاتِل, مُقَاتَل; مُقَتِّل, مُقَتَّل.

(*e*) The existence of passive participles of Pa"ēl and Aph'ēl after the *Hebrew* formation is not certain in Mandaitic, but Noeldeke gives for the Pa"ēl the possible instances of מוּלִיא, "the highlands," for מְעֻלָּיָא, and משניא כושטא, a name of Paradise, lit. "the taken away of righteousness," i.e. "the (land) of righteousness that has been taken away," = מְשֻׁנֶּה. On the other hand, the existence of Pu"al and Hoph'al participles in modern Syriac seems tolerably certain. For example, in Pu"al, ܒܣܘܡܣܘܡܠܗ ܠܒ "I have healed thee," is literally ܡܒܘܣܡܐ ܐܢܬ ܠܒ "thou hast been healed by me," the fem. being ܒܣܘܡܣܡܠܗ ܠܒ, for ܡܒܣܘܡܬܐ ܐܢܬܝ ܠܒ. So also in Pu"al, ܙܒܝܢܐ, *zūbinnē*, for ܙܒܝܢ ܠܗ, for ܡܙܘܒܢ ܠܗ; in Hoph'al, ܡܘܩܡܐ "raised up," ܡܘܪܡܐ "exalted"; with weakening of the vowel in the 2nd syllable.

CHAPTER IX.

THE IRREGULAR VERBS.

I NOW proceed, with the Hebrew Grammar in hand, to explain to you the principal forms of the Irregular Verbs, comparing them, as before, with the corresponding forms in Arabic and Syriac, and more rarely in other dialects.

I. *Verbs* ע״ע *or Geminate Verbs.*

I begin with the verbs ע״ע, or, as they are called in Arabic Grammars, the *doubled* or *geminate verbs* or the *solid verbs.* The peculiarity here is the contraction of the trisyllabic root into a disyllable by the rejection of the vowel of the second radical or some other modification.

In classical Arabic the rules of contraction are few and simple.

(*a*) If all three radicals have vowels, the 2nd radical loses its vowel, and unites with the 3rd, so as to form a double letter. Hence سَبَبَ, "to cause," becomes سَبَّ; مَسِسَ "to touch," مَسَّ; حَبُبَ "to become dear" (to one), حَبَّ. The original form may be retained in poetry, for the sake of the metre, as ضَنِنُوا for ضَنُّوا, "they are stingy"; and in some verbs of the forms فَعِلَ and فَعُلَ the contraction does not take place, as صَكِكَ "to be knock-kneed," لَحِحَ "to be sore" (of the eyes), لَبُبَ "to be wise," دَمُمَ "to be ugly." Vulg. Arab., *madd, 'add, ẓann.*

(*b*) If the first radical has no vowel, and the 2nd and 3rd have, then the 2nd radical throws back its vowel on the 1st, and unites with the 3rd, so as to form a double letter. Hence يَسْبِبُ becomes يَسِبُّ; يَمْسَسُ, يَمَسُّ; يَفْرِرُ, يَفِرُّ. The original forms may be used by poetic license, as يَحْلَلُ for يَحِلُّ. Vulg. Arab., *yeẓunn, ye'idd, yiṣaḥḥ*.

(*c*) If the 3rd radical is vowelless, no contraction, generally speaking, takes place. The forms in ordinary use are سَبَبْتُ, حَبِبْتُ, مَسِسْتُ.

(*d*) Forms that might by rule remain uncontracted are sometimes contracted in different ways. For example, the jussive of سَبَّ is يَسْبِبْ, and the imperative اُسْبُبْ; but both are usually contracted, with the help of a supplementary vowel, into يَسُبَّ and سُبَّ. Vulg. Arab., *ẓunn, 'idd*.

Bearing these rules in mind, we may proceed to compare the Arabic forms with those of the Hebrew and Syriac, using chiefly as our paradigms رَدَّ, סַב, and ܒܙ.

Ḳal. Here the uncontracted forms are relatively far more common in Hebrew than in Arabic, as סָבַב, סָרַר, חָנַן, חָלַל, fem. נָדְדָה, plur. נָדְדוּ, שָׁחֲחוּ, סְבָבוּנִי, סְבָבוּנִי. The contracted 3rd sing. masc. סַב and ܒܙ stand for *sabb* and *bazz*, and these for *sabba* and *bazza*, *sababa* and *bazaza*, like رَدَّ for رَدَدَ. Add a suffix, and the doubling immediately becomes audible, קַבֹּה, חַנַּנִי for *ḳabba-hu*; Aram. ܒܙܗ; like Arabic رَدَّنِي. In the same way in the 3rd pers. plur. סַבּוּ, תַּמּוּ, J. Aram. דַּקּוּ, Syr. ܒܙܘ, for *sababū, tamamū, daḳaḳū*, as in Arabic رَدُّوا for رَدَدُوا. The retention of the tone on the 1st syllable is in accordance with the primitive accent, but it is often shifted to the last syllable, as רַבּוּ, זַכּוּ. The real existence of forms like רֹבּוּ, Gen. xlix. 23, and רֹמּוּ, Job xxiv. 24, is somewhat doubtful; but if genuine, they would find their analogy in the Arabic forms of praise and blame, حُبَّ for حَبُبَ, حُسْنَ for حَسُنَ, and بُعْدَ for بَعُدَ. In the 3rd p. fem. sing., Syr. ܒܶܙܰܬ stands for *bazzath* (Bibl. Aram. נַדַּת, עַלַּת, Mand. פאסאת, שאראת, אלאת), *bazazat*; and similarly סַבָּה, for *sabbath*, *sababat*, as رَدَّتْ for رَدَدَتْ. The primitive accent is often retained, as in חַתָּה, מָרָה, but may be shifted, as in וְרַבָּה, Is. vi. 12. In the 1st and 2nd persons, the normal form is the uncontracted Arabic رَدَدْتُ, رَدَدْتَ, رَدَدْنَا, which we find in Hebrew only in the forms זַמֹּתִי, Zech. viii. 14, 15; בַּזֹּנוּ, Deut. ii. 35. But these forms may be altered in two ways even in Arabic. Firstly, the 2nd radical may be dropped, and its vowel go with it, or it may be transferred to the 1st radical; as رَدْتُ for رَدَدْتُ, ظَلْتُ or ظِلْتُ for ظَلِلْتُ, مِسْتُ for مَسِسْتُ. So in Aramaic ܒܶܙܬ, ܒܙܰܬܘܢ, ܒܙܰܢ, for *basasta*, *basastôn*, *basasnan*. So in Hebrew, תַּמְנוּ for *tamamnû*, Num. xvii. 28. The 1st pers. sing., however, in Aramaic, is דַּקֵּת, Mand. פאסית, מאכית, אלית, Syr. ܒܶܙܬ for *bazzēth*, *bazzit*, *bazazti*. Secondly, the 3rd radical may coalesce in the usual way with the second, and to make the doubling audible a vowel-sound may be inserted after it. This vowel-sound seems to have been that of the diphthong *au* or *ai*, which was favoured by the corresponding forms of the verbs 3rd و and ي, as نَدَوْتُ, رَمَيْتُ. More probably however it was *ai*, which is far more frequent in the language than *au*, occurring alone for instance in all the derived conjugations. Hence رَدَدْتَ, would become (through the impossible *raddta*) *raddaita*, and this is the ordinary form at the present day, *raddait*, *raddêt*, and in Algiers *raddît*. We have seen, however, that the diphthong *ai* passed in some cases into *â*; for instance, Arab. أَيْنَ, Heb. אָן, אָנָה; בָּתִּים, from בַּיִת, بَيْت; דְּבָרָיו or דְּבָרָו, from דְּבָרַיְהוּ; and in Arabic itself تُوابَّة for دُوَيْبَّة, dimin. of دَابَّة. Hence out of رَدَيْتَ sprang the form رَدَّاتَ, the dialectical existence of which is vouched for by the grammarians; and hence the Hebrew סַבֹּתִי, חַגֹּתָם, זַמּוֹת, for *sabbâti*, *sababtī*. Of course the Hebrew *ô* in these forms might be as readily derived from an original *au*, but we have no evidence of the existence of a form *raddauta*, whereas *raddâta* is a known dialectical variety of *raddaita*.

The infinitive construct in Hebrew exhibits two forms: uncontracted, גְּזֹז, לִסְבֹב, far more rarely with *a*, לְחַנַנְכֶם, Is. xxx. 18, לְחֶנְנָהּ, Ps. cii. 14; and contracted, גֹּז, חֹג, סֹב, far more rarely with *a*, רַד, Is. xlv. 1, שַׁךְ, Jerem. v. 26. These are, of course, nothing but segolates of the same form as the Arabic رَدٌّ, وُدٌّ.

The Arabic imperative presents to us, as I explained above, the forms رُدَّ (اُرْدُدْ), فِرَّ, مَسَّ. These are exactly equivalent to the Hebrew סֹב, דֹּם, גֹּל, perhaps also גַּל, Ps. cxix. 22; in Aramaic, דֹּק, Mand. הוף "wash," דאר "dwell"; Syr. ܦܘܩ, ܡܘܣ, ܩܘܡ (from ܢܦܩ, ܢܦܘܩ). An example of the uncontracted form is שִׁדְדוּ, Jerem. xlix. 28, corresponding to an Arabic اُرْدُدُوا for رُدُّوا.

The Arabic imperfect has, as I explained to you, the forms

يمس، يفر، يرد. The first of these is reproduced exactly in the Hebrew יָסֹב for *yasubb, yasubbu, yasbubu*, with suffix יְסֻבֵּנִי, plural, יָסֹבּוּ for *yasubbū, yasubbūna*. This *ō* has rarely been weakened into *ū*, but we find examples in יָרוּץ Is. xlii. 4, יָרוּן Prov. xxix. 6, יָשׁוּד Ps. xci. 6. These may not improbably have been influenced by the imperfect of verbs ע״ו, as in Mand., where נימוך (from מאך) is identical with ניקום from קאם, and conversely נידאר "dwells," ניגאר "commits adultery," cannot be distinguished from ניהאם "be hot," תיראג "desirest." In intransitives like the Arabic مس، يمس, where the characteristic vowel of the imperfect is *a*, the Hebrew no longer maintains the ancient *yaḳṭal*, but employs the more recent *yiḳṭal*. Thus the imperfect of מַר is not יָמֹר but יֵמַר, for *yimrar, yamrar*. So יֵרַךְ, יֵרַע, and a few more. In 1 Kings i. 1 the form is pointed יִחַם instead of יֵחַם. The reason of this deviation from the form with *a* in the first syllable probably was that יֵמַר, יֵרַךְ, יֵרַע, too closely resembled in their vocalisation that of the *perfect*. Indeed יָמַר, יָרַךְ, and יָרַד, rightly appear as verbal roots in our lexicons. This has not however prevented the substitution of the form יָזְמוּ for יָזֹמּוּ in Gen. xi. 6, because the singular must actually have been יָזֹם, not יָזַם. In the fem. plur. תְּסֻבֶּינָה, תְּצִלֶּינָה, the diphthong *ai* has again been inserted to facilitate the pronunciation of the contracted forms, which stand respectively for *tasbubna* and *taṣlilna*, the intermediate steps being *tasubbna, taṣillna*, then *tasubbaina, taṣillaina*.

The Aramaic dialects go their own way in the formation of the imperfect and infinitive. They throw back the lost doubling of the 2nd and 3rd radicals upon the 1st. Hence יִדֹּק, ܢܒܘܙ, ܢܥܘܠ, ܢܦܓ, ܢܬܡܗ, for *yidukk, nĕbuzz*, etc., from *yadukku, nabuzzu*; and in the infinitive, מִדַּק, ܡܒܙܙ, for *midḳaḳ, mebzaz*. The

Hebrew also has this form in such words as יָדֹּם, יִדְּמוּ; יִקֹּד, יִקְּדוּ; יִתֹּם, יִתְּמוּ; תִּצַּלְנָה, Jerem. xix. 3, for תִּצְלַלְנָה; and so forth.

The participle active has in Hebrew the uncontracted form גֹּזֵז, חֹנֵן, חוֹגֵג, whereas in Arabic the contraction is prevalent, حالّ, حاجّ, and the uncontracted حَالِلٌ occurs as a rare poetic license. In vulg. Arab. however the uncontracted حاجِج is common in the masc. sing., whereas in the fem. sing. and in the plur. masc. and fem. the contracted form is more usual. In Syriac the form has been influenced by that of verbs ע"ו. The sing. masc. is therefore ܥܳܐܠ, ܥܳܐܶܠ, like ܩܳܐܶܡ, but the fem. sing. and the plurals are regular, ܥܳܠܠܳܐ, ܥܳܠܠܺܝܢ, ܥܳܠܠܳܢ, for *'âlilat, 'âlilîn, 'âlilân*[1]. In Bibl. Aram. we find the uncontracted plur. עָלְלִין, Dan. iv. 5, v. 8, as *Kěthîbh*, the *Ḳĕrē* being עָלִּין, as also in Samarit. עֲלֵל, עללה[2].

Let us now glance rapidly at the derived conjugations.

Niphʻal. Here the chief peculiarity in Hebrew is the pure vowel of the 1st syllable, נָסַב, נָחַר, נָקַל, for *nasabb, naḥarr, naḳall*, from *nasbab, naḥrar, naḳlal.* Curiously enough, however, we find here the intransitive vowels of the *Ḳal* also used in the 2nd syllable; e.g. נָמֵס, נָקֵל, נָרֹץ; and so in the fem., נָשַׁמָּה, but נָסַבָּה; and in the plur., נָסַבּוּ, נָשַׁמּוּ, but also נָגֹלּוּ, נָבֹזּוּ. This seems due to the resemblance of נָסַב to the ordinary *Ḳal* נָגַשׁ, whence the same variations that were admissible in the one came in course of time to be thought allowable in the other. Others think that the *ô* forms are due to the influence of verbs ע"ו. There is a fourth form, which altogether gives up the

[1] A possible instance of this Aramaic form in Hebrew is שֹׁאֲסַיִךְ, Jerem. xxx. 16 (*Kěthîbh*), if we derive it from שָׁסָה=שָׁסַס, the sing. being שֹׁאֵס for שֹׁסֵס.

[2] [עללל occurs also in Palmyrene; in Palestinian Syriac both עלל and חשש "suffering" are found: the former word makes its plural עלין.]

doubling and inflects exactly like the *Ḳal* of נָגַשׁ, for the same reason as the first three; e.g. נָסַבָּה, נָבְקָה, נָזֹלּוּ. A fifth form resembles the ordinary Niph'al in the vowel of the first syllable, as נִחַר, נִחַת, נִחַל, and gives the plur. נִחֲרוּ, נִחֲלוּ; participp. נְחַמִּים, נְאָרִים. This seems to be a secondary formation from נָחַר, נָחַת, נָחַל, after the fashion of Niph'al נִגַּשׁ from Ḳal נָגַשׁ. —Of the 2nd person examples are very rare; but we find נְמַקֹּתֶם side by side with נְמַלְתֶּם and נִחַלְתְּ.—Similarly in the first person we have נְקַלּוֹתִי, with the plur. נְשַׁדֻּנוּ, Micah ii. 4, where the supplementary vowel *ô* has been weakened into *û*.—For the sake of comparison with the above I need only mention the Arabic forms اِنْجَرَّ for *ingarara*; 2nd pers. اِنْجَرَرْتَ, uncontracted.—In the imperfect, the ordinary form is יִסֹּב, for *yissabb*, by assimilation and contraction for *yansabib*; as יִזַּח, יִמַּר, יִגַּל. The uncontracted form occurs in יִלָּבֵב, Job xi. 12. The corresponding plural naturally exhibits the double letter, יִסַּבּוּ, יִמַּדּוּ, contracted for *yansabibû(na)*, *yanmadidû(na)*. Such words as יֵרוֹעַ, Prov. xi. 15, xiii. 20, and תֵּרוֹץ, Ezek. xxix. 7, follow the analogy of verbs ע״ו. In Arabic, for the sake of comparison, take يَنْجَرُّ for يَنْجَرِرُ, plur. يَنْجَرُّونَ.

Hiph'îl. In the perfect the Arabic form is أَجَرَّ for أَجْرَرَ, 2nd pers. أَجْرَرْتَ. Contractions like أَحَسْتُ and أَحْسَيْتُ, for أَحْسَسْتُ, are very rare in the classical language. The Hebrew follows the form *hiḳṭal* or *hiḳṭêl* instead of *haḳṭal*; e.g. הֵדַק, הֵקַל, הֵסֵב, הֵחֵל, which stand for *hēdaḳḳ*, *hēsēbb*, etc., by contraction for *hidḳaḳ*, *hisbēb*. The uncontracted form in its latest stage appears in הֵרְנִין, הֵילִיל, which never undergo contraction (also in Syriac ܐܝܠܠ, Mand. האוליל), and in the participle

מַשְׁמִים, Ezek. iii. 15. The fem. sing. and plur. actually exhibit the doubling הֵחֵלָּה, הֵחֵלּוּ, הֵקַלּוּ, הֵתַמּוּ, הֵרֵעוּ, הֵפֵרוּ. The 2nd pers. usually has the form הֲרֵעֹתָה, (הֲחִלּוֹתָ), הֲרֵעֹתֶם. The original 1st pers. *haḳṭalti* occurs in all its purity in וְהַחְתַּתִּי, Jerem. xlix. 37; and a modification of the 2nd pers. in הֵתַלְתָּ and וַהֲפֵרֹתָה, for *hithlalta* and *hiphrarta*.—In the imperfect the Arabic form is يَجُرُّ for يَجْرُرُ. The Hebrew preserves a purer vowel in the 1st syllable, יָסֹב for *yāsēbb*, contracted from *yasbēb* for *yasbibu*, יָגֵן, יָפֵר; plur. יָחֵלּוּ for *yaḥlilū(na)*.

In the Aramaic dialects the doubling is thrown back upon the 1st radical, as in the imperfect Pʿal, whence arise the forms הַדֵּק, הַעֵל or הַנְעֵל, أَصَّن, for הַדְקֵק, أَصْنِن, impf. יַדֵּק, نُصُّن. To these correspond such Hebrew imperfects as יִסֹּב, יִתֹּם, יֵחַל. The plural however has two formations, one of which retains the doubling of the 2nd radical, whilst the other is purely Aramaic in dropping it. The former is exemplified by וַיָּסֵבּוּ, the latter by וַיַּכְּתוּ, Deut. i. 44.

The passive is in Arabic أُجِرَّ for أُجْرِرَ, 2nd pers. أُجْرِرْتَ, impf. يُجَرُّ for يُجْرَرُ. The Hebrew form הוּסַב stands for *husbab*, but has been influenced by the corresponding form of verbs ע"ו, הוּקַם; e.g. הוּחַל, הוּתַל, fem. הוּחַדָּה. In the imperfect we find a treble formation, as in the Hiph'il, there being forms (1) like יוּדַק, in pause for יוּדָק, resembling יָסֵב; (2) like יֻכַּת, plur. יֻכַּתּוּ, resembling יִסַּב, plur. יִסַּבּוּ; and (3) like הֻמְּכוּ, Job xxiv. 24; יֻחָקוּ, in pause for יֻחַקוּ, Job xix. 23, resembling the Aramaic הַדֵּק and יִדְּקוּן.

II. A. *Verbs of which the 1st radical is* w *or* y.

Of these the former, פ"ו, are by far the more common in the

Semitic languages. The number of verbs first *y* in Arabic and Ethiopic is very small indeed; in Hebrew and Syriac it appears to be larger, but this phenomenon is due to a peculiar change which verbs first *w* undergo in these two languages.

1. The normal form of verbs first *w* in the perfect of the first or simple form is that of the Arabic, وَلَدَ, وَعَدَ, وَعَظَ, وَدَعَ. وَجِعَ, وَجِلَ, وَجِرَ. Similarly in Ethiopic, ወለደ፡ ወረሰ፡ ወረደ፡ ወፅአ፡ ወዐየ፡. The only example that I remember in Ethiopic of the change of *w* into *y* is in አይድዐ፡ "to make known," the causative of an unused የድዐ፡ Heb. יָדַע. The corresponding Arabic verb is وَدَعَ "to put, place, store up, deposit"; what we "know" is that which we have "placed" or "stored up" in the mind for use[1]. In Hebrew the initial *w* almost invariably passes into *y*, unless protected by a preceding consonant; hence ילד, יעד, יעץ, ידע, יָגֹר, ינע, ירש, ירד, יָצָא. The same remark applies to the Aramaic; e.g. in Biblical Aramaic, יְהַב, יְדַע, further יְלַד, יְקַד, יְקַר, יְרַת. But the later Aramaic dialects vocalise this יְ, and turn it into a simple vowel *ī*. Hence in Syriac ܝܺܠܶܕ, ܝܺܪܶܬ, ܝܺܢܶܩ, ܝܺܩܶܕ, ܝܺܩܰܪ, which are commonly written in the oldest MSS. with prefixed *aleph*, ܐܺܝܠܶܕ, ܐܺܝܪܶܬ, etc.; and in Mandaitic עתיב, עקאר or עקיד, עתאר. The verb יְהַב, Mand. עהאב, also occurs in Syriac as ܝܺܗܶܒ, but the more common form is ܝܰܗܒ݂, which appears in the Talmūd Yĕrūshalmī as יַב, in which form the ה is elided and its vowel

[1] [The explanation of ידע, "know," from the Arabic ودع is due to Schultens but has not found general acceptance. The first radical of the verb "to know" is י not only in Hebrew, Aramaic and Ethiopic, but also in Sabaean, and perhaps in Assyrian (see Delitzsch, *Assyr. Gramm.* p. 308). The verb therefore is now generally taken to be true פ״י. Even in Arabic, as Nöldeke observes, there is a trace of a root يدع distinct from ودع (ايدع). The forms with ו after a prefix (הוֹדִיעַ, נוֹדַע etc.) are to be explained in the same way as הוביש, ܐܘܒܫ, *infra*, p. 242.]

thrown back on the initial letter. The Assyrian exhibits a further modification of the ground-form, since, according to the grammarians, the initial syllable is written with א, אשב for ישב, אצא for יצא, ארד for ירד. There is nothing antecedently improbable in this change of sound, since in Syriac we find these sounds confounded in ܝܒܫ compared with ܐܝܒܫ, ܝܠܦ compared with ܐܠܦ, whilst in Arabic we have أَرَخَ from ወርኅ: יֶרַח. In Arabic every initial و may be pronounced with hamza, if accompanied by the vowel *i* or *u* (but not *a*); e.g. one may say إِشَاح for وِشَاح, إِسَادَة for وِسَادَة, أُقِّتَ for وُقِّتَ, أُحِيَ for وُحِيَ (but not أَقَتَ for وَقَتَ).

In the imperfect indicative of the first form the Ethiopic retains the *w*, ይወልድ: ይወርስ:, with the exception of ይሁብ: (=ይህውብ:) from ወሀበ: (by transposition for ይውሁብ:). In the subjunctive the *w* is occasionally retained, as in ይውግር: "throw, pelt," ይውቅሥ: or ይውቀሥ: "argue, go to law," ይውስድ: "lead, carry," ይውጋእ: "butt"; but ordinarily the ወ is rejected, and the subjunctive appears as ይስድ: or ይሰድ: ይለድ: ይሬስ: ይግር: የሁብ: ይፃእ:: This rejection of the initial *w* is the rule in Arabic with all verbs which have *i* as the characteristic vowel of the imperfect, and with a few that have *a*; e.g. وَرِثَ، يَرِثُ ; وَعَدَ، يَعِدُ ; وَلَدَ، يَلِدُ ; وَسِعَ، يَسَعُ ; وَقَعَ، يَقَعُ ; وَهَبَ، يَهَبُ. But the و is retained when the characteristic vowel is *u*, and generally when it is *a*; e.g. وَجِرَ، يَوْجَرُ ; وَجِعَ، يَوْجَعُ ; وَدَّ، يَوَدُّ (for يَوْدَدُ) ; وَبُؤَ، يَوْبُؤُ "have murrain"; وَضُؤَ، يَوْضُؤُ "be clean and fair." There are, however, some interesting dialectical varieties, which I must notice. Firstly, initial و passes into *y*, yielding the forms يِيجَلُ، يِيجَعُ، يِيهَمُ "make mistake." Next, the sound of the *a* in this diphthong prevails over the other element, and the forms pass into يَاجَلُ,

يَاهَمُ، يَاجَعُ. Thirdly, the vowel of the first syllable may be weakened into *i*, and give us the forms يِيهَمُ، يِيجَعُ، يِيجَلُ.

Lastly, the vulgar forms of the present day are يُوقَف، يُوصَل، يُوعَد، يُولَد، يُوزَن، instead of يَصِلُ، يَقِفُ، يَعِدُ، يَلِدُ، يَزِنُ. We also find at the present day in Egypt the forms *yiḳaf, yiḳa', yiṣal*, and *yaḳif, yaḳi'*, but they are comparatively rare.

Let us glance now at Hebrew. Here one form of the imperfect is represented by תֵּלֵד, יֵרֵד, יֵשֵׁב, יֵדַע, יֵקַד, apparently identical with the normal Arabic تَلِدُ، يَرِدُ. The *a* was weakened as usual into *i*, and then lengthened before the tone into *ē*, תֵּלֵד, יֵרֵד, for *tilid, yirid*. A form like יֵקַד is against Arabic rule; and forms like יֵדָעֵם, יֵדָעֻנוּ, show that the *ṣêrê* was retained in the 2nd syllable before the tone, which has led some to think that it might have a diphthongal origin. They would derive תֵּלֵד, יֵרֵד, יֵדַע, from תֵּילֵד, יֵירֵד, יֵידַע, according to the dialectical Arabic يَيْجَلُ، يَيْجَعُ. Another form of the Hebrew imperfect is represented by יִירַשׁ, יִיקַד (as well as יֵקַד), יִישַׁן.

Here we have, no doubt, the dialectical Arabic يِيجَلُ، يِيجَعُ. The original *a* of the 1st syllable became *i*, and this worked the change of *w* into *y*. In one word, יָכֹל, the imperfect יוּכַל resembles in form the vulgar Arabic يُوصَل. We may consider it as the last weakening of an original יְוַכַּל, יוֹכַל[1].

Passing on to the Aramaic dialects, we find in Syriac the imperfect written with an *ālaph*, ܢܐܠܕ, ܢܐܪܬ. It seems to me that the original pronunciation was *nâladh, nârath*, as in the dialec-

[1] [But comp. p. 180.]

tical Arabic يَاجَلُ ,يَاجَعُ; and that *ā* was weakened into *ē* (for which we have abundant analogies), whence the Eastern forms ܢܹܐܒܲܐ ,ܢܹܐܟܘܿܠ. Others think, however, that this form arose by assimilation of the verbs פ״י and פ״א, such as ܢܹܐܡܲܪ ,ܢܹܐܘܲܠܹܦ. The Western Syrians weakened the *ē* still further into *ī*, ܢܺܐܟܘܿܠ, ܢܺܐܒܲܐ, as in the verbs פ״א ܢܺܐܡܲܪ. In Mandaitic the first syllable has ׳, probably *ī*, as עהאב, "I give," ניקאר, ניקאד or ניקוד; עדול and תידול, from עדל = ילד. These forms with *u* in the second syllable are remarkable.

Let us next examine the imperative mood.

In Ethiopic, where the initial *w* is lost in the subjunctive, it also disappears in the imperative. We occasionally find such forms as ወቅር: or ወቀር: "hew, cut out," ወግር: "pelt, stone"; but the usual ones are ቅር: or ቀር:, ግር: or ገር:, ረድ:, ሁበ:, ፀእ:: In Arabic, all verbs that lose the و in the imperfect, also drop it in the imperative; hence عِدْ ,رِثْ ,رِدْ ,قَعْ ,هَبْ. In those that retain the و, it is necessarily changed, on account of the prosthetic vowel, into a letter of prolongation; إِيجَلْ for إِوْجَلْ from وَجِلَ; اُوضُو for اُوْضُو from وَضُوَ. The vulgar form of the present day in Egypt is *ūḳaf, ūṣal, ūḳaʿ, ūzin, ūlid*; more rarely *ḳaf, ḳaʿ, ṣal*, or *ḳif*.

In Hebrew the forms waver somewhat: שֵׁב, רֵד, צֵא, דַּע; but perhaps יְרַד (Judg. v. 13). On the other hand, יְרֵה, יְרָא, יְרָשָׁה (Deut. xxxiii. 23) but also רֵשׁ and רַשׁ, and even יְצֹק as well as צַק "pour." In Syriac, on the contrary, the initial letter is retained in the imperative, with the exception of ܗܲܒ from ܝܗܲܒ, ܕܥ from ܝܕܲܥ, and ܬܸܒ from ܝܬܸܒ. In Mandaitic the form is not common in the extant literature. Noeldeke gives no examples but עתיב and תיב "sit"; האב "give," with the curious variations עהוב, אהוב, and before enclitics with ל, in the singular, הבא and ארבא, plur. הבו and ארבו.

In Arabic, the verbs which drop the initial و in the imperfect and imperative usually lose it also in one of the commonest forms of the infinitive, taking, as a sort of compensation, the feminine termination; e.g. لِدَةٌ as well as وَلْدٌ, and وِلَادَةٌ or إِلَادَةٌ; رِثَةٌ, as well as وِرْثٌ or إِرْثٌ; عِدَةٌ, as well as وَعْدٌ; عِظَةٌ, as well as وَعْظٌ. Precisely corresponding infinitives in Hebrew, as לֵדָה, דֵּעָה; generally however, לֶדֶת, רֶדֶת, רֶשֶׁת, שֶׁבֶת, צֵאת (for צֵאֶת), for *lidat*, etc. In דַּעַת the *pathachs* are due to the guttural, as in سَعَةٌ, ضَعَةٌ. The masculine form דֵּעַ in Job is a rarity, and equally so the contracted feminine לַת in 1 Sam. iv. 19. Examples of the fuller form are יְרֹא, יְסֹר, יְרֹד (Ps. xxx. 4), יְצֹק. The Ethiopic supplies us with many substantives of this class, but not infinitives, as ልደት፡ ርደት፡ ዕበት፡ ፀእት፡፡ In Aramaic there are likewise a few, e.g. עֵטָא, Dan. ii. 14; ܡܕܥܐ, ܡܫܟܒܐ, ܡܐܬܐ; ܥܕܬܐ is probably to be regarded as borrowed from the Hebrew עֵדָה.

Passing on to the derived conjugations, I would first direct your notice to the transitive or causative *Hiph'il*, in Hebrew הוֹלִיד. The presence of the ו is sufficient guarantee that the verb originally began with this letter; an original י must have yielded הֵילִיד. The Arabic and Ethiopic have preserved for us the purer form أَوْلَدَ, አውለደ፡, in Syriac ܐܘܠܕ, ܐܘܬܒ, ܐܘܕܥ. In the passive *Hoph'al*, the weak consonant is vocalised, הוּשַׁב for הָוְשַׁב, as in Arabic أُولِدَ for أُوْلِدَ.

In the same way, in the reflexive and passive *Niph'al*, the Hebrew נוֹלַד stands for נַוְלַד, according to the form נִקְטַל, whereas יִוָּלֵד is by assimilation from יִנְוָלֵד, corresponding to an Arabic يَنْوَلِدُ from اِنْوَلَدَ. Such forms, though not uncommon in the modern language, are not deemed classical.

The *reflexive conjugations* formed with the prefix *ta* require a little more attention.

The simplest is the Aramaic *Ethpe'el*. Of this the oldest shape is to be discerned in the Ethiopic ተወልደ: "be born," ተወሀበ: "be given." In Syriac it always appears with vocalised *y*, ܐܶܬܝܺܠܶܕ for *'eth-y-lēdh*, and that from *'eth-w-lēdh*, ܐܶܬܝܗܶܒ. In Mandaitic however the vowelless *yodh* is dropped, giving מיתליד, עתהיב; but "she was given" is עתיאהבאת, as in Syr. ܐܶܬܝܰܗܒܰܬ. The corresponding conjugation in Arabic is, as you may remember, the 8th, *ifta'ala*, اِقْتَتَلَ for تَقَتَّلَ. This should give us اِوْتَكَلَ, اِوْتَفَقَ; but these impossible forms necessarily become اِيتَكَلَ, اِيتَفَقَ, اِيتَعَدَ, اِيتَصَلَ, the existence of which is admitted, although the assimilation of *wt* into *tt* is greatly preferred: اِتَّكَلَ, اِتَّفَقَ, اِتَّعَدَ, اِتَّصَلَ. The imperf. of the former is يَاتَكِلُ, يَاتَفِقُ, يَاتَعِدُ; of the latter يَتَّكِلُ, يَتَّفِقُ, يَتَّعِدُ. So usual has this assimilation become that many secondary roots beginning with *t* have been formed from this conjugation; e.g. تَلَدَ "to be born in one's house, be hereditary"; تَسِعَ "be wide," تَقِيَ "fear God," تَكَلَ "rely on," اَتْلَجَ "insert," اَتْهَمَ "suspect." In Syriac ܬܟܶܠ is an example of this sort[1].

[1] [Prof. Wright's MS. cites also ܬܩܶܢ, late Heb. תָּקַן, which some scholars

On the reflexive of the Hebrew *Pi"ēl*, viz. *Hithpa"al*, in Syr. ܐܶܬܦܰܥܰܠ, I will merely remark that the prefixed syllable sometimes preserves the initial *w* from passing into *y*. So in הִתְוַדָּה, הִתְוַדַּע, הִתְוַכַּח; whence in post-biblical Hebrew the substantives וִדּוּי and וִכּוּחַ. The Syriac ܐܶܬܘܰܟܰܪ is hardly a parallel, because in that language we have the Pa"ēl ܘܰܟܰܪ and the noun ܘܽܟܪܳܐ.

The tendency to assimilate the *w* to the following letter, which we saw in the Arabic 8th conj. اِتَّلَدَ, appears in the other dialects in some other forms. In Hebrew, for instance, יצע = وَضَعَ assimilates in Hiph'il and Hoph'al, הִצִּיעַ, הֻצַּע. The same is the case with הִצִּיג and הֻצַּג; and with the rad. יצת, impf. יִצַּת, Niph. נִצַּת, Hiph. הִצִּית. In other instances the assimilation is merely sporadic, as in יִצַּק, יִסַּר, and even הִלֶּדֶת (inf. Hoph'al). In Aramaic instances of a similar kind are יִכֻּל from יְכֵל = יִכַּל, יִתַּב, Dan. vii. 26 [Compl., Norzi, Baer], from יְתִב; Syr. ܢܶܬܶܒ, ܢܶܕܰܥ, from ܝܺܬܶܒ, ܝܺܕܰܥ, whence in Bibl. Aram. יִנְדַּע, with dissimilation of *dd* into *nd*.

2. The verbs which are really פ״י are very few in number in the Semitic languages, and call for but little notice. In Hebrew there are only seven or eight altogether; יאשׁ, يَئِسَ, not used in Kal; יָבֵשׁ, يَبِسَ; יטב, not used in the perf. Kal; יָנַק; יָקַץ, يَقِظَ, not used in perf. Kal; יָשַׁר; and the Hiph'ils הֵילִיל and

connect with يَقِنَ; أَتْقَنَ: so still Mühlau and Volck, 11th ed., 1890. But يقن like the Syriac ܬܰܩܶܢ seems rather to be a denominative from ܬܽܘܩܳܢܳܐ, *εἰκόνα* (so Nöldeke; cf. Fränkel, *Lehnww.* p. 273), and therefore quite distinct from תקן, تقن, ܬܩܢ.]

הֵימִין. יצר is doubtful, and may be פ"ו; at least the Niph'al is נוֹצַר, Is. xliii. 10. The imperfects are יִיקַץ, יִינַק, יִיטַב, יִיבַשׁ, יִישַׁר, according to the Arabic form يَيْاَسُ for يَيْأَسُ; but instances of assimilation occur, as יִקַּץ (1 Kings iii. 15), יִשַּׁר (1 Sam. vi. 12), יִצַּר. The Hiph'il is הֵיטִיב for הֵיטִיב, הֵינִיק, הֵילִיל, הֵימִין, but the original diphthong is retained in הַיְשִׁיר, Prov. iv. 25, Ps. v. 9 (Ḳĕrē). In two cases the form הוֹשִׁיר seems to be used, falsely conforming to verbs פ"ו, viz. Ps. v. 9 (Kĕthībh) and Is. xlv. 2 (Kĕthībh). The same has happened with הוֹבִישׁ, Syr. ܐܘܒܫ; and with the Niph'al נוֹאָשׁ. The Niph'al of יָצַר is likewise, as we have seen, נוֹצַר (Is. liii. 10), and its Hoph'al יוּצַר (Is. liv. 17). The latter form would be quite *en règle* from a verb פ"י, because in Arabic too أَيْبَسَ would become in the passive أُوبِسَ, for أُيْبِسَ, the ي conforming to the preceding vowel. In Syriac ܐܝܠܠ and ܐܝܢܩ are the only words that exhibit the radical *y*, and the latter of these has a second form ܐܘܢܩ, which seems to have carried the day in Mandaitic, if we may judge by the word מונקא "foster, guardian," for מאנקא. The Mand. equivalent of ܐܝܠܠ is also האוליל. In the 8th conj. of the Arabic the same assimilation takes place as in verbs פ"ו, e.g. اِتَّقَنَ, اِتَّسَرَ, اِتَّبَسَ.

II. B. *Verbs of which the middle radical is* w *or* y.

In treating of these verbs, ע"ו and ע"י in Hebrew Grammar, we must, at the outset, distinguish carefully between verbs that never undergo contraction, and those which, according to my view, are generally or always contracted. To the former class, for example, belong in Arabic many verbs of the form فَعِلَ, as سَوِلَ "to be flaccid" or "pendulous," حَوِرَ "to be very white and black" (of the eye), عَوِرَ "to be one-eyed," حَوِلَ "to squint," صَيِدَ "to have the disease called صَيَدٌ" (of a camel), غَيِدَ "to be tender and flexible"; in Hebrew, חָוַר "be white," גָּוַע "expire," צָוַח "cry out," רָוַח "be airy and wide," אָיַב "be hostile to," עָיֵף "be weary"; in Syriac, ܚܘܰܪ "be white," ܫܘܰܪ "leap," ܪܘܰܙ "rejoice"; and in all three languages verbs that are also ל״ו or ל״י, as رَوِيَ, רָוָה, ܪܘܳܐ; هَوِيَ, הָיָה, ܗܘܳܐ. What principle guided the Semitic languages in the contraction or non-contraction of verbs ע״ו and ע״י, I am unable to state. I do not know why خَوِفَ became خَافَ, and مَوِتَ, مَاتَ, whilst حَوِلَ and عَوِرَ remained uncontracted; neither can I tell you why the Hebrew says צָוַח, while the Arab changed his صَيَحَ into صَاحَ[1].

The uncontracted verbs ע״ו and ע״י we may pass over altogether, as their inflexion is exactly like that of the regular verb. It is only the contracted ones that require our attention. And here I may remark that some grammarians of note, among them Aug. Müller, Noeldeke and Stade, regard this class as actual specimens of biliteral roots. Stade, for example, calls them *mittelvocalig*, "having a vowel in the middle," and denies altogether the correctness of the term ע״ו, for says he (p. 109) "these roots never had a consonant ו in the second place." For my own part, I prefer the older view, which is held by the Arab grammarians themselves, and for which I think we shall discover many good reasons as we go along.

The question of the existence of verbs ע״י in Hebrew has been

[1] [With the exception of verbs which have י as their third radical (e.g. לוה, لوي), all those verbs in which middle ו or י is treated as a consonant, appear to be denominatives and to have been formed at a relatively late period.—N.]

finally settled by Noeldeke in the *ZDMG.* xxxvii. p. 525, in the affirmative [as against the view of Ewald that such forms as שִׂים and בִּין are not true ע״י verbs but shortened Hiph'īls from roots ע״ו]. To this article I refer you for all necessary information on the subject.

If you consult the Arab grammarians, they will tell you that such words as قَامَ, خَافَ and طَالَ, had originally a و in the second place, which has generally been vocalised; whence it comes that its place is occupied by a long vowel, which must under certain circumstances be shortened. The rules for these processes are few and simple.

(1) If three open syllables follow one another in succession the first of which has short *ă* and the other two any of the three vowels, then the vowel of the second syllable is rejected, and the second radical is changed into long *ā*. Hence قَوَلَ becomes قَالَ, خَوِفَ becomes خَافَ, طَوُلَ becomes طَالَ. If, however, the first radical has *u* and the second *i*, the latter vowel, as being the clearer, generally predominates, so that قُوِلَ becomes قِيلَ; although some of the Arabs contracted the form more regularly into قُولَ, whilst others gave the long vowel the intermediate sound of *ü*, *ḳûla*.

(2) If the 1st radical be vowelless, and the 2nd and 3rd radicals have vowels, then the vowel of the second is thrown back upon the 1st, and the و or ي becomes the corresponding letter of prolongation or long vowel. Hence يَقْوُلُ becomes يَقُولُ, يَخْوَفُ يَخَافُ, يُقْوَلُ يُقَالُ, أَقْوَمَ أَقَامَ, يَقْوِمُ يُقِيمُ. Should the final radical under any circumstances lose its vowel, then the preceding long vowel must be shortened. The jussive يَقُولْ becomes يَقُلْ, يَخَافْ يَخَفْ, يُقَالْ يُقَلْ, يُقِيمْ يُقِمْ, أَقَامْتُ أَقَمْتُ, يُقِيمْنَ يُقِمْنَ. A further consequence of these changes is that the imperative of the 1st conjugation drops the now

useless prosthetic *alif*; اُقْوُلْ becomes اُقُوْلْ, اُقُلْ, قُلْ; or perhaps we may rather say that it never required the prosthetic *alif*, for the original قْوُلْ would naturally become قُوْلْ and then قُلْ.

(3) In the perfect of the 1st conjugation, when the first radical has *a* and the third is vowelless, contraction takes place, but the vowel of the first radical is affected either by the consonant or the vowel of the middle syllable. Hence قَوَمْتَ becomes, not قَمْتَ, but قُمْتَ, through the influence of the و, and سَيَرْتَ becomes سِرْتَ, through the influence of the ي; but خَوِفْتَ becomes خِفْتَ, not خَفْتَ or خُفْتَ, through the influence of the vowel *i*, which is characteristic of the intransitive form. Where these influences are combined, their operation is of course the more certain; طَوُلْتَ can become nothing but طُلْتَ, and هَيِبْتَ nothing but هِبْتَ.

So much for the Arabic rules. Let us next study the forms of the Ethiopic, Hebrew and Syriac paradigms as compared with those of the Arabic.

The Arabic قَامَ stands, as we have seen, for قَوَمَ, خَافَ for خَوِفَ, طَالَ for طَوُلَ. The corresponding Ethiopic forms ሮጸ: "run," ቆእ: "conquer," ሖረ: "go," ቦእ: "come," ሤመ: "set," ሜጠ: "turn," are not identical with the Arabic, for the Arabic long *â* does not ordinarily become *ô* or *ê* in Ethiopic. The Ethiopic forms have been obtained by simple rejection of the vowel of the second radical, and subsequent change of the resulting diphthongs *au*, *ai*, into *ô*, *ê*. Thus *rawaṣa*, *sayama*, became *rauṣa*, *sayma*, and then *rôṣa*, *sêma*. These vowels are retained throughout the whole inflexion of the perfect, ሮጽተ: ሮጽከ: ሤምተ: ሤምከ: etc. The Hebrew form of the 3rd pers. sing. masc. is still more peculiar, and indeed very hard to explain. As Arabic long *â* regularly becomes *ô* in Hebrew, we should have expected

קָוֹם to yield *ḳôm* as the equivalent of قَامَ *ḳâma*, and not *ḳām*. How then is this form *ḳām*, קָם, from *ḳăm*, to be explained? Assimilation to the class ע״ע can scarcely have been in operation, for קָם is always carefully distinguished from סַב in its punctuation, and besides the fem. and plur. are קָ֫מָה, קָ֫מוּ, not קַמָּה, קַמּוּ. It would seem as if, in this case, the Hebrew, attaching more weight than the Arab did to the characteristic vowel of the form, had shortened the original *ḳawam* into *ḳam*, and then derived the other persons from this shortened form as a base[1]. Similarly, the Hebrew differs from the Arabic in the turn which it gives to verbs with *u* and *i* in the second syllable. The Arab changes مَوِتَ into مَاتَ, and طَوُلَ into طَالَ; but the Hebrew attached more weight to the vowels as characteristic of the intransitive form, and spoke not *mâth*, but מֵת *mêth* (for *mit*, from *mawit*); not *bâsh* or *'âr*, but בּוֹשׁ *bôsh* and אוֹר *'ôr* (for *bush* and *'ur*, from *bawush*, *'awur*). These forms resemble those of the Arabic 2nd pers. مِتَّ, خِفْتَ, طُلْتَ, for مَوِتْتَ, خَوِفْتَ, طَوُلْتَ. In Aramaic the ordinary form is precisely what we should expect, with long *â* corresponding to the Arabic *â*; e.g. קָם, שָׂם, ܩܳܡ, ܣܳܡ; Mand. קאם, פאש "remain"; but ܡܺܝܬ, Mand. מית, corresponding to Heb. מֵת. The 3rd pers. sing. fem. is in Arabic قَامَتْ, مَاتَتْ, خَافَتْ, طَالَتْ, سَارَتْ. The Heb. קָ֫מָה, בָּ֫אָה, מֵ֫תָה, בּ֫וֹשָׁה, with the tone ordinarily on the 1st syllable, are derived directly from the forms of the masc. קָם, מֵת, בּוֹשׁ; but we also find וְשָׁבַת, with older termination, Ezek. xlvi. 17. The Aramaic forms are סָ֫פַת, Dan. iv. 30; Syr.

[1] It may be, however, that the sound of the vowel was even still somewhat longer than that of *ă*, something between it and *â*, as the spelling קָאם in Hos. x. 14 may seem to indicate.

ܩܳܡܬ݂, ܩܳܡܬ݁, ܡܺܝܬܶܬ݂; Mand. קאמאת, נאראת. Similarly in the 3rd pers. plur., قَامُوا, مَاتُوا, خَافُوا, طَالُوا, سَارُوا, corresponding to Aramaic, שָׂמוּ, Dan. iii. 12, קָמוּ, Ezra v. 2; Syr. ܩܳܡܘ, ܩܳܡܘܿ, ܡܺܝܬܘ; Mand. קאמבה, פאשבה (without ו), in the fuller form קאמיון, פאשיון. The Heb. קָמוּ, סָרוּ, מֵתוּ, בֹּשׁוּ, אֹרוּ, with the tone usually on the 1st syllable, are derived directly from the corresponding singulars, קָם, etc.

In the 2nd pers. sing. and its analogous forms we find a still greater variety among the dialects. In Arabic the 2nd pers. sing. masc. is قُمْتَ, خِفْتَ, مِتَّ, طُلْتَ, or from a verb medial ي, سِرْتَ, هِبْتَ. Here the vowels *u* and *i* are due respectively either to the influence of the last radical و or ي, or of the characteristic vowel *u* or *i*: قَوَمْتَ = قُمْتَ, خَوِفْتَ = خِفْتَ, سَيَرْتَ = سِرْتَ, هَيِبْتَ = هِبْتَ, طَوُلْتَ = طُلْتَ, مَوِتَّ = مِتَّ. In Hebrew the form is קַמְתָּ, בַּנְתָּה, שַׂמְתָּ, סַרְתֶּם, גַּרְתִּי, with short *ă*, and *ķāmeṣ* (*ā*) appears only in pause, קָמְתִּי, Micha vii. 8, סָרְתִּי, Ps. cxix. 102, שָׂמְתִּי, Jerem. xxxiii. 25. Before Ķimḥi's time, however, even the ordinary forms used to be pointed with *ķāmeṣ*, קָמְתָּ, שָׂמְתָּ, at least when the accent was *mil'êl*. From מֵת we have, unexpectedly, מַתָּה, מַתְנוּ (we should have expected מֵתָּה, מֵתְנוּ), and in pause וָמַתִּי, Gen. xix. 19, but also וָמָתְנוּ. From verbs with *ô* we get בֹּשְׁתְּ, בֹּשְׁתִּי, בֹּשְׁנוּ (for *busht*, *bushti*, *bushnū*). On the other hand, the long vowel is steadily preserved in the Aramaic, not merely in the 1st pers., שָׂמֶת Ezra vi. 12, Syr. ܩܳܡܶܬ, ܩܳܡܶܬ݂, Mand. קאמית, נאמית; but also in the second, שַׂמְתְּ Dan. iii. 10, Syr. ܣܳܡܬ݁, ܣܡܶܬ݁, Mand. האקת = ܐܰܩܶܬ݁, לאפת = ܐܰܠܶܦܬ݁ "didst teach."

Passing on to the imperative, we find the Arabic forms to be such as قُمْ, خَفْ, سِرْ. But the plurals are قُومُوا, خَافُوا, سِيرُوا; fem. قُومِي, خَافِي, سِيرِي. In vulgar Arabic the shortening of the sing. forms is neglected, قول *ḳûl*, بيع *bîʿ*; unless an accus. suffix or an enclitic prep. follows, as *shil-nî* "carry me," *ḳul-lî*, *ḳul-lûhum*. In Geʿez the corresponding forms are ቁም፡, ሖር፡ or ሑር፡, ባእ፡, ሢም፡, exactly like the Heb. קוּם, קוּמוּ; בֹּא, בֹּאוּ; בּוֹשִׁי, בּוֹשׁוּ; שִׂים, גִּיל. In Hebrew קוּם stands for קְוֻם; but בֹּא was originally *bâ'*, for בְּוָא, בְּוַא; בּוֹשׁוּ *bâshû*, for *bĕwashû*; אוֹרִי *'ârî*, for *'ăwarî*. In Geʿez the form ሖር፡ is difficult to explain; perhaps we may regard it as an example of the change of *â* into *ô*, and as therefore standing for *ḥâr*; if so, then the other form ሑር፡ is only a weakening of the original ሖር፡, brought about by the influence of the common form ቁም፡. In Aramaic we find nothing unusual; Bibl. קוּמִי Dan. vii. 5, שִׂימוּ Ezra iv. 21; Syr. ܩܽܘܡ, ܣܺܝܡ; Mand. קום, תוב, but also סום. The verb مَاتَ, מֵת, ܡܺܝܬ݂, has مُتَّ, מַתָּ, ܡܺܝܬ݂ܬ݁, Mand. מות; and in Mand. there is one example with *a*, viz. דאר "dwell," by assimilation to the class ע"ע.

For the imperfect indicative the Arabic has the three forms يَقُومُ, يَخَافُ, يَسِيرُ, standing respectively for يَقْوُمُ, يَخْوَفُ, يَسْيِرُ. The peculiar Geʿez indicative may be exemplified by such words as ይቀውም፡, የሐውር፡, ይበውእ፡, ይሠይም፡. It is only the forms of the subjunctive that we can compare with the Arabic indicative. Here then we have ይሩጽ፡, ይዑድ፡, ይባእ፡, ይሢም፡. The verb ሖር፡ "to go," has the same double formation as in the imperative, viz. ይሖር፡ as well as ይሑር፡, which we must explain in the same way.—In Hebrew the preformatives have usually retained the original vowel *a*, as יָקוּם, יָבוֹא, יָשִׂים, corresponding exactly to the three Arabic forms, since יָבוֹא was originally *yabû'u*; other examples may be the very doubtful יָדוֹן, Gen. vi. 3, and יָקוֹט, Job viii. 14. The only instance of the weakening of the preformative to *i* is יֵבוֹשׁ, for *yabwashu, yabâsh, yibâsh, yēbôsh*. The jussives of يَقُومُ، يَخَافُ، يَسِيرُ are in Arabic يَقُمْ، يَخَفْ، يَسِرْ, and to these correspond in Hebrew יָקֹם, תָּרֹם, יָשֵׂם, יָגֵל, still farther shortened with vâv conversive into וַיָּקָם, וַתָּרָם, וַיָּגֶל, וַיָּשֶׂם. If however the last radical be ר or a guttural, then *ă* is substituted for *ŏ* or *ĕ*, as וַיָּנַע, וַיָּנַח, וַיָּסַר, וַיָּרַח; except וַיָּגָר, וַתָּגָר. In the 3rd pers. plur. fem. we should expect, after the analogy of the Arabic يَقُمْنَ، يَخَفْنَ، يَسِرْنَ, a Hebrew form תָּקֹמְנָה, and this actually occurs in תָּשֹׁבְןָ, Exod. xvi. 55, תָּבֹאןָ (for *tabâna, tabwa'na*), תָּגֹלְנָה; but more frequently this form is assimilated to that of verbs ע״ע, and a diphthongal י ֶ inserted, with consequent restoration of the long vowel, תְּשׁוּבֶינָה, תְּמוּטֶינָה. The Aramaic forms of the imperfect are just what we should naturally expect, viz. יְקוּם, ܢܩܘܡ, ܢܩܘܡ. There is however another form in use, viz. Syr. ܢܩܘܡ, Mand. and Talmud. ניקום. In Syriac I can scarcely remember any but singular forms, ܢܩܘܡ, ܬܩܘܡ, though ܢܩܘܡܘܢ is quoted[1]; but in Mand. the plural is נימיתון, f. נימיתא, נידינון, etc., while in the verb קום the vowel of the 2nd syllable is rejected, ניקמון, f. ניקמא. These Mandaitic forms coincide with those from verbs ע״ע in the same dialect, as תירינון from רנג, נינזון "sprinkle," from נזז, and the Syriac variation must be traced to a similar assimilation of ע״ו

[1] [ܢܩܘܡܘܢ is demanded by the metre in Ephr. Syr., iii. 316 A.—N.]

to ע"ע. The verb مات, מֵת, ܡܺܝܬ has in all the dialects يَمُوتُ, יָמוּת, ܢܡܽܘܬ, like יִבֹּל from נָבֵל, or ܢܶܣܒܳܘܣ from ܣܒܶܣ. In Mandaitic we find a future in *a*, נידאר, עדאר, "dwell," by assimilation to the class ע"ע.

The infinitive construct in Hebrew has the simple form קוּם, for קְוֹם, as in the regular verb קְטֹל for קְטָל. The form בּוֹא, אוֹר, בּוֹשׁ, probably springs from a long *â*, *bâ'*, *'âr*, *bâsh*, for *bawa'*, *'awar*, *bawash*.—In the infinitive absolute on the contrary, סוֹר, שׁוֹב, מוֹת, are contractions of *sawâr*, *shawâb*, *mawâth*.—The Aramaic infinitive is מְקָם, Syr. ܡܶܩܳܡ, for ܡܩܳܘܳܡ; the same variation occurs as in the imperfect, especially in Mandaitic and Talmudic, i.e. ܡܩܽܘܡ, מיקאם, מידאן, Talm. מיקם, מימת, מידן; but the emphatic form of מיקאם in Mandaitic is מיקמא, as if from a verb ע"ע.

The original form of the participle active must have been قَاوِم, سَايِر; but in the contracted verbs the و at the beginning of the syllable was changed into *hamsa*, قَائِم, and the verbs mediae ي followed this analogy, سَائِر. These forms are liable to a rare contraction into قَام, سَار as شَاكٌ for شَائِك "armed," هَارٌ for هَائِر "feeble," طَافٌ for طَائِف "going about," سَاسٌ for سَائِس "decayed" (a tooth), مَاهُ الفُوَاد for مَائِه "cowardly." To this corresponds the rare Hebrew form לוֹט, Is. xxv. 7, בּוֹסִים, Zach. x. 5, קוֹמִים, 2 Kings xvi. 7, for *lût*, *bûs*, *kûm*. The more usual form is however analogous to that of the perf., viz. בָּא, fem. בָּאָה, זָר, רָץ, צָם, sometimes written with א, as לָאט, Judg. iv. 21, שָׁאטִים Ezek. xxviii. 24, 26, שָׁאטוֹת, Ezek. xvi. 57, רָאשׁ, 2 Sam. xii. 1, 4, Prov. x. 4 (compare the perf. קָאם, Hos. x. 14). This form seems to me to be best explained as arising from a nominal *ḳaṭal*, i.e. *ṣawdm*, *rawdṣ*, *bawd'*, contracted after the analogy of the perfect into *ṣam*, *raṣ*, *ba'*. In the same way in intrans. verbs, with *ē* and *ō* in the second syllable, e.g. מֵת for מָוֵת (*mawit*, *mit*), לֵץ for לָוֵץ (*lawiṣ*, *liṣ*), בּוֹשׁ for בָּוֹשׁ (*bawush*, *bush*), according to the Heb. כָּבֵד, יָגֹר, or the Arabic adjectives حَذِر, يَقُظ. In Aramaic similar phenomena recur. In Bibl. Aram. the form is קָאֵם Dan. ii. 31, plur. in *Kᵉthībh* דָּאֲנִין, דָּאֲרִין, וְאָעִין, emph. קָאֲמַיָּא, constr. דָּאֲרֵי. The *Ḳĕrē* usually substitutes י for א in these plur. forms, דָּיְנִין, זָיְעִין, דָּיְרֵי. In Syriac only the singular is written with ܐ, ܩܳܐܶܡ, pronounced however, we are told, *ḳâyēm*. The fem. and plurals are invariably with *yūd*, ܩܳܝܡܳܐ, ܩܳܝܡܺܝܢ, ܩܳܝܡܳܢ. In Mandaitic the י is written in the sing. masc. too, קאיים, מאיית, fem. קאימא.—The passive participle of the Hebrew is exemplified by מוּל, סוּג, fem. לוּטָה, for *mawūl*, *sawūg*, *lĕwūṭāh*. In Aramaic the corresponding form is שִׂים, ܣܺܝܡ, Mand. ציר, "depicted," כיל "measured," for *sĕyīm*, *lĕwīṭ*, etc.

I shall now proceed to the derived conjugations of these verbs, and go through them as rapidly as possible.

1. *Pi"ēl.* The uncontracted verbs form their Pi"ēl quite regularly; e.g. عَوَّر, עִוֵּר, ܥܰܘܰܪ, "to blind of one eye," עִוֵּת "bend," ܩܰܘܰܪ "leap in numbers." The contracted ones too exhibit the normal form, that is to say, the weak letter, being strengthened by doubling, undergoes no change or only a slight one. In Arabic, for example, we have قَوَّم, صَوَّر, ذَيَّل, عَيَّن; in Ge'ez ሐወጸ: "inspect," "visit," ጸወዐ: "cry out"; in Heb. עִוֵּד "surround," Ps. cxix. 61; Aram. זַוֵּג, זַוֵּד, כַּוֵּן, Syr. ܙܰܘܶܕ, ܥܰܘܶܩ, ܙܰܘܶܓ, ܚܰܘܶܪ, ܐܶܬܚܰܘܰܪ; Mand. זאויד. But more frequently the middle consonant appears as a *y*, the origin of which I explain thus.

In a form like *ḳauwēm*, the initial of the second syllable was changed in Hebrew and Aramaic into *y*, *ḳauyēm* (comp. דְּיוֹ, دَوَاةٌ; הָיָה, הֲוָא, هَوِيَ), whence, by assimilation of the preceding letter, *ḳaiyēm*, and finally *ḳiyyēm*. So in Aram. קַיֵּם, ܩܰܝܶܡ, חַיֵּב, ܚܰܝܶܒ, ܐܰܝܶܢ̈, etc. In Hebrew forms like קִיֵּם, חִיֵּב, belong to the later stage of the language. In place of Pi"ēl the Hebrew frequently exhibits another formation, viz. *Pi'lēl*, of which the older form was *Pa'lal*, as קוֹמֵם, רוֹמֵם, עוֹרֵר, בּוֹסֵס, etc., for *ḳaumam*, *raumam*, etc.

2. *Hiph'îl* and *Hoph'al*. The contracted Arabic form is أَقَامَ, أَبَانَ, for أَقْوَمَ, أَبْيَنَ. To this correspond in Ge'ez አሮጸ:, አሐረ:, አቤየ:, which seem to be taken directly from the simple forms ሮጸ:, ሐረ:, ቤየ:. Some verbs however exhibit a short *a* in the 2nd syllable, which before a final guttural may become *ĕ*; e.g. አቀመ: *'aḳáma*; አነመ: *'anáma*, as well as አኖመ:; አጠቀ: *'aṭáḳa*, "hem in," as well as አጥወቀ:; አነኀ: *'anáḫa* or አንኀ: *'anĕḫa*, "lengthen"; አብአ: *'abĕ'a* "bring or put in"; አብሐ: *'abĕḥa*, "permit." Such words seem to be really derived from the old form *'aḳwáma*, *'anwáma*, *'abwĕ'a*, etc.; perhaps with doubling of the first letter by way of compensation, as in הֵסִּית, הֵנִּיחַ.—The Hebrew form הֵקִים stands far below the Arabic and Ge'ez. The original *haḳwáma* must have already passed through the stages of *haḳwám*, *hiḳwám*, *hiḳwîm*, *hiḳîm*, before it could become *hēḳîm*. The 2nd pers. of the Hebrew is likewise far removed from the purity of the Arabic أَقَمْتَ, for أَقَامْتَ, أَقْوَمْتَ. The purer form does indeed occur in such cases as הֲנַפְתָּ, הֲמִתָּה, הֲבֵאתָ, הֲנַחֹתָ, plur. הֲבֵאתֶם, הֲמִתֶּם; but commonly an assimilation to verbs ע"ע is effected by the insertion of *ô*, for original *ā*, in which case the vowel of the preformative is usually *ă*, sometimes *ĕ*, and the vowel of the radical syllable sometimes *ē* instead of *î*; as הֲעִירֹתָ, הֲרִימוֹתָ, הֲבִיאֹתָ, וַהֲסִירֹתָ, הֲבִישׁוֹתָ, הֲשִׁיבוֹתָ, הַעֲרֹתָה, וַהֲקִמֹתָ; and in the plur. הֲפִצֹתֶם,

הֲשֵׁבֹתֶם, הֲבִיאֹתֶם, הֲבִינוֹתֶם. The Aramaic perfect is in the Old Testament הֲתִיב, וַהֲקִים, הֲקִים; 2nd sing. הֲקֵימְתָּ, 1st sing. הֲקֵימֶת, 3rd plur. הֲקִימוּ; in Syr. ܐܩܝܡ, ܐܬܝܒ; in Mand. ארים, אקים. In this last dialect the 1st pers. seems often to be identical in form with that of verbs ע״ע, e.g. האשטית, אקמית "I despised," but ארימית, אריקית.—The imperfect is in Arabic يُقِيمُ for يُقْوِمُ, with the jussive يُقِمْ and imperative أَقِمْ. In Ge'ez the imperfect indicative is ያጸውር: ያከይድ:, the subjunctive ያጹር: ያኪድ:, imperative አጹር: አኪድ:. But verbs of the form አቀመ: አብአ: have in the subjunctive ያቅም: *yâkîm*, ያብእ:, imperative አቅም: አብእ:. In Hebrew יָקִים stands for *ya-hakwim, yakwim*; the jussive is יָקֵם, the vowel of which is still further shortened with ו *conversive* into וַיָּקָם. In Aramaic the corresponding form is יְקִים, ܢܩܝܡ; but in Syriac the form ܢܩܝܡ, participle ܡܩܝܡ, is admissible, and this is the only one found in Mandaitic, e.g. נארים, מארים, מאקים. These are all assimilated to verbs ע״ע, as appears from the plur. מאקמילון as compared with מאהיקילון, "afflicting them."—The passive of this conjugation in Arabic is أُقِيمَ for أُقْوِمَ. In Hebrew the original *hukwáma* would naturally become *hukāma, hukâm*, but the form in actual use has been entirely assimilated to that of verbs פ״ו, הוּשַׁב, הוּקַם. In Syriac we have only the passive participle ܡܩܳܡ, for *mukwam, mukâm*; but in Biblical Aramaic there is the remarkable survival הֳקִימַת Dan. vii. 4, wrongly pointed הֳקְמַת in verse 5.

3. Of the reflexive conjugations with prefixed *ta*, I will only notice the *Ethpĕ'ĕl*, corresponding to the 8th conjugation of the Arabic. In Arabic the form is, of course, اِجْتَازَ, contracted for

اِجْتَوَزَ; but the uncontracted form is used in many verbs either by itself or along with the other; e.g. اِجْتَوَرُوا or اِجْتَارُوا, اِعْتَوَرُوا. In Ge'ez the corresponding forms are ተሀውከ: "be agitated," ተሠይመ:. The Aramaic of the Bible exhibits יִתְּשָׂם, יִתְּשָׂמוּן, מִתְּשָׂם, but also יִתְזִין. The one form, הִתְּשָׂם, comes directly from the original *tasayama, tasâma.* The doubling of the *t* may be an attempt to compensate for the radical which has disappeared by contraction, and so to give the word something of the outward form of the normal הִתְקְטֵל; or it may be merely imitated from the *Ethtaf'al* (*Ittaf'al*). The other form, הִתְזִין, has no doubt arisen by assimilation to the *Ethtaf'al* or reflex of *Af'el,* the two being completely confounded in Syriac. E.g. הִתְזִין is *Ethpe'el* of זָן, ܐܶܬ݂ܣܺܝܡ or ܐܶܬ݁ܬ݁ܣܺܝܡ of ܣܳܡ; but ܐܶܬ݁ܬ݁ܚܶܕ, ܐܶܬ݁ܬ݁ܺܝܒ, ܐܶܬ݁ܬ݁ܚܶܡ are *Ethtaf'als* from ܐܰܚܶܕ, ܐܰܘܬܶܒ, ܐܰܚܶܡ. In Mandaitic however the two conjugations can be readily distinguished; ניתליפון is *Ethpe'el* from לוף; ניתאראם, *Ethtaf'al* from רום. I find however עתניהית "I was quieted," which seems to be *Ethpe'el,* whereas ܐܶܬ݁ܬ݁ܢܺܝܚ must be regarded as *Ethtaf'al.*

4. The last form to which I shall direct your attention is the reflexive and passive *Niph'al.* The Arabic form may be exemplified by اِنْقَاد, اِنْدَاس, for اِنْقَوَدَ, اِنْدَوَسَ, imperf. يَنْقَادُ, يَنْدَاسُ. In Hebrew נָדוֹשׁ was originally *nadâsh,* contracted from *nadwash,* as in the Arabic 4th conj. أَقَامَ from أَقْوَمَ; and so fem. נְפֹוצָה, plur. נָפֹצוּ. One verb, נֵעוֹר, exhibits the weakening of *a* to *i* in the preformative. The 1st and 2nd persons are assimilated to verbs ע"ע by the insertion of a vowel; viz. 2nd plur. נְפֻצוֹתֶם, נְקֹטֹתֶם, with *ô*; 1st pers. sing. נְסוּגֹתִי, נְפוּגֹתִי, נְבוּכֹתִי, with sinking of *ô* to *û.* The infinitives have the form

הֵמוֹל, הֵפוֹחַ. The vowel *ô* (for *â*) is sunk to *û* in הוּדוּשׁ (Isaiah xxv. 10); and the preformative is absorbed in לֵאוֹר (Job xxxiii. 30), if the reading be correct. The imperative is exemplified by הָכֵן for *hinkân* (*hinkawin*), הֵמֹּלוּ, הֵרֹמּוּ, the last with irregular doubling of the *m*. The imperfect is, for example, יָכוֹן for *yinkân*, from *yankawin*, יָנוּעַ, יָעוּר; יִסֹּגוּ, יֵרוֹמּוּ, with irregular doubling of the *m*.

Of the frequent and close resemblances in form between verbs ע״ו and ע״ע we have already had many examples. I may add to these such Hiph'îls as הִסִּיג, with its Hoph'al הֻסַּג, and הִסִּית, which latter differs only in form from הֵסִית; whereas in some other cases the difference perhaps extends to the meaning as well, as הֵנִיחַ "cause to rest" and הִנִּיחַ "lay down." Similar is the Niph'al נִמּוֹל for *namâl* (*namwal*), Gen. xvii. 26, participle נִמֹּלִים, Gen. xxxiv. 22, for *namâlîm* (*namwalîm*).

II. C. *Verbs of which the 3rd radical is* w *or* y.

We now proceed to the large and important class of verbs in which the weak letter occupies the third place in the root. In our Hebrew Grammars these are generally called verbs ל״ה, but as the ה is merely a vowel-letter, I prefer speaking of them as verbs ל״ו or ל״י, according to circumstances. Verbs ל״ה, strictly so called, are such as גָּבַהּ, which pertain to a quite different class, *verba tertiae gutturalis*.

In the *first conjugation*, the fullest form of the verbs of this class has been preserved in Ethiopic, where no contraction takes place in the perfect 3rd pers. sing. masc.: ተለወ፡ *talâwa*, "follow"; በከየ፡ *bakâya*, "weep"; ሐየወ፡ *ḥâywa*, "live"; ዐበየ፡ *'âbya*, "be large"; ርእየ፡ *re'ya*, "see." The solitary instance that I remember of contraction is in a form corresponding to Heb. Pi"ēl, viz. ሀሎ፡ *hallô*, for ሀለወ፡ *hallâwa* ["he was"], which are both in use. The final vowel was obviously dropped in this exceedingly common word, and the resulting diphthong *aw* then naturally passed into *ô*.—In Arabic the final *w* appears as such only in verbs of the form فَعُلَ, as سَرُوَ "to be noble," حَلُوَ "to be sweet." In verbs third ي such a form would be impossible; the final ي would at once influence the vowel *u* so as to change it into *i*, and the form فَعُلَ, if it ever occurred, would be indistinguishable from فَعِلَ, as خَزِيَ "be ashamed," رَوِيَ "be sated with drink." Not only so, however, but verbs third و of the form فَعِلَ are indistinguishable from verbs third ي, because the influence of the vowel *kesr* necessarily changes و into ي, as رَضِيَ "be pleased with," for رَضِوَ, سَلِيَ "be comforted *or* consoled," for سَلِوَ, حَيِيَ for حَيِوَ. These forms, be it observed, are all uncontracted (with the exception of حَيِيَ, which a false analogy has shortened into حَيَّ); but in the most common form of all, فَعَلَ, the contraction, of which we found but a trace in Ethiopic, has become customary. *Tálawa* and *bákaya* drop their final vowel, but the resulting diphthongal terminations *aw* and *ay* both pass in Arabic into *á*, *tálá*, *bákâ*. For distinction's sake the grammarians bid us write تَلَا with *alif*, when the final radical is *w*, and بَكَي with *y*, when the final radical is *y*, but the sound is one and the same.

In Hebrew the tendency of the ו to pass into י has almost obliterated the differences between verbs ל״ו and ל״י. The radical שלו alone has preserved the final *w* in such forms as שָׁלַוְתִּי, Job iii. 25, and, which is more remarkable, in an adjective of the form فَعِلٌ, viz. שָׁלֵו or שְׁלֵיו, Job xvi. 12, xxi. 23, Jerem. xlix. 31 (written שְׁלֵיו). Neither do intransitive verbs of the form فَعِلَ seem to occur in Hebrew, so that we have only verbs of the form فَعَلَ to deal with. These follow exactly the same course as in Arabic; the final vowel was dropped, and the resulting diphthongal terminations passed into *â*, which the Hebrews expressed by the vowel-letter ה. In this way the original *talâwa*, *bakâya*, became *talâw, talâ*; *bakây, bakâ*; and were written תָּלָה "hang," בָּכָה "weep."

In Aramaic the intransitive forms are not very common, e.g., in Syriac, ܫܠܶܐ, ܚܕܺܝ, which stand for *shalîya, shalîwa,* and *ḥadîya, ḥadîwa.* So in Mandaitic, עמיליא "he swore to me." The transitives have undergone the same contraction as in Hebrew, only that the termination is here usually expressed by ا א, and the door thereby opened for further confusion, as in vulgar Arabic, with the entirely different verbs ל״א, like ܢܣܐ, ܡܠܐ. The words ܬܠܐ, ܒܟܐ stand for *talâwa, bakâya*; whereas ܢܣܐ, ܡܠܐ, were originally *ḥaṭâ'a, malâ'a.* Similarly in Mandaitic הזא "saw," שתא "drank," בא "sought for" (for בעא). In the Bibl. Aram. א and ה are used indifferently.

One verb in Aramaic constantly takes prosthetic aleph, viz. אִשְׁתִּי Dan. v. 3, 4, ܐܶܫܬܺܝ, for ܫܬܺܝ. I mention this for the sake of calling attention to the same phenomenon in vulgar Arabic (Spitta, p. 232), e.g. *iḥkâ* "he narrated," *iskâ* "he gave water," *irmâ* "he threw or pelted."

The 3rd pers. sing. fem. must of course originally have been, as in Ethiopic, ተለወት፡ *talâwat*, በከየት፡ *bakâyat.* (The contracted ሀሎ፡ *hallô* [*infra*, p. 271] admits of a contracted ሀሎት፡ *hallôt*, for ሀለወት፡ *hallâwat.*) In Arabic and Aramaic the intransitives are regular in formation, حَلُوَتْ, خَزِيَتْ, رَضِيَتْ; Syr. ܫܠܝܰܬ, for *shaliyat, shaliwat*; Mand. מיטיאת "arrived," מיסיאת "became dense *or* firm"; vulgar Arabic of Egypt, *mishiyet* "she went," from *mishî*, or more commonly *mishyet, bikyet, nisyet, riḍyet.* In the Targûms the punctuation is סְנִיאַת, סְנֵית, but this I consider doubtful. But the transitives undergo contraction: *galâwat* or *galâyat* becomes in Aramaic *galât*, which appears in

Biblical Aramaic as מְטָת, הֲוָת, רְבָת, עֲדָת; the form with *pathach*, though equally common, seems to be less correct, e.g. הֲוַת, מְחַת, מְטַת, עֲנַת; in Syr. as ܡܛܳܬ, ܪܡܳܬ; in Mand. as הואת, באת (for ܡܛܳܬ); in the Talmûd as הֲוָת, חֲוָת, or more commonly חזאי, הואי, אתאי, where the י must be a trace either of the lost radical or of the evanishing final soft *t*, which wholly disappears in Mandaitic before enclitics, as עמאלה, "she swore to him." In Arabic the same contraction takes place, but the Arab has a certain dislike to a long vowel in a shut syllable, and has consequently shortened *ât* into *at*, جَلَتْ, رَمَتْ, for جَلَاتْ, رَمَاتْ, and these for جَلَيَتْ or جَلَوَتْ and رَمَيَتْ. In Hebrew, according to the analogy of קָטְלָה for קָטְלַת, we should expect the 3rd pers. sing. fem. to be גָּלְיָה (for גָּלְיַת), and this form is actually once found, with the older accentuation in pause, viz. חָסָיָה, Ps. lvii. 2. More frequently, however, the Hebrew takes the same course as the Arabic, and contracts the original *galáyat* into *galât*, whence with suffix-pronouns in sundry derived conjugations, צִוָּתוּ, Ruth iii. 6, כִּלַּתּוּ, Zach. v. 4, הִטַּתּוּ, Prov. vii. 21. But in pause the vowel is slightly lengthened, עָשָׂתְנִי Job xxxiii. 4, רָאָתְךָ Job xlii. 5, חִיָּתְנִי, Ps. xcix. 50, כִּסָּתְנִי Ps. xliv. 16; and so also in the separate form עָשָׂת Lev. xxv. 21, הית 2 Kings ix. 37 *kêthîbh*, Siloam inscription l. 3, and from derived conjugations הִרְצָת, Lev. xxvi. 34, הֶלְאָת (in pause), Ezek. xxiv. 12, הָגְלָת, Jerem. xiii. 19. Far more frequently, however, the Hebrew uses separately the form עָשְׂתָה, רָאֲתָה, in pause עָשָׂתָה, רָאָתָה. Herein there is no great mystery. The language had got accustomed to the form קָטְלָה, and as the old עָשָׂת (for עָשְׂיַת) was no longer perspicuous and intelligible, the usual termination ה ָ

was once more appended to it. We ourselves do much the same thing when we say *thou love*ST, with a double pronominal termination, to distinguish this form externally from *he loves* or *loveth*. It is curious, however, to observe the Mandaite using a similar form when he connects the verb with an enclitic, as הנאתאלה, "it pleased him," גלאתאלכון, "she revealed to you," אתאתאלון, "she came to them." Here הנאתא etc. stand for הנאתאת etc., the final *t* having disappeared as in the ordinary נפאלאלה or נפילאלה, "she fell," compared with the separate ניפלאת.

On the 3rd pers. dual, which occurs only in Arabic, I will merely remark that the masc. form is uncontracted, نَدَوَا, رَمَيَا، رَضِيَا. حَلَوَا; whereas the fem. is directly derived from the contracted singular. The form in use is جَلَتَا, رَمَتَا, not, as we should have expected, جَلَاتَا, رَمَاتَا, though these latter are said to occur dialectically. The ear having once got accustomed to رَمَتْ, the dual was naturally taken from this form, as was قَتَلَتَا from قَتَلَتْ.

The 3rd pers. plur. masc. requires a little more explanation. Reverting to the Ethiopic, we find in use the uncontracted ተለዉ፡ *taláwū*, በከዩ፡ *bakáyū*, ዐበዩ፡ *'ábyū*; to which correspond in Hebrew the pausal חָסָיוּ, Deut. xxxii. 37, נָטָיוּ, Num. xxiv. 6, הֶתָיוּ, Is. xxi. 14, Jerem. xii. 9; and so too probably, though out of pause, Ps. lxxiii. 2, נָטָיוּ רַגְלָי (for נטוי *kĕthībh*), and Prov. xxvi. 7, [where some copies read] דַּלְיוּ שֹׁקַיִם מִפִּסֵּחַ (for [the Massoretic] דַּלְיוּ = דַּלּוּ). More usually, however, contraction takes place in Arabic, Hebrew and Aramaic. In Arabic the form varies according to the characteristic vowel; حَلَوُوا becomes حَلَوْا: رَضِيُوا and خَزِيُوا also become رَضُوا and

خزوا ; but a preceding *fatha* produces a diphthong, غزوا for غزووا، رموا for رميوا. The vulgar forms in Egypt are *ramû* from *ramâ*, but *mishiyû* or *mishyû* from *mishî* "go," *bikyû*, *nisyû*, *ridyu*. In Aramaic we may also remark a difference between the intransitive and the transitive forms: ܡܠܝ makes ܡܠܝܘܢ, shortened into ܡܠܝܘ, but ܓܠܐ makes ܓܠܐܘܢ, contracted, after dropping the final *n*, into ܓܠܐܘ *gĕlâw* for *gĕlâ'û*. The corresponding form in Biblical Aramaic texts is usually read with *ô* for *au*, רְמוֹ, שְׁנוֹ, עֲנוֹ, הֲווֹ, מְטוֹ; but also אִשְׁתִּיו Dan. v. 3, 4. In the later Jewish writings I find such forms as בְּנוֹ, גְּלוֹ, and אִשְׁתִּיאוֹ. In Syriac the original *gĕlâ'û* is used with suffixes, as ܒܥܐܘܢܝ or ܒܥܘܢܝ, "they sought me." In our Jewish Aramaic texts the punctuation is exemplified by שְׁנוֹהִי Dan. v. 6, in later texts רְמוּנִי, רְמוֹהִי. In Mandaitic the usual form is הזון, אתון, שתון, בון (for בעון), but the *u* is sometimes dropped, רמו, צבו, בנו; this latter form is always used with enclitics, צבוביא, אתוליך. With suffixes the shorter form is employed, e.g. הזון "saw me," בון "sought me"; but the fuller form with י often occurs, as היזיון "saw me," שיביון, עניון. In Hebrew the prevalent form is identical with that of the vulgar Arabic. The normal גָּלְיוּ (for *galayû*) has been contracted into גָּלוּ.

The corresponding fem. in Ethiopic is *taláwâ*, *bakáyâ*, *'ábyâ*. In Aramaic the yet fuller form with final *n* is preserved, e.g. Chald. הֲוָן, קְרָאָן (for הֲוָאָן); Syr. ܪ̈ܘܝܢ, ܒ̈ܢܝܢ; but far more common are the shortened גְּלָאָה, סְגִיאָה, ܪ̈ܘܝ, ܒ̈ܢܝ. With suffixes, however, the Syriac exhibits the purer forms intact, ܓ̈ܠܝܢܢ, ܓ̈ܠܝܢܗ. In Mandaitic this form is rare, but Noeldeke gives as examples עהזויא and עקניא or קניא, which are probably to be read *ehzê* and *eknê* or *k'nê*, for ܒ̈ܢܝ

and صَفَت. The Arabic, as you may remember, has adopted the form قَتَلْنَ instead of the original *ḳatalâna*; whence in this class of verbs we meet, according to the vowel of the 2nd syllable, with the forms نَدَوْنَ, رَمَيْنَ, رَضِيْنَ, حَلَوْنَ. The form رَضِيْنَ stands for رَضِوْنَ, and حَلَوْنَ for حَلُوْنَ.

In the 2nd pers. sing. masc. the Ethiopic exhibits the oldest form ተለውከ: *talâwka*, በከይከ: *bakâyka*, ዐበይከ: *'abayka*, from ዐበየ:: The contracted form too is common in verbs 3rd *w*, as ተሎከ: ሐዮከ:, much rarer in those 3rd *y*, as ኀሬከ:: Verbs 3rd *y*, of which the 2nd radical is a guttural, weaken the diphthong still further into *î*, as ርኢከ: *rĕ'îka*, ርዒከ: *rĕ'îka*, from ርእየ: and ርዕየ:: In classical Arabic the forms are precisely what we should expect from analogy: حَلَو makes حَلَوْتَ; رَضِيَ and خَزِيَ, رَضِيتَ and خَزِيتَ; but تَلَا and رَمَي make تَلَوْتَ and رَمَيْتَ. In the modern dialects these words may be pronounced nearly as *t'lôt* and *r'mêt*, which are weakened in the dialect of N. Africa to *ñ* and *î*, غزوت *gh'zût* and *r'mît*. Spitta gives the Egyptian forms as *saḳêt* and *mishît*. In the Aramaic dialects there is a considerable variety. The Biblical Aramaic of Daniel exhibits חֲזַיְתָ ii. 41, 43, 45, iv. 17, הֲוַיְתָ ii. 31, 34, and רְבַיְתָ iv. 19 (*kĕthîbh*, where I do not understand the Massoretic alteration into רְבַת), בְּנַיְתַהּ (in some MSS. even בְּנַיְתַהּ, with incomprehensible ־ or ־) Dan. iv. 27, all with soft *t*, which I do not find it easy to explain; in later books we find גְּלֵיתָ as well as גְּלַיְתָ, but in the plural the weaker form גְּלֵיתוּן has prevailed, e.g. חֲזֵיתוּן Dan. ii. 8. Intransitive verbs of the form סְגִי have of course סְגִיתָ, סְגִיתוּן. In Syriac only the form ܓܠܝܬ, ܓܠܝܬܘܢ is used; and from the intransitive ܚܕܝ, ܚܕܝܬ, ܚܕܝܬܘܢ likewise with hard *t*, by way of distinction from the 1st pers. ܚܕܝܬ. The Mandaitic appears to have weakened the original vowels most, for though the plural exhibits the diphthong קראיתון, הואיתון, more frequently than the weaker קריתון, עתיתון (*ē* or *ī*?), yet in the singular we find only קרית, הזית, בית (for בעית). Lastly in Hebrew the weakest form of all has prevailed; בָּנִיתָ, בְּנִיתֶם, stand for *banêtha*, *bᵉnêthém*, and these for *banáyta*, *banaytúm*.

The 1st pers. sing. and plur. deviate but little from the analogy of the 2nd. In Gĕ'ĕz and Arabic the forms, apart from the pronominal affix, are identical; and in the vulgar dialects the forms are *saḳêt*, *saḳênâ*, *mishît*, *mishînâ*. In Hebrew too עָשִׂיתִי, עָשִׂינוּ, are the exact counterparts in vocalisation of עָשִׂיתָ, standing for *'asáytî*, *'asáynû*. The one form שָׁלַוְתִּי is remarkable as corresponding exactly with the Arabic سَلَوْتُ.

The Aramaic forms we must notice with a little more detail. The book of Daniel and the Targûms offer us הֲוֵית, חֲזֵית, בְּעֵינָא, רְמֵינָא, with *ê* for *ai*; the weaker צְבִית occurs in Dan. vii. 19; intrans. verbs have naturally the vowel *î*, סְגִית, סְגִינָא. Similarly in Syriac, in the singular, ܪܡܝܬ *rᵉmêth* (eastern) or ܪܡܝܬ *rᵉmîth* (western); but the plural retains the older diphthong ܪܡܝܬܘܢ or ܪܡܝܬܝܢ. Intransitives have always *î*, ܚܕܝܬ, ܚܕܝܬܘܢ or ܚܕܝܬܝܢ. In Mandaitic the usual form is הזית, קרית, בית (for בעית), but whether with *ê* or *î* is uncertain. The plural has not only the weaker form בין, אתין, הזין, but also the stronger diphthongal מטאינין, קראינין, הטאינין. Before enclitics the plural exhibits both forms, הואינאלה, קרינאלה. The singular in the same position has only the weak form, but in two varieties. Firstly, the final ת may be rejected, as הריבה, קרילה; or, secondly, the original termination of the 1st person may be restored, שריתיבה, קריתילה, "I dwelt in it." In the Talmûd the ordinary form of the 1st pers. sing. has also lost the final *t*, as אתאי "I came," בעאי "I asked," לָךְ קְרָאִי לָךְ תְּנָאִי "for thee have I read (the Scriptures), for thee have I repeated" (the Mishnah); but the fuller form is found occasionally both in it and in the Targūms, as אתיתי, גְּלֵיתִי, סְגִיתִי.

Passing on to the *imperfect*, I will first invite your attention to the forms in Gĕ'ĕz of the indic. and subj. In the indic. the original forms must have been *yĕtâlĕwu, yĕbâkĕyu*; but the final short vowels were dropped, yielding *yĕtâlĕw, yĕbâkĕy*; and the contraction took place, giving as the actual forms in use *yĕtâlû, yĕbâkî, yĕwâ'î*, ይወዒ፡ 3 sing. f. *tĕtalĕ́wî, tĕbakĕ́yî*; 3 pl. m. *yĕtalĕ́wû, yĕbakĕ́yû*. In the subj., which corresponds with the ordinary imperf. of the other Semitic languages, the fuller *yĕtlĕ́w, yĕbkĕ́y*, were contracted into *yĕtlû, yĕbkî*; 3 sing. f. *tĕtlĕ́wî, tĕbkĕ́yî*; 3 pl. m. *yĕtlĕ́wû, yĕbkĕ́yû*. The forms with *a* in the 2nd syllable may be exemplified by *yĕftaw, yĕ'bay*, which become *yĕftau, yĕ'bai*; the former may be further vocalised into *yĕftô*.

The form of the Arabic imperfect is, as you remember, identical with that of the Ethiopic subjunctive; Ar. *yăḳtulu* = Eth. *yĕḳtĕl*. We therefore obtain in the imperf. indic. the forms *yătluwu, yăbkiyu, yarḍayu*. The rejection of the final short vowels reduces these to *yătluw, yăbkiy, yărḍay*, which then become *yătlû* يتلو, *yăbkî* يبكي, *yărḍâ* يرضي. The subjunctive differs from the indic. only in its final vowel *a*, instead of *u*; but as the combinations *uwa* and *iya* do not undergo contraction, the forms in use are *yătluwa* يتلو, and *yăbkiya* يبكي; whereas the combination *aya* becomes first *ay* and then *â*, يرضي *yărḍâ*, which is therefore indistinguishable from the indic. The corresponding vulgar forms are *yimshî* and *yirḍâ*. The 3rd Arabic form, the jussive, is marked in the regular verb by the absence of any final vowel, يقتل. Hence in verbs 3rd و and ي the original form must have been يتلو, يبكي, يرضي, which would necessarily become *yătlû, yăbkî, yarḍâ*, and thus coincide with the indicative. To obviate this, the language shortened the final vowels, and the result was the forms *yátlu* يَتْلُ, *yábki* يَبْكِ, *yarḍa* يَرْضَ.

These Arabic forms in their turn cast much light on the corresponding ones in Hebrew. If we regard the word יִגְלֶה by itself, we might readily suppose that the final vowel *ĕ* was merely a dulling or obscuration of an older *û*; that *yiglĕ* stood for *yiglû*, just as *pĕ* פֶּה stands for *pû*, Ar. فُو, or *zĕ* זֶה for *zû*, Ar. ذُو. Were this the case, יִגְלֶה would correspond letter for letter to the Ar. *yaglû*, يَجْلُو. Other circumstances, however, militate against this explanation. For instance, if יִגְלֶה = يَجْلُو, then the 3rd pl. fem. ought to be תִּגְלוּנָה = يَجْلُونَ, for *yagluwna*, whereas the form in use is תִּגְלֶינָה. And how about יִבְכֶּה = يَبْكِي, and יִחְיֶה = يَحْيَى *yaḥyâ*? It would seem therefore that in verbs of this class the vowel *a* gained the upper hand in Hebrew as the characteristic vowel of the 2nd syllable; and final *w* everywhere gave place to *y*; so that the oldest Hebrew forms were *yaglay*, *yabkay*, most nearly resembling the Arabic يَرْضَى *yarḍâ* for *yarḍay*, for the *alif maksûra* of the Arabic is represented in Hebrew by the termination ־ֶה. In the jussive this vowel would naturally be shortened to the utmost, whence such words are וַיֵּרְדְּ, וַיֵּבְךְּ, וַיִּשְׁבְּ, וַיֵּרְא. In course of time, however, as the final letter became absolutely vowelless, a difficulty would be experienced in the utterance of the two consecutive consonants. Words like יַעְשׂ, יִגְל, יִבְן, יִחְד, יִשְׁע, יִרְא, were unpronounceable by the Hebrew organs, and a supplementary or furtive vowel had to be introduced to facilitate their utterance. Hence such forms as יַעַשׂ, יִגֶל, יִבֶן, יִחַד (with hard ד), יִשַׁע, יֵרֶא. In הָיָה and חָיָה, the jussives יְהִי and יְחִי became יְהִי and יְחִי,

just like the similar nominal forms בְּכִי, עֲנִי, for בְּכְיְ, עֲנְיְ. A trace of the original *a* of the first syllable remains, both in verb and noun, in the pausal forms יֶהִי, יֶחִי, בֶּכִי, for the original בְּכְיְ, יְחְיְ, יְהְיְ.

In Aramaic the same form is dominant as in Hebrew, the imperfect being usually of the forms יִבְנֵה or יִבְנֵא, ܢܒܢܐ, Mand. ניקריא. Very remarkable is לֶהֱוֵא or לֶהֱוֵה in Ezra and Daniel, with the plur. masc. לֶהֱוֹן and fem. לֶהֶוְיָן. The verb ܗܘܐ has also in Syriac a shorter form ܢܗܐ for the common ܢܗܘܐ, and in Mand. Noeldeke gives ניהיא or לִיהִיא as well as ניהויא or לִיהויא. Similar varieties occur in Samaritan, יהי, and in Talmudic, לִיהוֵי and נהי. In Syriac too the verb ܚܝܐ, "to live," contracts its imperf. into ܢܚܐ or ܢܚܐ (for ܢܚܝܐ), but in Mand. this does not seem to be the case (ניהייא).

The contractions which the augmented persons of the imperfect undergo, I will illustrate by the 2nd pers. sing. fem. and the 3rd pers. plural.

In Ethiopic no contraction takes place: the 2nd pers. sing. fem. is *tĕtalĕwī, tĕbakĕyī*; *tĕtlĕwī, tĕbkĕyī, tĕftāwī*; the 3rd pers. plur. masc. *yĕtalĕwū*, f. *-wā*, *yĕbakĕyū -yā*; *yĕtlĕwū -wā*, *yĕbkĕyū -yā*, *yĕbdyū -yā*.

In the other dialects these forms are more or less contracted. In Arabic the 2nd pers. sing. fem. is, for example, تَجْلِينَ from جَلَا, تَرْمِينَ from رَمَي. In the former case, تَجْلِينَ stands for *tagluwīna*; in the latter, تَرْمِينَ stands for *tarmiyīna*. A verb like رَضِيَ gives the form تَرْضَيْنَ, for *tarḍayīna*. The vulgar forms are *timshī, tirḍī*. The corresponding Hebrew forms are תַּעֲשִׂין, תַּעֲשִׂי, תֶּהֱמִי, תִּבְכִּי, תִּרְאִי, תִּהְיִי. Here תַּעֲשִׂין stands for *ta'sayín*, *tibkí* for *tabkayí*, etc. The Syriac has the advantage over the Hebrew in having the vowel *ê* instead of the weaker *î*, ܬܒܟܶܝܢ for *tabkaytu*.

The 3rd pers. plur. masc. in Arabic has the forms يَجْلُونَ, يَرْمُونَ, يَرْضَوْنَ. The first of these is contracted from *yagluwûna*, the second from *yarmiyûna*, the third from *yarḍayûna*. The vulgar forms are *yimshû*, *yirḍû*. The corresponding Hebrew form occurs not unfrequently in its uncontracted shape, יֶאֱתָיוּן, יֶחֱזָיוּן, יִבְכָּיוּן, יִשְׁתָּיוּן; without final *n*, יֶאֱתָיוּ, יִשְׁלָיוּ; with a weaker vowel in the 2nd syllable, יִרְבְּיֻן Deut. viii. 13, יִרְוְיֻן Ps. xxxvi. 9. These stand for *yabkayûna*, *yarbayûna*, etc. More frequently, however, a still further change takes place: יִרְבְּיֻן becomes יִרְבּוּן. Hence יַעֲשׂוּן, יַעֲשׂוּ; יֶהְגּוּ, יֶחֱזוּ; יִבְכּוּ, יִרְאוּ. In Syriac the masc. form is ܢܶܪܡܽܘܢ *nĕrmôn*, according to the Eastern pronunciation, for *narmayûn*; the Westerns weaken the vowel of the 2nd syllable to *û*, *nĕrmûn*, ܢܶܪܡܽܘܢ. The corresponding Mand. form is written ניקרון, ניהוון; with an enclitic, נירמובה; and in Biblical Chaldee we also find יִבְנוֹן, יִשְׁתּוֹן, לֶהֱוֺן.

The 3rd pers. plur. fem. in Arabic is يَجْلُونَ, يَرْمِينَ, يَرْضَيْنَ; the first of which, according to the norm يَقْتُلْنَ, stands for *yagluwna*, the second for *yarmiyna*, the third for *yarḍayna*. The corresponding Hebrew form is תַּעֲשֶׂינָה, תֶּחֱזֶינָה, תִּבְכֶּינָה, for *ta'sayna*, *taḥzayna*, *tabkayna*. The Aramaic preserves here an older shape than the other dialects, and does not contract. In Jewish Aramaic we have יִגְלְיָן, לֶהֶוְיָן Dan. v. 16; in Syriac ܢܶܪܡܝܳܢ; in Mand. ניבעיאן or ניבייאן (ܢܶܒܟܝܳܢ), corresponding very closely to the Ethiopic subjunctive *yĕbkĕyâ*, for *yĕbkĕyân*.

Passing on to the imperative, we find the minimum of contraction in the Ethiopic where the masc. sing. is *tĕlû* (for *tĕlĕw*),

f. *tĕlĕwt*, pl. m. *tĕlĕwā*; *bĕkī* (for *bĕkĕy*), f. *bĕkĕyt*, pl. m. *bĕkĕyā*; *'ĕbai* (for *'ĕbay*), f. *'ĕbdyt*, pl. m. *'ĕbdyā*; *fĕtau* or *fĕtō* (for *fĕtaw*), f. *fĕtāwt*, pl. m. *fĕtāwā*. In Arabic the 3rd radical has altogether disappeared, as in the jussive, and only a vowel remains: أُجْلُ *uglu* for *ugluw*, اِرْمِ *irmi* for *irmiy*, اِرْضَ *irḍa* for *irḍay* or *irḍā*. The vulgar forms have the long vowels, *imshī*, *irḍā*. The different persons undergo contraction precisely as in the imperfect. For instance the feminines of the above words are أُجْلِي *uglī* for *ugluwī*, اِرْمِي *irmī* for *irmiyī*, and اِرْضَيْ *irḍay* for *irḍayī*; their plurals masc., أُجْلُوا *uglū* for *ugluwū*, اِرْمُوا *irmū* for *irmiyū*, and اِرْضَوْا *irḍau* for *irḍayū*. The vulgar forms are: fem. *imshī*, *irḍī*; plur. *imshū*, *irḍū*. In Hebrew the termination of the imperat. sing. masc. is substantially the same as that of the imperfect, but with a slight lengthening of the vowel, גְּלֵה, רְאֵה, עֲלֵה, הֱיֵה, for *gĕlai*, etc. This lengthening is sometimes found in the imperfect, especially in pause and with a jussive sense; as יֵרֶא Gen. xli. 33, יַעֲשֶׂה Is. lxiv. 3, אַל־תִּהְיֵה Jerem. xvii. 17. The sing. fem. is גְּלִי, עֲשִׂי, רְאִי, for *gil'yī*, and that for *gĕlayī*. The plur. masc. is found in the oldest form *ḳĕṭālū* in such words as אֵתָיוּ and בְּעָיוּ; but far more common are words like עֲשׂוּ, הֱיוּ, רְאוּ, בְּכוּ, for *bikh'yū*, etc. The corresponding fem. is exemplified by רְאֶינָה, Cant. iii. 11, for *rĕ'ayna*, in Arabic رَيْنَ, *raina*. In Syriac we find a very few imperatives with the original diphthong in the 2nd syllable, e.g. ܒܥܝ, ܚܕܝ, ܐܬܝ; and in the Targūms the punctuation with *ē* occurs, גְּלֵי; but generally speaking, in Aramaic the sound of *ī* prevails. So in Dan. ii. 4, חֱיִי; in Syr. ܚܕܝ, ܒܢܝ, ܩܪܝ; in Mand. קריא, הויא. The fem. and plurals retain more of the ancient forms than in Hebrew.

Thus the fem. sing. in Syriac is ܪܡܳܝ; in Mand. קראי, הואי, and in the Talmūd חדאי "rejoice," גבאי "get thyself paid." Hence it appears that the fem. form גלי in the Targūms is to be read גְּלַי (and not גְּלִי, as indeed we might infer from the variant גְּלָא (for גְּלַאי). The plural masc. in Syriac is ܪܡܰܘ, for *rĕmaʿū*, and that for *rĕmaʿūn* ܪܡܰܘܢ. The Mand. exhibits the contraction הזון, הדון; the Bibl. Aram. the still greater one of אֲתוֹ, הֲוֹ. The corresponding fem. in Syriac is ܪܡܰܝܶܢ *rĕmâyĕn*, for *rĕmâyân*, to which answer the Jewish Aram. רְמָאָה or רְמָן, and the Mand. אתיאן, in Syr. ܐܬܝܶܢ.

With regard to the infinitive I will merely remark that the Hebrew form גְּלֹה, בְּנֹה, הֱיוֹ, עֲשׂוֹ, has lost its 3rd radical. Originally these were words of same form as the Arabic infinitive خَفَآءٌ, بِنَآءٌ, بُكَآءٌ, where the 3rd rad. و or ي appears as a *hamza*. In Hebrew however the *hamza* fell away after the loss of the final vowels, and the preceding *â* passed as usual into *ô*. The other infinitive גְּלוֹת, בְּנוֹת, עֲשׂוֹת, stands for *galāth*, *banāth*, by contraction for *galawat*, *banayat*; just as in Arabic صَلَاةٌ stands for صَلَوَةٌ, حَيَاةٌ for حَيَوَةٌ, فَتَاةٌ for فَتَيَةٌ. The Aramaic infinitive with prefixed *m* varies slightly in form in the several dialects. In Bibl. Aramaic we have מִבְנֵא, מִגְלֵא, מֶחֱוֵא, with suff. כְּמִצְבְּיֵהּ, as contrasted with the Syriac ܡܶܓܠܳܐ, ܡܶܒܢܳܐ, with suff. ܡܶܓܠܝܶܗ. In the form ܡܶܓܠܳܐ I see the influence of verbs ל״א, as well as in the imperatives of Paʿʿēl, Aphʿēl, etc. In Mand. both forms seem to occur, מיבניא, מידריא, as well as מיסנא, מירבא; and so also in the Talmūd מִטְעֵי, מִבְעֵי, מֶחֱזֵי, as well as מִיגְבָּא "to get paid." There also occurs in Bibl. Aram. the form לְמִבְנְיָה Ezra v. 9, like מִבְזְיָא in Targ. Prov. xxv. 27 and

מִשְׁתְּיָא in Targ. Esther v. 14. The form לְבְנֵא or לִבְנֵא in Ezra v. 3, 13, is probably corrupt; in any case it must be meant for an infin. Pe'al and not Hithpe'ēl.

The Arabic participle active has the same form as in the regular verb, but contracted; جَالٍ، رَامٍ، رَاضٍ، for جَالِيٌ، رَامِيٌ، رَاضِيٌ، fem. جَالِيَةٌ, etc. The vulgar form is *bâkî, mâshî, râḍî*, fem. *bâkiye* or *baḳye* (with short *a*), etc. The Aramaic has preserved an older form *ḳâṭal*, instead of the prevalent *ḳâṭil*; e.g. in Biblical Aramaic עָנֵה, שָׁתֵה, plur. בָּנַיִן, שָׁתַיִן, fem. דָּמְיָה, plur. שָׁנְיָן; in Syriac ܓܳܠܶܐ, ܓܳܒܶܐ, fem. ܓܳܠܝܳܐ, ܓܳܠܝܳܢ; and in Mandaitic האויא, באייא. The form בָּנַיִן, ܒܳܢܰܝܢ, for *bânayîn*, is analogous to the Hebrew plurals מַיִם, שָׁמַיִם, for *mayîm* and *shâmayîm*, and is probably due to an effort to preserve the consonant power of the *yōd* unimpaired. Similar to the Aramaic is the Hebrew form, which appears in its integrity in the proper name חֹזַי; but ordinarily *ai* has passed into *ĕ*, and we get the form חֹזֶה, רֹעֶה, construct חֹזֵה, רֹעֵה, like שָׂדַי, שָׂדֶה, שְׂדֵה. The corresponding fem. is exemplified by פֹּרָת, רֹעָה, זֹנָה, which stand for *pârayat, râ'ayat, zânayat*. The fem. עֹטְיָה, Cant. i. 7, is like the Aramaic דָּמְיָה, or it may rather be taken as = Arabic جَالِيَةٌ, with *ĭ* in the 2nd syllable; if so, the other form בֹּכִיָּה, הֹמִיָּה, פֹּרִיָּה, צֹפִיָּה, is only a slight variation, with emphatic utterance of the 3rd radical.

The passive participle of the Hebrew presents the regular form *ḳâṭûl*, בָּנוּי, עָשׂוּי, fem. בְּנוּיָה, עֲשׂוּיָה, with י at the end, whether the third radical be really י or ו. The final radical is sometimes rejected, עָשׂוּ, צָפוּ, which some derive from עָשׂוּי, צָפוּי, others from עָשׂוּו, צָפוּו. The original *w* reappears in the two plurals *kĕthîbh* עֲשׂוּוֹת, 1 Sam. xxv. 18, and נְטוּוֹת, Is. iii. 16.

In Esther ii. 9 הָרְאֻיוֹת seems to be a mistake for הָרְאוּיוֹת, which is found in some MSS. and editions. The corresponding Aramaic participle has the form בְּנֵה, חֲזֵה, מְנֵא, שְׁרֵא; Syr. ܫܪܐ, Mand. הזויא; the plur. is שְׁרַיִן Dan. iii. 25, in Syr. ܡܪܝܢ, ܡܪܝܢ; the fem. שְׁנָיָא, ܫܪܝܐ. The form would seem then to be that of adjectives like ܣܚܠ, ܣܚܠܐ; ܣܟܠ (or ܣܟܠ), ܣܟܠܐ; ܫܦܝܪ, ܫܦܝܪܐ; ܙܥܘܪ, ܙܥܘܪܐ; which spring from an original *katal* or *katil*, like بَطَلٌ "brave," حَسَنٌ "handsome," جَذِلٌ "glad," دَنِسٌ "dirty." The nearest Arabic equivalent would be شَجٍ "in grief," رَدٍ "perishing," for شَجِيٌ, رَدِيٌ, but either the Aramaic words had *a* in the second syllable, or the termination was influenced by that of the active participle. On this supposition בְּנֵה would stand for *banay*, plur. בְּנַיִן for *banayîn*, fem. בְּנָיָא for *banaya*, *banayat*. Lastly, the Arabic passive participle has the form *maktûl*, and therefore appears in these verbs as مَجْلُوٌّ, مَرْمِيٌّ, مَرْضِيٌّ. In the case of مَرْمِيٌّ, مَرْضِيٌّ, the influence of the final *y* has sufficed to transform the original *û* of مَرْمُويٌ, مَرْضُويٌ, into *î*. The vulgar forms may be exemplified by مَهْدِيٌّ *mahdîyun*, which has become *mdhdî*, fem. *mahdîye*, plur. *mahdiyîn*.

In treating of the derived conjugations I can be somewhat more brief[1].

In the intensive or Pi‘‘ēl the Ethiopic form alone is pure in the third person of the perfect: ሐለወ: *ḥallâwa*, "watch,"

[1] [Of the sketch of the derived conjugations of these verbs there is, among Prof. Wright's papers, only a rough draft in pencil, not going beyond the intensive or Pi‘‘ēl. There are indications in the MS. that the writer intended to add, in a separate paragraph, some remarks on the other derived conjugations; but, as these are for the most part constructed on exactly the same model as the Pi‘‘ēl, it has seemed sufficient to refer to them from time to time, in the course of the discussion of the intensive, by foot-notes or insertions within square brackets.]

ሐለየ: *hallâya*, "meditate," ሐሰወ: *hassâwa*, "lie," ሠናየ: *sannâya*, "be beautiful," ሀለወ: *hallâwa* "become, be," contracted ሀሎ *hallô*[1]. The Arabic exhibits ي for و in the 3rd pers. sing., not only here, but throughout all the derived conjugations; جَلَّى for *gallaya*, whence plur. masc. جَلَّوْا for *gallayû*, fem. جَلَّيْنَ. The vulgar form of the plur. masc. would be *gallû*. In Hebrew we find similar forms prevailing, viz. גִּלָּה for *gallaya*, גִּלּוּ for *gallayû* [Niph'al נִגְלָה plur. נִגְלוּ, and so forth]. In Aramaic the vowel of the first syllable has been retained intact, but that of the second has been weakened to the utmost, the resulting form being in Bibl. Aram. מַנִּי, רַבִּי [Haph'el הַגְלִי, הַיְתִי from אֲתָה, etc.], Syr. ܪܰܒܺܝ, ܡܰܢܺܝ, Mand. אסיא, שאניא for *mannaya*, etc., [and so throughout the other derived conjugations]. The lengthening of the final vowel by the complete vocalisation of the radical *y* has affected the form of the 3rd plur. masc., which is now שַׁנִּיו, שְׁרִיו; Syr. ܡܰܢܺܝܘ, ܪܰܒܺܝܘ; the Mand. however gives us שאנון, מאטון for *shannayûna*. Of the 3rd plur. fem. there are no examples in Biblical Aramaic. The Syriac form is ܪܰܒܺܝ, shortened from ܪܰܒܺܝ̈ܶܢ from an original *rabbayân(a)*; Mand. [Aph'ēl] אסגיא, אודיבון = ܐܰܘܕܺܝܘ ܐܰܣܺܝ.—The 3rd sing. fem. of the Arabic is جَلَّتْ for *gallayat*, which appears in Hebrew (before suffixes) as *gillath*, e.g. צִוָּתָה, כִּלָּתוּ, or, with slight tone-lengthening of the vowel חִיִּתָנִי, כִּסָּתְנִי. The ordinary form in Hebrew of course is כִּלְּתָה, כִּסְּתָה, with double termination. The Aramaic inflects regularly, ܪܰܒܝܰܬ for *rabbayat*, Mand. שאניאת, שאריאת. The Targûms give, it is true, the forms גַּלִּיאַת, גַּלִּית, but this punctuation seems as doubtful as

[1] [And so in the other derived conjugations *ǎtlawa*, *ǎstaya*, *tafâtwa*, *taḫâdrya*, etc.; so that the whole inflexion of the perfects is the same as in the strong verb.]

in the 1st conjugation. The 2nd pers. always retains the diphthong in Arabic, جَلَيْتَ *gallaita* for *gallayta*, of which the vulgar form would be *gillêt*. In Hebrew the vowel is weakened to *î*, צִוִּיתָ, כִּסִּיתָ, fem. גִּלִּית, plur. masc. כִּלִּיתֶם, עֲשִׂיתֶם, but the older *ê* is sometimes retained in the first pers., e.g. גִּלֵּיתִי, קִוֵּיתִי, נִקֵּיתִי and צִוֵּיתִי, גִּלִּיתִי and צִוִּיתִי[1]. In Biblical Aramaic the only form that occurs is מַנִּיתָ, Dan. iii. 12. Syriac distinguishes the second person ܪܰܒܺܝܬ (plur. ܪܰܒܺܝܬܽܘܢ) by giving it hard *t*, while the first person is ܪܰܒܺܝܬ with soft *t*[2]. The former word was originally *rabbaita*, the latter *rabbaiti*, and so the reason for the different treatment of the two cases lies merely in the wish to differentiate the later forms. Whether the same rule applies to the Mand. מטית, שאנית, זאכית, we cannot tell; probably not, as the Targūms seem to make the difference in the vowels, גַּלֵּיתָ fem. גַּלֵּית, but גַּלֵּיתִי, גַּלֵּית, supposing the punctuation to be correct[3].

In Ethiopic the form of the subjunctive mood of the imperfect is ይፈኑ: *yĕfánnū*, የሀሉ: *yahállû*, ይጸሊ: *yĕṣallî*, የሐሊ: *yaḥallî* for *-nĕw*, *-lĕy*. The corresponding indicative, 3rd pers. sing., in Arabic is يُجَلِّي by regular contraction for يُجَلِّيُ,

[1] [In the other derived conjugations the older *ê* occurs also in the second person. In the Niph'al it is commoner than *î*, and in the perfects of Po''el and Hoph'al *ê* is never thinned to *î* before consonantal affixes.]

[2] [So in all the derived conjugations, as in the intransitive form of Pe'al; *supra*, p. 261 *sq*.]

[3] [This distinction is not uniformly carried out in the printed texts: e.g., in the first person, the Bomberg editions have צְלִיתִי Ps. xxx. 3 (Nebiensis צַלִּיתִי), אַחֲזִיתָךְ Deut. xxxiv. 4 (where the same pronunciation is indicated by means of the Babylonian vowels in the MS. of the Brit. Mus. used by Merx, *Chrest. Targ.* p. 54), side by side with אִיתֵיתִי Gen. xxxi. 39, Deut. xxvi. 10 (where the edition of Sabbioneta, according to Berliner, has אַיְתֵיתִי, but Compl. agrees with Bomb.), אִיתְגְּלֵיתִי Ezek. xvi. 3. These examples shew how precarious are the rules formulated in ordinary "Chaldee" grammars, which for the most part are not even based on the fundamental editions of the Targūms.]

according to the norm يَقْتِلُ, the preceding *kesr* changing every *w* into *y*. We are therefore surprised to find in Hebrew יִגְלֶה instead of יִגְלִי. I can only explain this by supposing that it is due to an effort at uniformity. We found reason to suppose that the *a*-form prevailed in the first conjugation; and it is in its proper place in the passives: יְגֻלֶּה for *yagullay*, Ar. يُجَلَّى; יָגְלֶה for *yahuglay*, Ar. يُجْلَى[1]; whence, I imagine, it spread to the *Pi"el*, [*Hiph'îl*]. and *Niph'al*, giving יְגַלֶּה instead of יְגַלִּי, Ar. يُجَلِّي. [יַגְלֶה instead of יַגְלִי, Ar. يُجْلِي], and יִגָּלֶה instead of יִגָּלִי, Ar. يَنْجَلِي. As regards the plural of the imperfect we find in Hebrew examples of uncontracted forms, תְּדַמְּיוּן, Is. xl. 18, תְּדַמְּיוּנִי, ibid. ver. 25, ch. xlvi. 5, יְכַסְיֻמוּ, Exod. xv. 5; but the ordinary form is יְגַלּוּ, Arabic يُجَلُّونَ, *yugallûna*, for *yugalliyûna*. A similarly uncontracted participle is the Pu"al מְמֻחָיִם in Isa. xxv. 6. The shortened or jussive form of the Imperfect is in Arabic يُجَلِّ, to which correspond closely the Hebrew יְצַו, Deut. xxviii. 8, וַיְצַו, תְּעַר, Ps. cxli. 8[2].

The Aramaic form of the Imperfect differs from the Hebrew,

[1] [In like manner יִתְגַּלֶּה corresponds to يَتَجَلَّى.]

[2] [Similarly in the Hiph'îl the forms without a helping vowel יֹסְףְּ, וַיַּשְׁקְ, וַיַּרְא correspond to the Arabic يُجْلِ, while the forms with a helping vowel like יָגֶל, וַיַּעַל stand for *yagl*, *ya'l*, as, in the case of nouns, מֶלֶךְ, נַעַר stand for *malk*, *na'r*. In the Hithpa"el the Jussive is וַיִּתְגַּל for *yithgall*, pl. יִתְכַּסּוּ, in pause וַיִּתְחָל, 2 Sam. xiii. 6, and so without pause תִּתְגָּר, Deut. ii. 9, 19 (under the influence of the virtually doubled guttural), also יִתְאָו. The Pi'lēl הִשְׁתַּחֲוָה has Jussive יִשְׁתַּחוּ for יִשְׁתַּחְוְ.]

being in Biblical Aramaic יִמְחֵא, יִבְלֵא, often written with י ֵ in the Targūms; [and this *ṣērē* runs through all the conjugations], while *seghol* appears in the termination only a very few times in pause, as אֲחַוֶּה, Dan. ii. 24, נְהַחֲוֶה, Dan. ii. 4,—a doubtful punctuation. The plural is יִבְעוֹן, יִשְׁנוֹן. The Syriac and Mandaitic forms are nearly identical, viz. نِڤِتا, pl. نِڤِتون; נישאניא, נידאליא, pl. נישאנון, נידאלון. In Biblical Aramaic the final *ṣērē* is however shortened with suffixes into *ī*, יְחַוִּנַּנִי, Dan. v. 7, and יְחַוִּנַּהּ, Dan. ii. 11, which might raise a doubt whether א ֵ, י ֵ arises out of *ai*, as in Hebrew, or out of *i*. I prefer the former view because of the plural יִשְׁנוֹן, and because the participle is מְצַלֵּא, Dan. vi. 11, with the plural מְצַלַּיִן, Ezra vi. 10, Syr. ܡܨܠܐ, ܡܨܠܝܢ, which could only arise out of *mĕṣallayīn* not *mĕṣalliyīn*. The striving after unity of termination in the same part of the different verbal forms has here been pushed to its utmost.

The Imperative has in Ethiopic the form ፈነ: *fănnī*, ጸሊ: *ṣallī* for *fannĕw*, *ṣallĕy*; fem. ፈንዊ: *fannĕwī*, ጸልዪ: *sallĕyī*; plur. masc. ፈንዉ: *fannĕwū*, ጸልዩ: *ṣallĕyū*. In Arabic the corresponding form has a short vowel in the singular, جَلِّ for *galliy*, but the feminine is جَلِّي for *galliyī*, and the plural masc. جَلُّوا for *galliyū*. Identical herewith is the shorter Hebrew form צַו, מַן, Ps. lxi. 8, גַּל, Ps. cxix. 18, 22, נַס, Dan. i. 12, for *ṣauwi* etc. The longer and commoner form צַוֵּה, קַוֵּה, has arisen under the combined influence of the Qal גְּלֵה and the normal קַטֵּל.—In the Aramaic dialects similar forms prevail. The Bibl. Aram. yields the form מַנִּי for מַנִּי, Ezr. vii. 25. In the Targūms you will find both גַּלִּי and גַּלֵּי, but the former is probably correct. So in Mand. ואכיא, האריא; in the Talmūd שַׁנִּי "change," "remove," in Samaritan סלי, in modern Syriac ܣܰܦܶܝ, ܣܦܶܝ, *sāpī* for *sappī*. In ancient Syriac alone do we encounter a different form ܓܠܳܐ, which is probably owing to the influence of verbs ל״א, which would naturally have this vowel[1]. The fem. in Syriac is ܓܠܳܝ, in the Targūms גְּלַאי for גְּלַאִי; the plur. m. in Syriac is ܓܠܰܘ, in the Targūms גְּלוֹ, Mand. דאכון, כאסון; the plur. fem. in Syriac ܓܠܳܝܶܝܢ for *gallāyān*, in the Targūms גְּלַיָא.

The Infinitive is remarkable for the variety of its forms. In Arabic the preference is given to the form تَفْعِلَة, the real origin of which I explained to you before [*supra*, p. 204]; thus تَسْلِيَة، تَعْزِيَة, which become in vulgar Arabic, under the influence of the accent, *taslīye, ta'zīye, tarbīye*. In Hebrew the usual form of the inf. abs. is כַּלֵּה, קַוֵּה, according to the norm קַטֵּל [and similarly Hiph. הַגְלֵה, Hoph. הָגְלֵה on the norm הַקְטֵל, הָקְטֵל], but קַוֹּה occurs in Ps. xl. 2, which was originally

[1] [As in the infinitive Pe'al ܡܶܓܠܳܐ; see p. 268, *supra*. An original *gallay* (with *a* in the last syllable, according to the principle of effort after uniformity of termination explained in the text) would give *gallē*, *gallī*, but an original *malla'* (from ܡܠܳܐ = ܡܠܐ) might naturally become *mallā*. Now, in Syriac, verbs ל״א (with a very few exceptions in the intensive stem, such as ܣܰܢܳܐ and ܛܰܡܳܐ) have become entirely fused with verbs ל״ו and ל״י, and in the main it is the latter class of verbs that have prevailed to determine the form of the verbal inflexions. But in the inf. Pe'al and also in the imperatives Pa''el, Aph'el and Ethpa'al (ܓܰܠܳܐ, ܐܰܓܠܳܐ, ܐܶܬܓܰܠܳܐ) the ל״א form may be supposed to have prevailed. The imperative Ethpe'el on the other hand has the unweakened termination *ay* ܐܶܬܓܠܰܝ, in Eastern Syriac ܐܶܬܓܠܺܝ *ethgal*, with transposition of the vowel and double silent ܝ. Duval, p. 193, thinks that the imperatives in *ā*, to which must be added a single Pe'al form, ܬܳܐ "come," are relics of the energetic form in *an*, *ā*; cf. p. 195 *supra*.]

ḳauwâ, corresponding to the Arabic form (with weakened vowel) *kittâl*. The inf. const. is כַּלּוֹת, חַיּוֹת, גַּלּוֹת, formed as an intensive from the *Ḳal* גְּלוֹת etc.; originally therefore *gallâth*. In Aramaic the different dialects vary considerably. The Targūms have גַּלָּאָה [with suf. גַּלָּיוּתִי; Aph'el in Biblical Aramaic הַשְׁנָיָה, הַחֲוָיָה, Targumic אַגְלָאָה and so forth], the Talmūd Bablī אַפּוּיֵי, צַלּוּיֵי, Mand. נאסוייא, אסוייא, which form sometimes occurs in the later Targūms, e.g. רַצּוּיֵי. In these dialects forms with prefixed *m* sometimes occur, e.g. Mand. מישאנוייא; and the same prefix appears in the Syriac forms ܡܓܰܠܳܝܽܘ constr. ܡܓܰܠܳܝܽܘܬ, [Aph'ēl ܡܰܓܠܳܝܽܘ and so forth, which, apart from the initial *m*, are of the same type as the Biblical and Targumic forms].

The active participle is in Arabic مُجَلٍّ for *mugalliy^un*, the passive مُجَلًّى for *mugallay^un*. Here all is clear and distinct, as also in Hebrew מְגַלֶּה, מְגֻלָּה. But in Aramaic a considerable amount of confusion has been introduced by the unlucky assimilation of active and passive forms. Thus the absolute singular masc. מְגַלֵּא, מְגַלֵּי, ܡܓܰܠܶܐ is, it is true, sufficiently distinct from the passive מְצַלַּי, ܡܓܰܠܰܝ, but all the other forms are hopelessly confounded, and can only be distinguished with the help of the context. [Similarly in the causative stem the Arabic active part. مُجْلٍ and the passive مُجْلًى, the Hebrew active מַגְלֶה and the passive מָגְלֶה are clearly distinguished, but in Syriac the active ܡܰܓܠܶܐ and the passive ܡܰܓܠܰܝ assume identical forms with inflexional additions, ܡܰܓܠܝܳܐ, ܡܰܓܠܝܺܢ etc.]

[*Appendix. Verbs of which one radical is an* א.

Here we must distinguish, in general, between forms in which the א retains its original force as a guttural consonant (*hamza*) and forms in which the א is weakened or disappears, according to the principles laid down above, pp. 44 *sqq*. In the former case there is no irregularity, properly so called, though the א exerts the usual influence of a guttural on neighbouring vowels; in the latter case weak forms arise, some of which can be at once explained by the general rules at pp. 44 *sqq.*, while others involve also the operation of the law of analogy, and the influence of weak verbs of the class that have a ו or י among their radicals.

In Ethiopic verbs a radical א is throughout treated as a guttural. Similarly in Arabic verbs a radical *hamza* commonly remains consonantal in all positions (except where two *hamzas* come together in the same syllable) and the inflexion is essentially regular, though a certain tendency to soften the guttural pronunciation in the direction of و or ي, under the influence of an *u* or *i* immediately preceding or following the *hamza*, is indicated by the orthographic rules which bid us write بؤس for بأس, يبؤس for يبأس, يؤثر for يأثر etc. For the details of these rules it is sufficient to refer to the Arabic Grammar. Further weakenings of a radical *hamza*, involving the entire disappearance of the consonant or its conversion into *w* or *y*, occur in old Arabic in certain parts of very common verbs, or, sporadically, under the influence of metrical necessity. It is recorded that in the time of Moḥammed the people of the Ḥijāz retained the guttural force of *hamza* less firmly than many other tribes, and to the influence of the Ḥijāzī pronunciation may be ascribed such readings in the Ḳor'ân as يَاتِي, مُومِن for *ya'tî*, *mu'min*[1]. In modern Arabic the

[1] In all cases where radical ا is represented by و, ى or simple ء the consonants, taken by themselves, indicate a pronunciation in which the radical has ceased to be heard as a guttural; and this is very intelligible if we remember that the laws of Arabic orthography are mainly based on the text of the Ḳor'ân, which was first written down in the Ḥijāz, and without ء or other diacritical points. But as regards

weakening of *hamza* has gone much further, so that, for example, verbs *tertiae hamzatae* are entirely merged in verbs *tertiae* ي. The extreme is reached in the Aramaic dialects, where consonantal א is maintained only as an initial or between two full vowels. The Hebrew holds a middle position between the Arabic and the Aramaic, but there is reason to think that at the time when the oldest Biblical Books were written it retained the consonantal force of א much more fully than the Massoretic tradition admits. (See below, p. 284.) Of the details a brief sketch will suffice.

A. *Verbs* פ״א. In the perfect of the simple stem א is initial, and retains its guttural force, so that the inflexion is essentially regular. In Syriac initial ܐ demands a full vowel instead of a mere vocal *shĕvâ*, and in the perfect this vowel is commonly *e*, ܐܶܡܰܪ, with the same thinning of the original *a* as in the fem. ܩܶܛܠܰܬ, ܐܶܡܪܰܬ. But in some verbs the Eastern Syrians have the older and stronger pronunciation ܐܰܟ݂ܶܠ, ܐܰܟ݂ܡܶܕ, ܐܰܠܶܡ, ܐܰܡܰܪ[1]. In Mandaitic also the vowel of the first syllable is generally *a*, אמאר, and so too in the fem. we have אמראת, אולאת as well as עמראת, עולאת. In Biblical Aramaic the vowel appears to be shorter, אֲמַר, אֲזַל[2]. In Syriac a few verbs assume in the perfect the form of verbs פ״י, ܐܺܠܶܦ, ܝܺܠܶܦ, ܝܺܒܶܫ, ܝܺܟ݂ܡܶܕ.

In the imperfect the Arabic has يَأْكُلُ, يَأْلَفُ, to which such

the pronunciation of the text the influence of the Ḥijâz was limited, and most readers preserved something of the guttural sound in very many cases where there was nothing to indicate this in the consonantal text. The insertion of the sign ء is therefore a sort of corrective, warning the careful reader to retain, in spite of the consonants, at least a trace of the original guttural.

[1] So too ܐܰܪܥܳܐ, for ארע = عرض. The Western Syrians write ܐܰܪܥܳܐ, and even ܟܰܗܢܳܐ, the ܥ before ܗ being pronounced by them as ܐ.

[2] A fuller vowel, אָ, אֶ, is given in MSS. and early editions of the Targums and even in some copies of the Bible; but these forms, and others to be mentioned below, with אֵ, אָ instead of a *ḥateph*, are now explained as due to transcription from MSS. with Assyrian punctuation in which there were no distinctive signs for the *ḥatephs*.

Hebrew forms as יֹאמַר, תֹּאמַר closely correspond. But in Heb., where the א retains its guttural force, the pronunciation is usually facilitated by the insertion of a *ḥateph* or a short vowel, יֶאֱסֹף, יֶאֱהַב, 2 fem. תַּאַסְפִי etc. By this means the radical א may remain consonantal even in the first person, אֶאֱסֹף, whereas in Arabic أأكل necessarily becomes آكل *âkulu*, because two hamzas cannot be pronounced in one syllable. The same contraction sometimes appears in old Arabic in the other persons, and in modern Arabic the pronunciation *yâkul*, *yâmur* is the rule. Similarly Hebrew אָבַד, אָבָה, אָכַל, אָמַר, אָפָה form the imperfects יֹאבַד, יֹאפֶה, יֹאכַל etc.; *yô-* standing as usual for *yâ-*. The first persons are written אֹבַד etc. with a single א, which probably indicates that the contraction began, as in Arabic, with the part in which two hamzas came together. King Mēsha' also writes ואמר, "and I said," l. 24, ואחזה l. 11, 20, but ויאמר l. 6, 14. The *ē* of the second radical, which becomes *a*, *ĕ* in current discourse or with retracted accent, יֹאבַד, וַיֹּאכַל, וַיֹּאמֶר, extends through all these verbs, and similarly אָחַז makes יֶאֱחֹז and יֹאחֵז; אָסַף, יֶאֱסֹף, תַּאֱסֹף and וַיֹּסֶף, תֹּסֵף (with omission of the א). In all these cases the broader prefix seems to have thinned the *u*, *ô* of the second radical to *ĭ*, *ē*, a vowel which the Hebrew imperfect usually avoids. Similar forms from stative verbs with imperfect *a* are וָאֹהַב, Mal. i. 2, וַיּוֹחֶר (for וַיֹּאחֶר), 2 Sam. xx. 5, *Ḳ'rê*; but beside these we find also אֹהֵב, Prov. viii. 17, וָאֵחַר, Gen. xxxii. 5, and probably וַיִּיחֵר, 2 Sam. xx. 5 *K'thîbh*, with similar forms from אתה and אזל. Those from the two last verbs may be mere Aramaisms; the others seem to be genuine Hebrew forms and may be compared with the dialectic Arabic تِيثَم from أَثِم.

In the Aramaic imperfect (and inf.) the contraction into *ê* (for *ă*, *a'*, as in the particle نِ = נָא, *na'*) is universal; Jewish Ar.

יֵאכֻל, יֵאמַר, inf. מֵאמַר etc., Syr. ܢܐܟܘܠ, ܡܐܟܠ. But in verbs imperfect *a* the West Syrians further thin *ê* to *î*; thus ܢܐܡܪ, ܡܐܡܪ are in the East *nêmar, mêmar*, but in the West *nîmar, mîmar.*

The Arabic imperative is necessarily ايسِرْ not اِئْسِرْ, اُوجَلْ not اوْجَلْ[1]. Three verbs commonly reject the first radical, أَخَذَ, أَمَرَ, أَكَلَ, making خُذْ, مُرْ, كُلْ, whence in vulgar Arabic we even find the perfects *ḥad* and *kal.* So from أَتَى we have ايتِ and تِ, in pause تِهْ. A similar apocope takes place in Syriac in the imperatives ܬܐ "come" and ܙܠ "go"[2]. Apart from these anomalous forms the only point to be noted about the Syriac imperative is that the full vowel necessarily assumed by the initial ܐ is *a* before *ô* but *e* before *a*, ܐܟܘܠ, ܐܡܪ—a distinction which does not appear to be carried out in the other dialects of Aramaic. In Biblical Aramaic and Targumic, as in Hebrew, a *ḥateph* commonly takes the place of a full vowel; yet we find in the Targums such forms as אֵימַר, אֵיכוֹל, and even in Hebrew the plurals אִסְפוּ and אֵתָיוּ. In the passive participle the Syriac has ܐ, but in Dan. iii. 22 we have אֲזֵה.

In the reflexive of the simple stem the Arabic اِيتَثَرَ, imperfect يَاتَثِرُ, perf. pass. اُوتُثِرَ, requires no explanation. But the verb أَخَذَ makes اِتَّخَذَ, and so also we find اِتَّزَرَ as well as اِيتَزَرَ. اِتَّجَرَ.

[1] But فَاسِرْ, وَاوجَلْ and so forth. So also وَأْمُرْ as well as وَمُرْ, but وَخُذْ, وَكُلْ.

[2] Talm. B. תָּא, זִיל; but in Bibl. Aram. אֵזֶל, Ezra v. 15 (in the Targums אִיזִיל, Numb. xxii. 35, Compl., Bomb.); אֲתוֹ, Dan. iii. 26 (in the Targums אִיתוֹא, אֲתָא).

as well as ايتجر, and more rarely a few other cases of the same kind. Similarly in Aramaic ܐܶܬܒܪܝܡ, אִתְּחַד with sporadic cases of the same kind in other verbs. The ordinary Syriac reflexive is ܐܶܬܐܟܶܠ, fem. ܐܶܬܐܰܟܠܰܬ, by the general rule of Syriac that ܐ gives up its vowel to a vowelless consonant and disappears in pronunciation. In the Targums this elision seems not to take place and the forms are regular. In the intensive stem the ܐ in Syriac also mostly surrenders its vowel and is elided after prefixes with a vanishing vowel: imperf. ܢܰܐܟܶܠ for *n'akkel* (1st person ܐܰܟܶܠ) part. ܡܰܐܟܶܠ etc. Similar forms are found, though less consistently, in Jewish Aramaic and occasionally in Hebrew, וַתַּזְרֵנִי, 2 Sam. xxii. 40, for וַתְּאַזְּרֵנִי, Ps. xviii. 40, מַלְּפֵנוּ, Job xxxv. 11, and so forth. In Aramaic the extensive stem (Aph'el and Shaph'el with their reflexives) passes wholly over into the forms of verbs פ״י, except in the two verbs הֵימֵן, ܗܰܝܡܶܢ and הַיְתִי, אֵיתִי, Palmyrene אתי, De Vog. 15, l. 4, ܐܝܬܝ, where the א becomes י; compare the Hebrew imper. Hiph. הֵתָיוּ, Jer. xii. 9, and the part. מֵזִין "giving ear," Prov. xvii. 4. The Hebrew forms are generally regular, but in a few cases we find the contraction of אֲ into *ô*, as אוֹכִיל, Hosea xi. 4, and so in the Niph'al נֹאחֲזוּ, Numb. xxxii. 30, or even into *â*, וַיָּאצֶל, Numb. xi. 25, וַיָּרֶב, 1 Sam. xv. 5. The passage of א into ו, which plays so large a part in Syriac, is sometimes found also in the Arabic verb, but in a different connexion and mainly in the later language. Thus *a'â* often becomes *awâ*, تَوَامَرُوا for تَآمَرُوا "they deliberated together," and so too initial *'â* sometimes becomes *wâ* in stem III., وَاكَلَ for آكَلَ. In modern Egyptian Arabic we even find *wakkil* for أكَّلَ, perf. of اكل II.

B. *Verbs* ע״א. In Ethiopic, Arabic and Hebrew the forms are generally strong throughout; and strong forms are also common in Eastern Syriac[1]. But in Arabic these verbs are sometimes assimilated to hollow verbs, or, when the hamza begins a syllable and is preceded by a vowelless consonant, it is elided and throws back its vowel on the consonant before it. This happens mainly with the verb سَأَلَ "ask," from which we have such forms as سَالَ, سِلْتُ, يَسَالُ, or more frequently, with elision, يَسَلُ. Similarly the common يَرَى for يَرْأَى "he will see," and a few others. In Western Syriac the elision of ܐ is the rule, whether at the beginning or end of a syllable, unless it stands between two full vowels; but the otiant letter is generally allowed to remain in writing; thus perf. Peal ܫܳܐܶܠ (E. Syr. ܫܐܶܠ), imperf. ܢܶܫܐܰܠ, pl. ܢܶܫܐܠܽܘܢ (E. Syr. ܢܶܫܐܰܠ, pl. ܢܶܫܐܠܽܘܢ, where the subscript line denotes a kind of vocal *shĕva*), Ethpe'el ܐܶܫܬܐܶܠ (E. Syr. ܐܶܫܬܐܶܠ), 1st pers. ܐܶܫܬܐܶܠܶܬ, and so forth. When the first or third radical is an aspirate we sometimes find forms like ܒܳܐܬ, ܢܒܽܐܫ, where the hardening of the aspirate represents an older doubling, presumably due to assimilation of the ܐ. In Biblical Aramaic the א maintains itself, as in E. Syriac, and so apparently in the Targums. In the latter א may pass into י when it is doubled, e.g. שייר (שַׁיֵּר) Pa''el of שְׁאַר. So too many Syrians pronounced ܒܐܶܫ as *bayesh*, and the verb ܛܐܶܒ forms the Pa''el ܛܰܝܶܒ; but in the latter case it is the form of the Pĕ'al that is secondary. The transition of verbs ע״א to hollow verbs, of which we have found some examples in Arabic, prevails within the Aramaic field in

[1] See for the Syriac Nestle in *Beitr. zur Assyriologie*, i. 153 *sqq.* (where however in Nöldeke's judgment the case is overstated, and insufficient weight is given to the numerous instances in which the ancient Nestorian Massora (of A.D. 899) forbids the ܐ to be pronounced). All Syriac verbs of this class are stative in form. In Hebrew the only cases of contraction are נָאווּ pl. of the Pi'lēl נָאוָה (if this is not rather an old Niph'al from אוה) and possibly יָנֵאץ, Eccles. xii. 5.

Mandaitic. A transition to פ״א sometimes occurs in Syriac, e.g. ܐܶܬ݂ܐܰܟܰܦ, ܢܶܐܟܰܦ (from ܟܦܐ), ܢܶܐܠܰܦ, Ps. xli. 2; but most forms of this kind are only graphical errors.

C. *Verbs* ל״א. Here the tendency of the languages, completely carried out in vulgar Arabic, and almost completely in Aramaic, is to entire assimilation with verbs ל״י. In the intensive stem of a very few Syriac verbs a final ܐ, though it is no longer actually pronounced, retained its guttural force to so late a date that the forms are still ܛܰܢܰܐ, ܐܶܬ݂ܛܰܢܰܐ, ܢܛܰܢܰܐ (with *a* for *e* in the last syllable under the influence of the guttural), and are commonly inflected regularly, except that the ܐ throws back its vowel in forms like 3rd pl. perf. ܛܰܢܰܐܘ etc. In Hebrew alone do the ל״א form a distinct class of weak verbs, the א retaining its consonantal force whenever it has a vowel, מְצָאוֹ, יִמְצָאוּ, יִמְצָאֻנִי, or even a vocal *shᵉva*, אֶמְצָאֲךָ, but being absorbed into the previous vowel when it closes a syllable. In a final syllable this absorption produces no change in the quality of the vowel, though it lengthens *a* to *â*, מָצָא, stative מָלֵא, imperf. יִמְצָא (for *yimṣa'*, with characteristic *a* before the guttural), Niph'al נִמְצָא, יִמָּצֵא, Hiph. הִמְצִיא etc. In the perfect of the simple stem the normal vowel is also retained in syllables not final מָצָאתָ, מָלֵאתָ, but the other perfects in such cases uniformly take *ê* נִמְצֵאתָ, הִמְצֵאתָ etc. A similar law of uniformity prevails in all imperfects (so far as the few examples allow us to judge), but here the vowel is *sᵉghol*; תִּמְצֶאנָה, תִּמָּצֶאנָה etc. So also the imper. of the simple stem מְצֶאןָ; in the derived stems there are no examples of the imperative with consonantal affix. If we compare these forms with the corresponding parts of verbs third guttural we see that the *ē* of the perfect and the *sᵉghol* of the imperfect alike represent an older *a'*, and it seems most likely that the deflection to *ê*, *è*, has been produced under the influence of verbs ל״י. The two classes of verbs often run into one another, as may be seen from the lists of mixed forms in any Hebrew Grammar.

In what has been said above as to the treatment of radical א in Hebrew we have had to do with the stage of the language represented by the Massoretic pronunciation; but before we leave the subject it will be well to glance at the reasons, already alluded to on p. 278, for concluding that traces of a more primitive pronunciation are preserved in the spelling of the consonantal text. It is not doubtful that when Hebrew and the neighbouring Canaanite dialects were first committed to writing, spelling went by sound and not by etymology, so that א would not be written unless it was actually heard as a guttural. Let us first apply this consideration to ancient inscriptions, in which we are sure that we have the actual orthography of the first writers, untouched by subsequent correction. On the stele of Mēsha' we have רש, "head," רית, "gazingstock," ואמר "and I said," all with omission of a radical א which was already lost in pronunciation. But on the other hand we have ויאמר, מאתן (Heb. מָאתַ֫יִם), צאן "sheep." The last example is particularly noticeable in contrast with רש; for while the spelling מאתן might conceivably be aided by the singular מאת (l. 20) there was nothing to help the retention of the א in צאן unless it was actually sounded when this spelling was chosen. So again when the Phoenician writes בנת "I built" (*C. I. S.* 3, l. 4) but קראת "I called" (*Ib.* 1, l. 7) we are certainly not justified by the rules of Phoenician spelling in taking the א to be merely the sign of the vowel *a*. When we pass from inscriptions to the Biblical texts we are met by the difficulty that the spelling has undergone later revision, especially by the insertion of vowel letters in cases where these were not used in old times. But א is not a mere *mater lectionis*; the rule that prevails is that א is inserted wherever it is etymologically justified, whether it is sounded or not, and the exceptions to this rule are merely sporadic, except in such cases as אמר for אאמר, where the second א must have lost its sound in very ancient times. It is incredible that any systematic correction of the orthography, by the lights that the later Hebrew scribes possessed, could have given us a system so correct etymologically as the Old Testament displays; and the same degree of correctness already appears on a small scale in the Siloam inscription (מאתים, מוצא, ראש, against Moabite and Phoenician רש). The conclusion is inevitable that when Hebrew first came to be written to an extent sufficient to give a tolerably fixed orthography, radical א still retained in most cases its guttural sound.]

ADDITIONAL NOTES AND CORRECTIONS.

P. 3, l. 35. Since this was printed Prof. Kautzsch, now of Halle, has brought out the 25th edition of Gesenius' *Heb. Gr.* (Leipzig, 1889) with considerable additions and improvements.

P. 7, l. 35. For 421 read 420.

P. 12, *footnote*. Still later are the cursive tablets of the Arsacid period, some of which Strassmeier has published in *Zeitschr. f. Assyr.* vol. iii. (1888) p. 129 *sqq*. One of these (p. 135) of the year 80 B.C. is, as Mr E. A. W. Budge kindly informs me, the latest example of the Assyrian writing of which we have certain knowledge.

P. 17. The Aramaic inscriptions will form the second part of the great Paris Corpus. The first fasciculus, edited by M. de Vogüé, has appeared (Paris, 1889).

P. 20, l. 10. For 1865 read 1855.

Ibid., *footnote* 1. Further information about the dialect of Ma'lūlā is given by Mr F. J. Bliss in the *Qu. Statement* of the *Pal. Expl. Fund*, April, 1890, p. 74 *sqq*.

P. 25, *footnote*. The text of the inscription, in Hebrew square characters, with translation and notes, is given in Prof. Driver's *Notes on . . . Samuel* (Oxf. 1890), p. lxxxv *sqq*.

P. 29, *footnote*. A substantial addition to our stock of dated Himyaritic inscriptions is promised by E. Glaser from the epigraphic collections formed during his journeys in S. Arabia.

P. 34. In *Zeitschr. f. aegypt. Spr. u. Alterthumsk.* 1889, p. 81, Erman has indicated the existence in Egyptian of a tense precisely corresponding to the Semitic Perfect. (Nöld.) The forms of the singular and plural are as follows—

SING.		PLUR.	
3 m.	ḥbs	3.	ḥbsw
3 f.	ḥbsti'		
2 m.	ḥbsti'	2 c.	ḥbstïnī
1.	ḥbskwi' (cf. Aeth. -kū)	1.	ḥbswïn

P. 35. For the history of Semitic, and especially of Hebrew, writing the student will do well to consult the introduction to Prof. Driver's *Notes on . . . Samuel*, Oxf. 1890 (with facsimiles).

P. 40, *footnote*. It should be stated that the quotation at the close of this note is from Prof. Müller's article "Yemen" in the *Encyclopaedia Britannica*. His paper in the Vienna *Denkschriften*, which had not reached England when the note was printed, deals with the Minaean inscriptions of Euting's collection, of which the dialect and character are S. Arabian, and with one group of inscriptions of N. Arabian type, which, on the ground of their contents, are called Liḥyānite. A large number of inscriptions, provisionally classed together as Proto-Arabic, are reserved for future publication. Thus it is not yet possible to say anything definitive about the history of the old Arabian alphabets; the materials already published have given rise to lively controversy.

P. 44, l. 24. Prof. Nöldeke observes that the form derived from *sham'al^un* by elision of أ would be *shamal^un*, not *shamāl^un*. The latter therefore must be derived from a secondary form *sham'āl^un*; cf. the Hebrew and Aramaic forms.

P. 48, l. 15. See p. 51, *footnote* 1.

P. 48, l. 21. Prof. Nöldeke "cannot recognise the weakening or loss of ע in any one of the three cases adduced. In מתאב the change of ע to א has been deliberately introduced to change the sense" [Geiger, *Urschrift und Uebers.* p. 349], "בֵּל is Babylonian, and that בִּי stands for בְּעִי is improbable." There are, however, other probable examples of the occasional weakening of ע in Hebrew, notably פִּתְאֹם side by side with פֶּתַע. Such readings as נשקה for נִשְׁקְעָה, Amos viii. 8, *Kethîbh*, לָמוֹ for לְעַמּוֹ, Ps. xxviii. 8 (LXX. τοῦ λαοῦ αὐτοῦ), are probably due to a pronunciation in which ע was not sounded; but to ascribe this vicious pronunciation to the original writers is not justifiable; the readings in question are presumably errors of later scribes.

P. 51, l. 5. "In many parts of Syria ج seems to be pronounced like the French *j*"—(Nöld.). In upper Egypt one sometimes hears a pronunciation intermediate between English hard and soft *g*, but nearly approaching the latter. In Arabia ج is hard in Nejd, and soft (*g* in *gem*) in the Ḥijāz (Mecca, Ṭāif).

P. 58, l. 4. This paragraph and those that follow it should be read in the light of p. 41, where the author takes it to be probable that the proto-Semitic had three sibilants besides *z* and *ṣ*. All three appear distinct in Hebrew as שׁ, שׂ and ס respectively; but in later times the sounds of שׂ and ס were so much alike that the one was sometimes written for the other. In Syriac (but not in the oldest Aramaic; see p. 74 *footnote*) שׂ has been absorbed in ס (ܣ); in Arabic, on the contrary, the primitive sound represented by Hebrew שׁ remains distinct (as ش), while the other two old sounds (שׂ, ס) are both represented by س. For an attempt to work out the history of the Semitic sibilants see D. H. Müller, *Zur Gesch. d. Sem. Zischlaute*, Vienna, 1888 (from the *Abhandlungen* of the 7th International Congress of Orientalists, Sem. Sect., p. 229 *sqq.*).

P. 73, l. 9 *sqq.*; and p. 256, l. 16. Prof. Nöldeke observes that the distinction between تلا and بكى cannot be regarded as the invention of the grammarians, inasmuch as it was carefully observed by the writers of the oldest copies of the Ḳor'ān. These scribes, he believes, made a distinction in pronunciation between ـَا and ـَى; we know indeed that many Ḳor'ān teachers pronounced ـَى with *Imāla*. See *Geschichte des Qorāns*, p. 252 *sqq.*

P. 94, l. 14. For ܡܣܡܘܟܬܐ read ܡܣܡܘܟܬܐ.

P. 100, l. 17. Prof. Nöldeke remarks that to connect שִׁחֵר with شَكَدَ appears to be inadmissible, since to do so involves *two* irregularities (Hebrew שׁ should correspond to Arabic س), and that ܦܛܝܟܐ is a mere transcription of the Arabic بطّيخ. The genuine Syriac form is ܦܰܛܺܘܚܳܐ.

THE END.

CAMBRIDGE: PRINTED BY C. J. CLAY, M.A. AND SONS, AT THE UNIVERSITY PRESS.